London

LONDON

A History in Verse

Edited by

Mark Ford

The Belknap Press of Harvard University Press

CAMBRIDGE, MASSACHUSETTS
LONDON, ENGLAND · 2012

Book design by Dean Bornstein

Library of Congress Cataloging-in-Publication Data

London : a history in verse / edited by Mark Ford.
   p.   cm.
Includes bibliographical references and index.
ISBN 978-0-674-06568-0 (alk. paper)
1. London (England—Poetry).   2. English poetry.   I. Ford, Mark, 1962 June 24–
PR1195. L6L64   2012
821.008′0358421–dc23   2011053028

Contents

Preface

Children growing up in England, and in many other countries where English is spoken, have for centuries been inducted into the poetry of London before they can walk or talk: "London Bridge is falling down, / Falling down, falling down, / London Bridge is falling down, / My fair lady"; "Oranges and lemons, / Say the bells of St. Clement's"; "Pussy cat, pussy cat, where have you been? / I've been to London to look at the queen"; "Up and down the City Road, / In and out the Eagle, / That's the way the money goes, / Pop goes the weasel!" It is thought that the rhyme of "London Bridge is falling down" dates back as far as 1016, and an attack by a marauding Danish army on a Lundúnum stoutly defended by King Edmund Ironside.

This anthology begins in the mid-fourteenth century, by which time Old English had evolved into Middle English, and London had established itself definitively as the capital of England. The land on which the city stands had been inhabited for many millennia by this point; there is evidence of humans having lived in what is now Greater London during the Palaeolithic, Mesolithic, Neolithic, Bronze, and Iron ages. It was not, however, until the Romans arrived in AD 43, and settled the low hills of Ludgate and Cornhill on the north bank of the Thames, that London, or Londinium—a Roman version of a Celtic name—was really founded. The nascent *urbs* was famously destroyed when only a decade or so old by Boudicca of the Iceni, an event movingly recorded by Tacitus and commemorated in a striking mid-Victorian bronze statue of the warrior queen now sited on the Victoria Embankment. On recovering from Boudicca's devastating attack Londinium evolved, during three and a half centuries of Roman rule, into one of the area's most important trading stations, only for its fortunes to wax and wane in the 650 years between the Romans' departure and the arrival in 1066 of William of Normandy, following his triumph at the Battle of Hastings. William the Conqueror, as he became known, would be the last overseas invader to seize control of the city by force.

It was the London of Richard II that saw the first real efflorescence of poetry in the vernacular, in the writings of Gower and Langland and Chaucer and Hoccleve. All four present scenes explicitly set in London, and it is with their work that this anthology opens. It ends with the present day.

While it is not easy to develop useful generalizations about the six and a half centuries of London poetry gathered in this anthology, I have in my introduction attempted to suggest how certain tropes and themes link poems written in radically different eras. My attention is predominantly directed, however, at the way poetry refracts the political and cultural history of the city in a given period, and how particular historical events and social shifts are figured in the work of individual poets.

While researching this anthology I developed a rather rigorous definition of what constitutes a London poem; I came to feel it must contain some explicit reference to London, or to places in London, or to events that happened in London, or, as is the case with, say, Keats's sonnet "On Seeing the Elgin Marbles," to artworks housed in London. I decided, further, to include only poems written in English, not feeling competent to make selections from languages such as Chinese or Japanese or Arabic, and wanting to avoid the impression that I was presenting a judicious selection of non-English-language poems about London by simply including a piece or two by Paul Verlaine or Valery Larbaud.

The reader will find here, as well as celebrated poems by canonical figures such as John Donne, Ben Jonson, John Dryden, Jonathan Swift, Alexander Pope, Samuel Johnson, William Wordsworth, Lord Byron, T. S. Eliot, Ezra Pound, Louis MacNeice, Philip Larkin, and Sylvia Plath, the work of many less famous poets: these include Anne Askew, Isabella Whitney, Everard Guilpin, John Taylor, Thomas Freeman, Abraham Holland, Simon Ford, John Oldham, Thomas Jordan, Elizabeth Tollet, Charles Jenner, Hannah More, Charles Dibdin, John Hamilton Reynolds, Frederick Locker-Lampson, and Henry S. Leigh. My selections range from love lyrics to light verse, from mock-epics to limericks, from anonymous ballads to scathing satires, from stately sonnets to the cries of London:

> Dust or ash this chap calls out,
> With all his might and main,
> He's got a mighty cinder heap
> Somewhere near Gray's Inn Lane.
>
> Here's taters hot, my little chaps,
> Now just lay out a copper,
> I'm known up and down the Strand,
> You'll not find any hotter.
>
> Any old pots or kettles,
> Or any old brass to mend?

Come my pretty maids all,
To me your aid must lend.

This man, from Covent Garden comes,
With his green wares early,
Singing out carrots and turnips, oh,
Making a hurly-burly.

Sprats alive, oh! sprats alive,
Just up from Billingsgate;
Come buy some sprats of me, my deary,
For yourself or for your mate.

The poetry of London reflects all strata of the culture of London, and an anthology such as this might be said to replicate the way so many different types of Londoner, or types of visitor to London, find themselves crammed into the same tube carriage, so to speak—that is, forced to share the contested spaces and resources of the city. The collection is arranged chronologically according to the author's date of birth, thus allowing, I hope, a sense of the successive waves of the city's history, as the eras leach into each other, marked, now and again, by some singular crisis or decisive event. The range of poems and authors collected here seems to me a moving and eloquent testimony to the power of London to attract and absorb and inspire and give voice to its residents, and to the power of poetry to create, layer by layer by layer, its own history of the city.

Acknowledgments

I would like to express my thanks to all members of the English Department at University College London for assistance with this project. I am particularly grateful for advice and suggestions to Matthew Beaumont, Kasia Boddy, Marilyn Corrie, Jane Darcy, Gregory Dart, Paul Davis, Helen Hackett, Chris Laoutaris, Neil Rennie, Nick Shepley, Daniel Starza Smith, and Henry Woudhuysen. I would also like to thank my editors, John Kulka, Christine Thorsteinsson, and Heather Hughes, for all their hard work on this project.

London

Introduction

"London, thou art of townes A per se," opens a poem composed by an unknown Scottish poet around 1500. By "A per se" he means unique or preeminent, and the poem's seven eight-line stanzas proceed to celebrate this "sovereign of cities," this "pryncesse of townes" for a rich variety of reasons: for its beauty (it is "semeliest in sight" and "in beawtie beryng the crone imperiall"); for its wealth (its merchants are "full of substaunce and myght" and its streets thronged with knights wearing "velvet gownes and cheynes of fyne gold"); for its military impregnability (its walls are strong and its "artillary with tonge may not be told"); for its many churches with their "wele sownyng" bells and "famous prelatis in habitis clericall"; for its river whose "beryall stremys" are "pleasaunt and preclare" (bright), and crowded with barges, ships, and swans; for its women ("Fair be thy wives, right lovesom, white and small; / Clere be thy virgyns, lusty under kellis" [head-dresses]); and finally for the "pryncely governaunce" of its "famous Maire," who is praised as "exampler, loodester, and guye" (example, lodestar, and guide), as "principall patrone and roose orygynalle." "London," concludes each stanza, "thou art the flour of Cities all."

The poem was long thought to have been written by William Dunbar, who certainly visited London as a member of a Scottish delegation that was sent, in 1501, to negotiate the marriage of James IV to Henry VII's elder daughter, Margaret. While that attribution no longer stands, there seems no doubt that the poem was written on commission for some mayoral function by an official Scottish bard; its sublime vision of London as a "Swete paradise precelling in pleasure" might well have struck even the city's proud, princely mayor as a little extravagant.

A somewhat earlier anonymous poem, "London Lickpenny," also allows us to view the city through the eyes of an outsider. It recounts a trip made to London by a Kentish farmer who has been defrauded of his goods and is seeking legal redress; like "London, thou art . . . ," it is written in eight-line stanzas that conclude with a repeated final line (or version thereof), in this case: "For lacke of money I may not spede" (prosper). Almost on arrival the farmer has his hood stolen from him as he pushes his way through the crowds; he is rebuffed by lawyer after lawyer, for his "purs is faynt," and "they that lacked money mowght not spede." The streets are packed with vendors urging him to buy all manner of goods—felt hats, spectacles, ribs of beef, cherries, spices, hot sheep's feet, cod, and mackerel. In Cornhill, "where is moche stolne gere," he even spies his own hood for sale. After drowning his sorrows in a pint of wine he tries to persuade a bargeman moored by Billingsgate to give him a free ride downriver, but to no avail. He must make his own way back to Kent, where he resolves never to meddle again with London or the law: "By-caus no man to me would take entent [pay attention], / I dight me to the plowe, even as I ded before."

The tradition of the panegyric to the city inaugurated by "London, thou art . . ." can be traced through many succeeding London poems; a number, such as Edmund Spenser's "Prothalamion" or Edmund Waller's "A Poem on St. James's Park, As Lately Improved by His Majesty" or the concluding stanzas of John Dryden's "Annus Mirabilis," testify directly, like "London, thou art . . . ," to the pressures of patronage, but there are also plenty of poems written in the postpatronage era that celebrate London's power to inspire in the poet a sense of the sublime: "Earth," to quote the most obvious example,

> has not anything to show more fair:
> Dull would he be of soul who could pass by
> A sight so touching in its majesty.

Or consider the closing lines to "Londoner," by the New Zealand–born poet Fleur Adcock. The speaker has just returned to the city from abroad, and is struck, like Wordsworth, by the prospect from Westminster Bridge:

> It's cold, it's foggy,
> the traffic's as abominable as ever,
> and there across the Thames is County Hall,
> that uninspired stone body, floodlit.
> It makes me laugh. In fact, it makes me sing.

Undoubtedly, however, many more London poems follow in the cautionary tradition of "London Lickpenny" and present satirical or realist or jaundiced perspectives on the capital: as the rain drives all before it, to take another famous example, in Jonathan Swift's "A Description of a City Shower," the waste products of London are caught up into a single feculent stream that might be seen as summarizing the unwholesome, indifferent brutality of urban life:

> Sweepings from butchers' stalls, dung, guts, and blood,
> Drowned puppies, stinking sprats, all drenched in mud,
> Dead cats, and turnip-tops, come tumbling down the flood.

Readers of this anthology, then, will find the squalid and the sublime jostling each other for elbow room, as they do in the experience of any city-dweller: Spenser's Sweet Thames metamorphosing into the ominously post-apocalyptic river that "bears no empty bottles, sandwich papers, / Silk handkerchiefs, cardboard boxes, cigarette ends / Or other testimony of summer nights" in T. S. Eliot's *The Waste Land*. And as for the nymphs who gathered violets and daisies and primroses and lilies and braided posies from them to adorn the stately swans on their fast approaching bridal day, they are departed, and have left no addresses. "Let the petals fall," observes Louis MacNeice in his bleak, late poem "Goodbye to London," "Fast from the flower of cities all."

In the second stanza of "London, thou art . . . ," the Scottish visitor addresses the capital as "lusty Troy Novaunt, / Citie that some tyme cleped was New Troy." He is here alluding to the claim first launched by Geoffrey of Monmouth in the 1130s that London had been founded by a grandson of Aeneas called Brutus. The popularity of the myth owed much to the way it linked London to that other triumphant offshoot of Troy, imperial Rome. While not giving rise to a poem to compare with Virgil's *Aeneid*, it was widely circulated through the *Brut* chronicles and played a significant role in imbuing London's growing commercial dominance in the medieval period with an aura of destiny and common purpose. As late as 1590 Spenser felt able to make use of it, declaring in Book III of *The Faerie Queene* that *"Troynovant"* was founded by the *"Troian Brute"* where the waves "of wealthy *Thamis* washed is along." Further, Spenser boldly and, as it turned out, accurately predicted that the nation whose capital was Troynovant "in all glory and great enterprise, / Both first and second *Troy* shall dare to equalise."

Such myths bring sharply into focus the complex relationships poetry establishes with the power structures of its day, relationships often foregrounded in poems set in the city that has been the dominant seat of power in England since at least 1066. This anthology opens with a passage that presents a direct encounter between a poet and his sovereign; it is taken from the dedication by John Gower of his enormously long poem *Confessio Amantis* to Richard II, a dedication later rescinded after Gower's political allegiances shifted toward Henry of Lancaster. (Henry would in due course oust Richard and seize the throne, and it is to Henry IV that the last version of Gower's poem is addressed.) In this first dedication the poet describes how he came rowing in his boat on the Thames, "Under the toun of newe Troye, / Which took of Brut his ferste joye," and whom should he run into but King Richard on his royal barge; the poet is at once invited to join his sovereign, who proceeds to instruct him to write some "newe thing" in "oure Englissh" rather than in Latin or French. "Myn hert," observes Gower, "is wel the more glad / To write so as he me bad," for Richard's royal favor will serve to protect him, or at least so he hopes, from the envy of all those eager to "feyne" (misconstrue) or "blame" what he writes—an early glimpse into the long tradition of literary backbiting and Grub Street politics that would reach its apogee in the work of Alexander Pope.

John Lydgate, writing a little later, also refers to the myth of London's Trojan founder in his account of the festivities with which the ten-year-old Henry VI was welcomed to London in 1432: "make grete joye," he enthuses, "Citee of Citees, of noblesse precellyng, / In thy bygynnynge called Newe Troye." Pageants and Joyous Entries played a crucial role in disseminating myths of sovereignty in the early modern period, and we are fortunate to have Lydgate's detailed poetic description of the various allegorical tableaux with which the young ruler was both entertained and subtly instructed in the arts of just kingship. These "noble devyses" include a giant on a pillar on London Bridge, "of looke and chere [expression] sterne as a lyoun," to symbolize martial prowess; three "emperesses" representing Nature, Grace, and Fortune from whom he receives gifts that signify not only science and cunning and strength but also fairness; and seven virgins dressed in white whose gifts range from a sword of "myht and victorie" to a "mantel of prudence" and a "girdyll of love and parfyte pees." Like the poet of "London, thou art . . . ," Lydgate is profuse in his praise of the mayor, one John Welles, who organized the pageant and commissioned the poem, and beneath its celebration of Henry's triumphant entry into a rapturous London lurk familiar tensions between the business interests of the civic authorities who controlled the city—the area now known as the City or the Square Mile—and the royal prerogatives of the court a mile or so away at Westminster.

For London's greatness, its unflagging ability to consolidate its gains and expand into new economic areas as well as the surrounding countryside, has always been powered by the energies of trade and consumption rather than by the dictates of a wise ruler. "Hote pies, hote! / Goode gees and grys!" (pork) yell the vendors in Langland's *The Vision of Piers Plowman*, "Whit wyn of Oseye and wyn of Gascoigne" (Alsace and Gascony). Arthur Hugh Clough, in the high-Victorian era, rather loftily complained that London was simply a "huge Bazaar," lacking the higher virtues of "Nobleness, Learning, Piety," and obsessed only with "Competition and Display." Many poems, like Clough's "To the Great Metropolis," echo the complaints of the author of "London Lickpenny" and Langland's ascetic dreamer, and decry the commercial realities of city life. Rather than a New Troy or New Rome, such poems either figure London as a place of confusion ("Why how now Babel," demands the Jacobean poet Thomas Freeman in *London's Progress*, "whither wilt thou build?"), of corruption and dissipation, or view it as governed entirely by money and self-interest, as "gain-devoted," to borrow William Cowper's disapproving term. In a rather more jaunty second poem about the city that borrows the form of a glee-club tavern song, Clough summed up the ethos of commercial London:

> Each for himself is still the rule
> We learn it when we go to school—
>   The devil take the hindmost, o!
>   ("In the Great Metropolis")

Instead of a noble epic or lyrical visions of an urban utopia, this London inspires a series of comic or tragic visions of London's failure to match classical or biblical ideals; it drives the excremental pseudo-quest of Ben Jonson's adventurers in "On the Famous Voyage," and the absurd mock-epic contests of Pope's vain and grasping dunces and stationers. In the poetry of Blake it results in a melding of the idioms of political protest and psalm-like lament to create a wholly original mythology of the city as fallen, a lost paradise, betrayed and doomed:

> Jerusalem fell from Lambeth's Vale,
> Down through Poplar & Old Bow,
>   Through Maldon & across the sea,
> In war & howling, death & woe.

Dissent and misrule permeate much of the poetry of London, the New Troy and Augusta and heart of empire myths notwithstanding. Chaucer's Perkyn, from the fragmentary *The Cook's Tale*, might be seen as the boisterous progenitor of this line. Perkyn, though an apprentice in the victualling trade in London, is yet as "gaillard" (merry) as a "goldfynch in the shawe" (wood). Perkyn can dance "so wel and jolily" that he is known as Perkyn Revelour, and he dances with a purpose, for we learn he is "as ful of love and paramour / As is the hyve ful of hony sweete; / Wel was the wenche with hym myghte meete." This sprightly lad about town is also a dab hand with the dice, and prone to stealing from his master's cashbox. The master eventually decides that "bet is roten appul out of hoord / Than that it rotie al the remenaunt," and fires him. In the fragment's concluding lines we learn that the disgraced

Perkyn, who will now never achieve full citizenship (for this was controlled by the guilds), has moved in with a pal of a similar ilk, whose wife "heeld for contenance / A shoppe, and swyved for hir sustenance"—in other words, she worked as a prostitute.

It is perhaps odd that the most vivid description of the capital made by the well-connected Chaucer, who rose to become controller of customs in the port of London, should focus on a riotous apprentice, though it's also worth pointing out that Chaucer lived through the Peasants' Revolt of 1381, to which an oblique reference is made in *The Nun's Priest's Tale*. The antics of the low-born, pleasure-seeking Perkyn might be contrasted with the more dainty dissipations of his youth recounted by Chaucer's near contemporary, Thomas Hoccleve; in his autobiographical "La Male Regle" the poet reports himself as too shy to engage in love or fights, but more than happy to spend his days drinking at the "Poules Heed" tavern, surrounded by "Venus femel lusty children deer."

Sex and alcohol are among the crucial catalysts for the formation of a kind of counter-mythology of London that brazenly ignores or defies or subverts the official institutions of the city and the rhetoric in which they are commended. A good instance of this at work is Rochester's "A Ramble in St. James's Park," which was circulating in manuscript in 1673. Some twelve years earlier Edmund Waller had celebrated Charles II's improvements to the park in the most fulsome of terms, and even used them as a metaphor for the wonderful reforms with which the restored king was about to improve the nation. Admire, we are encouraged by Waller, this perfect park, fit for a perfect sovereign:

> Here, a well-polished Mall gives us the joy
> To see our prince his matchless force employ:
> His manly posture and his graceful mien,
> Vigour and youth in all his motions seen;
> His shape so lovely and his limbs so strong
> Confirm our hopes we shall obey him long . . .
> Near this my Muse, what most delights her, sees
> A living gallery of agèd trees:
> Bold sons of Earth, that thrust their arms so high,
> As if once more they would invade the sky . . .
> Here Charles contrives the ordering of his states,
> Here he resolves his neighbouring princes' fates:
> What nation shall have peace, where war be made,
> Determined is in this oraculous shade.

With this compare Rochester's ribald account of a stroll in the same park by night:

> Much wine had passed, with grave discourse
> Of who fucks who, and who does worse,
> Such as you usually do hear
> From those that diet at the Bear,
> When I, who still take care to see
> Drunkenness relieved by lechery,
> Went out into St. James's Park
> To cool my head, and fire my heart.
> But though St. James has th' honour on't,
> 'Tis consecrate to prick and cunt.
> There, by a most incestuous birth,
> Strange woods spring from the teeming earth:
> For they relate how heretofore,
> When ancient Pict began to whore,
> Deluded of his assignation
> (Jilting, it seems, was then in fashion),
> Poor pensive lover, in this place
> Would frig upon his mother's face;
> Whence rows of mandrakes tall did rise,
> Whose lewd tops fucked the very skies.
> Each imitative branch does twine
> In some loved fold of Aretine;
> And nightly now beneath their shade
> Are buggeries, rapes, and incests made.
> Unto this all-sin-sheltering grove
> Whores of the bulk and the alcove,
> Great ladies, chamber-maids, and drudges,
> The rag-picker and heiress trudges;
> Car-men, divines, great lords, and tailors,
> 'Prentices, pimps, poets, and jailers,
> Footmen, fine fops, do here arrive,
> And here promiscuously they swive.

Waller's stately, venerable trees become mandrakes (half-human trees growing from spilled semen) whose "lewd tops fucked the very skies," while the king's "oraculous shade," where Waller imagines him solemnly pondering foreign policy, is transformed by Rochester into "an all-sin-sheltering grove," the site of a sexual free-for-all. One wonders which poetic version of the park was preferred by Charles II himself, who fathered fourteen or more illegitimate children with a range of mistresses.

It was Rochester's contemporary John Dryden, the first poet laureate, who most fully and effectively used poetry as a means of recording, and responding to, particular events in the history of the city. His "Annus Mirabilis," published in 1667, had plenty to record and respond to: naval battles with the Dutch, the "spotted deaths" and "poisoned darts" of an outbreak of the bubonic plague, which killed about 100,000 people, and then the Great Fire that started in Thomas Faryner's bakehouse in Pudding Lane on September 2 and raged for four days, eventually engulfing much of the city. Dryden, like Waller, presents Charles II as an exemplary ruler, who is shown acting throughout the crisis with courage and determination; it is even suggested that the distraught citizens' greatest fear, as they survey the smoking ruins of London, is that the dispiriting sight might drive "the father of the people" to abandon the capital once and for all.

Dryden's elegant *abab* quatrains combine royalist flattery with superb depictions of the spread of the fire itself, and the flight of Londoners from it:

> The next to danger, hot pursued by fate,
>   Half-clothed, half-naked, hastily retire;
> And frighted mothers strike their breasts, too late,
>   For helpless infants left amidst the fire.

Each night they gather in fields on the outskirts of London, and there

>   like herded beasts, lie down,
> To dews obnoxious on the grassy floor:
>   And while their babes in sleep their sorrows drown,
> Sad parents watch the remnants of their store.

Eighty-seven churches were destroyed by the fire, forty-four livery halls, and over thirteen thousand houses. The Guildhall, the Royal Exchange, and St. Paul's Cathedral all fell victim to it. The ravaging of St. Paul's allowed Dryden to air a theological dilemma that he rather speciously solves in the poem by evoking the conflict of two decades earlier: how could God consent to the destruction of a building sacred to

Himself? Well, Dryden replies, "since it was profaned by civil war, / Heaven thought it fit to have it purged by fire."

At the time Dryden wrote "Annus Mirabilis," soon after the terrible events it records, London was still in shock. Eighty thousand people had fled the city, and even five years on, only a quarter of them had returned. Yet Dryden was, in the event, right to envision in the poem's concluding stanzas a city "of more precious mould" arising from the ashes, courtesy, in particular, of Sir Christopher Wren. This rebuilding process was commemorated by numerous poets. Simon Ford, in *London's Resurrection* of 1669, notes how many "foreign realms" are contributing to the process—"Spain brings steel, / Libanus cedar sends, and Denmark deal." Ireland supplies oak. It is as a "famed emporium" that London will reestablish itself, Dryden argues, and it is notable that the "glorious day" ("mayst thou be writ in gold") that Ford most excitedly celebrates is that on which Charles II inaugurated the rebuilding of the Royal Exchange.

Often, however, London poems reflect specific historical events less directly than is the case with a poet as insistently public as Dryden. Sir Thomas Wyatt, for instance, in the haunting lyric "Who list his wealth and ease retain," only hints at the terrible sight he witnessed from his dungeon in the Tower, normally taken to be the execution of Anne Boleyn:

> The bell tower showèd me such sight
> That in my head sticks day and night.
> There did I learn out of a grate,
> For all favour, glory, or might,
> That yet *circa Regna tonat.*

"It thunders around the throne"—the line is borrowed from Seneca's *Phaedra.* The poem's Latin epigraph seems also to be a coded reference to the political dangers besetting the courtier poet, and can even be seen as a plea that he not be condemned to the same fate as Anne Boleyn. *Veritas Viat Fides,* its second line reads, that is *Viat,* or rather Wyatt, with truth on one side and faith on the other. And directly above *Viat* on the epigraph's first line is the word *Innocentia.*

It could also, of course, thunder for the monarch *on* the throne, and the beheading of Charles I in 1649 elicited what is perhaps the subtlest of all meditations on political power, Andrew Marvell's "An Horatian Ode upon Cromwell's Return from Ireland." At the heart of this poem is the execution itself, figured by Marvell as the last act of a play:

That thence the royal actor born
The tragic scaffold might adorn:
    While round the armèd bands
    Did clap their bloody hands.

An endless series of monarchs, from the eponymous hero of *Gorboduc* of 1561 on, had been dispatched on the stages of London theaters such as the Globe and the Rose; here it was happening in reality. Marvell's profoundly ambivalent lines do piercing justice to Charles's bravery as he approached the block:

He nothing common did or mean
Upon that memorable scene;
   But with his keener eye
   The axe's edge did try:
Nor called the gods with vulgar spite
To vindicate his helpless right;
   But bowed his comely head
   Down as upon a bed.

Marvell's delicacy here might be compared to that exhibited by David Kennedy in his attempt to respond to the bombs detonated on July 7, 2005, by terrorists on three London Underground trains and a London bus. "Trying to join words," Kennedy's poem opens, "to four bombs, // words that are not, / words that are not, // words that are not, / that are not, // are not / like carnage, // atrocity, screens / around the bombs." Marvell's ever-shifting metaphors enact a similar sense of a mind grappling with a turn of events whose reality and implications seem impossible to grasp; Kennedy's hesitations and repetitions and Marvell's sinuous ironies model ways of responding to the cataclysmic in a manner that effectively reclaims for the individual a sense of, or at least the illusion of, privacy—that most precious of commodities for a city-dweller bombarded with news, and opinions about that news, from all sides.

    The relationship between the individual's body and the city's body is often stressed in London poems that deal specifically with moments of historical crisis. In his plague poem of 1625 "London, Look Back," Abraham Holland creates an elaborate analogy between the plague victim and the city under siege: the infection is figured as a swarm of "remorseless enemies" who first "batter down, / The clayey bulwarks of our mud-walled town" and then, once inside the stomach, which is compared to the marketplace, spread swiftly and unstoppably:

> some are ready first
> To break the sluices, which do raging burst
> And drown low buildings, some with flaming brands
> Fire holy temples, some with swords in hands,
> Sharp-pointed javelins, mauls, and poisonous darts
> Make massacres through all the trembling parts
> Of the distressed fabric.

Holland would himself learn the truth of this analogy, for he died of the plague the following year.

Blitz poems also often refract a heightened awareness of correspondences between the individual's body and that of the city. Mervyn Peake's "London Buses," for example, develops a complex, almost metaphysical conceit between the workings of the body and those of bombed-out London: the gallant, defiant "blood-red" buses "winding / Through corridors of broken stone" are pictured as

> binding
> The city's body with a living thread
> That like a vessel weaving through grey flesh
> Its crimson mesh
> Of anger, surges onward like a tide
> Among the empty ruins and the dead—
> And those who have not died.

This sense of being in a kind of symbiotic relationship with the body of the city is even more concisely rendered in one of Roy Fuller's war poems, "London Air-Raid, 1940": "My reading and the alimentary city / Freeze."

In another Blitz poem, "In Westminster Abbey," John Betjeman gives us the prayer of a woman begging God to preserve all the things that Britain stands for; these include "Free speech, free passes, class distinction, / Democracy and proper drains," after which she adds:

> Lord, put beneath Thy special care
> One-eighty-nine Cadogan Square.

The Almighty's preservation of class distinction means most British readers of the poem will know, from her address, the echelon of the class system to which the

speaker belongs—one that means even the Holy Father must submit to the impera-
tives of her social diary: the poem concludes, "And now, dear Lord, I cannot wait /
Because I have a luncheon date."

The poetry of London offers a precisely nuanced topography of class and social
distinctions, from the impoverished street cleaners of the eighteenth-century poet
William Whitehead's "The Sweepers" to Betjeman's aristocratic denizen of Belgra-
via, from D. H. Lawrence's tramps sleeping rough on the Embankment to the Duke
of Wellington commemorated in Tennyson's great elegy of 1852. Poetry's ability to
register, or indeed foment, social change is particularly marked in the poetry of Lon-
don; new styles of poetry can be seen as emanating from new urban types. A striking
example of this is the emergence of what its critics dubbed the Cockney School in
the early nineteenth century. "The grand distinction of the new school of poets,"
wrote Byron to his publisher John Murray in 1821 of Leigh Hunt and his followers,
"is their *vulgarity*. By this I do not mean that they are *coarse*, but 'shabby-genteel,'
as it is termed." Byron was particularly withering about Keats, whose poetry he de-
scribed as "a sort of mental masturbation"; "I don't mean he is *indecent*," he ex-
plained, "but viciously soliciting his own ideas into a state, which is neither poetry
nor any thing else but a Bedlam vision produced by raw pork and opium." A flagrant
example of this vicious soliciting of his imagination is Keats's sonnet on the Elgin
Marbles, pillaged from the Parthenon by the Earl of Elgin and placed on display in
the British Museum in 1816. Rather than the coolly admiring appraisal of classical
proportions or harmonies that one familiar, from his public school days, with the
culture of Ancient Greece might record, the vulgarly nouveau Keats, the son of an
ostler, sullies, or so Byron would have seen it, the stately sculptures with an ill-bred,
unmanly hysteria. Contemplation of the Parthenon frieze brings "round the heart
an undescribable feud," an aesthetic rapture felt physically, and one that knows no
bounds. How different is "the dizzy pain" Keats experiences on entering the world
of "Grecian grandeur" to the response of the gentleman he met on a visit to the Mar-
bles, and who observed: "I believe, Mr Keats, we may admire these works safely."

Keats's poetry, though pretty much devoid of overt references to London, em-
bodies, then, the emergence of a new London type, or social phenomenon. So too
does, say, John Davidson's "Thirty Bob a Week," a poem that T. S. Eliot declared
"one of the great poems of the end of the nineteenth century," and one that "made a
terrific impact" on him on account of its "colloquial idiom" and "spoken rhythm."
The new kind of Londoner it introduces to poetry is one who journeys by tube each
day to his lowly white-collar job "like a mole," "A-travelling along the underground /
From my Pillar'd Halls and broad Suburban Park." Class distinction may, as Betje-

man's Belgravian hostess prays, remain a fundamental and ineradicable aspect of British life, but London's relentless expansion and sponge-like absorption of newcomers from all parts of Britain and from the world at large have kept the tectonic plates of social change not just active but often whirring and grinding. It is notable that in his description of the deputation assembled to greet Henry VI at Blackheath, John Lydgate lists the various "alyens" admitted to the official welcoming party— Genoese, Florentines, Venetians, and "Esterlinges" (Hansa merchants). London has always depended for its economic survival on its ability to attract fresh waves of workers—partly because mortality rates in the city were for so long so high. Not all immigrants, of course, found themselves invited to participate in mayoral pageants, or indeed welcomed with open arms by grateful Londoners; this anthology includes poems by such as James Berry, Grace Nichols, and Linton Kwesi Johnson that reveal in unsparing detail the difficulties to be overcome by some of those lured to London from Commonwealth countries in the postwar era, a phase of immigration inaugurated by the arrival of the *Empire Windrush* from Kingston, Jamaica, in June 1948. James Berry's "Two Black Labourers on a London Building Site" deftly catches the mistrust and suspicion with which these new arrivals to London were greeted by some:

> Been a train crash.
> > Wha?
> Yeh—tube crash.
> > Who the driver?
> Not a black man.
> > Not a black man?
> I check that firs.
> > Thank Almighty God.
> Bout thirty people dead.
> > Thirty people dead?
> Looks maybe more.
> > Maybe more?
> Maybe more.
> > An black man didn drive?
> No. Black man didn drive.

More unsettling still is Linton Kwesi Johnson's "Sonny's Lettah," which Johnson later recorded with a dub soundtrack; the poem is in the form of an anguished letter written by Sonny to his mother back in the Caribbean from Brixton Prison, where

Sonny finds himself after killing a policeman in an attempt to defend his brother from an unprovoked police assault.

London is often described as being made up of a series of discrete villages—Greenwich, Tottenham, Hampstead, Putney, and so on—and therefore as not being a coherent city in quite the way Paris or Rome is. There is certainly a disparate, even tribal element in the poetry it has generated, a range of idioms and dictions that reflects this diversity or, to be more Darwinian, these struggles for power and prestige. By making such effective use of dialect in their poetry, poets like Berry and Johnson widen our sense of the possibilities of verse. These infusions of the demotic have been the lifeblood of much London poetry, from the street cries of Langland to the ballads of Kipling, from the slang of Elizabethan and Jacobean city comedy to the argot of Peter Reading's buskers on the Underground ("missiz gone arse-over-ed on da fuggin / down eshcalator / tryin to swing for some cuntinna bowler / wot giver two pee"). New forms of enjoyment, such as coffee houses or the pleasure gardens at Vauxhall or Ranelagh or the advent of Music Hall, register not only as topics for poems but as catalysts for poetic change. Consider the way Thomas Hood's "Sonnet to Vauxhall" mimes the fireworks display as observed by someone about to eat a forkful of ham:

> All noses are upturned! Whish—ish!—On high
> The rocket rushes—trails—just steals in sight—
> Then droops and melts in bubbles of blue light—
> And Darkness reigns—Then balls flare up and die—
> Wheels whiz—smack crackers—serpents twist—and then
> Back to the cold transparent ham again.

This might be glossed as the Cockney sublime, as the thrilling but short-lived rockets and catherine wheels and crackers momentarily dazzle the observer, but not enough to make him forget, when they're over, the ham, still waiting to be consumed on his fork.

In their heyday of the early to mid-eighteenth century the Vauxhall Gardens attracted many thousands of visitors each night, but during the Victorian era they slowly declined in popularity, finally closing permanently in 1859. The land was sold for building, and by 1865 not a trace was left of the pleasure grounds where, during the season, Londoners had sought and found entertainment for almost two centuries—though their charms were still being nostalgically celebrated, by Austin Dobson, as late as 1885. To live in a city is to live with change, change normally ac-

complished by an anonymous "they": "they're pulling down . . . ," or "they're build-
ing . . . ," or sometimes one misses the process altogether: "they've pulled down . . . ,"
"they've built . . ." Siegfried Sassoon, out "strolling one afternoon along a street,"
looks for but fails to find Devonshire House (demolished in 1924); where formerly
"Byron rang the bell and limped upstairs," he sees only industrious workmen: "And
not one nook survived to screen a mouse / In what was Devonshire (God rest it)
House." London poems frequently brood on the inexorably changing fabric of the
city. U. A. Fanthorpe watches, fascinated, as bulldozers destroy some mock-Tudor
villas as part of a plan to widen the Westway, while in "River History" Lavinia Green-
law traces the rise and fall and rise and fall of buildings in the area now known as
Docklands. John Heath-Stubbs laments the disappearance of the pub the Old Swan
in Notting Hill Gate and, conversely, the shooting up, seemingly overnight, of so
many terrible high-rise eyesores in the 1960s. Their appearance prompts a witty take
on the legend of Amphion, who supposedly sang so sweetly that the walls of Thebes
built themselves:

> Everyone is complaining
> About these featureless new office blocks.
> And so am I. Each one recalls
> A rather larger than usual poem
> By . . . let's call him N. O. Packdrill
> The currently fashionable bard.
> The poems, you would say, reflect the architecture.
> Or does he, like a new Amphion,
> Evoke this other Thebes?

The relationship between poetry and the streets and buildings and parks and
bridges and railway lines and flyovers and cul-de-sacs and mews that make up the
city is particularly strong in poetry of the postwar era; many, many poems of the last
fifty years or so bristle with street names or other signifiers of London-ness, as if to
ground the poet's perceptions in a kind of documentary realism, and thus to anchor
experience to place. A poet such as the German-born Michael Hofmann often uses
street scenes as a means of registering the zeitgeist through relentless accumulations
of detail; see, in particular, his poem "From Kensal Rise to Heaven," an oddly uplift-
ing hymn to change and decay, to the "friable, broken and dirty" surfaces of this not-
particularly-anything corner of Northwest London in the conflict-ridden, Thatch-
erite 1980s.

Postwar poets are also much given to excavating the layers of literary association that have accreted around particular London sites such as Westminster Bridge—has any bridge in the world inspired quite so many sonnets?—or Bunhill Fields, where John Bunyan, Daniel Defoe, and William Blake are buried, or Wentworth Place, where Keats spent his last two years in London, or Westbourne Park Villas, where Thomas Hardy lived in the 1860s, a fact commemorated by the Australian-born Peter Porter:

> Here, rather than in death-filled Dorset, I see him,
>   The watchful conspirator against the gods
> Come to the capital of light on his own grim
> Journey into darkness.

Hardy of course initially trained as an architect, and while resident in the "capital of light" found his imagination frequently drawn to reflections upon the earlier lives of buildings, and those who once inhabited them or, in the case of Westminster Abbey, were buried within them. In "The Coronation" he pictures the various kings and queens of England being wakened from their slumbers by preparations for the coronation of George V, and speculating on the cause for this "throbbing thudding" sound of "chisels, augers, planes, and saws." Surely, complains one, royal corpses should be able to rest in peace, undisturbed by such typical urban commotions; "Alas," responds another dead regent, they've no choice but to "wait and listen, and endure the show. . . . / Clamour dogs kingship, afterwards not so!"

Another London poem by Hardy—who wrote a surprising number of them—recounts a visit to the British Museum, and finds a means of resuscitating a voice from an even more distant past; the poet is surprised to witness a fellow visitor to the museum lost in ecstasy before an ancient stone of no particular distinction. He asks why, and the man responds, "I'm a laboring man, and know but little, / Or nothing at all; / But I can't help thinking that stone once echoed / The voice of Paul"; the "time-touched stone" the laboring man contemplates was taken, it transpires, from the Areopagus near the Acropolis in Athens, where St. Paul preached his famous sermon. The great apostle is evoked in London even more fully in a poem entitled "In St. Paul's a While Ago," which imagines him proselytizing on the very steps of the church named after him. This poem uses Sir Christopher Wren's great cathedral as a kind of vertical probe into history; its "chasmal classic walls" momentarily free the poet, as he aimlessly wanders around it one July afternoon, from "the daemonian din outside," and allow him to see other "loiterers" there as timeless figures from the past; there goes a "brimming Hebe" (the Greek goddess of youth), "rapt in her adorning"; there an Artemisia—a reference to the Ancient Greek queen so upset by the death of her husband that she mixed a pinch of his ashes into her daily drink—"craped in mourning"; a young couple flirting become Beatrice "coquetting" with Benedick. How peculiar, Hardy muses, that a "strange Jew, Damascus-bound," should have inspired "architectural sages / To frame this pile," and to name it after him; for were St. Paul himself to appear here, and "lift his hand / In stress of eager, stammering speech," any who chanced to hear him "Would have proclaimed him as they passed / An epilept enthusiast."

While Hardy achieves a quirky access to the past by interrogating the fabric of London buildings such as Westminster Abbey or St. Paul's Cathedral or the ancient stone housed in the British Museum, Wordsworth presents himself, in Book VII of *The Prelude,* as constructing a London of the mind long before he actually visited the capital and its famous sights:

> Oh, wondrous power of words! How sweet they are
> According to the meaning which they bring!
> Vauxhall and Ranelagh—I then had heard
> Of your green groves and wilderness of lamps,
> Your gorgeous ladies, fairy cataracts
> And pageant fireworks! Nor must we forget
> Those other wonders, different in kind
> Though scarcely less illustrious in degree:
> The river proudly bridged, the giddy top
> And Whispering Gallery of St. Paul's, the tombs
> Of Westminster, the Giants of Guildhall,
> Bedlam and the two figures at its gates,
> Streets without end and churches numberless,
> Statues with flowery gardens in vast squares,
> The Monument and armoury of the Tower.

His account of the reality confronting him during his residence in the capital from February to August 1795 is perhaps the most richly detailed and vivid in the poetic history of the city, even though Wordsworth assumes the posture of morally condemning much of what he witnesses. His description of St. Bartholomew's Fair explicitly alludes to the parody of city-building in Book I of Milton's *Paradise Lost,* in which the fallen angels raise up their infernal Pandemonium, and yet the energy and specificity of Wordsworth's poetry suggest that, however "perverted" the spectacle, this "parliament of monsters" entered as deeply into his imagination as the scenery of the Alps or the Lake District. Indeed, for all his denunciations of the inorganic, inauthentic nature of city life, it was Wordsworth who first, and arguably most brilliantly, captured the experience of the subjective individual adrift in the baffling modern metropolis, restless, questing, alienated, time and again overwhelmed by the crowds ebbing and flowing through the city's streets, struggling to make sense of it all but repeatedly unable to parse into meaning so many disparate sights and sounds and presences, "the quick dance / Of colours, lights, and forms; the Babel din; / The endless stream of men, and moving things." And it was Wordsworth who first expressed what has since become a cliché of city poetry, the sense of being utterly cut off from all others in the midst of seething humanity:

> How often in the overflowing streets
> Have I gone forwards with the crowd, and said
> Unto myself "The face of everyone
> That passes by me is a mystery!"
> Thus have I looked, nor ceased to look, oppressed
> By thoughts of what and whither, when and how,
> Until the shapes before my eyes became
> A second-sight procession such as glides
> Over still mountains, or appears in dreams,
> And all the ballast of familiar life—
> The present and the past, hope, fear, all stays,
> All laws, of acting, thinking, speaking man—
> Went from me, neither knowing me, nor known.

We are not far here from the anxieties driving that other great epic of urban disaffection inspired by London, *The Waste Land:* "A crowd flowed over London Bridge, so many: / I had not thought death had undone so many."

In Eliot's poem the Thames, its "tent" of summer leaves "broken," an unwholesome rat dragging its slimy belly through the vegetation on its bank, is figured primarily as yet another instance of the deathly limbo of modernity into which London has collapsed; it also, however, occasionally affords brief, ironic glimpses into a golden past, as in the thrice-repeated line from Spenser's "Prothalamion," or the vision of Elizabeth and Leicester afloat on the royal barge, its stern "A gilded shell / Red and gold," a southwest wind bearing them downstream to the peal of bells from white towers. The river has always, at least before the flood-preventing Thames Barrier was built across it in the 1970s, glided at its own sweet will, as Wordsworth put it, though in the exceptionally bitter winter of 1683-1684 it froze solid for two months, and was fast transformed by profit-seeking London vendors into a sort of St. Bartholomew's Fair on ice (two anonymous poems commemorating this winter are included here). The part played by the river in the city's economic history is nicely caught in another anonymous poem, published in *The Gentleman's Magazine* in 1739, a period when the British Empire was expanding particularly rapidly:

> See how the Thames with dimpling motion smiles,
> And from all climes presents Augusta spoils:
> Eastward behold! a thousand vessels ride,
> Which like a floating city crowd her tide.

This happy vision of a boat-crowded Thames as emblem of spreading empire is neatly reversed in the St. Lucia–born Derek Walcott's postcolonial attack on London in his long poem *Omeros,* published in 1990, in which the symbolic shipping on the river is seen as far from beneficent—"the barges chained like our islands to the Thames."

Walcott's line distantly echoes Blake's devastatingly compacted image of the "chartered Thames" ("I wander through each chartered street / Near where the chartered Thames does flow") in his appalled and excoriating "London," for both refute the urge to project an illusion of freedom onto the river, a longing to believe that whatever takes place on its banks or bridges or the boats moored on it, the river is itself neutral and beyond the city's control or chronology. In his enchanting poem "The River's Tale" Rudyard Kipling pictured the life of the Thames before the founding of London, thus using it, like Eliot—or Joseph Conrad at the opening of *Heart of Darkness*—to sink back through the layers of history to some time almost unimaginably different from the present. (James Thomson, incidentally, uses Hampstead Heath in an analogous way in his "Sunday at Hampstead" of 1866.) Father Thames, it is often called, and Kipling's poem works on the premise that the young bridges that span it from the Tower of London to Kew are being inducted by the old river into the prehistoric mysteries of its being.

As is the case with all other aspects of the city, poetic figurations of the river veer dramatically from romance to realism. The Elizabethan poet George Turberville begs it to favor his lady as she passes over its "swelling tide" on which "snow-white swans do fish for needful meat," while, four centuries later, Wendy Cope suddenly realizes that she has fallen hopelessly in love with whomever it was that she shared lunch, just as she is crossing Waterloo Bridge ("After the Lunch"). It plays a significant role in structuring Michael Drayton's stirring nationalist vision of England, *Poly-Olbion,* and Drayton's language turns particularly lyrical when "this mighty flood," "the fair and goodly Thames," at last reaches London, and

> sees his crowded wharfs, and people-pestered shores,
> His bosom overspread with shoals of labouring oars;
> With that most costly bridge that doth him most renown,
> By which he clearly puts all other rivers down.

Against this one might place Alexander Pope's sordid riverside vignettes in his very early poem "The Alley. An Imitation of Spenser," rife with squalling children, foul-mouthed fishwives, and grunting hogs, or the site chosen for the fluvial contests of his writers in *The Dunciad,* just "where Fleet Ditch with disemboguing streams / Rolls the large tribute of dead dogs to Thames." The mud-nymphs dwelling in Pope's filthy river include Nigrina black and Merdamante brown, who compete for the love of one of the dunces, Smedley, or so he relates on eventually emerging from their "jetty bowers" in awesome "majesty of mud."

It took the revolution in sensibility inspired by the Decadents and the Impressionists to find this mud itself a thing of beauty. The paintings of the river and its bridges by such as Whistler and Monet made possible a new kind of urban riverine aesthetic, one that found beauty in steam and fog and industry; in poetry, something analogous is attempted by Oscar Wilde in his "Impression du Matin," which provocatively Frenchifies the capital's river:

> The Thames nocturne of blue and gold
>   Changed to a Harmony in grey:
>   A barge with ochre-coloured hay
> Dropped from the wharf: and chill and cold
>
> The yellow fog came creeping down
>   The bridges, till the houses' walls
>   Seemed changed to shadows and St. Paul's
> Loomed like a bubble o'er the town.

The fog that torments the inhabitants of London in the opening paragraph of Charles Dickens's *Bleak House* here becomes a choice aesthetic effect to be savored by the connoisseur of composition, while the grand dome of St. Paul's almost evanesces, becoming a mere watery bubble afloat in the foggy yellow dawn. John Davidson, in "The Thames Embankment," pursues these harmonies still further in a passage that follows Wilde and the Impressionists in celebrating the power of light to transform "uncouthest shapelessness" and "decoloured refuse" into "ornament." Terms from painting and metalworking serve to aestheticize an essentially nondescript stretch of the Thames Embankment:

> The glistening, close-grained canvas of the mud
> Like hammered copper shone, and all about
> The burning centre of the mirrored orbs
> Illimitable depth of silver fire
> Harmonious beams the overtones of light,
> Suffused the embossed, metallic river bank.

Aureoled in such light, and such extravagant, if syntactically puzzling, poetry, even the river's ungainly barges become "ethereal," while the figureheads of old ships preserved and erected along Baltic Wharf open vistas into Britain's fading imperial glories—"Forlorn / Elysium of the might of England!"

Now that the Thames is no longer the vital artery for Britain's maritime and imperial interests, it seems to have recovered some of its own sweet will, or at least a number of recent poems contrast its "lovely inattentive water," as Alice Oswald puts it in "Another Westminster Bridge," with the "teetering structures of administration" on its banks. Jamie McKendrick depicts, in terms that are rather more barbed, the river reflecting "gold glass from the wavering, // hollow towers of commerce where the profiteers / long for their 'strong and stable government.'" In this poem, "The Deadhouse," McKendrick summons, in a kind of shorthand, the baleful ghosts of both Blake and Eliot, but proceeds to find in the spangled reflections of the ever-moving river a momentary respite from the burdens of both earlier poetic figurations of London and the inexorable demands of capitalism:

> Mind-forged, unreal city. The weight
> of stone on each square foot of earth.
> At least the river is its own weight, give or take
>
> the passing traffic. Makes a silvery tear
> where the light floods in, pools in the soundwell.

The most significant building project undertaken on the banks of the Thames for anyone concerned with the literary history of the city was undoubtedly that of the Globe Theatre in 1599. Shakespeare never mentions London in his poetry, and most of his famous London scenes in plays such as *Henry IV,* Parts 1 and 2, are in prose. It was Ben Jonson who brought to the stage a poetry redolent of the verbal cut-and-thrust of Elizabethan and Jacobean street life in plays such as *The Devil Is an Ass* and *The Alchemist,* plays thickly cluttered with topical references and place-names. We are, however, vouchsafed an almost panoramic glimpse of the physical structure of the Globe, in which Shakespeare was a major shareholder, in the playwright's reference in the prologue to *Henry V* to the "wooden O" of the theater, in which the play's action is about to take place; the Chorus that speaks this prologue then invites the audience to imagine "within the girdle of these walls" the unfolding struggle between England and France. Speculations on the traffic between the London outside that wooden O and the Shakespearean stage itself are an endemic feature of bardolatry, and might be typified by a stanza from Kipling's "The Craftsman," which presents Shakespeare revealing to Ben Jonson one drunken evening in the Mermaid the original sources of his characters:

> How at Bankside, a boy drowning kittens
> Winced at the business; whereupon his sister—
> Lady Macbeth aged seven—thrust 'em under,
> > Sombrely scornful.

The verbal O that is any London poem will inevitably invite us to ponder the way it transmutes experiences, places, people, fantasies, events, into a fragment shored against the ruins of time and history, and how it performs itself in relation not only to the world at large but to all the other poems written about London. Often a crucial aspect of the performance of the poems gathered here is that of the poem's—and poet's—London-ness, that is, the markers of participating in the life of the capital, though these of course keep changing: *"it's a London thing,"* shouts a boy on a bus in the final poem in this anthology, by Ahren Warner, though the poem never discloses exactly what that *London thing* is.

The Satires of John Donne, who we know was a "great frequenter of plays"—plays that must have included those of Jonson and Shakespeare—offer a striking example of a poet performing his mastery of the codes of metropolitan sophistication, his *London thing.* Somewhat paradoxically, a crucial feature of the London-ness of the persona that Donne's Satires project is his unwillingness to adopt a role in the complex urban pageant unfolding around him. In Satire 4 he makes great play of his reluctance ever to go to court, though a court visit is exactly what the poem then goes on to describe, while at the opening of Satire 1 we find him vigorously driving away the "fondling motley humourist" friend who is attempting to lure him out of his study and away from his books and out on to the streets. Well, quite vigorously, for after fifty lines praising different kinds of authors and wittily anticipating the ways his "wild, uncertain" friend will behave in the throng—fawning over a "velvet Justice," servilely raising his hat to a height exactly commensurate with the status and wealth of each person they meet, or even abandoning his chum altogether should he run into "some more spruce companion"—the Donne persona eventually succumbs: "lo / I shut my chamber door, and come, let's go."

The snatches of their dialogue that Donne gives us, once they are out on the streets, echo the kinds of witty jousting between young men that one finds in Shakespearean comedy, or between such as Romeo and Mercutio:

> Now leaps he upright, jogs me, and cries, "Do you see
> Yonder well-favoured youth?" "Which?" "Oh, 'tis he
> That dances so divinely." "Oh," said I,
> "Stand still, must you dance here for company?"
> He drooped, we went . . .

While his social-climbing companion is naïvely excited by the various "silken painted fool[s]" they meet, including one reeking of tobacco (an exciting new product at this period), and one who has traveled and thus seems to be "perfect French, and Italian" ("So is the pox," comes the inevitable riposte), the Donne persona presents himself as brilliantly unimpressed by all those noticed or accosted in the course of their walk. Yet of course the poet's incisive put-downs of the various social performances he witnesses are themselves a performance, and the point of it is to show him as wittier, sharper, more knowing, more skeptical, more alert to what's happening than those he describes—as the King of the Cats, to use a phrase that W. B. Yeats once applied to himself.

There is something inherently metropolitan in the poetry of Donne, as there is in that of later poets such as Rochester and Byron, whose work operates by performing with a similar kind of charisma and panache. The insouciant, but exquisitely timed, shattering of taboos plays a key role in the poetry of all three, and leaves us in no doubt that we are being inducted into the most glamorous act in town: "Had she," to quote again from the vitriolic speaker of "A Ramble in St. James's Park,"

> picked out to rub her arse on
> Some stiff-pricked clown or well-hung parson,

> Each job of whose spermatic sluice
> Had filled her cunt with wholesome juice,
> I the proceeding should have praised
> In hope she had quenched a fire I raised.

The rhymes carry much of the humor here, as they do in Byron's *Don Juan*. In Canto XI Byron's Spanish hero finally reaches London, the sight of which, when glimpsed from Shooter's Hill, inspires in him an exalted meditation on British justice and freedom: "Here laws," he enthuses,

> "are all inviolate; none lay
> Traps for the traveller; every highway's clear.
> Here"–he was interrupted by a knife,
> With "Damn your eyes! your money or your life!"

Less picaresque writers of London satire found a model in the Roman poet Juvenal, in particular his third satire, which was adapted by John Oldham–a friend of Dryden's–in 1683, and then by Samuel Johnson some fifty-five years later. Juvenal's targets–political corruption, pushy foreigners, sycophants, money-lenders, jostling crowds, drunken brawlers–map fairly easily onto London and allow these poets to make a less flattering link between London and imperial Rome than that implicit in the mythology of New Troy. Oldham's version is the more vigorous, while Johnson's "London" imposes an elegant neo-Classical compression on the all-pervasive sins and crimes that afflict the city. It is the tension that the poem develops between its power to anatomize and contain, and the forces of social disorder that it castigates, which seems to drive each perfectly balanced couplet:

> Prepare for death, if here at night you roam,
> And sign your will before you sup from home.
>   . . .
> Scarce can our fields, such crowds at Tyburn die,
> With hemp the gallows and the fleet supply.

Impressive as the poem is, it is perhaps better approached as an experiment in the performance of Johnsonian rhetoric than as the Great Sage's true opinion of the capital where he lived for nearly fifty years, and made his name and his living, and of whose streets he so famously never tired. "What, is it you, you dogs," Boswell records him responding when awakened at three o'clock one morning by a couple of young blades requesting his company for a nocturnal ramble; "I'll have a frisk with you."

A vast proportion of the poetry put into print in Britain since Richard Tottel issued the first edition of his best-selling poetic Miscellany, in 1557, was published in the capital. An interesting study might be made of the influence exerted by the great power of the London book trade on poets from other regions: John Clare, for instance, who is about as regional a poet as one could get, was taken up and published by Keats's publisher, the Fleet Street–based John Taylor, and this had a significant impact, for good or ill, on the poetic oeuvre he created. Even today, when presses like Carcanet in Manchester and Bloodaxe in Newcastle are in such excellent health, together issuing many of the finest collections of the day, it is often lamented that the nation's poetry remains in thrall to the capital's coteries and bias.

Not all great poets, even those who, like Milton or Coleridge or Browning, spent long periods of their lives resident in the capital, wrote great London poems: only Milton's sonnet "When the Assault Was Intended to the City" really qualifies as a London poem; in Coleridge I found nothing beyond the famous lines in "Frost at Midnight" ("For I was reared / In the great city, pent 'mid cloisters dim"); and in Browning only the opening sections of "Waring." A comparison of the contents list of this volume with that of a general anthology of English poetry would reveal a number of conspicuous absences: Sir Philip Sidney, Christopher Marlowe, George Herbert, Thomas Gray, William Collins, Coleridge, Christina Rossetti, Gerard Manley Hopkins, Edward Thomas, and W. H. Auden would all be vying for places in my list of the top-ten great poets who never wrote a London poem, or at least one that advertised its London-ness in a manner sufficient to warrant inclusion in this volume. On the other hand, there are certain poets, such as Blake or Thomas Hood or John Betjeman or Jeremy Reed, whose poetic impulse seems as fundamentally wedded to the life of the city as, say, Frank O'Hara's was to New York, or Baudelaire's to Paris.

The poetry of London, like that of earth, is "ceasing never," to adapt a phrase from Keats: observing, from the upper deck of a gridlocked bus, the cranes wheel above some half-built shopping mall or office block—or, most likely, both; trying to gauge when the Shard, a development under construction near London Bridge Station, will finally glitter in the smokeless air as it does in the pictures on the hoardings that surround it; listening to the optimistic pronouncements of a government spokesperson on the radio about the likely "legacy" of the Olympic Games for Hackney, the borough where I live—all these trigger thoughts of the extent to which the city, like this anthology, is a work in progress. For the *London thing* will forever be metamorphosing, assuming new forms for each new generation of Londoners. Only the Thames, whose commonest crafts these days seem to be speeding police launches and Damien Hirst–spotted riverboats ferrying tourists between Tate Britain and Tate Modern, would have been recognizable to the Gower of the first poem in this volume. And it is perhaps when suspended on one of the city's many bridges, gazing at the river's turbid, churning waters, that one feels most strongly London's "mighty heart," to quote one last time from Wordsworth's extraordinary sonnet, and the pulsing tide of the work of all who have tried to describe it in verse.

John Gower (1330?–1408)

from *Confessio Amantis*

And for that fewe men endite
In oure Englissh, I thenke make
A book for King Richardes sake
To whom bilangeth my ligeance,
With al myn hertes obeissance,   5
In al that ever a liege man
Unto his king may doon or can;
So ferforth I me recomaunde
To him which al me may comaunde,
Prayend unto the hihe regne   10
Which causeth every king to regne,
That his corone longe stonde.
I thenke and have it understonde,
As it bifel upon a tyde,
As thing which scholde tho bityde,   15
Under the toun of newe Troye,
Which took of Brut his ferste joye,
In Temse whan it was flowende,
As I by bote cam rowende,
So as Fortune hir tyme sette,   20
My liege lord par chaunce I mette;
And so bifel, as I cam neigh,
Out of my bot, whan he me seigh,
He bad me come in to his barge.
And whan I was with him at large,   25
Amonges othre thinges seyde,

---

1. *endite* write
4. *ligeance* allegiance
10. *hihe regne* high ruler (here meaning God)
12. *corone* crown
14. *tyde* time
15. *tho* then
18. *Temse* Thames
19. *bote* boat

He hath this charge upon me leyde,
And bad me doo my busynesse,
That to his hihe worthinesse
Som newe thing I scholde booke,   30
That he himself it mighte looke
After the forme of my writyng.
And thus upon his comaundyng
Myn hert is wel the more glad
To write so as he me bad;   35
And eek my fere is wel the lasse
That non envye schal compasse,
Without a resonable wite,
To feyne and blame that I write. . . .

---

30. *booke* compose
36. *fere* fear
38. *wite* retribution
39. *feyne* misconstrue

William Langland (1330?–1386?)

from *The Vision of Piers Plowman*

Persons and parisshe preestes pleyned hem to the bisshop
That hire parisshes weren povere sith the pestilence tyme,
To have a licence and leve at London to dwelle,
And syngen ther for symonie, for silver is swete.
Bisshopes and bachelers, bothe maistres and doctours   5
That han cure under Crist, and crownynge in tokene
And signe that thei sholden shryven hire parisshens,
Prechen and praye for hem, and the povere fede
Liggen at Londoun, in Lenten and ellis.
Somme serven the King, and his silver tellen,   10
In Cheker and in Chauncelrie chalangen his dettes
Of wardes and of wardemotes, weyves and streyves.
And somme serven as servaunts lordes and ladies,
And in stede of stywardes sitten and demen.
Hire messe and hire matyns, and many of hire houres,   15
Arn doone undevoutliche; drede is at the laste
Lest Crist in Consistorie acorse ful manye!
. . .

---

1. *persons* parsons
1. *pleyned* complained
2. *povere* poor
2. *pestilence* plague
3. *leve* permission
4. *syngen . . . for symonie* sing . . . masses for payment
5. *bachelers . . . maistres and doctours* i.e., of divinity
6. *crownynge* tonsure
9. *liggen* reside
9. *ellis* other times
10. *tellen* keep accounts of
11. *Cheker* the court of the Exchequer
11. *chalangen his dettes* make claims for money owed
12. *wardes* guardianships of underage heirs
12. *wardemotes* meetings of the citizens of an urban ward
12. *weyves and streyves* lost property and strayed animals
14. *stede* position
14. *stywardes* stewards
14. *demen* judge
15. *messe* masses
15. *houres* divine offices
17. *Consistorie* Consistory court
17. *acorse* condemn

Yet hoved ther an hundred in howves of selk,
Sergeants, it seemed, that serveden at the Barre,
Pleteden for penyes and pounded the lawe,   20
And noght for love of Oure Lord unlose hire lippes ones.
Thow myghtest bettre meete myst on Malverne Hilles
Than get a "mom" of hire mouth til moneie be shewed!
   Barons and burgeises and bondemen als
I seigh in this assemblee, as ye shul here after;   25
Baksteres and brewesteres and bochiers manye,
Wollen webbesters and weveres of lynnen,
Taillours and tynkers and tollers in marketes,
Masons and mynours, and many othere craftes:
Of alle kynne lybbynge laborers lopen forth somme,   30
As dykeres and delveres that doon hire dedes ille,
And dryveth forth the longe day with *"Dieu save Dame Emme!"*
Cokes and hire knaves cryden, "Hote pies, hote!
Goode gees and grys! Go we dyne, go we!"
Taverners until hem tolden the same: 35
"Whit wyn of Oseye and wyn of Gascoigne,
Of the Ryn and of the Rochel, the roost to defie!"
—Al this I seigh slepyng, and sevene sythes more.

---

18. *hoved* milled
18. *howves* coifs
18. *selk* silk
19. *sergeants* lawyers
19. *Barre* bar
20. *pleteden* pleaded
21. *unlose* unloose
22. *meete* measure
22. *myst* mist
23. *"mom"* murmur, sound
26. *baksteres* bakers
26. *brewesteres* brewers
26. *bochiers* butchers
27. *webbesters* weavers
27. *lynnen* linen

28. *tollers in marketes* toll-collectors
29. *mynours* miners
30. *lybbynge* living
30. *lopen* ran
31. *dykeres* ditchers
31. *delveres* diggers
31. *dedes* work
33. *cokes* cooks
34. *grys* pork
36. *Oseye* Alsace
37. *Ryn* Rhine
37. *the Rochel* La Rochelle
37. *defie* digest
38. *sythes* times

Geoffrey Chaucer (1343?–1400)

from *The Canterbury Tales*

from GENERAL PROLOGUE

Bifil that in that seson on a day,
In Southwerk at the Tabard as I lay
Redy to wenden on my pilgrymage
To Caunterbury with ful devout corage,
At nyght was come into that hostelrye   5
Wel nyne and twenty in a compaignye
Of sondry folk, by aventure yfalle
In felaweshipe, and pilgrimes were they alle,
That toward Caunterbury wolden ryde.
The chambres and the stables weren wyde,   10
And wel we weren esed atte beste.
And shortly, whan the sonne was to reste,
So hadde I spoken with hem everichon
That I was of hir felaweshipe anon,
And made forward erly for to ryse,   15
To take oure wey ther as I yow devyse.

. . .

   A Cook they hadde with hem for the nones,
To boille the chiknes with the marybones,
And poudre-marchant tart and galyngale.
Wel koude he knowe a draughte of Londoun ale.   20
He koude rooste, and sethe, and broille, and frye,
Maken mortreux, and wel bake a pye.

---

1. *bifil* it happened
7. *aventure* chance
11. *esed* accommodated
11. *atte beste* in the best possible way
14. *anon* at once
15. *forward* agreement
16. *devyse* describe

17. *for the nones* for the occasion
18. *marybones* marrow bones
19. *poudre-marchant tart and galyngale* spices
20. *knowe* recognize
21. *sethe* simmer
22. *mortreux* stews

But greet harm was it, as it thoughte me,
That on his shyne a mormal hadde he.
For blankmanger, that made he with the beste.   25

. . .

    Greet chiere made oure Hoost us everichon,
And to the soper sette he us anon.
He served us with vitaille at the beste;
Strong was the wyn, and wel to drynke us leste.
A semely man Oure Hooste was withalle   30
For to been a marchal in an halle.
A large man he was with eyen stepe—
A fairer burgeys was ther noon in Chepe—
Boold of his speche, and wys, and wel ytaught,
And of manhod hym lakkede right naught.   35
Eek therto, he was right a myrie man,
And after soper pleyen he bigan.
And spak of myrthe, amonges othere thynges,
Whan that we hadde maad oure rekenynges,
And seyde thus: "Now, lordynges, trewely,   40
Ye been to me right welcome, hertely;
For by my trouthe, if that I shal nat lye,
I saugh nat this yeer so myrie a compaignye
Atones in this herberwe as is now.
Fayn wolde I doon yow myrthe, wiste I how.   45
And of a myrthe I am right now bythoght,
To doon yow ese, and it shal coste noght. . . ."

---

24. *mormal* ulcer
25. *blankmanger* milky stew of chicken
    or fish
28. *vitaille* victuals
29. *us leste* it pleased us
30. *semely* impressive
30. *withalle* indeed
31. *marchal* master of ceremonies

32. *stepe* prominent
33. *burgeys* burgher
33. *Chepe* Cheapside
39. *maad oure rekenynges* paid our bills
44. *atones* at one time
44. *herberwe* inn
45. *fayn* gladly
45. *wiste I* if I knew

THE COOK'S PROLOGUE

The Cook of Londoun, whil the Reve spak,
For joye him thoughte he clawed him on the bak.
"Ha! ha!" quod he, "For Cristes passion,
This millere hadde a sharp conclusion
Upon his argument of herbergage!   5
Wel seyde Salomon, in his langage,
'Ne bryng nat every man into thyn hous,'
For herberwynge by nyghte is perilous.
Wel oghte a man avysed for to be
Whom that he broghte into his pryvetee.   10
I pray to God, so yeve me sorwe and care,
If evere, sitthe I highte Hogge of Ware,
Herde I a millere bettre yset a-werk.
He hadde a jape of malice in the derk.
But God forbede that we stynte heere;   15
And therfore, if ye vouche-sauf to heere
A tale of me, that am a povre man,
I wol yow telle, as wel as evere I kan,
A litel jape that fil in oure citee."
    Oure Hoost answerde, and seide, "I graunte it thee. 20
Now telle on, Roger; looke that it be good,
For many a pastee hastow laten blood,
And many a Jakke of Dovere hastow soold
That hath been twies hoot and twies coold.
Of many a pilgrym hastow Cristes curs,   25
For of thy percely yet they fare the wors,
That they han eten with thy stubbel goos,

---

2. *For joye him thoughte he clawed him on the bak* enjoyed it so much it was as if the Reeve were scratching his back
5. *herbergage* accommodation
8. *herberwynge* providing lodgings
12. *highte* was called
13. *yset a-werk* duped
22. *laten blood* let blood (i.e., removed gravy from unsold pie to make it last longer)
23. *Jakke of Dovere* type of pie
26. *percely* parsley

For in thy shoppe is many a flye loos.
Now telle on, gentil Roger, by thy name.
But yet I pray thee, be nat wroth for game;   30
A man may seye ful sooth in game and pley."
    "Thou seist ful sooth," quod Roger, "by my fey!
But 'sooth pley, quaad pley,' as the Flemyng seith.
And therfore, Herry Bailly, by thy feith,
Be thou nat wrooth, er we departen heer,   35
Though that my tale be of an hostileer.
But nathelees I wol nat telle it yit;
But er we parte, ywis, thou shalt be quit."
And therwithal he lough, and made cheere,
And seyde his tale, as ye shul after heere.   40

THE COOK'S TALE

    A prentys whilom dwelled in oure citee,
And of a craft of vitailliers was hee.
Gaillard he was as goldfynch in the shawe,
Broun as a berye, a propre short felawe,
With lokkes blake, ykembd ful fetisly.   45
Dauncen he koude so wel and jolily
That he was cleped Perkyn Revelour.
He was as ful of love and paramour
As is the hyve ful of hony sweete.
Wel was the wenche with hym myghte meete.   50
At every bridale wolde he synge and hoppe;
He loved bet the taverne than the shoppe.

---

27. *stubbel goos* goose fed on stubble   43. *gaillard* merry
33. *'sooth pley, quaad pley'* 'a true joke is   43. *shawe* wood
    a bad joke'   45. *lokkes* locks
36. *hostileer* innkeeper   45. *ykembd* combed
41. *prentys* apprentice   45. *fetisly* neatly
42. *vitailliers* victuallers   48. *paramour* wenching

For whan ther any ridyng was in Chepe,
Out of the shoppe thider wolde he lepe—
Til that he hadde al the sighte yseyn,   55
And daunced wel, he wolde nat come ayeyn—
And gadered hym a meynee of his sort
To hoppe and synge and maken swich disport;
And ther they setten stevene for to meete,
To pleyen at the dys in swich a streete.   60
For in the toune, nas ther no prentys
That fairer koude caste a paire of dys
Than Perkyn koude, and therto he was free
Of his dispense, in place of pryvetee.
That fond his maister wel in his chaffare,   65
For often tyme he foond his box ful bare.
For sikerly a prentys revelour
That haunteth dys, riot, or paramour,
His maister shal it in his shoppe abye,
Al have he no part of the mynstralcye.   70
For thefte and riot, they been convertible,
Al konne he pleye on gyterne or ribible.
Revel and trouthe, as in a lowe degree,
They been ful wrothe al day, as men may see.
    This joly prentys with his maister bood   75
Til he were ny out of his prentishood,
Al were he snybbed bothe erly and late,
And somtyme lad with revel to Newegate.

---

53. *ridyng* horse procession
53. *Chepe* Cheapside
57. *meynee* group
59. *setten stevene* made an appointment
60. *dys* dice
63/4. *free / Of his dispense* extravagant in his expenditure
65. *chaffare* business
66. *box* strongbox
69. *abye* pay for it
71. *convertible* interchangeable
72. *gyterne* cithern
72. *ribible* fiddle
73. *as in a lowe degree* in a man of the lower orders
74. *ful wrothe* completely incompatible
75. *bood* remained
77. *snybbed* told off
78. *Newegate* i.e., Newgate Prison

But atte laste his maister hym bithoghte,
Upon a day, whan he his papir soghte,   80
Of a proverbe that seith this same word:
"Wel bet is roten appul out of hoord
Than that it rotie al the remenaunt."
So fareth it by a riotous servaunt;
It is ful lasse harm to lete hym pace,   85
Than he shende alle the servantz in the place.
Therfore his maister yaf hym acquitance,
And bad hym go, with sorwe and with meschance!
And thus this joly prentys hadde his leve.
Now lat hym riote al the nyght or leve.   90
And for ther is no theef withoute a lowke,
That helpeth hym to wasten and to sowke
Of that he brybe kan, or borwe may,
Anon he sente his bed and his array
Unto a compeer of his owene sort,   95
That lovede dys and revel and disport,
And hadde a wyf that heeld for contenance
A shoppe, and swyved for hir sustenance.

---

80. *papir* certificate of completion of ap-
  prenticeship
83. *rotie* rot
85. *pace* leave
86. *shende* corrupt
91. *lowke* accomplice

92. *sowke* suck
93. *brybe* steal
97. *for contenance* for the sake of appear-
  ances
98. *swyved* had sex

Thomas Hoccleve (1367?–1426)

from *La Male Regle de T. Hoccleue*

I dar nat telle how that the fressh repeir
Of Venus femel lusty children deer,
That so goodly, so shaply wer, and feir,
And so plesant of port and of maneere,
And feede cowden al a world with cheere,   5
And of atyr passyngly wel byseye,
At Poules Heed me maden ofte appeere,
To talke of mirthe and to disporte and pleye.

Ther was sweet wyn ynow thurghout the hous,
And wafres thikke, for this conpaignie   10
That I spak of, been sumwhat likerous.
Wheras they mowe a draght of wyn espie,
Sweete, and in wirkynge hoot for the maistrie
To warme a stommak with, therof they drank.
To suffre hem paie had been no courtesie.   15
That charge I took, to wynne loue and thank.

Of loues aart yit touchid I no deel.
I cowde nat, and eek it was no neede.
Had I a kus, I was content ful weel,
Bettre than I wolde han be with the deede.   20
Theron can I but smal, it is no dreede.
Whan that men speke of it, in my presence,
For shame I wexe as reed as is the gleede.
Now wole I torne ageyn to my sentence.

---

1. *fressh repeir* boisterous company
2. *femel* female
6. *atyr* attire
6. *byseye* supplied
7. *Poules Heed* Paul's Head (tavern)
10. *wafres* wafers
11. *likerous* greedy

12. *wheras* wherever
13. *hoot for the maistrie* powerfully hot
19. *kus* kiss
21. *can I but smal* I only know a little
21. *it is no dreede* there is no doubt
23. *gleede* burning coal
24. *my sentence* what I was saying

Of him that hauntith tauerne of custume,   25
At shorte wordes, the profyt is this:
In double wyse his bagge it shal consume,
And make his tonge speke of folk amis,
For in the cuppe seelden fownden is
That any wight his neigheburgh commendith.   30
Beholde, and see what auantage is his
That God, his freend, and eek himself offendith.

But oon auantage in this cas I haue:
I was so ferd with any man to fighte,
Cloos kepte I me. No man durste I depraue,   35
But rownyngly I spak, nothyng on highte.
And yit my wil was good, if that I mighte,
For lettynge of my manly cowardyse,
That ay of strokes impressid the wighte,
So that I durste medlyn in no wyse.   40

Wher was a gretter maistir eek than Y,
Or bet aqweyntid at Westmynstre yate,
Among the tauerneres namely,
And cookes, whan I cam eerly or late?
I pynchid nat at hem in myn acate,   45
But paied hem as that they axe wolde,
Wherfore I was the welcomer algate,
And for a verray gentilman yholde.

And if it happid on the someres day
That I thus at the tauerne hadde be,   50

---

25. *of custume* very often
27. *bagge* money bag
32. *that* who
32. *eek* also
34. *ferd* afraid
35. *depraue* disparage
36. *rownyngly* in a whisper
36. *on highte* out loud

38. *lettynge* hindering
39. *strokes* blows
39. *wighte* weight
40. *medlyn* fight
42. *yate* gate
45. *pynchid nat* found no fault with
45. *acate* purchase
47. *algate* always

Whan I departe sholde and go my way
Hoom to the Priuee Seel, so wowed me
Hete and vnlust and superfluitee
To walke vnto the brigge and take a boot,
That nat durste I contrarie hem all three,   55
But dide as that they stired me, God woot.

And in the wyntir, for the way was deep,
Vnto the brigge I dressid me also,
And ther the bootmen took vpon me keep,
For they my riot kneewen fern ago.   60
With hem I was itugged to and fro,
So wel was him that I with wolde fare,
For riot paieth largely eueremo.
He styntith neuere til his purs be bare.

Othir than maistir callid was I neuere   65
Among this meynee, in myn audience.
Methoghte I was ymaad a man for euere,
So tikelid me that nyce reuerence
That it me made larger of despense
Than that I thoghte han been. O flaterie,   70
The guyse of thy traiterous diligence
Is, folk to mescheef haasten and to hie. . . .

---

52. *wowed me* enticed me   59. *keep* notice
53. *vnlust* laziness   62. *so wel was him* so pleased was he
54. *brigge* bridge   70. *thoghte han been* intended to be
54. *boot* boat   71. *guyse* manner
57. *deep* deep in mud   72. *hie* hurry
58. *dressid* went

John Lydgate (1370?–1449/50)

from *King Henry VI's Triumphal Entry into London*

Towarde the end of wyndy Februarie,
Whanne Phebus was in the Fysshe eronne
Out of the synge, which called is Aquarie,
Newe kalendes wern entred and begonne
Of Marchis komyng, and the mery sonne   5
Upon a Thursday shewed his bemys briht
Uppon London, to make hem glade and liht.

The stormy reyne of alle theyre hevynesse
Were passed away, and alle her olde grevaunce,
For the sixte Herry, roote of here gladnesse,   10
Theyre hertis joye, theyre worldis suffisaunce,
By trewe dissent crounyd kyng of Fraunce,
The hevene rejoysyng the day of his repayre
Made his komyng the wedir to be so fayre.

A tyme, I trowe, of God, for hym provided;   15
In alle the hevenes there was no clowde seyn,
From other dayes that day was so devided,
And fraunchised from mistys and from reyn,
The eyre attempred, the wyndis smoth and pleyn,
The citezenis thurhoute the Citee   20
Halwyd that day with grete solempnyté.

And lyke for David, after his victorie,
Rejoyssed was alle Jerusalem,
So this Citee with laude, pris, and glorie,
For joye moustred lyke the sonne beem,   25

---

12. *dissent* descent   21. *halwyd* celebrated
13. *repayre* return   25. *moustred* gathered
18. *fraunchised* free

To geve ensample thurhout the reem;
Alle of assent, whoso kan conseyve,
Theyre noble kyng wern gladde to resseyve.

Theyr clothing was of colour ful covenable,
The noble Meire cladde in reede velvette,   30
The Sheryves, the Aldermen ful notable,
In furred clokes, the colour skarlette;
In statly wyse, when they were mette,
Eche oon well horsed made no delay,
But with here Meire roode forth in her way.   35

The citizenis echoon of the Citee
In here entent that they were pure and clene,
Chees hem of white a ful feyre lyveré,
In every crafte, as yt was well sene;
To showe the trouthe that they dyde mene   40
Toward the Kyng hadd made hem feythfully
In soundry devyses enbrowdred richely.

And forto remembre of other alyens;
First Jeneweys, though they were straungers,
Florentyns and the Venycyens,   45
And Esterlinges gladde in her maners,
Canveyed with sergeauntes and other officers
Estatly horsed, after the Meire rydyng,
Passed the subbarbes to mete with the kyng.

To the Blakeheeth whanne they dydde atteyne,   50
The Meire, of prudence in especyall,
Made hem hove in rengis tweyne,
A strete bitwene eche partye lyke a wall,

---

26. *reem* realm
29. *convenable* suitable
38. *lyveré* livery
42. *enbrowdred* embroidered
43. *alyens* foreigners

44. *Jeneweys* Genoese
46. *Esterlinges* Hansa merchants
48. *estatly* nobly
52. *rengis tweyne* two rows

Alle cladde in white; and the moste princypall
Afforn in reede with theire Meire rydyng   55
Tyl tyme that he sauh the kyng komyng.
. . .

But forto tellen alle the circumstaunces,
Of every thing shewed in sentence,
Noble devyses, dyvers ordenaunces
Conveyed by scripture with ful grete excellence,   60
Alle to declare I have noone eloquence;
Wherfore I pray to alle that shall yt rede,
Forto correcte where as they se nede.

First, whanne he passed was the fabour,
Entryng the Brigge of this noble town,   65
Ther was a pyler reysed lyke a tour,
And theron stoode a sturdy champeoun,
Of looke and chere sterne as a lyoun,
His swerde up rered proudely gan manace,
Alle foreyn enmyes from the kyng to enchace.   70

And in defence of his estate ryall
The geaunt wolde abyde eche aventure;
And alle assautes that wern marcyall,
For his sake he proudely wolde endure,
In tokne wherof he hadde a scripture   75
On eyther syde declaryng his entent,
Which seyde thus by goode avysement:

"Alle tho that ben enemyes to the Kyng,
I shall hem clothe with confusioun;
Make him myhty with vertuous levyng   80
His mortall foon to oppressen and bere adoun,
And him to encresen as Cristis champioun,

---

55. *afforn* before
60. *scripture* writing
64. *fabour* suburb

66. *pyler* pillar
66. *tour* tower
73. *marcyall* martial

Alle myscheffes from hym to abrigge
With the grace of God at th'entryng of the Brigge."

Twoo antelopes stondying on eytheyr syde   85
With the armes of Englond and of Fraunce,
In tokenyng that God shal for hym provyde,
As he hath tytle by juste enheritaunce
To regne in pees, plenté and plesaunce;
Sesyng of werre, that men mow ryde or goon,   90
As trewe lieges, theyre hertes made both oon.

Ferthermore, so as the Kyng gan ryde,
Midde of the Brigge ther was a tour on lofte,
The Lorde of Lordes beyng ay his guyde,
As He hath be and yitt wole be ful ofte;   95
The tour arrayed with velvettes softe,
Clothis of golde, sylke, and tapcerye,
As apperteynyth to his regalye.

And at his komyng, of excellent beauté,
Beyng of port most womanly of chere,   100
Ther yssed oute emperesses three;
Theyre heer dysplayed as Phebus in here spere,
With crounettes of golde and stones clere;
At whos out komyng they gaf such a liht,
That the byholders were stonyed in theire siht.   105

The first of hem called was Nature,
As she that hath under her demeyne,
Man, beeste, and foule, and every creature,
Withinne the bondys of hire goldyn cheyn;
Eke heven, and erthe, and every creature   110
This emperesse of custume doth enbrace;
And next hire komyth hire sustre called Grace.

---

90. *sesyng* ceasing   101. *yssed* issued
97. *tapcerye* tapestry   102. *heer* hair
98. *regalye* royalty   102. *spere* spheres

Passyng famous, and of grete reverence,
Moste desired in all regions;
For wher that ever she with here precence,   115
She bryngeth gladnes to citees and touns;
Of alle well fare she holdeth the possessions,
For, I dar say, prosperyté in no place
No while abydith, but yf ther be grace.

In tokne that Grace shulde longe contune   120
Unto the Kyng, she shewed hire full benyngne;
And next hire come the emperesse, Fortune,
Apperyng to hym with many a noble sygne,
And ryall toknes; to shewe that he was dygne,
Of God dysposed as Grace lyst to ordeyne,   125
Upon his heede to were crounes tweyne.

Thes three ladyes, all of oon entent
Three goostly giftes, hevenly and devyne,
Unto the Kyng anoon they dydde present,
And to his hyhnesse they dydd anoon enclyne;   130
And, what they were pleynly to termyne,
Grace gaf him first at his komyng
Twoo riche giftes, Sciens and Kunnyng.

Nature gaf him eke strenth and feyrenesse,
Forto be lovyd and dredde of every wiht;   135
Fortune gaf him eke prosperité and richesse,
With this scripture apperyng in theire siht,
To him applyed of verrey dewe riht;
"First undirstonde and joyfully procede
And lange to regne" the scripture seyde in dede.   140

This ys to mene, whoso undirstonde ariht,
Thow shalt be Fortune have lange prosperité;

---

120. *contune* continue   131. *termyne* declare
121. *benyngne* graciousness   138. *verrey dewe riht* very aptly
124. *dygne* worthy

And be Nature thow shalt have strenth and myht,
Forth to procede in lange felicité;
And Grace also hath graunted unto thee,   145
Vertuously lange in thy ryall citee,
With septre and croune to regne in equyté."

On the riht hande of thes emperesses
Stoode sevyn maydenys verrey celestyall;
Lyke Phebus bemys shone hire goldyn tresses,   150
Upon here heedes eche havyng a cornall,
Of porte and chere semyng inmortall,
In siht transendyng alle erthely creatures,
So aungelyk they wern of theyre figures.

Alle cladde in white, in tokne of clennesse,   155
Lyche pure virgynes as in theyre ententys,
Shewyng outward an hevenly fressh brihtnesse;
Stremed with sonys were alle their garmentis,
Aforne provyded for pure innocentis,
Most columbyne of chere and of lokyng,   160
Mekely roos up at komyng of the Kyng.

They hadde an bawdrykes alle of safir hewe,
Goynge outward gan the Kyng salewe,
Hym presentyng with her giftes newe,
Lyche as theym thouht yt was unto hem dewe,   165
Which goostly giftes here in ordre sewe,
Doune dessendyng as sylvere dewe fro hevyn,
Alle grace include withinne thes giftes sevyn.

Thes ryall giftes ben of vertue moste
Goostly corages, moste sovernynly delyte;   170
Thes giftes called of the Hooly Gooste,
Outward figured ben seven dowys white,

---

151. *cornall* coronet   163. *salewe* greet
158. *sonys* sun's rays   166. *goostly* spiritual
160. *columbyne* dove-like   166. *sewe* follow
162. *bawdrykes* sashes   172. *dowys* doves

And seyying to him, lyke as clerkes write,
"God thee fulfille with intelligence
And with a spyryt of goostly sapience.   175

"God sende also unto thy moste vaylle
Thee to preserve from alle hevynesse,
A spyrit of strenth, and of goode counsaylle,
Of konnyng, drede, pité, and lownesse."
Thus thes ladyes gan theire giftes dresse,   180
Graciously at theyre oute komyng,
Be influence liht upon the Kyng.

Thes emperesses hadde on theyre lefte syde
Other sevyne virgynes, pure and clene,
Be attendaunce contenuelly to abyde,   185
Alle cladde in white, smytte fulle of sterres shene;
And to declare what they wolde mene
Unto the Kyng with ful grete reverence
Thes were theire giftes shortly in sentence:

"God thee endewe with a crowne of glorie,   190
And with septre of clennesse and pytee,
And with a swerde of myht and victorie,
And with a mantel of prudence cladde thow be,
A shelde of feyth forto defende thee,
An helme of helthe wrouht to thyn encrees,   195
Girt with a girdyll of love and parfyte pees."

Thes sevyn virgyns, of siht most hevenly,
With herte, body, and handes rejoysynge,
And of othir cheris appered murely,
For the Kyngis gracious home komynge;   200

---

176. *vaylle* benefit   191. *clennesse* purity
179. *lownesse* humility   199. *cheris* gestures
180. *dresse* offer   199. *murely* joyfully
186. *smytte* studded

And for gladnesse they beganne to synge,
Moste aungelyk with hevenly armonye,
This same roundell, which I shall now specyfye:

"Sovereyne Lorde, welcome to youre citee;
Welcome, oure Joye, and oure Hertis Plesaunce,   205
Welcome, oure Gladnesse, welcome, our Suffisaunce,
Welcome, welcome, riht welcome mote ye be.

"Syngyng toforn thy ryall Magesté,
We say of herte, withoute variaunce,
Sovereyene Lorde, welcome, welcome ye be.   210

"Meire, citezenis and alle the comounté,
At youre home komyng now out of Fraunce,
Be grace relevyd of theyre olde grevaunce,
Syng this day with grete solempnyté,
Sovereyne Lorde, welcome to youre citee."   215
. . .

Be gladde, O London! be gladde and make grete joye,
Citee of Citees, of noblesse precellyng,
In thy bygynnynge called Newe Troye;
For worthynesse thanke God of alle thyng,
Which hast this day resseyved so thy Kyng   220
With many a signe and many an observaunce
To encrese thy name by newe remembraunce.

Suche joye was nevere in the Consistorie,
Made for the tryumphe with alle the surplusage,
Whanne Sesar Julius kam home with his victorie;   225
Ne for the conqueste of Sypion in Cartage;
As London made in every manere age,

---

209. *variaunce* hesitation
211. *comounté* common people
217. *precellyng* surpassing
220. *resseyved* received

223. *Consistorie* Council Chamber of the
      Roman senate
224. *surplusage* embellishments

Out of Fraunce at the home komyng
Into this citee of theyre noble Kyng.

Of sevyn thinges I preyse this citee: 230
Of trewe menyng, and feythfull observaunce,
Of rihtwysnesse, trouthe, and equyté,
Of stablenesse ay kepte in lygeaunce;
And for of vertue thow hast such suffisaunce,
In this lande here and other landes alle   235
The Kyngis Chambre of custume men thee calle.

    [*L'envoye.*

O noble Meir! be yt unto youre plesaunce
And to alle that duelle in this citee,
On my rudenesse and on myn ygnoraunce,
Of grace and mercy forto have pitee,   240
My symple makyng forto take at gree;
Considre this, that in moste lowly wyse
My wille were goode forto do yow servyse.

---

241. *at gree* at your pleasure

Anon. (15th century)

London Lickpenny

    In London there I was bent,
    I saw myselfe, where trouthe shuld be ateynte;
    Fast to Westminstar-ward I went
    To a man of lawe, to make my complaynt.
    I sayd, "For Marys love, that holy seynt,   5
    Have pity on the powre, that would procede.
    I would gyve sylvar, but my purs is faynt."
    For lacke of money I may not spede.

    As I thrast thrugheout the thronge
    Amonge them all, my hode was gonn;   10
    Netheles I let not longe,
    To kyngs benche tyll I come.
    Byfore a juge I kneled anon;
    I prayd hym for Gods sake he would take hede.
    Full rewfully to hym I gan make my mone;   15
    For lacke of money I may not spede.

    Benethe hym sat clerks, a great rowt;
    Fast they writen by one assent.
    There stode up one, and cryed round about,
    "Richard, Robert, and one of Kent!"   20
    I wist not wele what he ment,
    He cried so thike there in dede;
    There were stronge theves shamed and shent,
    But they that lacked money mowght not spede.

2. *ateynte* achieved
6. *procede* go to law
10. *hode* hood
15. *mone* complaint
22. *thike* fast
23. *shent* ruined

Unto the Comon Place I yowde thoo,   25
Where sat one with a sylken houde.
I dyd hym reverence as me ought to do;
I tolde hym my case, as well as I coude,
And seyd all my goods, by nowrd and by sowde,
I am defraudyd with great falshed;   30
He would not geve me a momme of his mouthe.
For lake of money I may not spede.

Then I went me unto the Rollis
Before the clerks of the Chauncerie.
There were many qui tollis,   35
But I herd no man speke of me.
Before them I knelyd upon my kne,
Shewyd them myne evidence, and they began to reade.
They seyde trewer things might there nevar be,
But for lacke of money I may not spede.   40

In Westminster Hall I found one
Went in a longe gowne of ray.
I crowched, I kneled before them anon,
For Marys love, of helpe I gan them pray.
As he had be wrothe, he voyded away   45
Bakward, his hand he gan me byd.
"I wot not what thou menest," gan he say.
"Ley downe sylvar, or here thow may not spede."

In all Westminstar Hall I could find nevar a one
That for me would do, thowghe I shuld dye.   50

---

25. *Comon Place* Court of Common
    Pleas
25. *yowde* went
29. *by nowrd and by sowde* by north and
    by south
30. *falshed* falsehood

31. *momme* murmur
33. *Rollis* Court of Rolls
35. *qui tollis* Latin legal formula to sum-
    mon to the bar
42. *gowne of ray* striped robe
45. *voyded* dismissed me

Without the dores were Flemings grete woon;
Upon me fast they gan to cry,
And sayd, "Mastar, what will ye copen or by—
Fine felt hatts, spectacles for to rede?"
Of this gay gere, a great cause why   55
For lake of money I might not spede.

Then to Westminster gate I went
When the sone was at highe prime.
Cokes to me, they toke good entent,
Called me nere, for to dyne,   60
And proferyd me good brede, ale, and wyne.
A fayre clothe they began to sprede,
Rybbes of befe, bothe fat and fine;
But for lacke of money I might not spede.

In to London I gan me hy;   65
Of all the lond it bearethe the prise.
"Hot pescods!" one gan cry,
"Strabery rype, and chery in the ryse!"
One bad me come nere and by some spice;
Pepar and saffron they gan me bede,   70
Clove, grayns, and flowre of rise.
For lacke of money I might not spede.

Then into Chepe I gan me drawne,
Where I sawe stond moche people.
One bad me come nere, and by fine cloth of lawne,   75
Paris thred, coton, and umple.
I seyde thereupon I could no skyle,
I am not wont thereto in dede.

---

51. *Flemings grete woon* a large number
    of Flemings
53. *copen* barter
59. *cokes* cooks
66. *it bearethe the prise* is the best
68. *ryse* branch

70. *bede* offer
71. *grayns* cereal
71. *flowre of rise* rice flour
73. *gan me drawne* went
76. *umple* fine gauze
77. *I could no skyle* I knew nothing about it

One bad me by an hewre, my hed to hele:
For lake of money I might not spede.   80

Then went I forth by London Stone
Thrwgheout all Canywike strete.
Drapers to me they called anon;
Grete chepe of clothe, they gan me hete;
Then come there one, and cried "Hot shepes fete!"   85
"Risshes faire and grene," an othar began to grete;
Both melwell and makarell I gan mete,
But for lacke of money I myght not spede.

Then I hied me into Estchepe.
One cried, "Ribes of befe, and many a pie!"   90
Pewtar potts they clatteryd on a heape.
Ther was harpe, pipe and sawtry.
"Ye by Cokke!" "Nay by Cokke!" some began to cry;
Some sange of Jenken and Julian, to get themselvs mede.
Full fayne I wold hadd of that mynstralsie,   95
But for lacke of money I cowld not spede.

Into Cornhill anon I yode
Where is moche stolne gere amonge.
I saw wher henge myne owne hode
That I had lost in Westminstar amonge the throng.   100
Then I beheld it with lokes full longe;
I kenned it as well as I dyd my Crede.
To be myne owne hode agayne, me thought it wrong,
But for lacke of money I might not spede.

Then came the taverner, and toke my by the sleve,   105
And seyd, "Ser, a pint of wyn would yow assay?"

---

79. *by* buy   87. *melwell* cod
79. *hewre* cap   92. *sawtry* psaltery
79. *hele* cover   93. *Cokke* God
82. *Canywike* Candlewick   94. *mede* rewards
84. *hete* offer   97. *yode* went
86. *risshes* rushes   103. *be* buy

"Syr," quod I, "it may not greve,
For a peny may do no more then it may."
I dranke a pint, and therefore gan pay;
Sore a-hungred away I yede;   110
For well London Lykke-peny for ones and eye,
For lake of money I may not spede.

Then I hyed me to Byllingesgate,
And cried "Wagge, wagge yow hens!"
I praye a barge man, for Gods sake,   115
That they would spare me myn expens.
He sayde, "Ryse up, man, and get the hens.
What wenest thow I will do on the my almes-dede?
Here skapethe no man, by-nethe ij. pens!"
For lacke of money I myght not spede.   120

Then I conveyed me into Kent,
For of the law would I medle no more;
By-caus no man to me would take entent,
I dight me to the plowe, even as I ded before.
Jhesus save London, that in Bethelem was bore,   125
And every trew man of law, God graunt hym souls med;
And they that be othar, God theyr state restore:—
For he that lackethe money, with them he shall not spede!

---

107. *it may not greve* it can do no harm
110. *yede* went
111. *for ones and eye* for once and for all
114. *wagge* move
118. *what wenest thow* why do you think

119. *by-nethe ij. pens* for under twopence
123. *take entent* pay attention
124. *dight me* gave myself over
126. *med* reward

John Skelton (1460?–1529)

from *Collyn Clout*

Avaunt, Syr Gye of Gaunt!
Avaunt, lewde preest, avaunt!
Avaunt, syr doctour Deuyas!
Prate of thy matens and thy mas,
And let our matters pas!   5
How darest thou, daucocke, mell?
Howe darest thou, losell,
Allygate the gospell
Agaynst us of the counsell?
Avaunt to the devyll of hell!   10

Take him, wardeyn of the Flete,
Set hym fast by the fete!
I say, lieutenaunt of the Toure,
Make this lurdeyne for to loure;
Lodge hym in Lytell Ease,   15
Fede hym with beanes and pease!
The Kynges Benche or Marshalsy,
Have hym thyder by and by!
The vyllayne precheth openly,
And declareth our vyllany;   20
And of our fee symplenes
He sayes that we are recheles,
And full of wylfulnes,
Shameles, and mercyles,
Incorrigible and insaciate;   25

---

2. *lewde* ignorant
6. *daucocke* simpleton
6. *mell* meddle
7. *losell* scoundrel
8. *allygate* cite

14. *lurdeyne* loafer
14. *loure* look frightened
21. *fee symplenes* unrestricted possession
22. *recheles* irresponsible

And after this rate
Agaynst us dothe prate.
At Poules Crosse, or elswhere,
Openly at Westmynstere,
And Saynt Mary Spytell   30
They set nat by us a shyttell;
And at the Austen Fryars
They counte us for lyars,
And at Saynt Thomas of Akers
They carpe of us lyke crakers;   35
Howe we wyll rule all at wyll
Without good reason or skyll,
And say howe that we be
Full of parcyallyte;
And howe at a pronge   40
We tourne ryght into wronge,
Delay causes so longe
That ryght no man can fonge.
They say many matters be borne
By the ryght of a rambes horne.   45
Is nat this a shamfull scorne
To be tered thus and torne? . . .

---

31. *shyttell* shuttlecock   40. *at a pronge* under pressure
35. *crakers* boasters   43. *fonge* seize
39. *parcyallyte* bias

Anon. (1500?)

"London, thou art of townes A per se"

London, thou art of townes A per se,
Sovereign of cities, semeliest in sight,
Of high renoun, riches, and royaltie,
Of lordis, barons, and many goodly knyght;
Of most delectable lusty ladies bright,   5
Of famous prelatis in habitis clericall,
Of merchauntis full of substaunce and myght:
London, thou art the flour of Cities all.

Gladdith anon, thou lusty Troy Novaunt,
Citie that some tyme cleped was New Troy,   10
In all the erth, imperiall as thou stant,
Pryncesse of townes, of pleasure, and of joy;
A richer restith under no Christen roy;
For manly power, with craftis naturall,
Fourmeth none fairer sith the flode of Noy: 15
London, thou art the flour of Cities all.

Gemme of all joy, jasper of jocunditie,
Most myghty carbuncle of vertue and valour,
Strong Troy in vigour and in strenuytie;
Of royall cities rose and geraflour;   20
Empresse of townes, exalt in honour,
In beawtie beryng the crone imperiall,
Swete paradise precelling in pleasure:
London, thou art the flour of Cities all.

---

9. *gladdith* be glad
10. *cleped* called
11. *stant* stands
13. *roy* king

15. *Noy* Noah
18. *carbuncle* jewel
20. *geraflour* gillyflower
23. *precelling* excelling

Above all ryvers thy Ryver hath renowne,   25
Whose beryall stremys, pleasaunt and preclare,
Under thy lusty wallys renneth down,
Where many a swanne doth swymme with wyngis fare,
Where many a barge doth saile, and row with are,
Where many a ship doth rest with toppe-royall.   30
O! towne of townes, patrone and not-compare:
London, thou art the flour of Cities all.

Upon thy lusty Brigge of pylers white
Been merchauntis full royall to behold;
Upon thy stretis goth many a semely knyght   35
In velvet gownes and cheynes of fyne gold.
By Julyus Cesar thy Tour founded of old
May be the hous of Mars victoryall,
Whos artillary with tonge may not be told:
London, thou art the flour of Cities all.   40

Strong be thy wallis that about the standis;
Wise be the people that within the dwellis;
Fresh is thy ryver with his lusty strandis;
Blith be thy chirches, wele sownyng be thy bellis;
Riche be thy merchauntis in substaunce that excellis;   45
Fair be thy wives, right lovesom, white and small;
Clere be thy virgyns, lusty under kellis:
London, thou art the flour of Cities all.

Thy famous Maire, by pryncely governaunce,
With swerd of justice the rulith prudently.   50
No Lord of Parys, Venyce, or Floraunce
In dignytie or honoure goeth to hym nye.

---

26. *preclare* bright   33. *Brigge* Bridge
29. *are* oars   33. *pylers* pillars
31. *patrone* pattern   44. *sownyng* sounding
31. *not-compare* beyond all comparison   47. *kellis* headdresses

He is exampler, loode-ster, and guye;
Principall patrone and roose orygynalle,
Above all Maires as maister moost worthy: 55
London, thou art the flour of Cities all.

---

53. *loode-ster* lodestar   53. *guye* guide

Sir Thomas Wyatt (1503–1542)

"Tagus, farewell, that westward with thy streams"

Tagus, farewell, that westward with thy streams
Turns up the grains of gold already tried;
With spur and sail for I go seek the Thames,
Gainward the sun that show'th her wealthy pride,
And, to the town which Brutus sought by dreams,
Like bended moon doth lend her lusty side.
My king, my country, alone for whom I live,
Of mighty love the wings for this me give.

"Who list his wealth and ease retain"

V. Innocentia
Veritas Viat Fides
Circumdederunt me inimici mei

Who list his wealth and ease retain
Himself let him unknown contain.
Press not too fast in at that gate
Where the return stands by disdain,
For sure, *circa Regna tonat.*

The high mountains are blasted oft
When the low valley is mild and soft.
Fortune with Health stands at debate.
The fall is grievous from aloft.
And sure, *circa Regna tonat.*

These bloody days have broken my heart.
My lust, my youth did them depart,
And blind desire of estate.
Who hastes to climb seeks to revert.
Of truth, *circa Regna tonat.*

The bell tower showèd me such sight
That in my head sticks day and night.
There did I learn out of a grate,
For all favour, glory, or might,
That yet *circa Regna tonat.*

By proof, I say, there did I learn:
Wit helpeth not defence too yerne
Of innocency to plead or prate.
Bear low, therefore, give God the stern,
For sure, *circa Regna tonat.*

Henry Howard, Earl of Surrey (1517?–1547)

"London, hast thou accusèd me"

London, hast thou accusèd me
    Of breach of laws, the root of strife?
    Within whose breast did boil to see,
So fervent hot thy dissolute life,
    That even the hate of sins, that grew
    Within thy wicked walls so rife,
For to break forth did convert so
    That terror could it not repress.
    The which, by words, since preachers know
What hope is left for to redress,
    By unknown means it likèd me
    My hidden burden to express,
Whereby it might appear to thee
    That secret sin hath secret spite;
    From justice' rod no fault is free;
But that all such as work unright
    In most quiet are next ill rest.
    In secret silence of the night
This made me, with a reckless breast,
    To wake thy sluggards with my bow:
    A figure of the Lord's behest,
Whose scourge for sin the Scriptures show.
    That, as the fearful thunder clap
    By sudden flame at hand we know,
Of pebble stones the soundless rap
    The dreadful plague might make thee see
    Of God's wrath, that doth thee enwrap;
That pride might know, from conscience free,
    How lofty works may her defend;
    And envy find, as he hath sought,
    How other seek him to offend;
    And wrath taste of each cruel thought

The just shape higher in the end;
   And idle sloth, that never wrought,
   To heaven his spirit lift may begin;
   And greedy lucre live in dread
   To see what hate ill got goods win;
   The lechers, ye that lust do feed,
   Perceive what secrecy is in sin;
   And gluttons' hearts for sorrow bleed,
Awakèd when their fault they find.
   In loathsome vice each drunken wight
   To stir to God, this was my mind.
Thy windows had done me no spite;
   But proud people that dread no fall,
   Clothèd with falsehood and unright
Bred in the closures of thy wall.
   But wrested to wrath in fervent zeal
   Thou hast to strife my secret call.
Indured hearts no warning feel.
   Oh shamles whore! is dread then gone
   By such thy foes as meant thy weal?
Oh member of false Babylon!
   The shop of craft! the den of ire!
   Thy dreadful doom draws fast upon.
Thy martyrs' blood, by sword and fire,
   In Heaven and earth for justice call.
   The Lord shall hear their just desire;
The flame of wrath shall on thee fall;
   With famine and pest lamentably
   Stricken shall be thy lechers all;
Thy proud towers and turrets high,
   Enemies to God, beat stone from stone;
   Thine idols burnt, that wrought iniquity;
When none thy ruin shall bemoan,
   But render unto the right wise Lord,
   That so hath judgèd Babylon,
Imortal praise with one accord.

Anne Askew (1521–1546)

The Ballad Which Anne Askew Made and Sang When She Was in Newgate

Like as the armèd knight
   Appointed to the field,
With this world will I fight,
   And faith shall be my shield.

Faith is that weapon strong
   Which will not fail at need;
My foes therefore among
   Therewith will I proceed.

As it is had in strength
   And force of Christes way,
It will prevail at length
   Though all the devils say nay.

Faith in the Fathers old
   Obtainèd righteousness,
Which makes me very bold
   To fear no world's distress.

I now rejoice in heart,
   And hope bid me do so,
For Christ will take my part
   And ease me of my woe.

Thou say'st, Lord, who so knock
   To them wilt thou attend.
Undo therefore the lock,
   And thy strong power send.

More en'mies now I have
   Than hairs upon my head.
Let them not me deprave,
   But fight thou in my stead.

On thee my care I cast,
    For all their cruel spite;
I set not by their haste
    For thou art my delight.

I am not she that list
    My anchor to let fall,
For every drizzling mist
    My ship substantial.

Not oft use I to write
    In prose nor yet in rhyme,
Yet will I show one sight
    That I saw in my time.

I saw a royal throne
    Where Justice should have sit,
But in her stead was one
    Of moody cruel wit.

Absorbed was righteousness
    As of the raging flood;
Satan in his excess
    Sucked up the guiltless blood.

Then thought I, Jesus Lord,
    When thou shall judge us all,
Hard is it to record
    On these men what will fall.

Yet, Lord, I thee desire
    For that they do to me,
Let them not taste the hire
    Of their iniquity.

George Turberville (1544?–1597?)

The Lover to the Thames of London, to Favour His Lady Passing Thereon

Thou stately stream that with the swelling tide
'Gainst London walls incessantly dost beat,
Thou Thames, I say, where barge and boat doth ride,
And snow-white swans do fish for needful meat:

When so my love, of force or pleasure, shall
Flit on thy flood as custom is to do,
Seek not with dread her courage to appall,
But calm thy tide and smoothly let it go,
As she may joy, arrived to siker shore,
To pass the pleasant stream she did before.

To welter up and surge in wrathful wise,
As did the flood where Helle drenchèd was,
Would but procure defame of thee to rise;
Wherefore let all such ruthless rigour pass.
So wish I that thou may'st with bending side
Have power for aye in wonted gulf to glide.

Isabella Whitney (1548?–?)

The Manner of Her Will, and What She Left to London and to All Those in It, at Her Departing

I whole in body and in mind,
    But very weak in purse,
Do make and write my testament
    For fear it will be worse.
And first, I wholly do commend
    My soul and body eke
To God the Father and the Son,
    So long as I can speak.
And, after speech, my soul to him
    And body to the grave,
Till time that all shall rise again
    Their judgement for to have.
And then I hope they both shall meet
    To dwell for aye in joy,
Whereas I trust to see my friends
    Released from all annoy.
Thus have you heard touching my soul
    And body, what I mean;
I trust you all will witness bear
    I have a steadfast brain.

And now let me dispose such things
    As I shall leave behind,
That those which shall receive the same
    May know my willing mind.
I first of all to London leave,
    Because I there was bred,
Brave buildings rare, of churches store,
    And Paules to the head.
Between the same, fair streets there be
    And people goodly store;

Because their keeping craveth cost,
    I yet will leave him more.
First for their food, I butchers leave,
    That every day shall kill;
By Thames you shall have brewers' store
    And bakers at your will.
And such as orders do observe
    And eat fish thrice a week,
I leave two streets full fraught therewith,
    They need not far to seek.
Watling Street and Canwick Street
    I full of woollen leave,
And linen store in Friday Street,
    If they me not deceive.
And those which are of calling such
    That costlier they require,
I mercers leave, with silk so rich
    As any would desire.
In Cheap of them they store shall find,
    And likewise in that street,
I goldsmiths leave with jewels such
    As are for ladies meet;
And plate to furnish cupboards with
    Full brave there shall you find,
With purl of silver and of gold
    To satisfy your mind;
With hoods, bongraces, hats or caps
    Such store are in that street
As, if on t'one side you should miss,
    The t'other serves you feat.
For nets of every kind of sort
    I leave within the Pawn,
French ruffs, high purls, gorgets and sleeves
    Of any kind of lawn.
For purse or knives, for comb or glass,
    Or any needful knack,

I by the Stocks have left a boy
    Will ask you what you lack.
I hose do leave in Birchin Lane
    Of any kind of size,
For women stitched, for men both trunks
    And those of Gascoyne guise.
Boots, shoes, or pantables good store
    St. Martin's hath for you;
In Cornhill, there I leave you beds
    And all that longs thereto.
For women shall you tailors have,
    By Bow the chiefest dwell;
In every lane you some shall find
    Can do indifferent well.
And for the men few streets or lanes
    But body-makers be,
And such as make the sweeping cloaks
    With guards beneath the knee.
Artillery at Temple Bar
    And dags at Tower Hill;
Swords and bucklers of the best
    Are nigh the Fleet until.

Now when thy folk are fed and clad
    With such as I have named,
For dainty mouths and stomachs weak
    Some junkets must be framed.
Wherefore I 'pothecaries leave,
    With banquets in their shop,
Physicians also for the sick,
    Diseases for to stop.
Some roisters still must bide in thee
    And such as cut it out,
That with the guiltless quarrel will
    To let their blood about.

For them I cunning surgeons leave,
    Some plasters to apply,
That ruffians may not still be hanged,
    Nor quiet persons die.
For salt, oatmeal, candles, soap,
    Or what you else do want,
In many places shops are full;
    I left you nothing scant.
If they that keep what I you leave
    Ask money when they sell it,
At Mint there is such store it is
    Unpossible to tell it.
At Steelyard store of wines there be
    Your dullèd minds to glad,
And handsome men that must not wed
    Except they leave their trade.
They oft shall seek for proper girls
    (And some perhaps shall find),
That needs compels or lucre lures
    To satisfy their mind.
And near the same, I houses leave
    For people to repair
To bathe themselves, so to prevent
    Infection of the air.
On Saturdays I wish that those
    Which all the week do drug
Shall thither trudge to trim them up
    On Sundays to look smug.
If any other thing be lacked
    In thee, I wish them look,
For there it is (I little brought
    But nothing from thee took).

Now for the people in thee left,
    I have done as I may,

And that the poor, when I am gone,
   Have cause for me to pray,
I will to prisons portions leave
   (What though but very small),
Yet that they may remember me,
   Occasion be it shall.
And first the Counter they shall have,
   Lest they should go to wrack,
Some coggers, and some honest men,
   That sergeants draw aback.
And such as friends will not them bail,
   Whose coin is very thin,
For them I leave a certain Hole
   And little ease within.
The Newgate once a month shall have
   A sessions for his share,
Lest, being heaped, infection might
   Procure a further care.
And at those sessions some shall 'scape
   With burning near the thumb,
And afterward to beg their fees
   Till they have got the sum.
And such whose deeds deserveth death,
   And twelve have found the same,
They shall be drawn up Holborn hill
   To come to further shame.
Well, yet to such I leave a nag
   Shall soon their sorrows cease,
For he shall either break their necks
   Or gallop from the press.
The Fleet not in their circuit is,
   Yet if I give him nought,
It might procure his curse ere I
   Unto the ground be brought.
Wherefore I leave some Papist old
   To underprop his roof,

And to the poor within the same,
    A box for their behoof.
What makes you standers-by to smile
    And laugh so in your sleeve?
I think it is because that I
    To Ludgate nothing give.
I am not now in case to lie,
    Here is no place of jest;
I did reserve that for myself
    If I my health possessed
And ever came in credit so
    A debtor for to be.
When days of payment did approach,
    I thither meant to flee,
To shroud myself amongst the rest
    That choose to die in debt.
Rather than any creditor
    Should money from them get
(Yet 'cause I feel myself so weak
    That none me credit dare),
I here revoke, and do it leave
    Some bankrupts to his share.
To all the bookbinders by Paul's,
    Because I like their art,
They every week shall money have
    When they from books depart.
Amongst them all my printer must
    Have somewhat to his share;
I will my friends these books to buy
    Of him, with other ware.
For maidens poor, I widowers rich
    Do leave, that oft shall dote,
And by that means shall marry them
    To set the girls afloat.
And wealthy widows will I leave
    To help young gentlemen,

Which when you have, in any case,
    Be courteous to them then,
And see their plate and jewels eke
    May not be marred with rust,
Nor let their bags too long be full,
    For fear that they do burst.
For every gate under the walls
    That compass thee about,
I fruit-wives leave to entertain
    Such as come in and out.
To Smithfield I must something leave,
    My parents there did dwell;
So careless for to be of it
    None would account it well.
Wherefore it thrice a week shall have
    Of horse and neat good store,
And in his spital, blind and lame
    To dwell for evermore.
And Bedlam must not be forgot,
    For that was oft my walk;
I people there too many leave
    That out of tune do talk.
At Bridewell there shall beadles be,
    And matrons that shall still
See chalk well chopped, and spinning plied
    And turning of the mill.
For such as cannot quiet be
    But strive for house or land,
At th'Inns of Court I lawyers leave
    To take their cause in hand.
And also leave I at each Inn
    Of Court or Chancery,
Of gentlemen, a youthful rut
    Full of activity;
For whom I store of books have left
    At each bookbinder's stall,

And part of all that London hath
　　To furnish them withal.
And when they are with study cloyed,
　　To recreate their mind,
Of tennis courts, of dancing schools
　　And fence, they store shall find.
And every Sunday at the least,
　　I leave, to make them sport,
In divers places players, that
　　Of wonders shall report.

Now London have I for thy sake
　　Within thee and without,
As comes into my memory,
　　Dispersèd round about
Such needful things as they should have
　　Here left now unto thee;
When I am gone, with conscience
　　Let them dispersèd be.
And though I nothing namèd have
　　To bury me withal,
Consider that above the ground
　　Annoyance be I shall.
And let me have a shrouding sheet
　　To cover me from shame,
And in oblivion bury me,
　　And never more me name.
Ringings nor other ceremonies
　　Use you not for cost,
Nor at my burial make no feast;
　　Your money were but lost.
Rejoice in God that I am gone
　　Out of this vale so vile,
And that, of each thing left such store
　　As may your wants exile;

I make thee sole executor
  Because I loved thee best,
And thee I put in trust to give
  The goods unto the rest.
Because thou shalt a helper need
  In this so great a charge,
I wish good fortune be thy guide, lest
  Thou shouldst run at large.
The happy days and quiet times
  They both her servants be,
Which well will serve to fetch and bring
  Such things as need to thee.
Wherefore, good London, not refuse
  For helper her to take.
Thus, being weak and weary both,
  An end here will I make.
To all that ask what end I made
  And how I went away,
Thou answer may'st like those which here
  No longer tarry may.
And unto all that wish me well
  Or rue that I am gone,
Do me commend and bid them cease
  My absence for to moan.
And tell them further, if they would
  My presence still have had,
They should have sought to mend my luck
  Which ever was too bad.
So fare thou well a thousand times,
  God shield thee from thy foe;
And still make thee victorious
  Of those that seek thy woe.
And though I am persuade that I
  Shall never more thee see,
Yet to the last I shall not cease
  To wish much good to thee.

This 20 of October, I,
    In Anno Domini
A thousand five hundred seventy three,
    As almanacs descry,
Did write this will with mine own hand
    And it to London gave
In witness of the standers-by;
    Whose names, if you will have,
Paper, Pen, and Standish were
    At that same present by,
With Time who promised to reveal
    So fast as she could hie
The same, lest of my nearer kin
    From anything should vary.
So finally I make an end,
    No longer can I tarry.

Edmund Spenser (1552?–1599)

Prothalamion

Calm was the day, and through the trembling air
Sweet breathing Zephyrus did softly play,
A gentle spirit, that lightly did delay
Hot Titan's beams, which then did glister fair;
When I, whose sullen care
Through discontent of my long fruitless stay
In prince's court, and expectation vain
Of idle hopes, which still do fly away
Like empty shadows, did afflict my brain,
Walked forth to ease my pain
Along the shore of silver streaming Thames,
Whose rutty bank, the which his river hems,
Was painted all with variable flowers,
And all the meads adorned with dainty gems,
Fit to deck maidens' bowers,
And crown their paramours,
Against the bridal day, which is not long:
    Sweet Thames, run softly, till I end my song.

There in a meadow by the river's side,
A flock of nymphs I chancèd to espy,
All lovely daughters of the flood thereby,
With goodly greenish locks all loose untied,
As each had been a bride;
And each one had a little wicker basket,
Made of fine twigs entrailèd curiously,
In which they gathered flowers to fill their flasket,
And with fine fingers cropped full featously
The tender stalks on high.
Of every sort, which in that meadow grew,
They gathered some; the violet pallid blue,
The little daisy, that at evening closes,

The virgin lily, and the primrose true,
With store of vermeil roses,
To deck their bridegrooms' posies,
Against the bridal day, which was not long:
   Sweet Thames, run softly, till I end my song.

With that I saw two swans of goodly hue
Come softly swimming down along the Lee;
Two fairer birds I yet did never see.
The snow, which doth the top of Pindus strew,
Did never whiter shew,
Nor Jove himself, when he a swan would be
For love of Leda, whiter did appear:
Yet Leda was they say as white as he,
Yet not so white as these, nor nothing near.
So purely white they were,
That even the gentle stream, the which them bare,
Seemed foul to them, and bade his billows spare
To wet their silken feathers, lest they might
Soil their fair plumes with water not so fair,
And mar their beauties bright,
That shone as heaven's light,
Against their bridal day, which was not long:
   Sweet Thames, run softly, till I end my song.

Eftsoons the nymphs, which now had flowers their fill,
Ran all in haste to see that silver brood,
As they came floating on the crystal flood.
Whom when they saw, they stood amazèd still,
Their wondering eyes to fill.
Them seemed they never saw a sight so fair,
Of fowls so lovely, that they sure did deem
Them heavenly born, or to be that same pair
Which through the sky draw Venus' silver team;
For sure they did not seem
To be begot of any earthly seed,
But rather angels or of angels' breed:

Yet were they bred of Somers-heat they say,
In sweetest season, when each flower and weed
The earth did fresh array,
So fresh they seemed as day,
Even as their bridal day, which was not long:
    Sweet Thames, run softly, till I end my song.

Then forth they all out of their baskets drew
Great store of flowers, the honour of the field,
That to the sense did fragrant odours yield,
All which upon those goodly birds they threw,
And all the waves did strew,
That like old Peneus' waters they did seem,
When down along by pleasant Tempe's shore,
Scattered with flowers, through Thessaly they stream,
That they appear through lilies' plenteous store,
Like a bride's chamber floor.
Two of those nymphs meanwhile, two garlands bound,
Of freshest flowers which in that mead they found,
The which presenting all in trim array,
Their snowy foreheads therewithal they crowned,
Whilst one did sing this lay,
Prepared against that day,
Against their bridal day, which was not long:
    Sweet Thames, run softly, till I end my song.

"Ye gentle birds, the world's fair ornament,
And heaven's glory, whom this happy hour
Doth lead unto your lovers' blissful bower,
Joy may you have and gentle heart's content
Of your love's couplement:
And let fair Venus, that is queen of love,
With her heart-quelling son upon you smile,
Whose smile, they say, hath virtue to remove
All love's dislike, and friendship's faulty guile
For ever to assoil.
Let endless peace your steadfast hearts accord,

And blessed plenty wait upon your board,
And let your bed with pleasures chaste abound,
That fruitful issue may to you afford,
Which may your foes confound,
And make your joys redound,
Upon your bridal day, which is not long:
    Sweet Thames, run softly, till I end my song."

So ended she; and all the rest around
To her redoubled that her undersong,
Which said, their bridal day should not be long.
And gentle echo from the neighbour ground
Their accents did resound.
So forth those joyous birds did pass along,
Adown the Lee, that to them murmured low,
As he would speak, but that he lacked a tongue,
Yet did by signs his glad affection show,
Making his stream run slow.
And all the fowl which in his flood did dwell
Gan flock about these twain, that did excel
The rest so far as Cynthia doth shend
The lesser stars. So they, enrangèd well,
Did on those two attend,
And their best service lend,
Against their wedding day, which was not long:
    Sweet Thames, run softly, till I end my song.

At length they all to merry London came,
To merry London, my most kindly nurse,
That to me gave this life's first native source;
Though from another place I take my name,
An house of ancient fame.
There when they came, whereas those bricky towers,
The which on Thames' broad agèd back do ride,
Where now the studious lawyers have their bowers
There whilom wont the Templar Knights to bide,
Till they decayed through pride:

Next whereunto there stands a stately place,
Where oft I gained gifts and goodly grace
Of that great lord, which therein wont to dwell,
Whose want too well now feels my friendless case.
But ah, here fits not well
Old woes, but joys to tell
Against the bridal day, which is not long:
   Sweet Thames, run softly, till I end my song.

Yet therein now doth lodge a noble peer,
Great England's glory and the world's wide wonder,
Whose dreadful name late through all Spain did thunder,
And Hercules' two pillars standing near
Did make to quake and fear.
Fair branch of honour, flower of chivalry,
That fillest England with thy triumph's fame,
Joy have thou of thy noble victory,
And endless happiness of thine own name
That promiseth the same:
That through thy prowess and victorious arms,
Thy country may be freed from foreign harms;
And great Elisa's glorious name may ring
Through all the world, filled with thy wide alarms,
Which some brave Muse may sing
To ages following,
Upon the bridal day, which is not long:
   Sweet Thames, run softly, till I end my song.

From those high towers this noble lord issuing,
Like radiant Hesper when his golden hair
In th'Ocean billows he hath bathèd fair,
Descended to the river's open viewing,
With a great train ensuing.
Above the rest were goodly to be seen
Two gentle knights of lovely face and feature
Beseeming well the bower of any queen,
With gifts of wit and ornaments of nature,

Fit for so goodly stature;
That like the twins of Jove they seemed in sight,
Which deck the baldric of the heavens bright.
They two forth pacing to the river's side,
Received those two fair birds, their love's delight,
Which at th'appointed tide,
Each one did make his bride,
Against their bridal day, which is not long:
    Sweet Thames, run softly, till I end my song.

George Peele (1556–1596)

from *King Edward the First*

KING EDWARD: Let Spanish steeds, as swift as fleeting wind,
      Convey these princes to their funeral:
      Before them let a hundred mourners ride.
      In every time of their enforced abode,
      Rear up a cross in token of their worth,
      Whereon fair Elinor's picture shall be placed.
      Arrived at London, near our palace-bounds,
      Inter my lovely Elinor, late deceased;
      And, in remembrance of her royalty,
      Erect a rich and stately carvèd cross,
      Whereon her stature shall with glory shine,
      And henceforth see you call it Charing Cross;
      For why the chariest and the choicest queen
      That ever did delight my royal eyes,
      There dwells in darkness, whilst I die in grief.

Chidiock Tichborne (1558?–1586)

Tichborne's Elegy

Written with his own hand in the Tower before his execution

My prime of youth is but a frost of cares,
    My feast of joy is but a dish of pain,
My crop of corn is but a field of tares,
    And all my good is but vain hope of gain;
        The day is past, and yet I saw no sun,
        And now I live, and now my life is done.

My tale was heard and yet it was not told,
    My fruit is fallen and yet my leaves are green;
My youth is spent and yet I am not old,
    I saw the world and yet I was not seen;
        My thread is cut and yet it is not spun,
        And now I live, and now my life is done.

I sought my death and found it in my womb,
    I looked for life and saw it was a shade;
I trod the earth and knew it was my tomb,
    And now I die, and now I was but made;
        My glass is full, and now my glass is run,
        And now I live, and now my life is done.

Michael Drayton (1563–1631)

from *Poly-Olbion*

from SONG XVII

But now this mighty flood, upon his voyage pressed,
That found how with his strength, his beauties still increased,
From where brave Windsor stood on tip-toe to behold
The fair and goodly Thames, so far as e'er he could,
With kingly houses crowned, of more than earthly pride,
Upon his either banks, as he along doth glide,
With wonderful delight doth his long course pursue,
Where Oatlands, Hampton Court, and Richmond he doth view.
Then Westminster, the next, great Thames doth entertain,
That vaunts her palace large, and her most sumptuous fane:
The land's tribunal seat that challengeth for her's,
The crowning of our Kings, their famous sepulchres.
Then goes he on along by that more beauteous strand,
Expressing both the wealth and bravery of the land.
So many sumptuous bowers, within so little space,
The all-beholding sun scarce sees in all his race.
And on by London leads, which like a crescent lies,
Whose windows seem to mock the star-befreckled skies;
Besides her rising spires, so thick themselves that show,
As do the bristling reeds within his banks that grow.
There sees his crowded wharfs, and people-pestered shores,
His bosom overspread with shoals of labouring oars;
With that most costly bridge that doth him most renown,
By which he clearly puts all other rivers down.

William Shakespeare (1564–1616)

from *Henry VI, Part II*

ACT IV, SCENE 4

Enter a MESSENGER.

KING: How now, what news? why com'st thou in such haste?
MESSENGER: The rebels are in Southwark; fly, my lord!
        Jack Cade proclaims himself Lord Mortimer,
        Descended from the Duke of Clarence' house,
        And calls your Grace usurper, openly,
        And vows to crown himself in Westminster.
        His army is a ragged multitude
        Of hinds and peasants, rude and merciless.
        Sir Humphrey Stafford, and his brother's death,
        Hath given them heart and courage to proceed.
        All scholars, lawyers, courtiers, gentlemen
        They call false caterpillars, and intend their death.
KING: O graceless men! they know not what they do.
BUCKINGHAM: My gracious lord, retire to Killingworth,
        Until a power be raised to put them down.
QUEEN: Ah, were the Duke of Suffolk now alive,
        These Kentish rebels would be soon appeased!
KING: Lord Say, the traitors hateth thee;
        Therefore away with us to Killingworth.
SAY: So might your Grace's person be in danger.
        The sight of me is odious in their eyes,
        And therefore in this city will I stay
        And live alone as secret as I may.

Enter another MESSENGER.

SECOND MESSENGER: Jack Cade hath gotten London Bridge:
        The citizens fly and forsake their houses;
        The rascal people, thirsting after prey,

       Join with the traitor, and they jointly swear
       To spoil the city and your royal court.
BUCKINGHAM: Then linger not, my lord, away, take horse.
KING: Come, Margaret, God, our hope, will succour us.
QUEEN: My hope is gone, now Suffolk is deceased.
KING: Farewell, my lord, trust not the Kentish rebels.
BUCKINGHAM: Trust nobody, for fear you be betrayed.
SAY: The trust I have is in mine innocence,
       And therefore am I bold and resolute.   *Exeunt.*

from *Henry V*

Enter PROLOGUE.

O for a Muse of fire, that would ascend
The brightest heaven of invention!
A kingdom for a stage, princes to act,
And monarchs to behold the swelling scene!
Then should the warlike Harry, like himself,
Assume the port of Mars, and at his heels,
Leashed in, like hounds, should famine, sword, and fire
Crouch for employment. But pardon, gentles all,
The flat unraisèd spirits that hath dared
On this unworthy scaffold to bring forth
So great an object. Can this cockpit hold
The vasty fields of France? Or may we cram
Within this wooden O the very casques
That did affright the air at Agincourt?
O, pardon! since a crooked figure may
Attest in little place a million,
And let us, ciphers to this great accompt,
On your imaginary forces work.
Suppose within the girdle of these walls
Are now confined two mighty monarchies,
Whose high, uprearèd, and abutting fronts
The perilous narrow ocean parts asunder.
Piece out our imperfections with your thoughts;
Into a thousand parts divide one man,
And make imaginary puissance;
Think, when we talk of horses, that you see them
Printing their proud hoofs i' th' receiving earth;
For 'tis your thoughts that now must deck our kings,
Carry them here and there, jumping o'er times,
Turning th' accomplishment of many years
Into an hour-glass: for the which supply,
Admit me Chorus to this history;

Who, Prologue-like, your humble patience pray,
Gently to hear, kindly to judge, our play.   *Exit.*

ACT V

Enter CHORUS.

Vouchsafe to those that have not read the story,
That I may prompt them; and of such as have,
I humbly pray them to admit th' excuse
Of time, of numbers, and due course of things,
Which cannot in their huge and proper life
Be here presented. Now we bear the King
Toward Callice; grant him there; there seen,
Heave him away upon your wingèd thoughts
Athwart the sea. Behold, the English beach
Pales in the flood with men, wives, and boys,
Whose shouts and claps out-voice the deep-mouthed sea,
Which like a mighty whiffler 'fore the King
Seems to prepare his way. So let him land,
And solemnly see him set on to London.
So swift a pace hath thought that even now
You may imagine him upon Blackheath;
Where that his lords desire him to have borne
His bruisèd helmet and his bended sword
Before him through the city. He forbids it,
Being free from vainness and self-glorious pride;
Giving full trophy, signal, and ostent
Quite from himself to God. But now behold,
In the quick forge and working-house of thought,
How London doth pour out her citizens!
The Mayor and all his brethren in best sort,
Like to the senators of th' antique Rome,
With the plebeians swarming at their heels,
Go forth and fetch their conquering Caesar in;

As by a lower but by loving likelihood,
Were now the general of our gracious Empress,
As in good time he may, from Ireland coming,
Bringing rebellion broachèd on his sword,
How many would the peaceful city quit,
To welcome him! Much more, and much more cause,
Did they this Harry. Now in London place him— . . .

from *Henry VIII*

Enter two GENTLEMEN, *meeting one another.*

1. GENTLEMAN: Y' are well met once again.

2. GENTLEMAN: So are you.

1. GENTLEMAN: You come to take your stand here, and behold
    The Lady Anne pass from her coronation?

2. GENTLEMAN: 'Tis all my business. At our last encounter,
    The Duke of Buckingham came from his trial.

1. GENTLEMAN: 'Tis very true; but that time offered sorrow,
    This, general joy.

2. GENTLEMAN: 'Tis well. The citizens
    I am sure have shown at full their royal minds—
    As, let 'em have their rights, they are ever forward
    In celebration of this day with shows,
    Pageants, and sights of honour.

1. GENTLEMAN: Never greater,
    Nor, I'll assure you, better taken, sir.

2. GENTLEMAN: May I be bold to ask what that contains,
    That paper in your hand?

1. GENTLEMAN: Yes, 'tis the list
    Of those that claim their offices this day
    By custom of the coronation.
    The Duke of Suffolk is the first, and claims
    To be High Steward; next the Duke of Norfolk,
    He to be Earl Marshal. You may read the rest.

2. GENTLEMAN: I thank you, sir; had I not known those customs
    I should have been beholding to your paper.
    But I beseech you, what's become of Katherine,
    The Princess Dowager? How goes her business?

1. GENTLEMAN: That I can tell you too. The Archbishop
    Of Canterbury, accompanied with other
    Learned and reverend fathers of his order,
    Held a late court at Dunstable, six miles off

From Ampthill, where the Princess lay, to which
She was often cited by them, but appeared not;
And, to be short, for not appearance and
The King's late scruple, by the main assent
Of all these learned men she was divorced,
And the late marriage made of none effect;
Since which she was removed to Kimmalton,
Where she remains now sick.

2. GENTLEMAN: Alas, good lady! [*Trumpets.*]
The trumpets sound; stand close, the Queen is coming. *Hoboys.*

The Order of the Coronation

1. *A lively flourish of trumpets.*
2. *Then, two* Judges.
3. Lord Chancellor, *with purse and mace before him.*
4. Choristers, *singing. Music.*
5. Mayor of London, *bearing the mace. Then* Garter, *in his coat of arms, and on his head he wore a gilt copper crown.*
6. Marquess Dorset, *bearing a sceptre of gold, on his head a demi-coronal of gold. With him, the* Earl of Surrey, *bearing the rod of silver with the dove, crowned with an earl's coronet. Collars of Esses.*
7. Duke of Suffolk, *in his robe of estate, his coronet on his head, bearing a long white wand, as High Steward. With him, the* Duke of Norfolk, *with the rod of marshalship, a coronet on his head. Collars of Esses.*
8. *A canopy borne by four of the* Cinque-Ports; *under it, the* Queen *in her robe, in her hair, richly adorned with pearl, crowned. On each side her, the* Bishops of London *and* Winchester.
9. *The old* Duchess of Norfolk, *in a coronal of gold, wrought with flowers, bearing the Queen's train.*
10. *Certain* Ladies *or* Countesses, *with plain circlets of gold without flowers.*

Exeunt, first passing over the stage in order and state, and then a great flourish of trumpets.

2. GENTLEMAN: A royal train, believe me. These I know.
Who's that that bears the sceptre?

1. GENTLEMAN: Marquess Dorset,
>   And that the Earl of Surrey, with the rod.

2. GENTLEMAN: A bold brave gentleman. That should be
>   The Duke of Suffolk.

1. GENTLEMAN: 'Tis the same: High Steward.

2. GENTLEMAN: And that my Lord of Norfolk?

1. GENTLEMAN: Yes.

2. GENTLEMAN: Heaven bless thee!

[*Looking on the Queen*]

>   Thou hast the sweetest face I ever looked on.
>   Sir, as I have a soul, she is an angel;
>   Our king has all the Indies in his arms,
>   And more and richer, when he strains that lady.
>   I cannot blame his conscience.

1. GENTLEMAN: They that bear
>   The cloth of honour over her, are four barons
>   Of the Cinque-Ports.

2. GENTLEMAN: Those men are happy, and so are all are near her.
>   I take it, she that carries up the train
>   Is that old noble lady, Duchess of Norfolk.

1. GENTLEMAN: It is, and all the rest are countesses.

2. GENTLEMAN: Their coronets say so. These are stars indeed.

1. GENTLEMAN: And sometimes falling ones.

2. GENTLEMAN: No more of that.

[*Exit the last of the procession; flourish of trumpets*]
Enter a third GENTLEMAN.

1. GENTLEMAN: God save you, sir! Where have you been broiling?

3. GENTLEMAN: Among the crowd i' th' Abbey, where a finger
>   Could not be wedged in more. I am stifled
>   With the mere rankness of their joy.

2. GENTLEMAN: You saw
>   The ceremony?

3. GENTLEMAN: That I did.

1. GENTLEMAN: How was it?

3. GENTLEMAN: Well worth the seeing.

2. GENTLEMAN: Good sir, speak it to us.

3. GENTLEMAN: As well as I am able. The rich stream
      Of lords and ladies, having brought the Queen
      To a prepared place in the choir, fell off
      A distance from her; while her Grace sat down
      To rest a while, some half an hour or so,
      In a rich chair of state, opposing freely
      The beauty of her person to the people.
      Believe me, sir, she is the goodliest woman
      That ever lay by man; which when the people
      Had the full view of, such a noise arose
      As the shrouds make at sea in a stiff tempest,
      As loud and to as many tunes. Hats, cloaks,
      Doublets, I think, flew up, and had their faces
      Been loose, this day they had been lost. Such joy
      I never saw before. Great-bellied women,
      That had not half a week to go, like rams
      In the old time of war, would shake the press
      And make 'em reel before 'em. No man living
      Could say, "This is my wife" there, all were woven
      So strangely in one piece.

2. GENTLEMAN: But what followed?

3. GENTLEMAN: At length her Grace rose, and with modest paces
      Came to the altar, where she kneeled, and saint-like
      Cast her fair eyes to heaven, and prayed devoutly;
      Then rose again and bowed her to the people;
      When by the Archbishop of Canterbury
      She had all the royal makings of a queen,
      As holy oil, Edward Confessor's crown,
      The rod, and bird of peace, and all such emblems
      Laid nobly on her; which performed, the choir,
      With all the choicest music of the kingdom,
      Together sung *Te Deum*. So she parted,
      And with the same full state paced back again

        To York-place, where the feast is held.

1. GENTLEMAN: Sir,

        You must no more call it York-place, that's past;
        For since the Cardinal fell that title's lost.
        'Tis now the King's, and called Whitehall.

3. GENTLEMAN: I know it;

        But 'tis so lately altered that the old name
        Is fresh about me.

2. GENTLEMAN: What two reverend bishops

        Were those that went on each side of the Queen?

3. GENTLEMAN: Stokesly and Gardiner, the one of Winchester,

        Newly preferred from the King's secretary,
        The other, London.

2. GENTLEMAN: He of Winchester

        Is held no great good lover of the Archbishop's,
        The virtuous Cranmer.

3. GENTLEMAN: All the land knows that.

        However, yet there is no great breach; when it comes,
        Cranmer will find a friend will not shrink from him.

2. GENTLEMAN: Who may that be, I pray you?

3. GENTLEMAN: Thomas Cromwell,

        A man in much esteem with th' King, and truly
        A worthy friend. The King has made him Master
        O' th' Jewel House,
        And one, already, of the Privy Council.

2. GENTLEMAN: He will deserve more.

3. GENTLEMAN: Yes, without all doubt.

        Come, gentlemen, ye shall go my way, which
        Is to th' court, and there ye shall be my guests;
        Something I can command. As I walk thither,
        I'll tell ye more.

BOTH: You may command us, sir.   *Exeunt.*

Thomas Nashe (1567?–1601)

from *Summer's Last Will and Testament*

Autumn hath all the summer's fruitful treasure;
Gone is our sport, fled is poor Croydon's pleasure.
Short days, sharp days, long nights come on apace;
Ah, who shall hide us from the winter's face?
Cold doth increase, the sickness will not cease,
And here we lie, God knows, with little ease.
   From winter, plague, and pestilence, good Lord,
      deliver us!

London doth mourn, Lambeth is quite forlorn;
Trades cry, woe worth that ever they were born.
The want of term is town and city's harm;
Close chambers we do want, to keep us warm.
Long banishèd must we live from our friends;
This low-built house will bring us to our ends.
   From winter, plague, and pestilence, good Lord,
      deliver us!

Everard Guilpin (1572?–?)

from *Skialetheia*

SATIRE V

Let me alone I prithee in this cell,
Entice me not into the city's hell;
Tempt me not forth this Eden of content,
To taste of that which I shall soon repent:
Prithee excuse me; I am not alone,
Accompanied with meditation
And calm content, whose taste more pleaseth me
Than all the city's luscious vanity.
I had rather be encoffined in this chest
Amongst these books and papers, I protest,
Then free-booting abroad purchase offence,
And scandal my calm thoughts with discontents.
Here I converse with those diviner spirits,
Whose knowledge and admire the world inherits:
Here doth the famous, profound Stagarite
With Nature's mystic harmony delight
My ravished contemplation: I here see
The now-old world's youth in an history:
Here may I be grave Plato's auditor;
And learning of that moral lecturer
To temper mine affections, gallantly
Get of my self a glorious victory:
And then for change, as we delight in change,
(For this my study is indeed m'Exchange)
Here may I sit, yet walk to Westminster
And hear Fitzherbert, Plowden, Brooke, and Dier
Canvass a law-case: or if my dispose
Persuade me to a play, I'll to the Rose,
Or Curtain, one of Plautus' comedies,
Or the Pathetic Spaniard's tragedies:

If my desire doth rather wish the fields,
Some speaking painter, some poet straitway yields
A flower-bespangled walk, where I may hear
Some amorous swain his passions declare
To his sun-burnt love. Thus my books' little case,
My study, is mine all, mine every place.
      What more variety of pleasures can
An idle city walk afford a man?
More troublesome and tedious well I know
'T will be, into the peopled streets to go:
Witness that hotch-potch of so many noises,
Black sanctus of so many several voices;
That chaos of rude sounds, that harmony,
And diapason of harsh Barbary,
Composed of several mouths, and several cries,
Which to men's ears turn both their tongues and eyes.
There squeaks a cart-wheel, here a tumbrel rumbles,
Here scolds an old bawd, there a porter grumbles;
Here two tough car-men combat for the way,
There two for looks begin a coward fray;
Two swaggering knaves here brabble for a whore,
There brawls an ale-knight for his fat-grown score.
      But oh purgation! yon rotten-throated slaves
Engarlanded with coney-catching knaves,
Whores, beadles, bawds, and sergeants filthily
Chant Kemp's jig, or the Burgonian's tragedy:
But in good time, there's one hath nipped a bong,
Farewell my hearts, for he hath marred the song.
      Yet might all this, this too bad be excused,
Were not an ethic soul much more abused,
And her still patience choked by vanity,
With unsufferable inhumanity:
For whose gall is't that would not overflow
To meet in every street where he shall go
With folly masked in divers semblances?
The city is the map of vanities,

The mart of fools, the magazine of gulls,
The painters' shop of antics: walk in Paul's
And but observe the sundry kinds of shapes,
Th'wilt swear that London is as rich in apes
As Afric Tabraca: one wries his face;
This fellow's wry neck is his better grace.
He coined in newer mint of fashion,
With the right Spanish shrug shows passion.
There comes one in a muffler of Cadiz-beard,
Frowning as he would make the world afeard;
With him a troupe all in gold-daubed suits,
Looking like Talbots, Percys, Montacutes,
As if their very countenances would swear.
The Spaniard should conclude a peace for fear:
But bring them to a charge, then see the luck,
Though but a false fire, they their plumes will duck;
What marvel, since life's sweet? But see yonder,
One like the unfrequented theatre
Walks in dark silence, and vast solitude,
Suited to those black fancies which intrude
Upon possession of his troubled breast:
But for black's sake he would look like a jest,
For he's clean out of fashion: what he?
I think the Genius of antiquity
Come to complain of our variety
Of tickle fashions: then you jest, I see.
Would you needs know? he is a malcontent:
A Papist? no, nor yet a Protestant,
But a discarded intelligencer.
Here's one looks like to a King Arthur's fencer,
With his case of rapiers, and suited in buff,
Is he not a sergeant? then say's a muff
For his furred satin cloak; but let him go,
Meddle not with him, he's a shrewd fellow.
      Oh what a pageant's this? what fool was I
To leave my study to see vanity?

But who's in yonder coach? my lord and fool,
One that for ape tricks can put Gue to school:
Heroic spirits, true nobility
Which can make choice of such society.
He more perfections hath than y'would suppose,
He hath a wit of wax, fresh as a rose,
He plays well on the treble violin,
He soothes his Lord up in his grossest sin;
At any rhymes sprung from his Lordship's head,
Such as Elderton would not have fathered,
He cries, *Oh rare my Lord;* he can discourse
The story of Don Pacolet and his horse,
To make my Lord laugh swear and jest,
And with a *simile non plus* the best,
Unless like Pace his wit be overawed;
But his best part is he's a perfect bawd:
Rare virtues; farewell they. But who's yonder
Deep mouthed hound, that bellows rhymes like thunder;
He makes an earthquake throughout Paul's churchyard;
Well fare his heart, his larum shall be heard:
Oh he's a puisne of the Inns of Court,
Come from th'university to make sport
With his friends' money here: but see, see,
Here comes Don Fashion, spruce formality,
Neat as a merchant's ruff, that's set in print,
New half-penny, skipped forth his laundry's mint;
Oh brave! what, with a feather in his hat?
He is a dancer you may see by that;
Light heels, light head, light feather well agree.
Salute him, with th'embrace beneath the knee?
I think 'twere better let him pass along,
He will so daub us with his oily tongue;
For thinking on some of his mistresses
We shall be curried with the brisk phrases,
And prick-song terms he hath premeditate,
Speak to him, woe to us, for we shall ha' it;

Then farewell he. But soft, whom have we here?
What brave Saint George, what mounted *cavaliere?*
He is all court-like, Spanish in's attire.
He hath the right duck, pray God he be no friar:
This is the dictionary of compliments,
The barber's mouth of new-scraped eloquence,
Synomic Tully for variety,
And Madame Conceit's gorgeous gallery,
The exact pattern which Castilio
Took for's accomplished courtier: but soft ho,
What needs that bound, or that curvet, good sir?
There's some sweet Lady, and 'tis done to her,
That she may see his jennet's nimble force:
Why, would he have her in love with his horse?
Or aims he at popish merit, to make
Her in love with him, for his horse's sake?
        The further that we walk, more vanity
Presents itself to prospect of mine eye:
Here swears some seller, though a known untruth,
Here his wife's bated by some quick-chapped youth.
There in that window Mistress Minkes doth stand,
And to some copesmate beckoneth her hand;
In is he gone, Saint Venus be his speed,
For some great thing must be adventured:
There comes a troupe of puisnes from the play,
Laughing like wanton school-boys all the way.
Yon go a knot to Blooms's ordinary,
Friends and good fellows all now; by and by
They'll be by the ears, vie stabs, exchange disgraces,
And bandy daggers at each other's faces.
        Enough of these then, and enough of all;
I may thank you for this time spent, but call
Henceforth, I'll keep my study, and eschew
The scandal of my thoughts, my follies view.
Now let us home, I'm sure 'tis supper time;
The home hath blown, have done my merry rhyme.

Ben Jonson (1572?–1637)

from *The Devil Is an Ass*

ACT I, SCENE 1

([*Enter*] DEVIL, PUG.)

SATAN: Hoh, hoh, hoh, hoh, hoh, hoh, hoh, hoh!
         To earth? And why to earth, thou foolish spirit?
         What would'st thou do on earth?
PUG: For that, great chief,
         As time shall work. I do but ask my month,
         Which every petty puisne devil has;
         Within that term, the court of Hell will hear
         Something may gain a longer grant, perhaps.
SATAN: For what? The laming a poor cow or two?
         Entering a sow, to make her cast her farrow?
         Or crossing of a market-woman's mare,
         'Twixt this and Tottenham? These were wont to be
         Your main achievements, Pug; you have some plot now,
         Upon a tunning of ale, to stale the yeast,
         Or keep the churn so, that the butter come not,
         Spite o' the housewife's cord, or her hot spit?
         Or some good ribibe, about Kentish Town
         Or Hogsden, you would bang now, for a witch,
         Because she will not let you play round robin.
         And you'll go sour the citizens' cream 'gainst Sunday,
         That she may be accused for't, and condemned
         By a Middlesex jury, to the satisfaction
         Of their offended friends, the Londoners' wives
         Whose teeth were set on edge with? Foolish fiend,
         Stay i' your place, know your own strengths, and put not
         Beyond the sphere of your activity.
         You are too dull a devil to be trusted
         Forth in those parts, Pug, upon any affair
         That may concern our name on earth. It is not

Every one's work. The state of Hell must care

Whom it employs, in point of reputation,

Here about London. You would make, I think,

An agent to be sent for Lancashire,

Proper enough; or some parts of Northumberland,

So you had good instructions, Pug.

PUG: O chief,

You do not know, dear chief, what there is in me.

Prove me but for a fortnight, for a week,

And lend me but a Vice, to carry with me,

To practise there with any play-fellow,

And you will see, there will come more upon't,

Than you'll imagine, precious chief.

SATAN: What Vice?

What kind wouldst th' have it of?

PUG: Why any; Fraud,

Or Covetousness, or Lady Vanity,

Or old Iniquity: I'll call him hither.

[*Enter* INIQUITY.]

INIQUITY: What is he calls upon me, and would seem to lack a Vice?

Ere his words be half spoken, I am with him in a trice,

Here, there, and everywhere, as the cat is with the mice,

True *vetus Iniquitas.* Lack'st thou cards, friend, or dice?

I will teach thee to cheat, child, to cog, lie and swagger,

And ever and anon, to be drawing forth thy dagger:

To swear by Gogs-nowns, like a lusty Juventus,

In a cloak to thy heel, and a hat like a pent-house.

Thy breeches of three fingers and thy doublet all belly.

With a wench that shall feed thee with cock-stones and jelly.

PUG: Is it not excellent, chief? How nimble he is!

INIQUITY: Child of hell, this is nothing! I will fetch thee a leap

From the top of Paul's steeple to the Standard in Cheap

And lead thee a dance through the streets without fail,

Like a needle of Spain, with a thread at my tail.

We will survey the suburbs, and make forth our sallies

Down Petticoat Lane, and up the Smock-alleys,
To Shoreditch, Whitechapel, and so to Saint Katherine's,
To drink with the Dutch there, and take forth their patterns.
From thence we will put in at Custom-house quay there,
And see how the factors and 'prentices play there,
False with their masters; and geld many a full pack,
To spend it in pies, at the Dagger, and the Woolsack.

PUG: Brave, brave, Iniquity! Will not this do, chief?

INIQUITY: Nay, boy, I will bring thee to the bawds, and the roysters
At Billingsgate, feasting with claret-wine and oysters;
From thence shoot the Bridge, child, to the Cranes i' the Vintry,
And see there the gimblets, how they make their entry!
Or, if thou hadst rather, to the Strand down to fall,
'Gainst the lawyers come dabbled from Westminster Hall,
And mark how they cling, with their clients together,
Like ivy to oak, so velvet to leather.
Ha, boy, I would show thee.

PUG: Rare, rare!

SATAN: Peace, dotard
And thou more ignorant thing, that so admir'it.

On the Famous Voyage

No more let Greece her bolder fables tell
    Of Hercules or Theseus going to hell,
Orpheus, Ulysses; or the Latin muse
    With tales of Troy's just knight our faiths abuse:
We have a Sheldon and a Heydon got,
    Had power to act what they to feign had not.
All that they boast of Styx, of Acheron,
    Cocytus, Phlegethon, our have proved in one:
The filth, stench, noise; save only what was there
    Subtly distinguished, was confusèd here.
Their wherry had no sail, too; ours had none;
    And in it two more horrid knaves than Charon.
Arses were heard to croak instead of frogs,
    And for one Cerberus, the whole coast was dogs.
Furies there wanted not; each scold was ten;
    And for the cries of ghosts, women and men
Laden with plague-sores and their sins were heard,
    Lashed by their consciences; to die, afeard.
Then let the former age with this content her:
    She brought the poets forth, but ours the adventer.

THE VOYAGE ITSELF

I sing the brave adventure of two wights,
And pity 'tis I cannot call 'em knights:
One was; and he for brawn and brain right able
To have been styled of King Arthur's table.
The other was a squire of fair degree,
But in the action greater man than he,
Who gave, to take at his return from hell,
His three for one. Now, lordings, listen well.
    It was the day, what time the powerful moon
Makes the poor Bankside creature wet it' shoon
In it' own hall, when these (in worthy scorn

Of those that put out moneys on return
From Venice, Paris, or some inland passage
Of six times to and fro without embassage,
Or him that backward went to Berwick, or which
Did dance the famous morris unto Norwich)
At Bread Street's Mermaid having dined, and merry,
Proposed to go to Holborn in a wherry.
A harder task than either his to Bristo',
Or his to Antwerp. Therefore, once more, list ho!
    A dock there is that called is Avernus,
Of some, Bridewell, and may in time concern us
All that are readers; but methinks 'tis odd
That all this while I have forgot some god
Or goddess to invoke, to stuff my verse,
And with both bombard-style and phrase rehearse
The many perils of this port, and how
Sans help of sibyl or a golden bough
Or magic sacrifice, they passed along.
Alcides, be thou succouring to my song!
Thou hast seen hell, some say, and know'st all nooks there,
Canst tell me best how every fury looks there,
And art a god, if fame thee not abuses,
Always at hand to aid the merry muses.
Great Club-fist, though thy back and bones be sore
Still, with thy former labours, yet once more
Act a brave work, call it thy last adventry;
But hold my torch while I describe the entry
To this dire passage. Say thou stop thy nose:
'Tis but light pains: indeed this dock's no rose.
    In the first jaws appeared that ugly monster
Ycleped Mud, which when their oars did once stir,
Belched forth an air as hot as at the muster
Of all your night-tubs, when the carts do cluster,
Who shall discharge first his merd-urinous load:
Thorough her womb they make their famous road
Between two walls, where on one side, to scar men

Were seen your ugly centaurs ye call car-men,
Gorgonian scolds and harpies; on the other
Hung stench, diseases, and old filth, their mother,
With famine, wants and sorrows many a dozen,
The least of which was to the plague a cousin.
But they unfrighted pass, though many a privy
Spake to 'em louder than the ox in Livy,
And many a sink poured out her rage anenst 'em;
But still their valour and their virtue fenced 'em,
And on they went, like Castor brave and Pollux,
Ploughing the main. When see (the worst of all lucks)
They met the second prodigy, would fear a
Man that had never heard of a Chimaera.
One said it was bold Briareus, or the beadle
(Who hath the hundred hands when he doth meddle);
The other thought it Hydra, or the rock
Made of the trull that cut her father's lock;
But coming near they found it but a lighter,
So huge, it seemed, they could by no means quite her.
Back, cried their brace of Charons; they cried, No,
No going back! On still, you rogues, and row.
How hight the place? A voice was heard: Cocytus.
Row close then, slaves! Alas, they will beshite us.
No matter, stinkards, row! What croaking sound
Is this we hear? of frogs? No, guts wind-bound,
Over your heads; well, row. At this a loud
Crack did report itself, as if a cloud
Had burst with storm, and down fell *ab excelsis*
Poor Mercury, crying out on Paracelsus
And all his followers, that had so abused him,
And in so shitten sort so long had used him;
For (where he was the god of eloquence,
And subtlety of metals) they dispense
His spirits now in pills and eke in potions,
Suppositories, cataplasms and lotions.
But many moons there shall not wane, quoth he,

(In the meantime, let 'em imprison me)
But I will speak—and know I shall be heard—
Touching this cause, where they will be afeard
To answer me. And sure, it was the intent
Of the grave fart, late let in parliament,
Had it been seconded, and not in fume
Vanished away: as you must all presume
Their Mercury did now. By this, the stem
Of the hulk touched and, as by Polypheme
The sly Ulysses stole in a sheepskin,
The well-greased wherry now had got between,
And bade her farewell sough unto the lurden.
Never did bottom more betray her burden:
The meat-boat of Bears' College, Paris Garden,
Stunk not so ill; nor, when she kissed, Kate Arden.
Yet one day in the year for sweet 'tis voiced,
And that is when it is the Lord Mayor's foist.
        By this time had they reached the Stygian pool
By which the masters swear when, on the stool
Of worship, they their nodding chins do hit
Against their breasts. Here several ghosts did flit
About the shore, of farts but late departed,
White, black, blue, green, and in more forms out-started
Than all those atomi ridiculous
Whereof old Democrite and Hill Nicholas,
One said, the other swore, the world consists.
These be the cause of those thick frequent mists
Arising in that place, through which who goes
Must try the unused valour of a nose:
And that ours did. For yet no nare was tainted,
Nor thumb nor finger to the stop acquainted,
But open, and unarmed, encountered all.
Whether it languishing stuck upon the wall
Or were precipitated down the jakes,
And after swam abroad in ample flakes,
Or that it lay heaped like an usurer's mass,

All was to them the same: they were to pass,
And so they did, from Styx to Acheron,
The ever-boiling flood; whose banks upon
Your Fleet Lane furies and hot cooks do dwell,
That with still-scalding steams make the place hell.
The sinks ran grease, and hair of measled hogs,
The heads, houghs, entrails, and the hides of dogs:
For, to say truth, what scullion is so nasty
To put the skins and offal in a pasty?
Cats there lay divers had been flayed and roasted
And, after mouldy grown, again were toasted;
Then selling not, a dish was ta'en to mince 'em,
But still, it seemed, the rankness did convince 'em.
For here they were thrown in wi' the melted pewter,
Yet drowned they not. They had five lives in future.
    But 'mongst these Tiberts, who d'you think there was?
Old Banks the juggler, our Pythagoras,
Grave tutor to the learned horse: both which
Being, beyond sea, burned for one witch,
Their spirits transmigrated to a cat;
And now, above the pool, a face right fat,
With great grey eyes, are lifted up, and mewed;
Thrice did it spit, thrice dived. At last it viewed
Our brave heroes with a milder glare,
And in a piteous tune began: How dare
Your dainty nostrils (in so hot a season,
When every clerk eats artichokes and peason,
Laxative lettuce, and such windy meat)
'Tempt such a passage? When each privy's seat
Is filled with buttock, and the walls do sweat
Urine and plasters? When the noise doth beat
Upon your ears of discords so unsweet,
And outcries of the damnèd in the Fleet?
Cannot the plague-bill keep you back? nor bells
Of loud Sepulchre's, with their hourly knells,
But you will visit grisly Pluto's hall?

Behold where Cerberus, reared on the wall
Of Holborn (three sergeants' heads) looks o'er,
And stays but till you come unto the door!
Tempt not his fury; Pluto is away,
And Madam Caesar, great Proserpina,
Is now from home. You lose your labours quite,
Were you Jove's sons, or had Alcides' might.
They cried out, Puss! He told them he was Banks,
That had so often showed 'em merry pranks.
They laughed at his laugh-worthy fate, and passed
The triple head without a sop. At last,
Calling for Rhadamanthus, that dwelt by,
A soap-boiler, and Aeacus him nigh,
Who kept an ale-house, with my little Minos,
An ancient purblind fletcher with a high nose,
They took 'em all to witness of their action,
And so went bravely back, without protraction.
    In memory of which most liquid deed,
The city since hath raised a pyramid.
And I could wish for their eternized sakes,
My muse had ploughed with his that sung A-jax.

John Donne (1572–1631)

Satire 1

Away thou fondling motley humourist,
Leave me, and in this standing wooden chest,
Consorted with these few books, let me lie
In prison, and here be coffined, when I die;
Here are God's conduits, grave divines; and here
Nature's secretary, the Philosopher;
And jolly statesmen, which teach how to tie
The sinews of a city's mystic body;
Here gathering chroniclers, and by them stand
Giddy fantastic poets of each land.
Shall I leave all this constant company,
And follow headlong, wild uncertain thee?
First swear by thy best love in earnest
(If thou which lov'st all, canst love any best)
Thou wilt not leave me in the middle street,
Though some more spruce companion thou dost meet,
Not though a captain do come in thy way,
Bright parcel gilt, with forty dead men's pay,
Nor though a brisk perfumed pert courtier
Deign with a nod, thy courtesy to answer.
Nor come a velvet Justice with a long
Great train of blue coats, twelve, or fourteen strong,
Wilt thou grin or fawn on him, or prepare
A speech to court his beauteous son and heir.
For better or worse take me, or leave me:
To take, and leave me is adultery.
Oh monstrous, superstitious Puritan,
Of refined manners, yet ceremonial man,
That when thou meet'st one, with inquiring eyes
Dost search, and like a needy broker prize
The silk, and gold he wears, and to that rate
So high or low, dost raise thy formal hat:

That wilt consort none, until thou have known
What lands he hath in hope, or of his own,
As though all thy companions should make thee
Jointures, and marry thy dear company.
Why shouldst thou (that dost not only approve,
But in rank itchy lust, desire, and love
The nakedness and barrenness to enjoy,
Of thy plump muddy whore, or prostitute boy)
Hate virtue, though she be naked, and bare?
At birth, and death, our bodies naked are;
And till our souls be unapparelled
Of bodies, they from bliss are banished.
Man's first blessed state was naked, when by sin
He lost that, yet he was clothed but in beast's skin,
And in this coarse attire, which I now wear,
With God, and with the Muses I confer.
But since thou like a contrite penitent,
Charitably warned of thy sins, dost repent
These vanities, and giddinesses, lo
I shut my chamber door, and come, let's go.
But sooner may a cheap whore, that hath been
Worn by as many several men in sin,
As are black feathers, or musk-colour hose,
Name her child's right true father, 'mongst all those:
Sooner may one guess, who shall bear away
The Infanta of London, heir to an India;
And sooner may a gulling weather spy
By drawing forth heaven's scheme tell certainly
What fashioned hats, or ruffs, or suits next year
Our subtle-witted antic youths will wear;
Than thou, when thou depart'st from me, canst show
Whither, why, when, or with whom thou wouldst go.
But how shall I be pardoned my offence
That thus have sinned against my conscience?
Now we are in the street; he first of all
Improvidently proud, creeps to the wall,

And so imprisoned, and hemmed in by me,
Sells for a little state his liberty;
Yet though he cannot skip forth now to greet
Every fine silken painted fool we meet,
He them to him with amorous smiles allures,
And grins, smacks, shrugs, and such an itch endures,
As 'prentices, or schoolboys which do know
Of some gay sport abroad, yet dare not go.
And as fiddlers stop lowest, at highest sound,
So to the most brave, stoops he nigh'st the ground.
But to a grave man, he doth move no more
Than the wise politic horse would heretofore,
Or thou O elephant or ape wilt do,
When any names the King of Spain to you.
Now leaps he upright, jogs me, and cries, "Do you see
Yonder well-favoured youth?" "Which?" "Oh, 'tis he
That dances so divinely." "Oh," said I,
"Stand still, must you dance here for company?"
He drooped, we went, till one (which did excel
Th' Indians, in drinking his tobacco well)
Met us; they talked; I whispered, "Let us go,
'T may be you smell him not, truly I do."
He hears not me, but, on the other side
A many-coloured peacock having spied,
Leaves him and me; I for my lost sheep stay;
He follows, overtakes, goes on the way,
Saying, "Him whom I last left, all repute
For his device, in handsoming a suit,
To judge of lace, pink, panes, print, cut, and pleat,
Of all the Court, to have the best conceit."
"Our dull comedians want him, let him go;
But Oh, God strengthen thee, why stoop'st thou so?"
"Why? he hath travelled." "Long?" "No, but to me,"
(Which understand none), "he doth seem to be
Perfect French, and Italian"; I replied,
"So is the pox." He answered not, but spied

More men of sort, of parts, and qualities;
At last his love he in a window spies,
And like light dew exhaled, he flings from me
Violently ravished to his lechery.
Many were there, he could command no more;
He quarrelled, fought, bled; and turned out of door
   Directly came to me hanging the head,
   And constantly a while must keep his bed.

To Mr. E. G.

Even as lame things thirst their perfection, so
The slimy rhymes bred in our vale below,
Bearing with them much of my love and heart,
Fly unto that Parnassus, where thou art.
There thou o'erseest London: here I have been,
By staying in London, too much overseen.
Now pleasure's dearth our city doth possess,
Our theatres are filled with emptiness;
As lank and thin is every street and way
As a woman delivered yesterday.
Nothing whereat to laugh my spleen espies
But bearbaitings or law exercise.
Therefore I'll leave it, and in the country strive
Pleasures, now fled from London, to retrieve.
Do thou so too: and fill not like a bee
Thy thighs with honey, but as plenteously
As Russian merchants, thyself's whole vessel load,
And then at winter retail it here abroad.
Bless us with Suffolk's sweets; and as that is
Thy garden, make thy hive and warehouse this.

Epithalamion Made at Lincoln's Inn

The sun-beams in the east are spread,
Leave, leave, fair bride, your solitary bed,
   No more shall you return to it alone;
It nurseth sadness, and your body's print,
Like to a grave, the yielding down doth dint;
    You and your other you meet there anon;
      Put forth, put forth that warm balm-breathing thigh,
Which when next time you in these sheets will smother
There it must meet another,
      Which never was, but must be, oft, more nigh;
Come glad from thence, go gladder than you came,
Today put on perfection, and a woman's name.

Daughters of London, you which be
Our golden mines, and furnished treasury,
   You which are angels, yet still bring with you
Thousands of angels on your marriage days,
Help with your presence, and device to praise
    These rites, which also unto you grow due;
      Conceitedly dress her, and be assigned,
By you, fit place for every flower and jewel,
Make her for love fit fuel,
      As gay as Flora, and as rich as Ind;
So may she fair, rich, glad, and in nothing lame,
Today put on perfection, and a woman's name.

And you frolic patricians,
Sons of these senators' wealth's deep oceans,
   Ye painted courtiers, barrels of others' wits,
Ye country men, who but your beasts love none,
Ye of those fellowships whereof he's one,
    Of study and play made strange hermaphrodites,
      Here shine; this bridegroom to the temple bring.
Lo, in yon path, which store of strewed flowers graceth,
The sober virgin paceth;

Except my sight fail, 'tis no other thing;
Weep not nor blush, here is no grief nor shame,
Today put on perfection, and a woman's name.

Thy two-leaved gates, fair temple, unfold,
And these two in thy sacred bosom hold,
   Till, mystically joined, but one they be;
Then may thy lean and hunger-starved womb
Long time expect their bodies and their tomb,
   Long after their own parents fatten thee;
     All elder claims, and all cold barrenness,
All yielding to new loves be far for ever,
Which might these two dissever,
     Always, all th'other may each one possess;
For, the best bride, best worthy of praise and fame,
Today puts on perfection, and a woman's name.

Oh winter days bring much delight,
Not for themselves, but for they soon bring night;
   Other sweets wait thee than these diverse meats,
Other disports than dancing jollities,
Other love tricks than glancing with the eyes,
   But that the sun still in our half sphere sweats;
     He flies in winter, but he now stands still,
Yet shadows turn; noon point he hath attained,
His steeds nill be restrained,
     But gallop lively down the western hill;
Thou shalt, when he hath run the world's half frame,
Tonight put on perfection, and a woman's name.

The amorous evening star is rose,
Why then should not our amorous star inclose
   Herself in her wished bed? Release your strings
Musicians, and dancers take some truce
With these your pleasing labours, for great use
   As much weariness as perfection brings;
     You, and not only you, but all toiled beasts

Rest duly; at night all their toils are dispensed;
But in their beds commenced
  Are other labours, and more dainty feasts;
She goes a maid, who, lest she turn the same,
Tonight puts on perfection, and a woman's name.

Thy virgin's girdle now untie,
And in thy nuptial bed (love's altar) lie
  A pleasing sacrifice; now dispossess
Thee of these chains and robes which were put on
T'adorn the day, not thee; for thou alone,
  Like virtue and truth, art best in nakedness;
   This bed is only to virginity
A grave, but, to a better state, a cradle;
Till now thou wast but able
  To be what now thou art; then that by thee
No more be said, I *may be,* but *I am,*
Tonight put on perfection, and a woman's name.

Even like a faithful man content,
That this life for a better should be spent,
  So, she a mother's rich style doth prefer,
And at the bridegroom's wished approach doth lie,
Like an appointed lamb, when tenderly
  The priest comes on his knees t'embowel her;
   Now sleep or watch with more joy; and O light
Of heaven, tomorrow rise thou hot, and early;
This sun will love so dearly
  Her rest, that long, long we shall want her sight;
Wonders are wrought, for she which had no maim,
Tonight puts on perfection, and a woman's name.

Satire 4

Well; I may now receive, and die; my sin
Indeed is great, but I have been in
A purgatory, such as feared hell is
A recreation to, and scant map of this.
My mind, neither with pride's itch, nor yet hath been
Poisoned with love to see, or to be seen.
I had no suit there, nor new suit to show,
Yet went to Court; but as Glaze which did go
To a Mass in jest, catched, was fain to disburse
The hundred marks, which is the Statute's curse,
Before he 'scaped, so it pleased my destiny
(Guilty of my sin of going), to think me
As prone to all ill, and of good as forget-
ful, as proud, as lustful, and as much in debt,
As vain, as witless, and as false as they
Which dwell at Court, for once going that way.
Therefore I suffered this: towards me did run
A thing more strange, than on Nile's slime, the sun
E'er bred; or all which into Noah's Ark came;
A thing, which would have posed Adam to name;
Stranger than seven antiquaries' studies,
Than Afric's monsters, Guiana's rarities;
Stranger than strangers; one, who for a Dane,
In the Danes' Massacre had sure been slain,
If he had lived then; and without help dies,
When next the 'prentices 'gainst strangers rise.
One, whom the watch at noon lets scarce go by,
One, to whom the examining Justice sure would cry,
"Sir, by your priesthood tell me what you are."
His clothes were strange, though coarse; and black, though bare;
Sleeveless his jerkin was, and it had been
Velvet, but 'twas now (so much ground was seen)
Become tufftaffaty; and our children shall
See it plain rash awhile, then naught at all.

This thing hath travelled, and saith, speaks all tongues
And only knoweth what to all states belongs;
Made of th' accents, and best phrase of all these,
He speaks one language; if strange meats displease,
Art can deceive, or hunger force my taste,
But pedant's motley tongue, soldier's bombast,
Mountebank's drugtongue, nor the terms of law
Are strong enough preparatives, to draw
Me to bear this: yet I must be content
With his tongue, in his tongue, called compliment:
In which he can win widows, and pay scores,
Make men speak treason, cozen subtlest whores,
Out-flatter favourites, or out-lie either
Jovius, or Surius, or both together.
He names me, and comes to me; I whisper, "God!
How have I sinned, that thy wrath's furious rod,
This fellow, chooseth me?" He sayeth, "Sir,
I love your judgment; whom do you prefer,
For the best linguist?" And I sillily
Said, that I thought Calepine's Dictionary.
"Nay but of men, most sweet Sir?" Beza then,
Some Jesuits, and two reverend men
Of our two Academies, I named; there
He stopped me, and said, "Nay, your Apostles were
Good pretty linguists, and so Panurge was;
Yet a poor gentleman, all these may pass
By travail." Then, as if he would have sold
His tongue, he praised it, and such wonders told
That I was fain to say, "If you had lived, Sir,
Time enough to have been interpreter
To Babel's bricklayers, sure the Tower had stood."
He adds, "If of Court life you knew the good,
You would leave loneness." I said, "Not alone
My loneness is; but Spartans' fashion,
To teach by painting drunkards, doth not taste
Now; Aretine's pictures have made few chaste;

No more can princes' Courts, though there be few
Better pictures of vice, teach me virtue."
He, like to a high stretched lute string squeaked, "O Sir,
'Tis sweet to talk of kings." "At Westminster,"
Said I, "the man that keeps the Abbey tombs,
And for his price doth with whoever comes,
Of all our Harrys, and our Edwards talk,
From king to king and all their kin can walk:
Your ears shall hear naught, but kings; your eyes meet
Kings only; The way to it, is King Street."
He smacked, and cried, "He's base, mechanic, coarse,
So are all your Englishmen in their discourse.
Are not your Frenchmen neat?" "Mine? as you see,
I have but one Frenchman, look, he follows me."
"Certes they are neatly clothed; I, of this mind am,
Your only wearing is your grogaram."
"Not so Sir, I have more." Under this pitch
He would not fly; I chaffed him; but as itch
Scratched into smart, and as blunt iron ground
Into an edge, hurts worse: so, I (fool) found,
Crossing hurt me; to fit my sullenness,
He to another key, his style doth address,
And asks, "What news?" I tell him of new plays.
He takes my hand, and as a still, which stays
A semi-breve, 'twixt each drop, he niggardly,
As loth to enrich me, so tells many a lie,
More than ten Holinsheds, or Halls, or Stows,
Of trivial household trash he knows; he knows
When the Queen frowned, or smiled, and he knows what
A subtle statesman may gather of that;
He knows who loves; whom; and who by poison
Hastes to an office's reversion;
He knows who hath sold his land, and now doth beg
A licence, old iron, boots, shoes, and egg-
shells to transport; shortly boys shall not play
At span-counter, or blow-point, but they pay

Toll to some courtier; and wiser than all us,
He knows what lady is not painted; thus
He with home-meats tries me; I belch, spew, spit,
Look pale, and sickly, like a patient; yet
He thrusts on more; and as if he undertook
To say *Gallo-Belgicus* without book
Speaks of all states, and deeds, that have been since
The Spaniards came, to the loss of Amiens.
Like a big wife, at sight of loathed meat,
Ready to travail: so I sigh, and sweat
To hear this Macaron talk: in vain; for yet,
Either my humour, or his own to fit,
He like a privileged spy, whom nothing can
Discredit, libels now 'gainst each great man.
He names a price for every office paid;
He saith, our wars thrive ill, because delayed;
That offices are entailed, and that there are
Perpetuities of them, lasting as far
As the last day; and that great officers,
Do with the pirates share, and Dunkirkers.
Who wastes in meat, in clothes, in horse, he notes;
Who loves whores, who boys, and who goats.
I more amazed than Circe's prisoners, when
They felt themselves turn beasts, felt myself then
Becoming traitor, and methought I saw
One of our giant Statutes ope his jaw
To suck me in; for hearing him, I found
That as burnt venomed lechers do grow sound
By giving others their sores, I might grow
Guilty, and he free: therefore I did show
All signs of loathing; but since I am in,
I must pay mine, and my forefathers' sin
To the last farthing; therefore to my power
Toughly and stubbornly I bear this cross; but the hour
Of mercy now was come; he tries to bring
Me to pay a fine to 'scape his torturing,

And says, "Sir, can you spare me?" I said, "Willingly."
"Nay, Sir, can you spare me a crown?" Thankfully I
Gave it, as ransom; but as fiddlers, still,
Though they be paid to be gone, yet needs will
Thrust one more jig upon you; so did he
With his long complimental thanks vex me.
But he is gone, thanks to his needy want,
And the prerogative of my crown: scant
His thanks were ended, when I, (which did see
All the Court filled with more strange things than he)
Ran from thence with such or more haste, than one
Who fears more actions, doth make from prison.

    At home in wholesome solitariness
My precious soul began, the wretchedness
Of suitors at Court to mourn, and a trance
Like his, who dreamed he saw hell, did advance
Itself on me; such men as he saw there,
I saw at Court, and worse, and more; low fear
Becomes the guilty, not the accuser; then,
Shall I, none's slave, of high-born, or raised men
Fear frowns? And, my mistress Truth, betray thee
To th' huffing braggart, puffed nobility?
No, no, thou which since yesterday hast been
Almost about the whole world, hast thou seen,
O sun, in all thy journey, vanity,
Such as swells the bladder of our Court? I
Think he which made your waxen garden, and
Transported it from Italy to stand
With us, at London, flouts our Presence, for
Just such gay painted things, which no sap, nor
Taste have in them, ours are; and natural
Some of the stocks are, their fruits, bastard all.

    'Tis ten a-clock and past; all whom the mews,
Balloon, tennis, diet, or the stews,
Had all the morning held, now the second
Time made ready, that day, in flocks, are found

In the Presence, and I, (God pardon me).
As fresh, and sweet their apparels be, as be
The fields they sold to buy them; "For a King
Those hose are," cry the flatterers; and bring
Them next week to the theatre to sell;
Wants reach all states; me seems they do as well
At stage, as Court; all are players; whoe'er looks
(For themselves dare not go) o'er Cheapside books,
Shall find their wardrobe's inventory. Now,
The ladies come; as pirates, which do know
That there came weak ships fraught with cochineal,
The men board them; and praise, as they think, well,
Their beauties; they the men's wits; both are bought.
Why good wits ne'er wear scarlet gowns, I thought
This cause: these men, men's wits for speeches buy,
And women buy all reds which scarlets dye.
He called her beauty lime-twigs, her hair net;
She fears her drugs ill laid, her hair loose set.
Would not Heraclitus laugh to see Macrine,
From hat, to shoe, himself at door refine,
As if the Presence were a moschite, and lift
His skirts and hose, and call his clothes to shrift,
Making them confess not only mortal
Great stains and holes in them, but venial
Feathers and dust, wherewith they fornicate;
And then by Dürer's rules survey the state
Of his each limb, and with strings the odds tries
Of his neck to his leg, and waist to thighs.
So in immaculate clothes, and symmetry
Perfect as circles, with such nicety
As a young preacher at his first time goes
To preach, he enters, and a lady which owes
Him not so much as good will, he arrests,
And unto her protests protests protests
So much as at Rome would serve to have thrown
Ten Cardinals into the Inquisition;

And whispered "By Jesu," so often, that a
Pursuivant would have ravished him away
For saying of Our Lady's psalter; but 'tis fit
That they each other plague, they merit it.
But here comes Glorius that will plague them both,
Who, in the other extreme, only doth
Call a rough carelessness, good fashion;
Whose cloak his spurs tear; whom he spits on
He cares not; his ill words do no harm
To him; he rusheth in, as if "Arm, arm,"
He meant to cry; and though his face be as ill
As theirs which in old hangings whip Christ, yet still
He strives to look worse, he keeps all in awe;
Jests like a licensed fool, commands like law.
     Tired, now I leave this place, and but pleased so
As men which from gaols to execution go,
Go through the great chamber (why is it hung
With the seven deadly sins?). Being among
Those Ascaparts, men big enough to throw
Charing Cross for a bar, men that do know
No token of worth, but "Queen's man," and fine
Living, barrels of beef, flagons of wine;
I shook like a spied spy. Preachers which are
Seas of wit and arts, you can, then dare,
Drown the sins of this place, for, for me
Which am but a scarce brook, it enough shall be
To wash the stains away, though I yet
With Maccabees' modesty, the known merit
Of my work lessen: yet some wise man shall,
I hope, esteem my writs canonical.

Twickenham Garden

Blasted with sighs, and surrounded with tears,
    Hither I come to seek the spring,
    And at mine eyes, and at mine ears,
Receive such balms, as else cure everything;
    But O, self traitor, I do bring
The spider love, which transubstantiates all,
    And can convert manna to gall,
And that this place may thoroughly be thought
    True paradise, I have the serpent brought.

'Twere wholesomer for me, that winter did
    Benight the glory of this place,
    And that a grave frost did forbid
These trees to laugh and mock me to my face;
    But that I may not this disgrace
Endure, nor yet leave loving, Love, let me
    Some senseless piece of this place be;
Make me a mandrake, so I may groan here,
    Or a stone fountain weeping out my year.

Hither with crystal vials, lovers, come
    And take my tears, which are love's wine,
And try your mistress' tears at home,
For all are false, that taste not just like mine;
    Alas, hearts do not in eyes shine,
Nor can you more judge woman's thoughts by tears,
    Than by her shadow, what she wears.
O perverse sex, where none is true but she,
    Who's therefore true, because her truth kills me.

John Taylor (1580–1653)

from *The Sculler*

EPIGRAM 22

As gold is better that's in fire tried,
So is the Bankside Globe that late was burned:
For where before it had a thatched hide,
Now to a stately theatre 'tis turned.
Which is an emblem, that great things are won,
By those that dare through greatest dangers run.

from *Sir Gregory Nonsense's News from No Place*

It was in June the eight and thirtieth day
That I embarkèd was on Highgate Hill,
After discourteous friendly taking leave
Of my young father Madge and mother John;
The wind did ebb, the tide flowed north south-east,
We hoist our sails of coloquintida,
And after thirteen days and seventeen nights
(With certain hieroglyphic hours to boot)
We with tempestuous calms and friendly storms
Split our main top-mast close below the keel.
But I with a dull quick congruity
Took eighteen ounces of the western wind,
And with the pith of the pole artichoke
Sailed by the flaming Coast of Trapezond.
There in a fort of melting adamant,
Armed in a crimson robe as black as jet,
I saw Alcides with a spider's thread
Lead Cerberus to the Pronontic Sea;
Then, cutting further through the marble main,
Mongst flying bulls and four-legged Turkicocks,
A dumb fair-spoken, wellfaced agèd youth,
Sent to me from the stout Stymphalides,
With tongueless silence thus began his speech:
"Illustrious flapjack, to thy hungry doom
Low as the ground I elevate my cause,
As I upon a gnat was riding late,
In quest to parley with the Pleiades,
I saw the Duke of Houndsditch gaping close,
In a green arbour made of yellow starch,
Betwixt two brokers howling madrigals.
A banquet was served in of lampreys' bones,
Well pickled in the tarbox of old time,
When Demogorgon sailed to Islington;
Which I perceiving with nine shads of steel,

Straight flew unto the coast of Pimlico,
To inform great Prester John and the Mogul
What excellent oysters were at Billingsgate.
The Mogul, all enragèd with these news,
Sent a black snail post to Tartaria,
To tell the Irishmen in Saxony
The dismal downfall of old Charing Cross.
With that, nine butter firkins in a flame
Did coldly rise to arbitrate the cause:
Guessing by the synderesis of Wapping,
Saint Thomas Watrings is most ominous.
For though an andiron and a pair of tongs
May both have breeding from one teeming womb,
Yet by the calculation of pickedhatch,
Milk must not be so dear as muscadel.
First shall Melpomene in cobweb lawn
Adorn great Memphis in a mussel boat,
And all the Muses clad in robes of air
Shall dance lavoltas with a whirligig;
Fair Pluto shall descend from brazen Dis,
And Polyphemus keep a seamster's shop;
The Isle of Wight shall like a dive-dapper
Devour the Egyptian proud pyramides,
Whilst Cassia Fistula shall gourmandize
Upon the flesh and blood of Croydon coal dust.
Then on the banks of Shoreditch shall be seen
What 'tis to serve the great Utopian queen."

Philip Massinger (1583–1640)

from *The City Madam*

[I.ii] Enter SIR MAURICE LACY *and* PAGE.

SIR MAURICE:
> You were with Plenty?

PAGE: Yes, sir.

SIR MAURICE: And what answer
> Returned the clown?

PAGE: Clown sir! he is transformed,
> And grown a gallant of the last edition;
> More rich than gaudy in his habit; yet
> The freedom and the bluntness of his language
> Continues with him. When I told him that
> You gave him caution, as he loved the peace
> And safety of his life, he should forbear
> To pass the merchant's threshold, until you,
> Of his two daughters, had made choice of her
> Whom you designed to honour as your wife,
> He smiled in scorn.

SIR MAURICE: In scorn?

PAGE: His words confirmed it.
> They were few, but to this purpose: "Tell your master,
> Though his lordship in reversion were now his,
> It cannot awe me. I was born a free man,
> And will not yield in the way of affection
> Precedence to him. I will visit 'em,
> Though he sat porter to deny my entrance.
> When I meet him next, I'll say more to his face.
> Deliver thou this"—then gave me a piece
> To help my memory, and so we parted.

SIR MAURICE:
> Where got he this spirit?

PAGE: At the academy of valor,
        Newly erected for the institution
        Of elder brothers, where they are taught the ways,
        Though they refuse to seal for a duelist,
        How to decline a challenge. He himself
        Can best resolve you.

Enter PLENTY *and three serving-men.*

SIR MAURICE: You, sir!
PLENTY: What with me, sir!
        How big you look! I will not loose a hat
        To a hair's breadth. Move your beaver, I'll move mine,
        Or if you desire to prove your sword, mine hangs
        As near my right hand, and will as soon out,
        Though I keep not a fencer to breathe me.
        Walk into Moorfields—I dare look on your Toledo.
        Do not show a foolish valor in the streets,
        To make work for shopkeepers and their clubs;
        'Tis scurvy, and the women will laugh at us.

SIR MAURICE:
        You presume on the protection of your hinds.

PLENTY:
        I scorn it:
        Though I keep men, I fight not with their fingers,
        Nor make it my religion to follow
        The gallant's fashion, to have my family
        Consisting in a footman and a page,
        And those two sometimes hungry. I can feed these,
        And clothe 'em too, my gay sir.
SIR MAURICE: What a fine man
        Hath your tailor made you!
PLENTY: 'Tis quite contrary,
        I have made my tailor, for my clothes are paid for
        As soon as put on, a sin your man of title
        Is seldom guilty of, but heaven forgive it.

I have other faults, too, very incident
To a plain gentleman. I eat my venison
With my neighbors in the country, and present not
My pheasants, partridges, and grouse to the usurer,
Nor ever yet paid brokage to his scrivener.
I flatter not my mercer's wife, nor feast her
With the first cherries, or peascods, to prepare me
Credit with her husband, when I come to London.
The wool of my sheep, or a score or two of fat oxen
In Smithfield, give me money for my expenses.
I can make my wife a jointure of such lands too
As are not encumbered, no annuity
Or statute lying on 'em. This I can do,
And it please your future honour, and why therefore
You should forbid my being a suitor with you
My dullness apprehends not.

PAGE: This is bitter.

SIR MAURICE:

I have heard you, sir, and in my patience shown
Too much of the stoic's. But to parley further,
Or answer your gross jeers, would write me coward.
This only: thy great grandfather was a butcher,
And his son a grazier; thy sire, constable
Of the hundred, and thou the first of your dunghill
Created gentleman. Now you may come on, sir,
You, and your thrashers.

PLENTY [*To his Serving-men*]: Stir not on your lives.—
This for the grazier, this for the butcher. [*They fight.*]

SIR MAURICE: So, sir!

PAGE:

I'll not stand idle.—[*To the Serving-men.*] Draw! My little rapier
Against your bumb blades. I'll one by one despatch you,
Then house this instrument of death and horror.

Francis Beaumont (1584–1616) and John Fletcher (1579–1625)

from *The Knight of the Burning Pestle*

SCENE 5

Enter RALPH, *dressed as a May-lord.*

RALPH: London, to thee I do present the merry month of May;
Let each true subject be content to hear me what I say:
For from the top of conduit-head, as plainly may appear,
I will both tell my name to you, and wherefore I came here.
My name is Ralph, by due descent though not ignoble I
Yet far inferior to the stock of gracious grocery;
And by the common counsel of my fellows in the Strand,
With gilded staff and crossèd scarf, the May-lord here I stand.
Rejoice, oh, English hearts, rejoice! rejoice, oh, lovers dear!
Rejoice, oh, city, town, and country! rejoice, eke every shere!
For now the fragrant flowers do spring and sprout in seemly sort,
The little birds do sit and sing, the lambs do make fine sport;
And now the birchen-tree doth bud, that makes the schoolboy cry;
The morris rings, while hobby-horse doth foot it feateously;
The lords and ladies now abroad for their disport and play,
Do kiss sometimes upon the grass, and sometimes in the hay;
Now butter with a leaf of sage is good to purge the blood;
Fly Venus and phlebotomy, for they are neither good.
Now little fish on tender stone begin to cast their bellies,
And sluggish snails, that erst were mewed, do creep out of their shellies;
The rumbling rivers now do warm, for little boys to paddle;
The sturdy steed now goes to grass, and up they hang his saddle;
The heavy hart, the bellowing buck, the rascal, and the pricket,
Are now among the yeoman's peas, and leave the fearful thicket.
And be like them, oh, you, I say, of this same noble town,
And lift aloft your velvet heads, and slipping off your gown,
With bells on legs, and napkins clean unto your shoulders tied,
With scarfs and garters as you please, and "Hey for our town!" cried.
March out, and show your willing minds, by twenty and by twenty,

To Hogsdon or to Newington, where ale and cakes are plenty;
And let it ne'er be said for shame, that we the youths of London
Lay thrumming of our caps at home, and left our custom undone.
Up, then, I say, both young and old, both man and maid a-maying,
With drums, and guns that bounce aloud, and merry tabor playing!
Which to prolong, God save our king, and send his country peace,
And root out treason from the land! and so, my friends, I cease. [*Exit.*

Francis Beaumont (1584–1616)

Letter to Ben Jonson

The sun, which doth the greatest comfort bring
To absent friends (because the self-same thing
They know they see, however absent), is
Here our best hay-maker (forgive me this,
It is our country style); in this warm shine
I lie, and dream of your full Mermaid wine.
Oh, we have water mixed with claret-lees,
Drink apt to bring in drier heresies
Than beer, good only for the sonnet strain,
With fustian metaphors to stuff the brain;
So mixed that given to the thirstiest one
'Twill not prove alms unless he have the stone.
I think with one draught man's invention fades,
Two cups had quite marred Homer's Iliads;
'Tis liquor that will find out Sutcliffe's wit,
Lie where it will, and make him write worse yet.
Filled with such moisture, in a grievous qualm,
Did Robert Wisdom write his singing psalm;
And so must I do this, and yet I think
It is a potion sent us down to drink
By special providence, keeps us from fights,
Makes us not laugh when we make legs to knights;
'Tis this that keeps our minds fit for our states,
A medicine to obey our magistrates.
For we do live more free than you; no hate,
No envy of another's happy state
Moves us, we are all equal, every whit;
Of land, that God gives men here, is their wit,
If we consider fully, for our best
And gravest man will, with his main house-jest,
Scarce please you; we want subtlety to do
The city tricks—lie, hate, and flatter too.

Here are none that can bear a painted show,
Strike when you wink, and then lament the blow,
Who, like mills set the right way to grind,
Can make their gains alike with every wind.
Only some fellow with the subtlest pate
Amongst us, may perchance equivocate
At selling of a horse, and that's the most.
Methinks the little wit I had is lost
Since I saw you; for wit is like a rest
Held up at tennis, which men do the best
With the best gamesters. What things have we seen
Done at the Mermaid! heard words that have been
So nimble and so full of subtle flame,
As if that everyone from whence they came
Had meant to put his whole wit in a jest,
And had resolved to live a fool the rest
Of his dull life; then when there has been thrown
Wit able enough to justify the town
For three days past; wit that might warrant be
For the whole city to talk foolishly
Till that were cancelled, and when we were gone,
We left an air behind, which was alone
Able to make the two next companies
Right witty, though they were downright cockneys.
When I remember this, and see that now
The country gentlemen begin to allow
My wit for dry-bobs, then I needs must cry;
I see my days of ballading are nigh.
I can already riddle, and can sing
Catches, sell bargains, and I fear shall bring
Myself to speak the hardest words I find
Over as fast as any, with one wind
That takes no medicines. But one thought of thee
Makes me remember all these things to be
The wit of our young men, fellows that show
No part of good, yet utter all they know;

Who like trees and the guard have growing souls
Only; strong destiny, which all controls,
I hope hath left a better fate in store
For me, thy friend, than to live evermore
Banished unto this home; 'twill once again
Bring me to thee, who wilt make smooth and plain
The way of knowledge for me, and then I
Who have no good in me but simplicity,
Know that it will my greatest comfort be
To acknowledge all the rest to come from thee.

On the Tombs in Westminster Abbey

Mortality, behold, and fear,
What a change of flesh is here!
Think how many royal bones
Sleep within this heap of stones,
Hence removed from beds of ease,
Dainty fare, and what might please,
Fretted roofs, and costly shows,
To a roof that flats the nose:
Which proclaims all flesh is grass;
How the world's fair glories pass;
That there is not trust in health,
In youth, in age, in greatness, wealth;
For if such could have reprieved
Those had been immortal lived.
Know from this the world's a snare,
How that greatness is but care,
How all pleasures are but pain,
And how short they do remain.
For here they lie had realms and lands,
That now want strength to stir their hands;
Where from their pulpits sealed with dust
They preach: "In greatness is not trust."
Here's an acre sown indeed
With the richest royalest seed,
That the earth did e'er suck in
Since the first man died for sin.
Here the bones of birth have cried,
"Though Gods they were, as men they died."
Here are sands (ignoble things)
Dropped from the ruined sides of kings;
With whom the poor man's earth being shown
The difference is not easily known.
Here's a world of pomp and state,
Forgotten, dead, disconsolate;

Think, then, this scythe that mows down kings
Exempts no meaner mortal things.
Then bid the wanton lady tread
Amid these mazes of the dead;
And these, truly understood,
More shall cool and quench the blood
Than her many sports aday,
And her nightly wanton play.
Bid her paint till day of doom,
To this favour she must come.
Bid the merchant gather wealth,
The usurer exact by stealth,
The proud man beat if from his thought,
Yet to this shape all must be brought.

Thomas Freeman (1590?–1630?)

from *London's Progress*

Why how now Babel, whither wilt thou build?
I see old Holborn, Charing Cross, the Strand,
Are going to Saint Giles's-in-the-field;
Saint Katherine's she shakes Wapping by the hand:
And Hogsdon will to Highgate ere't be long.
London is got a great way from the stream;
I think she means to go to Islington,
To eat a mess of strawberries and cream.
The City's sure in progress, I surmise,
Or going to revel it in some disorder
Without the walls, without the liberties,
Where she need fear nor Mayor nor Recorder.
Well, say she do; 'twere pretty, but 'twere pity
A Middlesex bailiff should arrest the City.

W. Turner (?)

from *Turner's Dish of Lenten Stuff, or a Gallimaufry*

My masters all, attend you,
If mirth you love to hear,
And I will tell you what they cry
In London all the year.
I'll please you if I can,
I will not be too long:
I pray you all attend awhile,
And listen to my song.

The fishwife first begins,
Any mussels lily-white!
Herrings, sprats or plaice,
Or cockles for delight.
Any Wellfleet oysters!
Then she doth change her note:
She had need to have her tongue be greased,
For the rattles in the throat.

For why, they are but Kentish,
To tell you out of doubt:
Her measure is too little;
Go, beat the bottom out.
Half a peck for twopence?
I doubt it is a bodge.
Thus all the City over
The people they do dodge.

The wench that cries the kitchen stuff,
I marvel what she ail,
She sings her note so merry,
But she hath a draggle tail:
An empty car came running,
And hit her on the bum;

Down she threw her greasy tub,
And away straight she did run.

But she did give her blessing
To some, but not to all,
To bear a load to Tyburn,
And there to let it fall:
The miller and his golden thumb,
And his dirty neck.
If he grind but two bushels,
He must needs steal a peck.

The weaver and the tailor,
Cozens they be sure.
They cannot work but they must steal,
To keep their hands in ure;
For it is a common proverb
Throughout the town,
The tailor he must cut three sleeves
To every woman's gown.

Mark but the waterman
Attending for his fare,
Of hot and cold, of wet and dry,
He always takes his share:
He carrieth bonny lasses
Over to the plays,
And here and there he gets a bit,
And that his stomach stays.

There was a singing boy
Who did ride to Rumford;
When I got my own school
I will take him in a comfort;
But what I leave behind
Shall be no private gain;
But all is one when I am gone:
Let him take it for his pain.

Old shoes for new brooms!
The broom-man he doth sing,
For hats or caps or buskins,
Or any old pouch-ring.
Buy a mat, a bed-mat!
A hassock or a press,
A cover for a close stool,
A bigger or a less.

Ripe, cherry ripe!
The costermonger cries;
Pippins fine or pears!
Another after hies
With basket on his head
His living to advance,
And in his purse a pair of dice
For to play at mumchance.

Hot pippin pies!
To sell unto my friends,
Or pudding pies in pans,
Well stuffed with candles ends.
Will you buy any milk?
I heard a wench that cries:
With a pale of fresh cheese and cream,
Another after hies.

Oh the wench went neatly;
Methought it did me good,
To see her cherry cheeks
So dimpled o'er with blood:
Her waistcoat washed white
As any lily flower;
Would I had time to talk with her
The space of half an hour.

Buy black! saith the blacking man,
The best that ere was seen;

'Tis good for poor citizens
To make their shoes to shine.
Oh! 'tis a rare commodity,
It must not be forgot;
It will make them to glister gallantly,
And quickly make them rot.

The world is full of threadbare poets
That live upon their pen,
But they will write too eloquent,
They are such witty men.
But the tinker with his budget,
The beggar with his wallet,
And Turner's turned a gallant man
At making of a ballad.

Abraham Holland (?–1626)

from *London, Look Back*

(The Description of the late great memorable and prodigious Plague, 1625)

Good God! what poison lurked in that first fruit
Whose surfeit left us wretches prostitute
To such a world of sorrow? Not confined
Only to tear and cruciate the mind
With sad remembrance of the bliss, wherein
We might have lived, but see, the cruel sin
Spares not our soul's weak houses, but doth spread
From viler parts unto the nobler head
A thousand maladies, which now, alas,
Through each small inlet of the body, pass,
Remorseless enemies, and batter down,
The clayey bulwarks of our mud-walled town.
Our throat is like that vast breach, which doth bring
In, like the Trojan Horse, dire surfeiting;
When in the stomach, like the market-place,
The foes let loose dare spread themselves, and trace
Through all the city: some are ready first
To break the sluices, which do raging burst
And drown low buildings, some with flaming brands
Fire holy temples, some with swords in hands,
Sharp-pointed javelins, mauls, and poisonous darts
Make massacres through all the trembling parts
Of the distressed fabric; no control
Can bar 'em but they will assault the soul
Itself, almost, while each small-breathing pore
Betrays unto the foe a postern door
To enter in at, every crawling vein
Affords him harbour, and doth entertain
The bloody enemy, each muscle, nerve
And film makes him a fortress to preserve

His longer durance, till the guest at last
With ruin pays his host for all that's past.
How many such foes, think you, secret lie
When hundreds of them ambush in one eye,
Which is the lantern and the watch and light,
Keeps sentry for all the body's night?

Robert Herrick (1591–1674)

An Ode for Him [Ben Jonson]

Ah Ben!
Say how or when
Shall we thy guests
Meet at those lyric feasts
Made at the Sun,
The Dog, the Triple Tun?
Where we such clusters had
As made us nobly wild, not mad;
And yet each verse of thine
Outdid the meat, outdid the frolic wine.

My Ben,
Or come again,
Or send to us
Thy wits' great overplus;
But teach us yet
Wisely to husband it,
Lest we that talent spend,
And having once brought to an end
That precious stock, the store
Of such a wit the world should have no more.

His Return to London

From the dull confines of the drooping West,
To see the day spring from the pregnant East,
Ravished in spirit, I come, nay more, I fly
To thee, blest place of my nativity!
Thus, thus with hallowed foot I touch the ground,
With thousand blessings by thy fortune crowned.
O fruitful Genius! that bestowest here
An everlasting plenty, year by year.
O Place! O People! Manners! framed to please
All nations, customs, kindreds, languages!
I am a freeborn Roman; suffer then
That I amongst you live a citizen.
London my home is, though by hard fame sent
Into a long and irksome banishment;
Yet since called back; henceforward let me be,
O native country, repossessed by thee!
For rather than I'll to the West return
I'll beg of thee first here to have mine urn.
Weak I am grown, and must in short time fall;
Give thou my sacred relics burial.

His Tears to Thamasis

I send, I send here my supremest kiss
To thee, my silver-footed Thamasis.
No more shall I reiterate thy Strand,
Whereon so many stately structures stand;
Nor in the summer's sweeter evenings go
To bathe in thee (as thousand others do).
No more shall I along thy crystal glide,
In barge (with boughs and rushes beautified)
With soft-smooth virgins (for our chaste disport)
To Richmond, Kingston, and to Hampton Court.
Never again shall I, with finny oar,
Put from, or draw unto thy faithful shore;
And landing here, or safely landing there,
Make way to my beloved Westminster;
Or to the golden Cheapside, where the earth
Of Julia Herrick gave to me my birth.
May all clean nymphs and curious water dames,
With swanlike state, float up and down thy streams,
No drought upon thy wanton waters fall
To make them lean, and languishing at all.
No ruffling winds come hither to disease
Thy pure, and silver-wristed Naiades.
Keep up your state, ye streams; and as ye spring,
Never make sick your banks by surfeiting.
Grow young with tides, and though I see ye never,
Receive this vow, *So fare ye well for ever.*

Anon. (1640s, pub. 1662)

London Sad London: An Echo

What wants thee, that thou art in this sad taking?
>*A King.*

What made him first remove his residing?
>*Siding.*

Did any here deny him satisfaction?
>*Faction.*

Tell me whereon this strength of faction lies.
>*On lies.*

What didst thou do when the King left Parliament?
>*Lament.*

What terms would'st give to gain his company?
>*Any.*

But how wouldst serve him, with thy best endeavour?
>*Ever.*

What wouldst thou do if here thou couldst behold him?
>*Hold him.*

But if he comes not what becomes of London?
>*Undone.*

Edmund Waller (1606–1687)

On the Statue of King Charles I at Charing Cross

That the First Charles does here in triumph ride,
See his son reign where he a martyr died,
And people pay that reverence as they pass,
(Which then he wanted!) to the sacred brass,
Is not the effect of gratitude alone,
To which we owe the statue and the stone;
But Heaven this lasting monument has wrought
That mortals may eternally be taught
Rebellion, though successful, is but vain,
And kings so killed rise conquerers again.
This truth the royal image does proclaim,
Loud as the trumpet of surviving Fame.

On St. James's Park, As Lately Improved by His Majesty

Of the first paradise there's nothing found;
Plants set by heaven are vanished, and the ground;
Yet the description lasts: who knows the fate
Of lines that shall this paradise relate?

   Instead of rivers rolling by the side
Of Eden's garden, here flows in the tide;
The sea, which always served his empire, now
Pays tribute to our prince's pleasure too.
Of famous cities we the founders know;
But rivers, old as seas to which they go,
Are nature's bounty; 'tis of more renown
To make a river than to build a town.

   For future shade young trees upon the banks
Of the new stream appear in even ranks;
The voice of Orpheus, or Amphion's hand,
In better order could not make them stand;
May they increase as fast, and spread their boughs,
As the high fame of their great owner grows!
May he live long enough to see them all
Dark shadows cast, and as his palace tall!
Methinks I see the love that shall be made,
The lovers walking in that amorous shade,
The gallants dancing by the river's side;
They bathe in summer, and in winter slide.
Methinks I hear the music in the boats,
And the loud echo which returns the notes,
While overhead a flock of new-sprung fowl
Hangs in the air, and does the sun control,
Darkening the sky; they hover o'er, and shroud
The wanton sailors with a feathered cloud.
Beneath, a shoal of silver fishes glides,
And plays about the gilded barges' sides;
The ladies, angling in the crystal lake,
Feast on the waters with the prey they take:

At once victorious with their lines, and eyes,
They make the fishes, and the men, their prize.
A thousand Cupids on the billows ride,
And sea-nymphs enter with the swelling tide,
From Thetis sent as spies, to make report,
And tell the wonders of her sovereign's court.
All that can, living, feed the greedy eye,
Or dead, the palate, here you may descry:
The choicest things that furnished Noah's ark,
Or Peter's sheet, inhabiting this park;
All with a border of rich fruit-trees crowned,
Whose loaded branches hide the lofty mound.
Such various ways the spacious alleys lead,
My doubtful Muse knows not what path to tread.
Yonder, the harvest of cold months laid up
Gives a fresh coolness to the royal cup;
There ice, like crystal firm, and never lost,
Tempers hot July with December's frost;
Winter's dark prison, whence he cannot fly,
Though the warm spring, his enemy, draws nigh.
Strange, that extremes should thus preserve the snow,
High on the Alps, or in deep caves below.

    Here, a well-polished Mall gives us the joy
To see our prince his matchless force employ:
His manly posture and his graceful mien,
Vigour and youth in all his motions seen;
His shape so lovely and his limbs so strong
Confirm our hopes we shall obey him long.
No sooner has he touched the flying ball
But 'tis already more than half the Mall;
And such a fury from his arm has got,
As from a smoking culverin 'twere shot.

    Near this my Muse, what most delights her, sees
A living gallery of agèd trees:
Bold sons of Earth, that thrust their arms so high,
As if once more they would invade the sky.

In such green palaces the first kings reigned,
Slept in their shades, and angels entertained;
With such old counsellors they did advise,
And, by frequenting sacred groves, grew wise.
Free from the impediments of light and noise,
Man, thus retired, his nobler thoughts employs.
Here Charles contrives the ordering of his states,
Here he resolves his neighbouring princes' fates:
What nation shall have peace, where war be made,
Determined is in this oraculous shade;
The world, from India to the frozen north,
Concerned in what this solitude brings forth.
His fancy, objects from his view receives;
The prospect, thought and contemplation gives.
That seat of empire here salutes his eye,
To which three kingdoms do themselves apply;
The structure by a prelate raised, Whitehall,
Built with the fortune of Rome's capitol;
Both, disproportioned to the present state
Of their proud founders, were approved by fate.
From hence he does that antique pile behold,
Where royal heads receive the sacred gold:
It gives them crowns, and does their ashes keep;
There made like gods, like mortals there they sleep;
Making the circle of their reign complete,
Those suns of empire, where they rise, they set.
When others fell, this, standing, did presage
The crown should triumph over popular rage:
Hard by that house, where all our ills were shaped,
The auspicious temple stood, and yet escaped.
So snow on Aetna does unmelted lie,
Whence rolling flames and scattered cinders fly;
The distant country in the ruin shares;
What falls from heaven the burning mountain spares.
Next, that capacious hall he sees, the room
Where the whole nation does for justice come;

Under whose large roof flourishes the gown,
And judges grave, on high tribunals, frown.
Here, like the people's pastor he does go,
His flock subjected to his view below;
On which reflecting in his mighty mind,
No private passion does indulgence find;
The pleasures of his youth suspended are,
And made a sacrifice to public care.
Here, free from court compliances, he walks,
And with himself, his best adviser, talks:
How peaceful olive may his temples shade,
For mending laws, and for restoring trade;
Or how his brows may be with laurel charged,
For nations conquered, and our bounds enlarged.
Of ancient prudence here he ruminates,
Of rising kingdoms and of falling states;
What ruling arts gave great Augustus fame,
And how Alcides purchased such a name.
His eyes, upon his native palace bent,
Close by, suggest a greater argument.
His thoughts rise higher when he does reflect
On what the world may from that star expect
Which at his birth appeared, to let us see
Day, for his sake, could with the night agree;
A prince on whom such different lights did smile,
Born the divided world to reconcile!
Whatever heaven, or high extracted blood
Could promise, or foretell, he will make good;
Reform these nations, and improve them more
Than this fair park, from what it was before.

John Milton (1608–1674)

When the Assault Was Intended to the City

Captain or colonel, or knight in arms,
    Whose chance on these defenceless doors may seize,
    If deed of honour did thee ever please,
    Guard them, and him within protect from harms;
He can requite thee, for he knows the charms
    That call fame on such gentle acts as these,
    And he can spread thy name o'er lands and seas,
    Whatever clime the sun's bright circle warms.
Lift not thy spear against the muses' bower;
    The great Emathian conqueror bid spare
    The house of Pindarus, when temple and tower
Went to the ground: and the repeated air
    Of sad Electra's poet had the power
    To save the Athenian walls from ruin bare.

Sir John Suckling (1609–1642)

A Ballad upon a Wedding

I tell thee, Dick, where I have been,
Where I the rarest things have seen,
    Oh things without compare!
Such sights again cannot be found
In any place on English ground,
    Be it at wake or fair.

At Charing Cross, hard by the way
Where we (thou know'st) do sell our hay,
    There is a house with stairs,
And there did I see coming down
Such folk as are not in our town,
    Forty, at least, in pairs.

Amongst the rest, one pestilent fine
(His beard no bigger, though, than thine)
    Walked on before the rest.
Our landlord looks like nothing to him;
The king (God bless him!), 'twould undo him
    Should he go still so dressed.

At course-a-park, without all doubt,
He should have first been taken out
    By all the maids i' th' town,
Though lusty Roger there had been,
Or little George upon the Green,
    Or Vincent of the Crown.

But wot you what? The youth was going
To make an end of all his wooing;
    The parson for him stayed.
Yet by his leave, for all his haste,

He did not so much wish all past,
 Perchance, as did the maid.

The maid (and thereby hangs a tale),
For such a maid no Whitsun-ale
 Could ever yet produce;
No grape, that's kindly ripe, could be
So round, so plump, so soft as she,
 Nor half so full of juice.

Her finger was so small the ring
Would not stay on, which they did bring;
 It was too wide a peck:
And to say truth (for out it must),
It looked like the great collar (just)
 About our young colt's neck.

Her feet beneath her petticoat,
Like little mice, stole in and out,
 As if they feared the light;
But oh, she dances such a way,
No sun upon an Easter day
 Is half so fine a sight!

He would have kissed her once or twice,
But she would not, she was so nice,
 She would not do 't in sight;
And then she looked as who should say,
"I will do what I list today;
 And you shall do't at night."

Her cheeks so rare a white was on,
No daisy makes comparison
 (Who sees them is undone);
For streaks of red were mingled there,
Such as are on a Catherine pear
 (The side that's next the sun).

Her lips were red, and one was thin
Compared to that was next her chin
    (Some bee had stung it newly);
But, Dick, her eyes so guard her face
I durst no more upon them gaze
    Than on the sun in July.

Her mouth so small, when she does speak,
Thou'dst swear her teeth her words did break,
    That they might passage get;
But she so handled still the matter,
They came as good as ours, or better,
    And are not spent a whit.

If wishing should be any sin,
The parson himself had guilty been
    (She looked that day so purely);
And did the youth so oft the feat
At night, as some did in conceit,
    It would have spoiled him, surely.

Passion o' me, how I run on!
There's that that would be thought upon,
    I trow besides the bride.
The business of the kitchen's great,
For it is fit that man should eat,
    Nor was it there denied.

Just in the nick the cook knocked thrice,
And all the waiters in a trice
    His summons did obey;
Each serving-man, with dish in hand,
Marched boldly up, like our trained band,
    Presented, and away.

When all the meat was on the table,
What man of knife or teeth was able
    To stay to be entreated?

And this the very reason was,
Before the parson could say grace,
    The company was seated.

Now hats fly off, and youths carouse;
Healths first go round, and then the house;
    The bride's came thick and thick:
And when 'twas named another's health,
Perhaps he made it hers by stealth;
    And who could help it, Dick?

O' th' sudden up they rise and dance,
Then sit again and sigh and glance,
    Then dance again and kiss.
Thus several ways the time did pass,
Till every woman wished her place,
    And every man wished his!

By this time all were stolen aside
To counsel and undress the bride,
    But that he must not know;
But yet 'twas thought he guessed her mind,
And did not mean to stay behind
    Above an hour or so.

When in he came, Dick, there she lay
Like new-fallen snow melting away
    ('Twas time, I trow, to part);
Kisses were now the only stay,
Which soon she gave, as who would say,
    "God b' w' ye, with all my heart."

But just as heaven would have, to cross it,
In came the bridesmaids with the posset.
    The bridegroom ate in spite,
For had he left the women to 't,
It would have cost two hours to do 't,
    Which were too much that night.

At length the candle's out, and now
All that they had not done, they do.
    What that is, who can tell?
But I believe it was no more
Than thou and I have done before
    With Bridget and with Nell.

Thomas Jordan (1612?–1685)

from *The Cheaters Cheated*

Soldiers fight and Hectors rant on
    Whilst poor wenches go to rack,
Who would be a wicked wanton
    Only for suppers, songs and sack,
To endure the alteration
    Of these times that are so dead;
Thus to lead a long vacation
    Without money, beer or bread.

Farewell Bloomsbury and Sodom,
    Lukeners Lane and Turnbull Street,
Woe was me when first I trod 'em
    With my wild unwary feet.
I was bred a gentlewoman,
    But our family did fall
When the gentry's coin grew common,
    And the soldiers shared it all.

from *The Triumphs of London*

You that delight in wit and mirth,
    And love to hear such news
As comes from all parts of the earth,
    Dutch, Danes, and Turks, and Jews;
I'll send ye to a rendezvous,
    Where it is smoking new;
Go hear it at a Coffee-house,
    It cannot but be true.

There battles and sea-fights are fought,
    And bloody plots displayed;
They know more things than e'er was thought,
    Or ever was betrayed:
No money in the Minting-house,
    Is half so bright and new;
And coming from a Coffee-house,
    It cannot but be true.

Before the navies fell to work,
    They knew who should be winner;
They there can tell ye what the Turk
    Last Sunday had to dinner.
Who last did cut De Ruyter's corns,
    Amongst his jovial crew;
Or who first gave the devil horns,
    Which cannot but be true.

A fisherman did boldly tell,
    And strongly did avouch,
He caught a shoal of mackerel,
    They parleyed all in Dutch;
And cried out *Yaw, yaw, yaw, mine hare,*
    And as the draught they drew,
They shook for fear that Monk was there—
    This sounds as if 'twere true.

There's nothing done in all the world,
    From monarch to the mouse,
But every day or night 'tis hurled
    Into the Coffee-house:
What Lilly or what Booker could
    By art not bring about,
At Coffee-house you'll find a brood
    Can quickly find it out.

They know who shall in times to come
    Be either made or undone;
From great St. Peter's Street in Rome
    To Turnbull Street in London.
And likewise tell at Clerkenwell,
    What whore hath greatest gain;
And in that place what brazen face
    Doth wear a golden chain.

They know all that is good or hurt,
    To damn ye or to save ye;
There is the college and the court,
    The country, camp, and navy.
So great an university,
    I think there ne'er was any,
In which you may a scholar be,
    For spending of a penny.

Here men do talk of everything,
    With large and liberal lungs,
Like women at a gossiping,
    With double tire of tongues;
They'll give a broadside presently,
    'Soon as you are in view,
With stories that you'll wonder at,
    Which they will swear are true.

You shall know there what fashions are,
    How perriwigs are curled;

And for a penny you shall hear
    All novels in the world;
Both old and young, and great and small,
    And rich and poor you'll see;
Therefore let's to the coffee all,
    Come all away with me.

A Song Sung at the Lord Mayor's Table in Honour of the City and the Goldsmiths Company

Let all the Nine Muses lay by their abuses,
    Their railing and drolling on tricks of the Strand,
To pen us a ditty in praise of the City,
    Their treasure, and pleasure, their power and command.
Their feast, and guest, so temptingly dressed,
    Their kitchens all kingdoms replenish;
In bountiful bowls they do succour their souls,
    With claret, Canary, and Rhenish:
Their lives and wives in plenitude thrives,
    They want neither meat nor money;
The Promised Land's in a Londoner's hand,
    They wallow in milk and honey.

For laws, and good orders, Lord Mayor and Recorders,
    And Sheriff, with Councils, keep all in decorum;
The simple in safety from cruel and crafty,
    When crimes of the times are presented before 'em.
No town as this in Christendom is
    So quiet by day and night;
No ruffian or drab dares pilfer or stab,
    And hurry away by flight;
Should danger come, at beat of drum
    (It is in such strong condition),
An army 'twould raise in a very few days,
    With money and ammunition.

For science, and reading, true wit, and good breeding,
    No city's exceeding in bountiful fautors;
No town under heaven doth give, or has given,
    Such portions to sons, or such dowries to daughters.
Their name and fame doth through all the world flame,
    For courage and gallant lives:
No nation that grows are more cursed to their foes,
    Or kinder unto their wives:

For bed and board, this place doth afford
    A quiet repose for strangers;
The Lord Mayor and Shrieves take such order with thieves
    Men sleep without fear of dangers.

For gownsmen and swordsmen, this place did afford men,
    That were of great policy, power, and renown;
A Mayor of this City, stout, valiant, and witty,
    Subdued a whole army by stabbing of one;
A traitor, that ten thousand men gat
    Together in warlike swarms;
And for this brave feat, his red dagger is set
    In part of the City arms.
Should I declare the worthies that are,
    And did to this place belong,
'Twould puzzle my wit: and I think it more fit
    For a chronicle than a song.

One meanly descended, and weakly attended,
    By Fortune befriended, in this city placed,
From pence unto crowns, from crowns unto pounds,
    Up to hundreds of thousands hath risen at last.
In chain of gold, and treasure untold,
    In scarlet, on horseback to boot;
(To th' joy of his mother) when his elder brother
    It may be, has gone on foot.
Such is the fate of temporal state,
    For Providence thinks it fit,
Since the eldest begat must enjoy the estate,
    The youngest shall have the wit.

Plague, famine, fire, sword, as our stories record,
    Did unto this city severely fix,
And flaming September will make us remember
    One thousand six hundred sixty-six,
When house, and hall, and churches did fall
    (A punishment due for our sin),

No town so quick burned, into ashes was turned
    And sooner was built again.
Such is the fate of London's estate;
    Sometimes sh' has a sorrowful sup
Of misery's bowl, but to quicken her soul,
    For mercy doth hold her up.

Our ruins did show, five or six years ago,
    Like an object of woe to all eyes that came nigh us:
Yet now 'tis as gay as a garden in May,
    Guildhall and th' Exchange are in *Statu quo prius.*
Our feasts in halls, each company calls,
    To treat 'em as welcome men:
The Muses, all nine, do begin to drink wine;
    Apollo doth shine again.
True union and peace make plenty increase,
    And every trade to spring;
The city so walled, may be properly called
    The chamber of Charles, our king.

Our princes have been (as on record is seen),
    Good authors and fautors of love to this place;
By many good charters, to strengthen our quarters,
    With divers indulgences, favour, and grace;
Their love so much to London is such,
    They do, as occasion calls,
Their freedom partake, for society's sake,—
    Kings have been made free of halls!
If city and court together consort,
    This nation can never be undone:
Then let the hall ring with God prosper the King!
    And bless the Lord Mayor of London.

Sir John Denham (1615–1669)

from *Cooper's Hill*

Sure there are poets which did never dream
Upon Parnassus, nor did taste the stream
Of Helicon; we therefore may suppose
Those made not poets, but the poets those.
And as courts make not kings, but kings the court,
So where the muses and their train resort,
Parnassus stands; if I can be to thee
A poet, thou Parnassus art to me.
Nor wonder, if (advantaged in my flight,
By taking wing from thy auspicious height)
Through untraced ways, and airy paths I fly,
More boundless in my fancy than my eye:
My eye, which swift as thought contracts the space
That lies between, and first salutes the place
Crowned with that sacred pile, so vast, so high,
That whether 'tis a part of earth, or sky,
Uncertain seems, and may be thought a proud
Aspiring mountain, or descending cloud,
Paul's, the late theme of such a muse whose flight
Has bravely reached and soared above thy height:
Now shalt thou stand though sword, or time, or fire,
Or zeal more fierce than they, thy fall conspire,
Secure, whilst thee the best of poets sings,
Preserved from ruin by the best of kings.
Under his proud survey the city lies,
And like a mist beneath a hill doth rise;
Whose state and wealth the business and the crowd,
Seems at this distance but a darker cloud:
And is to him who rightly things esteems,
No other in effect than what it seems:
Where, with like haste, though several ways, they run,
Some to undo, and some to be undone;

While luxury and wealth, like war and peace,
Are each the other's ruin, and increase;
As rivers lost in seas some secret vein
Thence reconveys, there to be lost again.
Oh happiness of sweet retired content!
To be at once secure, and innocent. . . .

Abraham Cowley (1618–1667)

from *The Civil War*

He spoke, and what he spoke was soon obeyed;
Haste to their London prey the Furies made.
The gaping ground with natural joy made room
For this old monstrous burden of her womb.
In a long dismal line through Earth they arise;
Th' affrighted night shuts close her trembling eyes.
It was the noon of Cynthia's silent course,
And sleep all senses bound with gentle force.
The subtle fiends themselves through London spread;
Softly, as dreams, they steal into every head:
There unawares the powers of soul surprise,
Whilst each at rest, unarmed and fearless, lies.
The will they poison and the reason wound;
Leave the pale conscience blinded, gagged and bound;
All ornaments of nature, art or grace,
Like zealots in fair churches, they deface.
The rebel passions they below unchain,
And licence that wild multitude to reign.
Their business done, home fled the night and they;
But scarce could nature's self drive on the day.
Pale as his sister's looks, the sun arose;
The sullen morn a night-like garment chose.
What strange, wild madness this ill morning brought!
So soon, in minds prepared, hell's poison wrought!
Up rose the mighty traitors, in whose breasts
The guilt of all our ills so tamely rests:
By sleeping now they advanced our ruin more
Than by long watchings they'd done oft before.
Straight, like thick fumes, into their brains arise
Thousand rich slanders, thousand useful lies.
A thousand arts and thousand sleights they frame
To avert the dangers of sweet peace's name.

To Westminster they haste, and fondly there
Talk, plot, conspire, vote, covenant, and declare.
New fears, new hopes, pretences new they show,
Whilst o'er the wondering town their nets they throw.
Up rose their priests (the viperous brood that dare
With their own mouths their beauteous mother tear);
Their walking noisy diligence ne'er will cease:
They roar and sigh and pray and eat 'gainst peace.
Up rose the base mechanics and the rout,
And cried, "No peace," the astonished streets throughout.
Here, injured Church, thy strong avengement see:
The same noise plucks down peace, that plucked down thee.
All strive who first shall go, who most shall give,
Gloucester and stiff-necked Massey to relieve.
Their only sons the frantic women send,
Earnest, as if in labour for their end.
The wives (what's that, alas?), the maidens too,
The maids themselves bid their own dear ones go.
The greedy tradesmen scorn their idol gain,
And send forth their glad servants to be slain.
The bald and grey-haired gownmen quite forsook
Their sleepy furs, black shoes, and City look:
All o'er in iron and leather clad they come;
Poor men that trembled erst at Finsbury's drum!
Forth did this rage all trades, all ages, call;
Religions, more than e'er before were all.

    Three thousand hot-brained Calvinists there came,
Wild men that blot their great Reformer's name.
God's image, stamped on monarchs, they deface,
And above the throne their thundering pulpits place.

Richard Lovelace (1618–1657/8)

To Althea, from Prison: Song

When love with unconfinèd wings
    Hovers within my gates,
And my divine Althea brings
    To whisper at the grates;
When I lie tangled in her hair
    And fettered to her eye,
The gods that wanton in the air
    Know no such liberty.

When flowing cups run swiftly round,
    With no allaying Thames,
Our careless heads with roses bound,
    Our hearts with loyal flames;
When thirsty grief in wine we steep,
    When healths and draughts go free,
Fishes that tipple in the deep
    Know no such liberty.

When, like committed linnets, I
    With shriller throat shall sing
The sweetness, mercy, majesty
    And glories of my king;
When I shall voice aloud how good
    He is, how great should be,
Enlargèd winds that curl the flood
    Know no such liberty.

Stone walls do not a prison make,
    Nor iron bars a cage;
Minds innocent and quiet take

That for an hermitage:
If I have freedom in my love
    And in my soul am free,
Angels alone that soar above
    Enjoy such liberty.

Simon Ford (1619?–1699)

from *London's Resurrection*

Hail, glorious day; mayst thou be writ in gold,
Which sawst the sceptered hand the trowel hold,
To lay that stone whence the Exchange became
Anew entitled to its royal name!
Henceforth, proud pillar, to thy readers' view
Tell thine own story, and thy founder's too.
    Fruitful example! From the royal hand
Each artist now takes pattern and command.
Hark, how the clattering tools' confusèd sound
Divides the ear! The pickaxe rends the ground
To load the spade, its loads bestowed between
The sifting ridder and the searching screen.
The saw the file, the axe the grindstone whets:
The knotty tree this hews, the other eats.
The arm the plane, and maul the chisel drives;
Through heart of oak the groaning auger dives.
The glowing steel the weighty sledge's stroke
Beats into form; which, quenched, doth hiss and smoke.
    Room, next, for miracles, profaned by use:
The issues of the famed Vitruvian Muse,
And that grave architect's whose ominous hand
Drew learned lines on Syracusan sand;
Whose dying gore did the choice figures drown,
And 's dying weight in *their* room stamped his *own!*
    Here twisted screws, whiles planted on the ground
They worm themselves through a like wreathèd round,
Prop tottering roofs. Versatile rundles there
By equal helps their fellows' burdens bear,
Transferred by clasping ropes; whence greatest weights
By a small force are wound to greatest heights.
The balance engine next, whose loaded end
The tenth part of its burden makes t' ascend.

Nor is 't less wondrous that the vastest beams,
On cylinders supporting both extremes,
Tough levers roll, whiles every lifting hand
One interjection jointly doth command.
     Thus goes the building on. Confusèd grounds
Just verdicts part; and, whiles they fix the bounds
To public streets by the imperious line,
Surveyors like unbounded sovereigns reign;
Each house clasps with its neighbour; and the square
Each front unto its fellow wall doth pair.
And sister piles, whiles thus they intermarry,
Like sister faces, uniformly vary.
     Lady enchantress of the ravished ear,
Ne'er did thy art effect what chance doth here!
Whiles building noises by the pleasèd mind
Are into all harmonious notes combined,
Orpheus to us would grate, Apollo jar:
Hammers and trowels sweeter music are.
By this one spell each melancholy breast
Is of its legion-devil dispossessed;
And where yet falling London's doleful knell
Doth in retentive apprehensions dwell,
By sympathetic cure these joyful sounds
With glad ideas heal the fancy's wounds.
     The fields are busy too. Bold miners found
In paunchèd hills a London under ground.
The realm of silence and eternal night
Is startled at the approach of noise and light.
Twin stones long claspèd in their mother bed,
Now severed, yield with foreign rocks to wed.
Each polished marble to a mirror grows,
Mocks its own workman, and retorts his blows.
     Here, the green robe pulled off, the unbowelled ground
Affords a clay which with chopped stubble bound
First, the sun fastens; then the brittle cakes
The rapid furnace to just hardness bakes:

An hardness that outstands the fiercest showers
Which heaven from its opened sluices pours;
Which winter frosts can't mellow, and the flame
Itself, that did beget it, cannot tame.
Scarce flint, or marble, lasts so long in prime:
This brittle stone grinds out the teeth of time.
With this th' immortal queen built Babel's spires,
And with burnt walls beguilèd future fires.

    There, the wood's glories fall, and where the eye
Of heaven scarce pierced, now mortal sight doth pry.
The shades by horror hallowed, the early dawn
Admitted doth illustrate and profane.
The reverend oaks presumptuous axes wound,
Measuring their lengths upon the furrowed ground,
Whiles rattling Echo (as great talkers do)
Reports at distance every blow for two.
The ring-dove sees her lofty nest o'erthrown,
And turtles that their love's bewrayèd, moan;
The magpie scolds whiles her arched roof doth fall;
And sharking rooks, their camp dislodgèd, brawl;
The hare forsakes her form; the rousèd deer
Their branched heads now above their thickets rear;
And all the game tall forests used to shield
Becomes a facile prey in the open field.
The traveller too, who setting forth designed
The crownèd hills, as certain guides, to mind,
At his return, admires the shavèd coast,
And finds his way, with his directors, lost.

    Yea, foreign realms contribute: Spain brings steel,
Libanus cedar sends, and Denmark deal;
A checkered gift the sunburnt India gives,
Whence th' whitest tooth and blackest wood arrives;
Our Ireland oak, on which no spider builds
(Arachne sure hanged on that timber), yields.
Marbles come varied by their native grains:
This, untrod snow with purer brightness stains;

That's pitchy black, a lump of solid night;
There, bloody veins creep through a lovely white;
Some in its speckled face, heaven's portrait bears,
An azure sky bespangled o'er with stars;
And some (on which Medusa's head did fall),
Wherein her snakes seem still to hiss and crawl....

Henry Vaughan (1621–1695)

A Rhapsody

*Occasionally Written upon a Meeting with Some of His Friends at the Globe Tavern,
in a Chamber Painted Over Head with a Cloudy Sky and Some Few Dispersed Stars
and on the Sides with Landscapes, Hills, Shepherds, and Sheep*

Darkness, & stars i' the mid day! They invite
Our active fancies to believe it night:
For taverns need no sun, but for a sign,
Where rich tobacco, and quick tapers shine;
And royal, witty sack, the poets' soul,
With brighter suns than he doth gild the bowl;
As though the pot, and poet did agree,
Sack should to both illuminator be.
That artificial cloud with its curled brow,
Tells us 'tis late; and that blue space below
Is fired with many stars; mark, how they break
In silent glances o'er the hills, and speak
The evening to the plains, where shot from far,
They meet in dumb salutes, as one great star.
   The room (me thinks) grows darker; & the air
Contracts a sadder colour, and less fair:
Or is't the drawer's skill? Hath he no arts
To blind us so, we can't know pints from quarts?
No, no, 'tis night; look where the jolly clown
Musters his bleating herd, and quits the down.
Hark! how his rude pipe frets the quiet air,
Whilst every hill proclaims Lycoris fair.
Rich, happy man! that canst thus watch, and sleep,
Free from all cares, but thy wench, pipe and sheep.
   But see the Moon is up; view where she stands
Sentinel o'er the door, drawn by the hands
Of some base painter, that for gain hath made
Her face the landmark to the tippling trade.

This cup to her, that to Endymion give;
'Twas wit at first, and wine that made them live.
Choke may the painter! and his box disclose
No other colours than his fiery nose;
And may we no more of his pencil see,
Than two churchwardens, and mortality.
    Should we go now a-wandering, we should meet
With catchpoles, whores, & carts in every street:
Now when each narrow lane, each nook & cave,
Sign-posts, & shop-doors, pimp for every knave,
When riotous sinful plush, and tell-tale spurs
Walk Fleet street, & the Strand, when the soft stirs
Of bawdy, ruffled silks, turn night to day,
And the loud whip, and coach scolds all the way;
When lust of all sorts, and each itchy blood
From the Tower-wharf to Cymbeline, and Lud,
Hunts for a mate, and the tired footman reels
'Twixt chair-men, torches, & the hackney wheels.
    Come, take the other dish; it is to him
That made his horse a Senator: each brim
Look big as mine; the gallant, jolly beast
Of all the herd (you'll say) was not the least.
    Now crown the second bowl, rich as his worth,
I'll drink it to—he! that like fire broke forth
Into the Senate's face, crossed Rubicon,
And the State's pillars, with their laws thereon:
And made the dull grey beards, & furred gowns fly
Into Brundusium to consult, and lie.
    This to brave Sylla! why should it be said,
We drink more to the living, than the dead?
Flatterers, and fools do use it: let us laugh
At our own honest mirth; for they that quaff
To honour others, do like those that sent
Their gold and plate to strangers to be spent.
    Drink deep; this cup be pregnant; & the wine
Spirit of wit, to make us all divine,

That big with sack, and mirth we may retire
Possessors of more souls, and nobler fire;
And by the influx of this painted sky,
And laboured forms, to higher matters fly;
So, if a nap shall take us, we shall all,
   After full cups have dreams poetical.

Let's laugh now, and the pressed grape drink,
Till the drowsy Day-Star wink;
And in our merry, mad mirth run
Faster, and further than the Sun;
And let none his cup forsake,
Till that Star again doth wake;
So we men below shall move
   Equally with the gods above.

Anon. (17th century)

The Cries of London

Here's fine rosemary, sage and thyme.
Come buy my ground ivy.
Here's fetherfew, gilliflowers and rue.
Come buy my knotted majorum, ho!
Come buy my mint, my fine greenmint.
Here's fine lavender for your clothes.
Here's parsley and winter-savory,
And hearts-ease, which all do choose.
Here's balm and hissop, and cinquefoil,
All fine herbs, it is well known.
Let none despise the merry, merry cries
Of famous London-town!

Here's fine herrings, eight a groat.
Hot codlins, pies and tarts.
New mackerel! have to sell.
Come buy my Wellfleet oysters, ho!
Come buy my whitings fine and new.
Wives, shall I mend your husbands' horns?
I'll grind your knives to please your wives,
And very nicely cut your corns.
Maids, have you any hair to sell,
Either flaxen, black or brown?
Let none despise the merry, merry cries
Of famous London-town!

Andrew Marvell (1621–1678)

An Horatian Ode upon Cromwell's Return from Ireland

The forward youth that would appear
Must now forsake his Muses dear,
 Nor in the shadows sing
 His numbers languishing.
'Tis time to leave the books in dust,
And oil the unusèd armour's rust;
 Removing from the wall
 The corslet of the hall.
So restless Cromwell could not cease
In the inglorious arts of peace,
 But through adventurous war
 Urgèd his active star.
And, like the three-forked lightning, first
Breaking the clouds where it was nursed,
 Did thorough his own side
 His fiery way divide.
For 'tis all one to courage high
The emulous or enemy;
 And with such to inclose
 Is more than to oppose.
Then burning through the air he went,
And palaces and temples rent;
 And Caesar's head at last
 Did through his laurels blast.
'Tis madness to resist or blame
The force of angry heaven's flame;
 And, if we would speak true,
 Much to the man is due,
Who, from his private gardens, where
He lived reservèd and austere,
 As if his highest plot
 To plant the bergamot,

Could by industrious valour climb
To ruin the great work of time,
   And cast the kingdoms old
   Into another mould.
Though justice against fate complain,
And plead the ancient rights in vain:
   But those do hold or break
   As men are strong or weak.
Nature, that hateth emptiness,
Allows of penetration less,
   And therefore must make room
   Where greater spirits come.
What field of all the civil wars,
Where his were not the deepest scars?
   And Hampton shows what part
   He had of wiser art;
Where, twining subtile fears with hope,
He wove a net of such a scope
   That Charles himself might chase
   To Carisbrook's narrow case:
That thence the royal actor born
The tragic scaffold might adorn:
   While round the armèd bands
   Did clap their bloody hands.
He nothing common did or mean
Upon that memorable scene;
   But with his keener eye
   The axe's edge did try:
Nor called the gods with vulgar spite
To vindicate his helpless right;
   But bowed his comely head
   Down as upon a bed.
This was that memorable hour
Which first assured the forcèd power.
   So when they did design
   The capitol's first line,

A bleeding head where they begun
Did fright the architects to run;
 And yet in that the state
 Foresaw its happy fate.
And now the Irish are ashamed
To see themselves in one year tamed:
 So much one man can do,
 That does both act and know.
They can affirm his praises best,
And have, though overcome, confessed
 How good he is, how just,
 And fit for highest trust;
Nor yet grown stiffer with command,
But still in the republic's hand;
 How fit he is to sway
 That can so well obey.
He to the Commons' feet presents
A kingdom, for his first year's rents;
 And, what he may, forbears
 His fame, to make it theirs;
And has his sword and spoils ungirt,
To lay them at the public's skirt:
 So when the falcon high
 Falls heavy from the sky,
She, having killed, no more does search
But on the next green bough to perch,
 Where, when he first does lure,
 The falconer has her sure.
What may not then our isle presume
While victory his crest does plume?
 What may not others fear
 If thus he crown each year?
A Caesar, he, ere long to Gaul,
To Italy an Hannibal,
 And to all states not free
 Shall climacteric be.

The Pict no shelter now shall find
Within his parti-coloured mind,
    But from this valour sad
    Shrink underneath the plaid:
Happy, if in the tufted brake
The English hunter him mistake,
    Nor lay his hounds in near
    The Caledonian deer.
But thou, the wars' and fortune's son,
March indefatigably on,
    And for the last effect
    Still keep thy sword erect:
Besides the force it has to fright
The spirits of the shady night,
    The same arts that did gain
    A power must it maintain.

John Dryden (1631–1700)

from *Annus Mirabilis*

TRANSITUM TO THE FIRE OF LONDON

But ah! how unsincere are all our joys!
    Which sent from heaven, like lightning make no stay.
Their palling taste the journey's length destroys,
    Or grief, sent post, o'ertakes them on the way.

Swelled with our late successes on the foe,
    Which France and Holland wanted power to cross,
We urge an unseen fate to lay us low,
    And feed their envious eyes with English loss.

Each element his dread command obeys,
    Who makes or ruins with a smile or frown;
Who, as by one he did our nation raise,
    So now he with another pulls us down.

Yet, London, empress of the northern clime,
    By a high fate thou greatly didst expire;
Great as the world's, which at the death of time
    Must fall, and rise a nobler frame by fire.

As when some dire usurper heaven provides
    To scourge his country with a lawless sway,
His birth perhaps some petty village hides,
    And sets his cradle out of fortune's way;

Till, fully ripe, his swelling fate breaks out,
    And hurries him to mighty mischiefs on;
His prince, surprised at first, no ill could doubt,
    And wants the power to meet it when 'tis known:

Such was the rise of this prodigious fire,
    Which, in mean buildings first obscurely bred,

From thence did soon to open streets aspire,
  And straight to palaces and temples spread.

The diligence of trades, and noiseful gain,
  And luxury, more late, asleep were laid;
All was the night's, and in her silent reign
  No sound the rest of nature did invade.

In this deep quiet, from what source unknown,
  Those seeds of fire their fatal birth disclose:
And first few scattering sparks about were blown,
  Big with the flames that to our ruin rose.

Then, in some close-pent room it crept along,
  And, smouldering as it went, in silence fed:
Till the infant monster, with devouring strong,
  Walked boldly upright with exalted head.

Now, like some rich or mighty murderer,
  Too great for prison, which he breaks with gold,
Who fresher for new mischiefs does appear,
  And dares the world to tax him with the old;

So scapes the insulting fire his narrow gaol,
  And makes small outlets into open air:
There the fierce winds his tender force assail,
  And beat him downward to his first repair.

The winds, like crafty courtesans, withheld
  His flames from burning but to blow them more:
And, every fresh attempt, he is repelled
  With faint denials, weaker than before.

And now, no longer letted of his prey,
  He leaps up at it with enraged desire,
O'erlooks the neighbours with a wide survey
  And nods at every house his threatening fire.

The ghosts of traitors from the bridge descend
   With bold fanatic spectres to rejoice;
About the fire into a dance they bend,
   And sing their sabbath notes with feeble voice.

Our guardian angel saw them where he sate
   Above the palace of our slumbering king:
He sighed, abandoning his charge to fate,
   And, drooping, oft looked back upon the wing.

At length the crackling noise and dreadful blaze
   Called up some waking lover to the sight;
And long it was ere he the rest could raise,
   Whose heavy eyelids yet were full of night.

The next to danger, hot pursued by fate,
   Half-clothed, half-naked, hastily retire;
And frighted mothers strike their breasts, too late,
   For helpless infants left amidst the fire.

Their cries soon waken all the dwellers near;
   Now murmuring noises rise in every street;
The more remote run stumbling with their fear,
   And in the dark men jostle as they meet.

So weary bees in little cells repose;
   But if night-robbers lift the well-stored hive,
A humming through their waxen city grows,
   And out upon each other's wings they drive.

Now streets grow thronged and busy as by day;
   Some run for buckets to the hallowed choir;
Some cut the pipes, and some the engines play,
   And some more bold mount ladders to the fire.

In vain; for from the east a Belgian wind
   His hostile breath through the dry rafters sent;
The flames impelled soon left their foes behind,
   And forward with a wanton fury went.

A quay of fire ran all along the shore,
   And lightened all the river with a blaze;
The wakened tides began again to roar,
   And wondering fish in shining waters gaze.

Old Father Thames raised up his reverend head,
   But feared the fate of Simois would return;
Deep in his ooze he sought his sedgy bed,
   And shrank his waters back into his urn.

The fire, meantime, walks in a broader gross;
   To either hand his wings he opens wide;
He wades the streets, and straight he reaches cross
   And plays his longing flames on the other side.

At first they warm, then scorch, and then they take;
   Now with long necks from side to side they feed;
At length, grown strong, their mother-fire forsake,
   And a new colony of flames succeed.

To every nobler portion of the town
   The curling billows roll their restless tide;
In parties now they straggle up and down,
   As armies, unopposed, for prey divide.

One mighty squadron, with a side-wind sped,
   Through narrow lanes his cumbered fire does haste,
By powerful charms of gold and silver led
   The Lombard bankers and the Change to waste.

Another backward to the Tower would go,
   And slowly eats his way against the wind;
But the main body of the marching foe
   Against the imperial palace is designed.

Now day appears, and with the day the king,
   Whose early care had robbed him of his rest:
Far off the cracks of falling houses ring,
   And shrieks of subjects pierce his tender breast.

Near as he draws, thick harbingers of smoke
    With gloomy pillars cover all the place;
Whose little intervals of night are broke
    By sparks that drive against his sacred face.

More than his guards his sorrows made him known,
    And pious tears, which down his cheeks did shower:
The wretched in his grief forgot their own;
    (So much the pity of a king has power.)

He wept the flames of what he loved so well,
    And what so well had merited his love;
For never prince in grace did more excel,
    Or royal city more in duty strove.

Nor with an idle care did he behold:
    (Subjects may grieve, but monarchs must redress;)
He cheers the fearful, and commends the bold,
    And makes despairers hope for good success.

Himself directs what first is to be done,
    And orders all the succours which they bring.
The helpful and the good about him run,
    And form an army worthy such a king.

He sees the dire contagion spread so fast
    That, where it seizes, all relief is vain;
And therefore must unwillingly lay waste
    That country which would, else, the foe maintain.

The powder blows up all before the fire:
    The amazed flames stand gathered on a heap,
And from the precipice's brink retire,
    Afraid to venture on so large a leap.

Thus fighting fires a while themselves consume,
    But straight, like Turks, forced on to win or die,
They first lay tender bridges of their fume,
    And o'er the breach in unctuous vapours fly.

Part stays for passage till a gust of wind
   Ships o'er their forces in a shining sheet;
Part, creeping under ground, their journey blind,
   And, climbing from below, their fellows meet.

Thus, to some desert plain, or old wood-side,
   Dire night-hags come from far to dance their round;
And o'er broad rivers on their fiends they ride,
   Or sweep in clouds above the blasted ground.

No help avails: for, Hydra-like, the fire
   Lifts up his hundred heads to aim his way;
And scarce the wealthy can one half retire
   Before he rushes in to share the prey.

The rich grow suppliant, and the poor grow proud;
   Those offer mighty gain and these ask more:
So void of pity is the ignoble crowd,
   When others' ruin may increase their store.

As those who live by shores with joy behold
   Some wealthy vessel split or stranded nigh;
And from the rocks leap down for shipwrecked gold,
   And seek the tempest which the others fly:

So these but wait the owners' last despair,
   And what's permitted to the flames invade:
E'en from their jaws they hungry morsels tear,
   And on their backs the spoils of Vulcan lade.

The days were all in this lost labour spent:
   And when the weary king gave place to night,
His beams he to his royal brother lent,
   And so shone still in his reflective light.

Night came, but without darkness or repose,
   A dismal picture of the general doom;
Where souls distracted when the trumpet blows,
   And half unready with their bodies come.

Those who have homes, when home they do repair,
  To a last lodging call their wandering friends.
Their short uneasy sleeps are broke with care,
  To look how near their own destruction tends.

Those who have none sit round where once it was,
  And with full eyes each wonted room require;
Haunting the yet warm ashes of the place,
  As murdered men walk where they did expire.

Some stir up coals and watch the vestal fire,
  Others in vain from sight of ruin run;
And, while through burning labyrinths they retire,
  With loathing eyes repeat what they would shun.

The most in fields like herded beasts lie down,
  To dews obnoxious on the grassy floor:
And while their babes in sleep their sorrows drown,
  Sad parents watch the remnants of their store.

While, by the motion of the flames, they guess
  What streets are burning now, and what are near;
An infant, waking, to the paps would press
  And meets, instead of milk, a falling tear.

No thought can ease them but their sovereign's care,
  Whose praise the afflicted as their comfort sing:
E'en those whom want might drive to just despair,
  Think life a blessing under such a king.

Meantime he sadly suffers in their grief,
  Outweeps a hermit, and outprays a saint:
All the long night he studies their relief,
  How they may be supplied, and he may want.

KING'S PRAYER

"O God," said he, "thou patron of my days,
  Guide of my youth in exile and distress!

Who me unfriended broughtst by wondrous ways,
  The kingdom of my fathers to possess:

"Be thou my judge, with what unwearied care
  I since have laboured for my people's good;
To bind the bruises of a civil war,
  And stop the issues of their wasting blood.

"Thou, who hast taught me to forgive the ill,
  And recompense, as friends, the good misled;
If mercy be a precept of thy will,
  Return that mercy on thy servant's head.

"Or, if my heedless youth has stepped astray,
  Too soon forgetful of thy gracious hand;
On me alone thy just displeasure lay,
  But take thy judgments from this mourning land.

"We all have sinned, and thou hast laid us low,
  As humble earth from whence at first we came:
Like flying shades before the clouds we show,
  And shrink like parchment in consuming flame.

"O let it be enough what thou hast done,
  When spotted deaths ran armed through every street,
With poisoned darts, which not the good could shun,
  The speedy could outfly, or valiant meet.

"The living few, and frequent funerals then,
  Proclaimed thy wrath on this forsaken place;
And now those few, who are returned again,
  Thy searching judgments to their dwellings trace.

"O pass not, lord, an absolute decree,
  Or bind thy sentence unconditional;
But in thy sentence our remorse foresee,
  And, in that foresight, this thy doom recall.

"Thy threatenings, lord, as thine thou mayst revoke;
  But if immutable and fixed they stand,

Continue still thyself to give the stroke,
    And let not foreign foes oppress thy land."

The eternal heard, and from the heavenly choir
    Chose out the cherub with the flaming sword;
And bade him swiftly drive the approaching fire
    From where our naval magazines were stored.

The blessed minister his wings displayed
    And like a shooting star he cleft the night;
He charged the flames, and those that disobeyed
    He lashed to duty with his sword of light.

The fugitive flames, chastised, went forth to prey
    On pious structures, by our fathers reared;
By which to heaven they did affect the way,
    Ere faith in churchmen without works was heard.

The wanting orphans saw, with watery eyes,
    Their founders' charity in dust laid low;
And sent to God their ever-answered cries,
    (For he protects the poor who made them so.)

Nor could thy fabric, Paul's, defend thee long,
    Though thou wert sacred to thy maker's praise;
Though made immortal by a poet's song,
    And poet's songs the Theban walls could raise.

The daring flames peeped in and saw from far
    The awful beauties of the sacred choir;
But, since it was profaned by civil war,
    Heaven thought it fit to have it purged by fire.

Now down the narrow streets it swiftly came,
    And, widely opening, did on both sides prey.
This benefit we sadly owe the flame,
    If only ruin must enlarge our way.

And now four days the sun had seen our woes,
    Four nights the moon beheld the incessant fire:

It seemed as if the stars more sickly rose,
    And farther from the feverish north retire.

In the empyrean heaven (the blessed abode)
    The thrones and the dominions prostrate lie,
Not daring to behold their angry God;
    And a hushed silence damps the tuneful sky.

At length, the almighty cast a pitying eye
    And mercy softly touched his melting breast:
He saw the town's one half in rubbish lie,
    And eager flames give on to storm the rest.

A hollow crystal pyramid he takes,
    In firmamental waters dipped above;
Of it a broad extinguisher he makes,
    And hoods the flames that to their quarry strove.

The vanquished fires withdraw from every place,
    Or, full with feeding, sink into a sleep:
Each household genius shows again his face,
    And from the hearths the little Lares creep.

Our king this more than natural change beholds,
    With sober joy his heart and eyes abound;
To the all-good his lifted hands he folds,
    And thanks him low on his redeemèd ground.

As, when sharp frosts had long constrained the earth,
    A kindly thaw unlocks it with mild rain,
And first the tender blade peeps up to birth,
    And straight the green fields laugh with promised grain:

By such degrees the spreading gladness grew
    In every heart, which fear had froze before;
The standing streets with so much joy they view,
    That with less grief the perished they deplore.

The father of the people opened wide
    His stores, and all the poor with plenty fed:

Thus God's anointed God's own place supplied,
   And filled the empty with his daily bread.

This royal bounty brought its own reward,
   And in their minds so deep did print the sense,
That, if their ruins sadly they regard,
   'Tis but with fear the sight might drive him thence.

CITY'S REQUEST TO THE KING NOT TO LEAVE THEM

But so may he live long, that town to sway,
   Which by his auspice they will nobler make,
As he will hatch their ashes by his stay,
   And not their humble ruins now forsake.

They have not lost their loyalty by fire,
   Nor is their courage or their wealth so low,
That from his wars they poorly would retire,
   Or beg the pity of a vanquished foe.

Not with more constancy the Jews of old,
   By Cyrus from rewarded exile sent,
Their royal city did in dust behold,
   Or with more vigour to rebuild it went.

The utmost malice of their stars is past,
   And two dire comets which have scourged the town,
In their own plague and fire have breathed their last,
   Or, dimly, in their sinking sockets frown.

Now frequent trines the happier lights among,
   And high-raised Jove from his dark prison freed,
(Those weights took off that on his planet hung,)
   Will gloriously the new-laid work succeed.

Methinks already, from this chemic flame,
   I see a city of more precious mould;

Rich as the town which gives the Indies name,
　　With silver paved, and all divine with gold.

Already, labouring with a mighty fate,
　　She shakes the rubbish from her mounting brow,
And seems to have renewed her charter's date,
　　Which heaven will to the death of time allow.

More great than human, now, and more august,
　　New deified she from her fires does rise:
Her widening streets on new foundations trust,
　　And, opening, into larger parts she flies.

Before she like some shepherdess did show,
　　Who sat to bathe her by a river's side;
Not answering to her fame, but rude and low,
　　Nor taught the beauteous arts of modern pride.

Now like a maiden queen she will behold
　　From her high turrets hourly suitors come;
The East with incense, and the West with gold,
　　Will stand like suppliants to receive her doom.

The silver Thames, her own domestic flood,
　　Shall bear her vessels like a sweeping train,
And often wind (as of his mistress proud)
　　With longing eyes to meet her face again.

The wealthy Tagus, and the wealthier Rhine,
　　The glory of their towns no more shall boast;
And Seine, that would with Belgian rivers join,
　　Shall find her lustre stained and traffic lost.

The venturous merchant, who designed more far,
　　And touches on our hospitable shore,
Charmed with the splendour of this northern star,
　　Shall here unlade him and depart no more.

Our powerful navy shall no longer meet,
   The wealth of France or Holland to invade:
The beauty of this town, without a fleet,
   From all the world shall vindicate her trade.

And while this famed emporium we prepare
   The British ocean shall such triumphs boast,
That those who now disdain our trade to share
   Shall rob like pirates on our wealthy coast.

Already we have conquered half the war,
   And the less dangerous part is left behind;
Our trouble now is but to make them dare,
   And not so great to vanquish as to find.

Thus to the Eastern wealth through storms we go;
   But now, the Cape once doubled, fear no more:
A constant trade-wind will securely blow,
   And gently lay us on the spicy shore.

from *MacFlecknoe*

All human things are subject to decay,
And when fate summons, monarchs must obey.
This Flecknoe found, who, like Augustus, young
Was called to empire, and had governed long;
In prose and verse, was owned, without dispute,
Through all the realms of Nonsense, absolute.
This aged prince, now flourishing in peace,
And blest with issue of a large increase,
Worn out with business, did at length debate
To settle the succession of the state;
And, pondering which of all his sons was fit
To reign, and wage immortal war with wit,
Cried: "'Tis resolved; for nature pleads, that he
Should only rule, who most resembles me.
Shadwell alone my perfect image bears,
Mature in dullness from his tender years:
Shadwell alone, of all my sons, is he
Who stands confirmed in full stupidity.
The rest to some faint meaning make pretence,
But Shadwell never deviates into sense.
Some beams of wit on other souls may fall,
Strike through, and make a lucid interval;
But Shadwell's genuine night admits no ray;
His rising fogs prevail upon the day.
Besides, his goodly fabric fills the eye,
And seems designed for thoughtless majesty;
Thoughtless as monarch oaks that shade the plain,
And, spread in solemn state, supinely reign.
Heywood and Shirley were but types of thee,
Thou last great prophet of tautology.
Even I, a dunce of more renown than they,
Was sent before but to prepare thy way:
And, coarsely clad in Norwich drugget, came
To teach the nations in thy greater name.

My warbling lute, the lute I whilom strung,
When to King John of Portugal I sung,
Was but the prelude to that glorious day,
When thou on silver Thames didst cut thy way,
With well-timed oars before the royal barge,
Swelled with the pride of thy celestial charge;
And big with hymn, commander of a host,
The like was ne'er in Epsom blankets tossed.
Methinks I see the new Arion sail,
The lute still trembling underneath thy nail.
At thy well-sharpened thumb, from shore to shore,
The treble squeaks for fear, the basses roar;
Echoes from Pissing Alley 'Shadwell' call,
And 'Shadwell' they resound from Ashton Hall.
About thy boat the little fishes throng,
As at the morning toast that floats along.
Sometimes, as prince of thy harmonious band,
Thou wield'st thy papers in thy threshing hand.
St. André's feet ne'er kept more equal time,
Not e'en the feet of thy own *Psyche's* rhyme;
Though they in number as in sense excel:
So just, so like tautology, they fell,
That, pale with envy, Singleton forswore
The lute and sword, which he in triumph bore,
And vowed he ne'er would act Villerius more."
Here stopped the good old sire, and wept for joy
In silent raptures of the hopeful boy.
All arguments, but most his plays, persuade,
That for anointed dullness he was made.

   Close to the walls which fair Augusta bind,
(The fair Augusta much to fears inclined,)
An ancient fabric raised to inform the sight,
There stood of yore, and Barbican it hight:
A watchtower once; but now, so fate ordains,
Of all the pile an empty name remains.
From its old ruins brothel-houses rise,

Scenes of lewd loves, and of polluted joys,
Where their vast courts the mother-strumpets keep,
And undisturbed by watch in silence sleep.
Near these a nursery erects its head,
Where queens are formed, and future heroes bred;
Where unfledged actors learn to laugh and cry,
Where infant punks their tender voices try,
And little Maximins the gods defy.
Great Fletcher never treads in buskins here,
Nor greater Jonson dares in socks appear;
But gentle Simkin just reception finds
Amidst this monument of vanished minds:
Pure clenches the suburban muse affords,
And Panton waging harmless war with words.
Here Flecknoe, as a place to fame well known,
Ambitiously designed his Shadwell's throne;
For ancient Dekker prophesied long since,
That in this pile should reign a mighty prince,
Born for a scourge of wit, and flail of sense;
To whom true dullness should some *Psyches* owe,
But worlds of *Misers* from his pen should flow;
Humourists and *Hypocrites* it should produce,
Whole Raymond families, and tribes of Bruce.
     Now Empress Fame had published the renown
Of Shadwell's coronation through the town.
Roused by report of Fame, the nations meet,
From near Bunhill, and distant Watling Street.
No Persian carpets spread the imperial way,
But scattered limbs of mangled poets lay;
From dusty shops neglected authors come,
Martyrs of pies, and relics of the bum.
Much Heywood, Shirley, Ogilby there lay,
But loads of Shadwell almost choked the way.
Bilked stationers for yeomen stood prepared,
And Herringman was captain of the guard.
The hoary prince in majesty appeared,

High on a throne of his own labours reared.
At his right hand our young Ascanius sate,
Rome's other hope, and pillar of the State.
His brows thick fogs, instead of glories, grace,
And lambent dullness played around his face.
As Hannibal did to the altars come,
Sworn by his sire a mortal foe to Rome;
So Shadwell swore, nor should his vow be vain,
That he till death true dullness would maintain;
And in his father's right and realm's defence,
Ne'er to have peace with wit, nor truce with sense.
The king himself the sacred unction made,
As king by office, and as priest by trade.
In his sinister hand, instead of ball,
He placed a mighty mug of potent ale;
Love's Kingdom to his right he did convey,
At once his sceptre, and his rule of sway;
Whose righteous lore the prince had practised young,
And from whose loins recorded *Psyche* sprung.
His temples, last, with poppies were o'erspread,
That nodding seemed to consecrate his head.
Just at that point of time, if fame not lie,
On his left hand twelve reverend owls did fly.
So Romulus, 'tis sung, by Tiber's brook,
Presage of sway from twice six vultures took.
The admiring throng loud acclamations make,
And omens of his future empire take.

Anon. (pub. 1680)

In the Fields of Lincoln's Inn

In the Fields of Lincoln's Inn
Underneath a tattered blanket,
On a flock-bed, God be thanked,
Feats of active love were seen.

Phyllis, who you know loves swiving
As the Gods love pious prayers,
Lay most pensively contriving
How to fuck with pricks by pairs.

Coridon's aspiring tarse
Which to cunt had ne'er submitted,
Wet with amorous kiss she fitted
To her less-frequented arse.

Strephon's was a handful longer,
Stiffly propped with eager lust;
None for champion was more stronger;
This into her cunt he thrust.

Now for Civil Wars prepare,
Raised by fierce intestine bustle,
When these heroes meeting jostle,
In the bowels of the fair.

They tilt, and thrust with horrid pudder,
Blood and slaughter is decreed;
Hurling souls at one another,
Wrapped in flakey clots of seed.

Nature had 'twixt cunt and arse
Wisely placed firm separation;

God knows else what desolation
Had ensured from warring tarse.

Though Fate a dismal end did threaten,
It proved no worse than was desired:
The nymph was sorely bollock-beaten,
Both the shepherds soundly tired.

John Wilmot, Earl of Rochester (1647–1680)

from *A Letter from Artemisa in the Town to Chloe in the Country*

Where I was visiting the other night
Comes a fine lady with her humble knight,
Who had prevailed on her, through her own skill,
At his request, though much against his will,
To come to London.
As the coach stopped, we heard her voice, more loud
Than a great-bellied woman's in a crowd,
Telling the knight that her affairs require
He for some hours obsequiously retire.
I think she was ashamed to have him seen—
Hard fate of husbands! The gallànt had been,
Though a diseased, ill-favoured fool, brought in,
"Dispatch," says she, "that business you pretend,
Your beastly visit to your drunken friend;
A bottle ever makes you look so fine!
Methinks I long to smell you stink of wine.
Your country drinking breath's enough to kill—
Sour ale corrected with a lemon peel.
Prithee, farewell—we'll meet again anon."
The necessary thing bows, and is gone.
She flies upstairs, and all the haste does show
That fifty antic postures will allow,
And then bursts out: "Dear Madam, am not I
The altered'st creature breathing? Let me die;
I find myself ridiculously grown
Embarrasseé with being out of town,
Rude and untaught, like any Indian Queen,
My country nakedness is strangely seen.
How is love governed, love, that rules the state—
And pray, who are the men most worn of late?

When I was married, fools were *à la mode;*
The men of wit were then held *incommode,*
Slow of belief, and fickle in desire,
Who, ere they'll be persuaded, must inquire,
As if they came to spy, not to admire.
With searching wisdom fatal to their ease,
They still find out why what may, should not please;
Nay, take themselves for injured, when we dare
Make 'em think better of us than we are:
And if we hide our frailties from their sights,
Call us deceitful jilts and hypocrites.
They little guess, who at our arts are grieved,
The perfect joy of being well deceived;
Inquisitive as jealous cuckolds grow,
Rather than not be knowing, they will know
What, being known, creates their certain woe.
Women should these of all mankind avoid;
For wonder by clear knowledge is destroyed.
Woman, who is an arrant bird of night,
Bold in the dusk before a fool's dull sight,
Should fly when reason brings the glaring light.
But the kind, easy fool, apt to admire
Himself, trusts us; his follies all conspire
To flatter his, and favour our desire.
Vain of his proper merit, he with ease
Believes we love him best, who best can please.
On him our gross, dull, common flatteries pass,
Ever most joyful when most made an ass:
Heavy to apprehend, though all mankind
Perceive us false, the fop concerned is blind,
Who doting on himself,
Thinks everyone that sees him of his mind.
These are true women's men." Here forced to cease
Through want of breath, not will to hold her peace,
She to the window runs, where she had spied
Her much esteemed dear friend, the monkey, tied.

With forty smiles, as many antic bows,
As if't had been the lady of the house,
The dirty, chattering monster she embraced,
And made it this fine tender speech at last:
"Kiss me, thou curious miniature of man;
How odd thou art! how pretty! how japan!
Oh, I could live and die with thee!"–then on
For half an hour in compliment she run.
   I took this time to think what Nature meant
When this mixed thing into the world she sent,
So very wise, yet so impertinent:
One who knew everything; who God thought fit
Should be an ass through choice, not want of wit:
Whose foppery, without the help of sense,
Could ne'er have rose to such an excellence.
Nature's as lame in making a true fop
As a philosopher; the very top
And dignity of folly we attain
By studious search and labour of the brain,
By observation, counsel, and deep thought:
God never made a coxcomb worth a groat.
We owe that name to industry, and arts:
An eminent fool must be a fool of parts.
And such a one was she, who had turned o'er
As many books as men; loved much, read more,
Had a discerning wit; to her was known
Everyone's fault and merit but her own.
All the good qualities that ever blessed
A woman so distinguished from the rest,
Except discretion only, she possessed.
But now, "*Mon cher,* dear pug," she cries, "*adieu,*"
And the discòurse broke off does thus renew:
"You smile to see me, whom the world perchance
Mistakes to have some wit, so far advance
The interest of fools, that I approve
Their merit more than men's of wit in love.

But in our sex too many proofs there are
Of such whom wits undo, and fools repair.
This in my time was so observed a rule,
Hardly a wench in town but had her fool;
The meanest common slut, who long was grown
The jest and scorn of every pit buffoon,
Had yet left charms enough to have subdued
Some fop or other, fond to be thought lewd.
Foster could make an Irish lord a Nokes,
And Betty Morris had her city cokes.
A woman's ne'er so ruined but she can
Be still revenged on her undoer, man.
How lost so e'er, she'll find some lover more
A lewd, abandoned fool, than she's a whore.
   "That wretched thing Corinna, who had run
Through all the several ways of being undone,
Cozened at first by love, and living then
By turning the too dear-bought trick on men:
Gay were the hours, and winged with joys they flew,
When first the town her early beauties knew;
Courted, admired, and loved, with presents fed,
Youth in her looks, and pleasure in her bed,
Till fate, or her ill angel, thought it fit
To make her dote upon a man of wit,
Who found 'twas dull to love above a day,
Made his ill-natured jest, and went away.
Now scorned by all, forsaken, and oppressed,
She's a *memento mori* to the rest;
Diseased, decayed, to take up half a crown
Must mortgage her long scarf, and manteau gown.
Poor creature! Who, unheard of as a fly,
In some dark hole must all the winter lie,
And want and dirt endure a whole half year,
That for one month she tawdry may appear.
In Easter Term she gets her a new gown,
When my young master's worship comes to town,

From pedagogue and mother just set free,
The heir and hopes of a great family,
Which with strong ale and beef the country rules,
And ever since the Conquest have been fools.
And now with careful prospect to maintain
This character, lest crossing of the strain
Should mend the booby breed, his friends provide
A cousin of his own to be his bride;
And thus set out
With an estate, no wit, and a young wife
(The solid comforts of a coxcomb's life),
Dunghill and pease forsook, he comes to town,
Turns spark, learns to be lewd, and is undone.
Nothing suits worse with vice than want of sense:
Fools are still wicked at their own expense.
This o'ergrown schoolboy lost Corinna wins,
And at first dash to make an ass begins:
Pretends to like a man who has not known
The vanities nor vices of the town.
Fresh in his youth, and faithful in his love,
Eager of joys which he does seldom prove,
Healthful and strong, he does no pains endure,
But what the fair one he adores can cure;
Grateful for favours, does the sex esteem,
And libels none for being kind to him;
Then of the lewdness of the times complains,
Rails at the wits and atheists, and maintains
'Tis better than good sense, than power or wealth,
To have a love untainted, youth, and health.
The unbred puppy, who had never seen
A creature look so gay, or talk so fine,
Believes, then falls in love, and then in debt,
Mortgages all, e'en to the ancient seat,
To buy this mistress a new house for life;
To give her plate and jewels robs his wife,
And when to th' height of fondness he is grown,

'Tis time to poison him, and all's her own.
Thus meeting in her common arms his fate,
He leaves her bastard heir to his estate;
And as the race of such an owl deserves,
His own dull lawful progeny he starves.
Nature, who never made a thing in vain,
But does each insect to some end ordain,
Wisely provides kind keeping fools, no doubt,
To patch up vices men of wit wear out."
Thus she ran on two hours, some grains of sense
Still mixed with volleys of impertinence.

    But now 'tis time I should some pity show
To Chloe, since I cannot choose but know
Readers must reap the dullness writers sow.
By the next post such stories I will tell
As joined with these shall to a volume swell,
As true as heaven, more infamous than hell;
But you are tired, and so am I.—Farewell.

Song ("Quoth the Duchess of Cleveland to Counselor Knight")

Quoth the Duchess of Cleveland to Counselor Knight,
I'd fain have a prick, but how to come by't?
I desire you'll be secret, and give your advice,
Though cunt be not coy, reputation is nice.

To some cellar in Sodom your Grace must retire,
There porters with black pots sit round a coal fire;
There open your case, and your Grace cannot fail
Of a dozen of pricks, for a dozen of ale.

Is't so? quoth the Duchess. Aye by God, quoth the whore.
Then give me the key that unlocks the back door;
For I had rather be fucked by porters and car-men,
Than thus be abused by Churchill and Jermyn.

A Ramble in St. James's Park

Much wine had passed, with grave discourse
Of who fucks who, and who does worse,
Such as you usually do hear
From those that diet at the Bear,
When I, who still take care to see
Drunkenness relieved by lechery,
Went out into St. James's Park
To cool my head, and fire my heart.
But though St. James has the honour on't,
'Tis consecrate to prick and cunt.
There, by a most incestuous birth,
Strange woods spring from the teeming earth:
For they relate how heretofore,
When ancient Pict began to whore,
Deluded of his assignation
(Jilting, it seems, was then in fashion),
Poor pensive lover, in this place
Would frig upon his mother's face;
Whence rows of mandrakes tall did rise,
Whose lewd tops fucked the very skies.
Each imitative branch does twine
In some loved fold of Aretine;
And nightly now beneath their shade
Are buggeries, rapes, and incests made.
Unto this all-sin-sheltering grove
Whores of the bulk and the alcove,
Great ladies, chamber-maids, and drudges,
The rag-picker and heiress trudges;
Car-men, divines, great lords, and tailors,
'Prentices, pimps, poets, and jailers,
Footmen, fine fops, do here arrive,
And here promiscuously they swive.
    Along these hallowed walks it was
That I beheld Corinna pass.

Whoever had been by to see
The proud disdain she cast on me
Through charming eyes, he would have swore
She dropped from heaven that very hour,
Forsaking the divine abode
In scorn of some despairing god.
But mark what creatures women are,
So infinitely vile and fair:
Three knights o'th' elbow and the slur
With wriggling tails made up to her.

    The first was of your Whitehall blades,
Near kin to the Mother of the Maids,
Graced by whose favour he was able
To bring a friend to the Waiters' table,
Where he had heard Sir Edward Sutton
Say how the King loved Banstead mutton;
Since when he'd ne'er be brought to eat,
By 's goodwill, any other meat.
In this, as well as all the rest,
He ventures to do like the best;
But wanting common sense, th' ingredient
In choosing well not least expedient,
Converts abortive imitation
To universal affectation.
So he not only eats and talks,
But feels and smells, sits down and walks,
Nay, looks, and lives, and loves by rote,
In an old tawdry birthday coat.

    The second was a Gray's Inn wit,
A great inhabiter of the pit,
Where critic-like he sits and squints,
Steals pocket handkerchiefs and hints
From 's neighbour and the comedy,
To court and pay his landlady.

    The third, a lady's eldest son
Within few years of twenty-one,

Who hopes from his propitious fate,
Against he comes to his estate,
By these two worthies to be made
A most accomplished, tearing blade.
    One in a strain 'twixt tone and nonsense
Cries, "Madam, I have loved you long since.
Permit me your fair hand to kiss."
When at her mouth her cunt says, "Yes."
In short, without much more ado,
Joyful and pleased, away she flew,
And with these three confounded asses,
From Park to hackney-coach she passes.
    So a proud bitch does lead about
Of humble curs the amorous rout,
Who most obsequiously do hunt
The savoury scent of salt-swollen cunt.
Some power more patient now relate
The sense of this surprising fate.
Gods! That a thing admired by me
Should fall to so much infamy!
Had she picked out to rub her arse on
Some stiff-pricked clown or well-hung parson,
Each job of whose spermatic sluice
Had filled her cunt with wholesome juice,
I the proceeding should have praised
In hope she had quenched a fire I raised.
Such natural freedoms are but just,
There's something generous in mere lust.
But to turn damned abandoned jade,
When neither head nor tail persuade,
To be a whore in understanding,
A passive pot for fools to spend in!
The devil played booty sure with thee
To bring a blot of infamy.
But why am I, of all mankind,
To so severe a fate designed?

Ungrateful! Why this treachery
To humble, fond, believing me?
Who gave you privileges above
The nice allowances of love?
Did ever I refuse to bear
The meanest part your lust could spare?
When your lewd cunt came spewing home,
Drenched with the seed of half the town,
My dram of sperm was supped up after
For the digestive surfeit-water.
Full-gorgèd at another time
With a vast meal of nasty slime,
Which your devouring cunt had drawn
From porters' backs and footmen's brawn,
I was content to serve you up
My ballock-full for your grace-cup.
Nor ever thought it an abuse
While you had pleasure for excuse.
You that could make my heart away
For noise and colour, and betray
The secrets of my tender hours
To such knight-errant paramours;
When leaning on your faithless breast,
Wrapped in security and rest,
Soft kindness all my powers did move,
And reason lay dissolved in love.
  May stinking vapour choke your womb,
Such as the men you dote upon.
May your depravèd appetite,
That could in whiffling fools delight,
Beget such frenzies in your mind
You may go mad for the north wind;
And fixing all your hopes upon't,
To have him bluster in your cunt,
Turn up your longing arse to the air,
And perish in a wild despair.

But cowards shall forget to rant,
Schoolboys to frig, old whores to paint;
The Jesuits' fraternity
Shall leave the use of buggery;
Crab-louse, inspired with grace divine,
From earthly cod to heaven shall climb;
Physicians shall believe in Jesus,
And disobedience cease to please us,
Ere I desist with all my power
To plague this woman and undo her.
But my revenge will best be timed
When she is married, that is: limed.
In that most lamentable state
I'll make her feel my scorn and hate,
Pelt her with scandals, truth or lies,
And her poor cur with jealousies,
Till I have torn him from her breech,
While she whines like a dog-drawn bitch,
Loathed and despised, kicked out of Town,
Into some dirty hole alone,
To chew the cud of misery,
And know she owes it all to me.
  And may no woman better thrive
  That dares profane the cunt I swive.

John Oldham (1653–1683)

from *A Satire in Imitation of the Third of Juvenal*

*The poet brings in a friend of his, giving him an account why he removes from
London to live in the country*

Though much concerned to leave my dear old friend,
I must however his design commend
Of fixing in the country: for were I
As free to choose my residence as he,
The Peak, the Fens, the Hundreds, or Land's End,
I would prefer to Fleet Street, or the Strand.
What place so desert, and so wild is there,
Whose inconveniencies one would not bear,
Rather than the alarms of midnight fire,
The falls of houses, knavery of cits,
The plots of factions, and the noise of wits,
And thousand other plagues, which up and down
Each day and hour infest the cursèd town?
    As fate would have it, on the appointed day
Of parting hence, I met him on the way,
Hard by Mile End, the place so famed of late
In prose and verse, for the great faction's treat;
Here we stood still, and after compliments
Of course, and wishing his good journey hence,
I asked what sudden causes made him fly
The once loved town, and his dear company:
When, on the hated prospect looking back,
Thus with just rage the good old Timon spake:
    "Since virtue here in no repute is had,
Since worth is scorned, learning and sense unpaid,
And knavery the only thriving trade;
Finding my slender fortune every day
Dwindle, and waste insensibly away,
I, like a losing gamester, thus retreat,

To manage wiselier my last stake of fate;
While I have strength, and want no staff to prop
My tottering limbs, ere age has made me stoop
Beneath its weight, ere all my thread be spun,
And life has yet in store some sands to run,
'Tis my resolve to quit the nauseous town.
    "Let thriving Morecraft choose his dwelling there,
Rich with the spoils of some young spendthrift heir:
Let the plot-mongers stay behind, whose art
Can truth to sham, and sham to truth convert:
Whoever has an house to build or set,
His wife, his conscience, or his oath to let:
Whoever has, or hopes for offices,
A navy, guard, or custom-house's place:
Let sharping courtiers stay, who there are great
By putting the false dice on king and state:
Where they, who once were grooms and footboys known,
Are now to fair estates and honours grown;
Nor need we envy them, or wonder much
At their fantastic greatness, since they're such
Whom Fortune oft in her capricious freaks
Is pleased to raise from kennels and the jakes
To wealth and dignity above the rest,
When she is frolic, and disposed to jest.
    "I live in London? What should I do there?
I cannot lie nor flatter nor forswear:
I can't commend a book, or piece of wit
(Though a lord were the author) dully writ:
I'm no Sir Sidrophel to read the stars,
And cast nativities for longing heirs,
When fathers shall drop off: no Gadbury
To tell the minute when the King shall die,
And you know what—come in: nor can I steer,
And tack about my conscience, whensoe'er
To a new point I see religion veer.
Let others pimp to courtier's lechery,

I'll draw no city cuckold's curse on me:
Nor would I do it, though to be made great,
And raised to the chief Minister of State.
Therefore I think it fit to rid the town
Of one that is an useless member grown.
    "Besides, who has pretence to favour now,
But he who hidden villainy does know,
Whose breast does, with some burning secret glow?
By none thou shalt preferred or valued be
That trusts thee with an honest secrecy:
He only may to great men's friendship reach,
Who great men, when he pleases, can impeach.
Let others thus aspire to dignity;
For me, I'd not their envied grandeur buy
For all th' Exchange is worth, that Paul's will cost,
Or was of late in the Scotch voyage lost.
What would it boot, if I, to gain my end,
Forego my quiet, and my ease of mind,
Still feared, at last betrayed, by my great friend?
. . .

    "'Tis now a common thing, and usual here,
To see the son of some rich usurer
Take place of nobles, keep his first-rate whore,
And for a vaulting bout or two give more
Than a guard-captain's pay: meanwhile the breed
Of peers, reduced to poverty and need,
Are fain to trudge to the Bankside, and there
Take up with porters' leavings, suburb ware;
There spend that blood, which their great ancestor
So nobly shed at Cressy heretofore,
At brothel-fights in some foul common shore.
    "Produce an evidence, though just he be
As righteous Job, or Abraham, or he
Whom Heaven, when whole nature shipwrecked was,
Thought worth the saving, of all human race;
Or t' other, who the flaming deluge 'scaped,

When Sodom's lechers angels would have raped;
How rich he is, must the first question be,
Next for his manners and integrity:
They'll ask what equipage he keeps, and what
He's reckoned worth in money and estate;
For shrieve how oft he has been known to fine,
And with how many dishes he does dine.
For look what cash a person has in store,
Just so much credit has he, and no more:
Should I upon a thousand Bibles swear,
And call each saint throughout the calendar
To vouch my oath, it won't be taken here:
The poor slight Heaven and thunderbolts, they think,
And Heaven itself does at such trifles wink.
   "Besides, what store of gibing scoffs are thrown
On one that's poor, and meanly clad in town;
If his apparel seem but overworn,
His stockings out at heel, or breeches torn:
One takes occasion his ripped shoe to flout,
And swears 't has been at prison-grates hung out;
Another shrewdly jeers his coarse cravat,
Because himself wears point; a third his hat,
And most unmercifully shows his wit
If it be old, or does not cock aright.
Nothing in poverty so ill is borne,
As its exposing men to grinning scorn,
To be by tawdry coxcombs pissed upon,
And made the jesting stock of each buffoon.
'Turn out there, friend!' cries one at church, 'the pew
Is not for such mean scoundrel curs as you:
'Tis for your betters kept': belike some sot
That knew no father, was on bulks begot,
But now is raised to an estate and pride,
By having the kind proverb on his side:
Let Gripe and Cheatwell take their places there,
And Dash, the scrivener's gaudy sparkish heir,

That wears three ruined orphans on his back.
Meanwhile, you in the alley stand and sneak,
And you therewith must rest contented, since
Almighty wealth does put such difference.
What citizen a son-in-law will take,
Bred ne'er so well, that can't a jointure make?
What man of sense, that's poor, e'er summoned is
Amongst the Common Council to advise?
At vestry-consults when does he appear,
For choosing of some parish officer,
Or making leather buckets for the choir?
    "'Tis hard for any man to rise, that feels
His virtue clogged with poverty at heels;
But harder 'tis by much in London, where
A sorry lodging, coarse and slender fare,
Fire, water, breathing, everything is dear:
Yet such as these an earthen dish disdain,
With which their ancestors, in Edgar's reign,
Were served, and thought it no disgrace to dine,
Though they were rich, had store of leather coin.
Low as their fortune is, yet they despise
A man that walks the streets in homely frieze:
To speak the truth, great part of England now
In their own cloth will scarce vouchsafe to go:
Only, the statute's penalty to save,
Some few perhaps wear woollen in the grave.
Here all go gaily dressed, although it be
Above their means, their rank and quality:
The most in borrowed gallantry are clad,
For which the tradesmen's books are still unpaid:
This fault is common in the meaner sort,
That they must needs affect to bear the port
Of gentlemen, though they want income for't.
    "Sir, to be short, in this expensive town
There's nothing without money to be done:
What will you give to be admitted there,

And brought to speech of some court minister?
What will you give to have the quarter-face,
The squint and nodding go-by of his Grace?
His porter, groom and steward must have fees,
And you may see the tombs and Tower for less:
Hard fate of suitors! who must pay, and pray
To livery-slaves, yet oft go scorned away.

    "Whoe'er at Barnet or St. Albans fears
To have his lodging drop about his ears,
Unless a sudden hurricane befall,
Or such a wind as blew old Noll to hell?
Here we build slight, what scarce outlasts the lease,
Without the help of props and buttresses:
And houses nowadays as much require
To be insured from falling as from fire.
There buildings are substantial, though less neat,
And kept with care both wind- and water-tight:
There you in safe security are blessed,
And nought but conscience to disturb your rest.

    "I am for living where no fires affright,
No bells rung backward break my sleep at night:
I scarce lie down, and draw my curtains here,
But straight I'm roused by the next house on fire:
Pale, and half-dead with fear, myself I raise,
And find my room all over in a blaze;
By this 't has seized on the third stairs, and I
Can now discern no other remedy,
But leaping out at window to get free:
For if the mischief from the cellar came,
Be sure the garret is the last takes flame.

    "The moveables of Pordage were a bed
For him and's wife, a piss-pot by its side,
A looking-glass upon the cupboard's head,
A comb-case, candlestick, and pewter spoon
For want of plate, with desk to write upon:
A box without a lid served to contain

Few authors, which made up his Vatican:
And there his own immortal works were laid,
On which the barbarous mice for hunger preyed.
Pordage had nothing, all the world does know,
And yet should he have lost this nothing too,
No one the wretched bard would have supplied
With lodging, house-room, or a crust of bread.
　　"But if the fire burn down some great man's house,
All straight are interested in the loss:
The court is straight in mourning sure enough,
The Act, Commencement, and the term put off:
Then we mischances of the town lament,
And fasts are kept, like judgments to prevent.
Out comes a brief immediately, with speed
To gather charity as far as Tweed.
Nay, while 'tis burning, some will send him in
Timber and stone to build his house again;
Others choice furniture: here some rare piece
Of Rubens or Van Dyck presented is,
There a rich suit of Mortlake tapestry,
A bed of damask or embroidery:
One gives a fine scrutoire, or cabinet,
Another a huge massy dish of plate,
Or bag of gold: thus he at length gets more
By kind misfortune than he had before:
And all suspect it for a laid design,
As if he did himself the fire begin.
Could you but be advised to leave the town,
And from dear plays, and drinking friends be drawn,
An handsome dwelling might be had in Kent,
Surrey, or Essex, at a cheaper rent
Than what you're forced to give for one half year
To lie, like lumber, in a garret here:
A garden there, and well that needs no rope,
Engine, or pains to crane its waters up:
Water is there through nature's pipes conveyed,

For which no custom or excise is paid.
Had I the smallest spot of ground, which scarce
Would summer half a dozen grasshoppers,
Not larger than my grave, though hence remote
Far as St Michael's Mount, I would go to't,
Dwell there content, and thank the Fates to boot.
   "Here want of rest a-nights more people kills
Than all the College, and the weekly bills:
Where none have privilege to sleep, but those
Whose purses can compound for their repose:
In vain I go to bed, or close my eyes;
Methinks the place the middle region is,
Where I lie down in storms, in thunder rise:
The restless bells such din in steeples keep,
That scarce the dead can in their churchyards sleep;
Huzzas of drunkards, bellmen's midnight rhymes,
The noise of shops, with hawkers' early screams,
Besides the brawls of coachmen, when they meet
And stop in turnings of a narrow street,
Such a loud medley of confusion make,
As drowsy Archer on the bench would wake.
   "If you walk out in business ne'er so great,
Ten thousand stops you must expect to meet:
Thick crowds in every place you must charge through,
And storm your passage wheresoe'er you go;
While tides of followers behind you throng,
And, pressing on your heels, shove you along:
One with a board or rafter hits your head,
Another with his elbow bores your side;
Some tread upon your corns, perhaps in sport,
Meanwhile your legs are cased all o'er with dirt.
Here you the march of a slow funeral wait,
Advancing to the church with solemn state:
There a sedan and lackeys stop your way,
That bears some punk of honour to the play:
Now you some mighty piece of timber meet,

Which tott'ring threatens ruin to the street:
Next a huge Portland stone, for building Paul's,
Itself almost a rock, on carriage rolls;
Which, if it fall, would cause a massacre,
And serve at once to murder and inter.

   "If what I've said can't from the town affright,
Consider other dangers of the night:
When brickbats are from upper storeys thrown,
And emptied chamber-pots come pouring down
From garret windows: you have cause to bless
The gentle stars, if you come off with piss:
So many fates attend, a man had need
Ne'er walk without a surgeon by his side,
And he can hardly now discreet be thought,
That does not make his will ere he go out.

   "If this you 'scape, twenty to one you meet
Some of the drunken scourers of the street,
Flushed with success of warlike deeds performed,
Of constables subdued, and brothels stormed:
These, if a quarrel or a fray be missed,
Are ill at ease a-nights, and want their rest:
For mischief is a lechery to some,
And serves to make them sleep like laudanum.
Yet, heated as they are, with youth and wine,
If they discern a train of flambeaux shine,
If a great man with his gilt coach appear,
And a strong guard of footboys in the rear,
The rascals sneak, and shrink their heads for fear.
Poor me, who use no light to walk about,
Save what the parish or the skies hang out,
They value not: 'tis worth your while to hear
The scuffle, if that be a scuffle where
Another gives the blows, I only bear:
He bids me stand: of force I must give way,
For 'twere a senseless thing to disobey,
And struggle here, where I'd as good oppose

Myself to Preston and his mastiffs loose.
'Who's there?' he cries, and takes you by the throat;
'Dog! are you dumb? Speak quickly, else my foot
Shall march about your buttocks: whence d'ye come?
From what bulk-ridden strumpet reeking home?
Saving your reverend pimpship, where d'ye ply?
How may one have a job of lechery?'
If you say anything, or hold your peace
And silently go off, 'tis all a case:
Still he lays on: nay well, if you 'scape so:
Perhaps he'll clap an action on you too
Of battery, nor need he fear to meet
A jury to his turn, shall do him right,
And bring him in large damage for a shoe
Worn out, besides the pains, in kicking you.
A poor man must expect nought of redress
But patience: his best in such a case
Is to be thankful for the drubs, and beg
That they would mercifully spare one leg
Or arm unbroke, and let him go away
With teeth enough to eat his meat next day.
    "Nor is this all which you have cause to fear:
Oft we encounter midnight padders here,
When the exchanges and the shops are close,
And the rich tradesman in his counting-house
To view the profits of the day withdraws.
Hither in flocks from Shooter's Hill they come,
To seek their prize and booty nearer home:
'Your purse!' they cry; 'tis madness to resist,
Or strive, with a cocked pistol at your breast.
And these each day so strong and numerous grow,
The town can scarce afford them jail-room now.
Happy the times of the old Heptarchy,
Ere London knew so much of villainy:
Then fatal carts through Holborn seldom went,
And Tyburn with few pilgrims was content:

A less, and single prison then would do,
And served the city and the county too.
    "These are the reasons, sir, which drive me hence,
To which I might add more, would time dispense
To hold you longer; but the sun draws low,
The coach is hard at hand, and I must go.
Therefore, dear sir, farewell; and when the town
From better company can spare you down,
To make the country with your presence blessed,
Then visit your old friend amongst the rest:
There I'll find leisure to unlade my mind
Of what remarks I now must leave behind:
The fruits of dear experience, which, with these
Improved, will serve for hints and notices;
And when you write again, may be of use
To furnish satire for your daring muse."

Anon. (1684)

A Winter Wonder; or, the Thames Frozen Over, with Remarks on the Resort There

When Neptune saw a wondrous bridge built o'er
His silver Thames, that reached from shore to shore,
He shook his trident and with awful frown,
Swore 'twas presumption in the haughty town,
Now laughs to see it standing useless o'er,
Whilst ice has made it one continued shore,
Under whose spreading roof he silent glides
And ebbs, and hews, unheard, unseen, his tides.
Greenland, Muscovy, sure their cold have lent,
And all their frigid blasts have hither sent,
Whilst Boreas with his keenest breath has blown,
To make our winter cold as is their own:
That if my ink was not congealed as it,
I'd on the subject show a poet's wit.
The fish lie closely in their watery bed,
And find an icy ceiling o'er their head.
They fear no anglers that do lie in wait,
Nor are deceived by the alluring bait.
The watermen with folded arms do stand,
And grieve to see the water firm as land,
Their boats haled up, their oars laid useless by,
Nor "Oars," nor "Skuller, master," do they cry,
Wishing kind Zephyrus with a warmer gale
Would once more launch their boat and fill their sail;
Or that the sun would with his gentle flames
Again set free their best of friends, the Thames.
The shores no longer sound with "Westward ho,"
Nor need men boats where they can firmly go.
See how the noble river in a trice
Is turned as 'twere one spacious street of ice.

And who'd believe to see revivèd there,
In January, Bartholomew Fair.
Where all the mobile in crowds resort,
As on firm land, to walk, and trade, and sport;
Now booths do stand where boats did lately row,
And on its surface up and down men go,
And Thames becomes a kind of raree-show.
Its upper rooms are let to mortal dweller,
And underneath it is god Neptune's cellar;
Now Vulcan makes his fires on Neptune's bed,
And saucy cooks roast beef upon his head;
As many tuns of ale and brandy flow
Above the ice, as water do below;
And folk do tipple, without fear to sink,
More liquors then the fish beneath do drink.
Here you may see a crowd of people flock,
One's heels fly up, and down he's on his dock;
Another steps, 'tis strange but true, no matter,
And in he flounces up to th' neck in water;
And third more sure his slippery footsteps guides,
And safely o'er the ice away he slides;
Another upon skates does swiftly pass,
Cutting the ice like diamonds upon glass.
Women, beware you come not here at all,
You are most like to slip and catch a fall;
This you may do, though in your gallant's hand,
And if you fall, he has no power to stand;
'Tis ten to one you tumble in a trice,
For you are apt to fall where there's no ice,
Oft on your back, but seldom on your face;
How can you stand then on such a slippery place?
Yet you will venture briskly to a booth,
To take a glass or two with youngster Smooth,
Then back again as briskly to the shore,
As wise and honest as you were before.
Here (like the great) on slippery place you stand,

They can nor fate, nor you your feet, command.
My muse to scribble further has no maw,
But for your good do wish a speedy thaw;
And let it ne'r be said 'twixt you and I,
The winter's cold, but move your charity.
Then let the poor meanwhile your bounty find,
And heaven to you, as you to them prove kind.

Anon. (1684)

from *The Wonders of the Deep*

The various sports behold here in this piece,
Which for six weeks were seen upon the ice;
Upon the Thames the great variety
Of plays and booths is here brought to your eye.
Here coaches, as in Cheapside, run on wheels,
Here man (out-tippling of the fishes) reels:
Instead of waves that used to beat the shore,
Here bulls they bait, till loudly they do roar;
Here boats do slide, where boats were wont to row,
Where ships did sail, the sailors do them tow;
And passengers in boats the river crossed,
For the same price as 'twas before the frost.
There is the printing booth of wondrous fame,
Because that each man there did print his name,
And sure, in former ages, ne'er was found,
A press to print, where men so oft were drowned.
In blanket booths, that sit at no ground rent,
Much coin in beef and brandy there is spent.
The Dutchmen here in nimble cutting skates,
To please the crowd do show their tricks and feats;
The rabble here in chariots run around,
Coffee, and tea, and mum doth here abound.
The tinkers here do march at sound of kettle,
And all men know that they are men of mettle:
Here roasted was an ox before the court,
Which to much folks afforded meat and sport;
At nine-pins here they play, as in Moorfields,
This place the pastime us of football yields:
The common hunt here makes another show,
As he to hunt an hare is wont to go;
But though no woods are here or hares so fleet,
Yet men do often foxes catch and meet;

Into a hole here one by chance doth fall,
At which the watermen began to bawl,
"What, will you rob our cellar of its drink?"
When he, alas! poor man, no harm did think.
Here men well mounted do on horses ride,
Here they do throw at cocks as at Shrovetide;
A chariot here so cunningly was made,
That it did move itself without the aid
Of horse or rope, by virtue of a spring
That Vulcan did contrive, who wrought therein.
The rooks at nine-holes here do flock together
As they are wont to do in summer weather.
Three ha'porth for a penny, here they cry,
Of gingerbread, come, who will of it buy?
This is the booth where men did money take,
For crape and ribbons that they there did make;
But in six hours, this great and rary show
Of booths and pastimes all away did go.

Pierre Antoine Motteux (1660–1718)

A Song

Slaves to London, I'll deceive you;
For the country now I leave you.
Who can bear, and not be mad,
Wine so dear, and yet so bad?
Such a noise, an air so smoky:
That to stun ye, this to choke ye?
Men so selfish, false, and rude,
Nymphs so young and yet so lewd?

If we play, we're sure of losing;
If we love, our doom we're choosing.
At the playhouse tedious sport,
Cant in City, cringe at Court,
Dirt in streets, and dirty bullies,
Jolting coaches, whores, and cullies,
Knaves and coxcombs everywhere:
Who that's wise would tarry here?

Quiet, harmless country pleasure
Shall at home engross my leisure.
Farewell, London! I'll repair
To my native country air:
I leave all thy plagues behind me—
But at home my wife will find me?
O ye gods! 'Tis ten times worse!
London is a milder curse.

Jonathan Swift (1667–1745)

A Description of the Morning

APRIL 1709

Now hardly here and there an hackney-coach
Appearing, showed the ruddy morn's approach.
Now Betty from her master's bed had flown,
And softly stole to discompose her own.
The slip-shod 'prentice from his master's door
Had pared the street and sprinkled round the floor.
Now Moll had whirled her mop with dexterous airs,
Prepared to scrub the entry and the stairs.
The youth with broomy stumps began to trace
The kennel edge, where wheels had worn the place.
The small-coal man was heard with cadence deep,
Till drowned in shriller notes of *"chimney-sweep."*
Duns at his lordship's gate began to meet;
And brickdust Moll had screamed through half a street.
The turnkey now his flock returning sees,
Duly let out a-nights to steal for fees.
The watchful bailiffs take their silent stands;
And schoolboys lag with satchels in their hands.

A Description of a City Shower

OCTOBER 1710

Careful observers may foretell the hour
(By sure prognostics) when to dread a shower:
While rain depends, the pensive cat gives o'er
Her frolics, and pursues her tail no more.
Returning home at night, you'll find the sink
Strike your offended sense with double stink.
If you be wise, then go not far to dine;
You'll spend in coach-hire more than save in wine.
A coming shower your shooting corns presage,
Old achès throb, your hollow tooth will rage.
Sauntering in coffeehouse is Dulman seen;
He damns the climate, and complains of spleen.

 Meanwhile the South, rising with dabbled wings,
A sable cloud athwart the welkin flings
That swilled more liquor than it could contain,
And, like a drunkard, gives it up again.
Brisk Susan whips her linen from the rope,
While the first drizzling shower is borne aslope;
Such is that sprinkling which some careless quean
Flirts on you from her mop, but not so clean:
You fly, invoke the gods; then turning, stop
To rail; she singing, still whirls on her mop.
Not yet the dust had shunned th'unequal strife,
But, aided by the wind, fought still for life,
And wafted with its foe by violent gust,
'Twas doubtful which was rain, and which was dust.
Ah! where must needy poet seek for aid,
When dust and rain at once his coat invade?
His only coat, where dust confused with rain
Roughen the nap, and leave a mingled stain.

 Now in contiguous drops the flood comes down,
Threatening with deluge this devoted town.
To shops in crowds the daggled females fly,

Pretend to cheapen goods, but nothing buy.
The Templar spruce, while every spout's abroach,
Stays till 'tis fair, yet seems to call a coach.
The tucked-up sempstress walks with hasty strides,
While streams run down her oiled umbrella's sides.
Here various kinds, by various fortunes led,
Commence acquaintance underneath a shed:
Triumphant Tories, and desponding Whigs,
Forget their feuds, and join to save their wigs.
Boxed in a chair the beau impatient sits,
While spouts run clattering o'er the roof by fits,
And ever and anon with frightful din
The leather sounds; he trembles from within.
So when Troy chairmen bore the wooden steed,
Pregnant with Greeks impatient to be freed
(Those bully Greeks, who, as the moderns do,
Instead of paying chairmen, run them through),
Laocoön struck the outside with his spear,
And each imprisoned hero quaked for fear.

   Now from all parts the swelling kennels flow,
And bear their trophies with them, as they go:
Filth of all hues and odours seem to tell
What street they sailed from, by their sight and smell.
They, as each torrent drives with rapid force,
From Smithfield or St. 'Pulchre's shape their course,
And in huge confluence joined at Snow Hill ridge,
Fall from the Conduit prone to Holborn-bridge.
Sweepings from butchers' stalls, dung, guts, and blood,
Drowned puppies, stinking sprats, all drenched in mud,
Dead cats, and turnip-tops, come tumbling down the flood.

Clever Tom Clinch

GOING TO BE HANGED

As clever Tom Clinch, while the rabble was bawling,
Rode stately through Holborn to die in his calling,
He stopped at the George for a bottle of sack,
And promised to pay for it when he came back.
His waistcoat, and stockings and breeches were white,
His cap had a new cherry ribbon to tie't.
The maids to the doors and the balconies ran,
And said, "Lack-a-day, he's a proper young man!"
But as from the windows the ladies he spied,
Like a beau in the box, he bowed low on each side.
And when his last speech the loud hawkers did cry,
He swore from his cart, "It was all a damned lie!"
The hangman for pardon fell down on his knee;
Tom gave him a kick in the guts for his fee:
Then said, "I must speak to the people a little;
But I'll see you all damned before I will whittle.
My honest friend Wild (may he long hold his place),
He lengthened my life with a whole year of grace:
Take courage, dear comrades, and be not afraid,
Nor slip this occasion to follow your trade;
My conscience is clear, and my spirits are calm,
And thus I go off, without prayer-book or psalm;
Then follow the practice of clever Tom Clinch,
Who hung like a hero, and never would flinch."

A Beautiful Young Nymph Going to Bed

WRITTEN FOR THE HONOUR OF THE FAIR SEX

Pars minima est ipsa Puella sui. Ovid Remed. Amoris.

Corinna, pride of Drury Lane,
For whom no shepherd sighs in vain;
Never did Covent Garden boast
So bright a battered, strolling toast!
No drunken rake to pick her up,
No cellar where on tick to sup;
Returning at the midnight hour,
Four stories climbing to her bower;
Then, seated on a three-legg'd chair,
Takes off her artificial hair;
Now picking out a crystal eye,
She wipes it clean, and lays it by.
Her eyebrows from a mouse's hide,
Stuck on with art on either side,
Pulls off with care, and first displays 'em,
Then in a play-book smoothly lays 'em.
Now dexterously her plumpers draws,
That serve to fill her hollow jaws,
Untwists a wire, and from her gums
A set of teeth completely comes;
Pulls out the rags contrived to prop
Her flabby dugs, and down they drop.
Proceeding on, the lovely goddess
Unlaces next her steel-ribbed bodice,
Which, by the operator's skill,
Press down the lumps, the hollows fill.
Up goes her hand, and off she slips
The bolsters that supply her hips;
With gentlest touch, she next explores
Her chancres, issues, running sores,
Effects of many a sad disaster;

And then to each applies a plaster:
But must, before she goes to bed,
Rub off the daubs of white and red,
And smooth the furrows in her front
With greasy paper stuck upon't.
She takes a *bolus* ere she sleeps,
And then between two blankets creeps.
With pains of love tormented lies;
Or, if she chance to close her eyes,
Of Bridewell and the Compter dreams,
And feels the lash, and faintly screams;
Or, by a faithless bully drawn,
At some hedge-tavern lies in pawn;
Or to Jamaica seems transported,
Alone, and by no planter courted;
Or, near Fleet-ditch's oozy brinks,
Surrounded with a hundred stinks;
Belated, seems on watch to lie,
And snap some cully passing by;
Or, struck with fear, her fancy runs
On watchmen, constables and duns,
From whom she meets with frequent rubs;
But never from religious clubs;
Whose favour she is sure to find
Because she pays 'em all in kind.

   Corinna wakes. A dreadful sight!
Behold the ruins of the night!
A wicked rat her plaster stole,
Half eat, and dragged it to his hole.
The crystal eye, alas, was missed;
And puss had on her plumpers p—ssed,
A pigeon picked her issue-peas.
And Shock her tresses filled with fleas.

   The nymph, though in this mangled plight,
Must every morn her limbs unite.
But how shall I describe her arts

To re-collect the scattered parts?
Or show the anguish, toil, and pain,
Of gathering up herself again?
The bashful Muse will never bear
In such a scene to interfere.
Corinna, in the morning dizened,
Who sees, will spew; who smells, be poisoned.

from *On Poetry: A Rhapsody*

Your poem in its modish dress,
Correctly fitted for the press,
Convey by penny-post to Lintot,
But let no friend alive look into't.
If Lintot thinks 'twill quit the cost,
You need not fear your labour lost.
And how agreeably surprised
Are you to see it advertised!
The hawker shows you one in print,
As fresh as farthings from the mint:
The product of your toil and sweating,
A bastard of your own begetting.

Be sure at Will's, the following day,
Lie snug, to hear what critics say;
And, if you find the general vogue
Pronounces you a stupid rogue,
Damns all your thoughts as low and little,
Sit still, and swallow down your spittle.
Be silent as a politician,
For talking may beget suspicion;
Or praise the judgment of the town,
And help, yourself, to run it down.
Give up your fond paternal pride,
Nor argue on the weaker side:
For, poems read without a name
We justly praise, or justly blame;
And critics have no partial views,
Except they know whom they abuse.
And since you ne'er provoked their spite,
Depend upon't their judgment's right.
But if you blab, you are undone;
Consider what a risk you run.

You lose your credit all at once;
The town will mark you for a dunce;
The vilest doggerel Grub Street sends,
Will pass for yours with foes and friends;
And you must bear the whole disgrace
Till some fresh blockhead takes your place. . . .

John Gay (1685–1732)

from *Trivia: or, The Art of Walking the Streets of London*

from BOOK II

FROSTY WEATHER

Winter my theme confines; whose nitry wind
Shall crust the slabby mire, and kennels bind;
She bids the snow descend in flaky sheets,
And in her hoary mantle clothe the streets.
Let not the virgin tread these slippery roads,
The gathering fleece the hollow patten loads;
But if thy footsteps slide with clotted frost,
Strike off the breaking balls against the post.
On silent wheel the passing coaches roll;
Oft look behind, and ward the threatening pole.
In hardened orbs the schoolboy moulds the snow,
To mark the coachman with a dexterous throw.
Why do ye, boys, the kennel's surface spread,
To tempt with faithless pass the matron's tread?
How can ye laugh to see the damsel spurn,
Sink in your frauds and her green stocking mourn?
At White's the harnessed chairman idly stands,
And swings around his waist his tingling hands:
The sempstress speeds to Change with red-tipped nose;
The Belgian stove beneath her footstool glows;
In half-whipped muslin needles useless lie,
And shuttlecocks across the counter fly.
These sports warm harmless; why then will ye prove,
Deluded maids, the dangerous flame of love?

THE DANGERS OF FOOTBALL

Where Covent Garden's famous temple stands,
That boasts the work of Jones' immortal hands,
Columns with plain magnificence appear,
And graceful porches lead along the square:
Here oft my course I bend, when lo! from far,
I spy the furies of the football war:
The 'prentice quits his shop to join the crew,
Increasing crowds the flying game pursue.
Thus, as you roll the ball o'er snowy ground,
The gathering globe augments with every round.
But whither shall I run? the throng draws nigh,
The ball now skims the street, now soars on high;
The dexterous glazier strong returns the bound,
And jingling sashes on the penthouse sound.

AN EPISODE OF THE GREAT FROST

O roving Muse, recall that wonderous year,
When winter reigned in bleak Britannia's air;
When hoary Thames, with frosted osiers crowned,
Was three long moons in icy fetters bound.
The waterman, forlorn along the shore,
Pensive reclines upon his useless oar;
Sees harnessed steeds desert the stony town,
And wander roads unstable, not their own:
Wheels o'er the hardened waters smoothly glide,
And raze with whitened tracks the slippery tide.
Here the fat cook piles high the blazing fire,
And scarce the spit can turn the steer entire.
Booths sudden hide the Thames, long streets appear.
And numerous games proclaim the crowded fair.

So when a general bids the martial train
Spread their encampment o'er the spacious plain,
Thick-rising tents a canvas city build,
And the loud dice resound through all the field.
'Twas here the matron found a doleful fate:
Let elegiac lay the woe relate,
Soft as the breath of distant flutes, at hours
When silent evening closes up the flowers;
Lulling as falling water's hollow noise;
Indulging grief, like Philomela's voice.
   Doll every day had walked these treacherous roads;
Her neck grew warped beneath autumnal loads
Of various fruit; she now a basket bore:
That head, alas! shall basket bear no more.
Each booth she frequent passed, in quest of gain,
And boys with pleasure heard her shrilling strain.
Ah Doll! all mortals must resign their breath,
And industry itself submit to death!
The cracking crystal yields, she sinks, she dies,
Her head, chopped off, from her lost shoulders flies;
"Pippins," she cried, but death her voice confounds,
And "pip-pip-pip" along the ice resounds.
So when the Thracian furies Orpheus tore,
And left his bleeding trunk deformed with gore,
His severed head floats down the silver tide,
His yet warm tongue for his lost consort cried;
"Eurydice" with quivering voice he mourned,
And Heber's banks "Eurydice" returned.

A THAW

   But now the western gale the flood unbinds,
And blackening clouds move on with warmer winds.

The wooden town its frail foundation leaves,
And Thames' full urn rolls down his plenteous waves:
From every penthouse streams the fleeting snow,
And with dissolving frost the pavements flow.

HOW TO KNOW THE DAYS OF THE WEEK

　　Experienced men, inured to city ways,
Need not the calendar to count their days.
When through the town with slow and solemn air,
Led by the nostril, walks the muzzled bear;
Behind him moves majestically dull,
The pride of Hockley-hole, the surly bull;
Learn hence the periods of the week to name:
Mondays and Thursdays are the days of game.
　　When fishy stalls with double store are laid;
The golden-bellied carp, the broad-finned maid,
Red-speckled trouts, the salmon's silver jowl,
The jointed lobster, and unscaly sole,
And luscious scallops to allure the tastes
Of rigid zealots to delicious fasts;
Wednesdays and Fridays you'll observe from hence,
Days, when our sires were doomed to abstinence.
　　When dirty waters from balconies drop,
And dexterous damsels twirl the sprinkling mop,
And cleanse the spattered sash, and scrub the stairs;
Know Saturday's conclusive morn appears.

REMARKS ON THE CRIES OF THE TOWN

　　Successive cries the seasons' change declare,
And mark the monthly progress of the year.
Hark, how the streets with treble voices ring,

To sell the bounteous product of the spring!
Sweet-smelling flowers, and elder's early bud,
With nettle's tender shoots, to cleanse the blood:
And when June's thunder cools the sultry skies,
Even Sundays are profaned by mackerel cries.

    Walnuts the fruiterer's hand, in autumn, stain,
Blue plums and juicy pears augment his gain;
Next, oranges the longing boys entice
To trust their copper fortunes to the dice.

OF CHRISTMAS

    When rosemary and bays, the poet's crown,
Are bawled in frequent cries through all the town,
Then judge the festival of Christmas near,
Christmas, the joyous period of the year.
Now with bright holly all your temples strow,
With laurel green and sacred mistletoe.
Now, heaven-born Charity, thy blessings shed;
Bid meagre Want uprear her sickly head:
Bid shivering limbs be warm; let plenty's bowl
In humble roofs make glad the needy soul.
See, see, the heaven-born maid her blessings shed.
Lo! meagre Want uprears her sickly head;
Clothed are the naked, and the needy glad,
While selfish Avarice alone is sad.

from BOOK III

THE EVENING

    When night first bids the twinkling stars appear,
Or with her cloudy vest enwraps the air,

Then swarms the busy street; with caution tread,
Where the shop-windows falling threat thy head;
Now labourers home return, and join their strength
To bear the tottering plank, or ladder's length;
Still fix thy eyes intent upon the throng,
And as the passes open, wind along.

OF THE PASS OF ST. CLEMENTS

Where the fair columns of Saint Clement stand,
Whose straitened bounds encroach upon the Strand;
Where the low penthouse bows the walker's head,
And the rough pavement wounds the yielding tread;
Where not a post protects the narrow space,
And strung in twines, combs dangle in thy face;
Summon at once thy courage, rouse thy care,
Stand firm, look back, be resolute, beware.
Forth issuing from steep lanes, the collier's steeds
Drag the black load; another cart succeeds,
Team follows team, crowds heaped on crowds appear,
And wait impatient, 'till the road grow clear.
Now all the pavement sounds with trampling feet,
And the mixed hurry barricades the street.
Entangled here, the waggon's lengthened team
Crack the tough harness; here a ponderous beam
Lies over-turned athwart; for slaughter fed,
Here lowing bullocks raise their hornèd head.
Now oaths grow loud, with coaches coaches jar,
And the smart blow provokes the sturdy war;
From the high box they whirl the thong around,
And with the twining lash their shins resound:
Their rage ferments, more dangerous wounds they try,
And the blood gushes down their painful eye;
And now on foot the frowning warriors light,

And with their ponderous fists renew the fight;
Blow answers blow, their cheeks are smeared with blood,
'Till down they fall, and grappling roll in mud.
So when two boars, in wild Ytene bred,
Or on Westphalia's fattening chestnuts fed,
Gnash their sharp tusks, and roused with equal fire,
Dispute the reign of some luxurious mire;
In the black flood they wallow o'er and o'er,
'Till their armed jaws distill with foam and gore.

OF PICK-POCKETS

    Where the mob gathers, swiftly shoot along,
Nor idly mingle in the noisy throng.
Lured by the silver hilt, amid the swarm,
The subtle artist will thy side disarm.
Nor is thy flaxen wig with safety worn;
High on the shoulder, in the basket born,
Lurks the sly boy; whose hand to rapine bred,
Plucks off the curling honours of the head.
Here dives the skulking thief, with practised slight,
And unfelt fingers make thy pocket light.
Where's now thy watch, with all its trinkets, flown?
And thy late snuff-box is no more thy own.
But lo! his bolder thefts some tradesman spies,
Swift from his prey the scudding lurcher flies;
Dexterous he scapes the coach, with nimble bounds,
While every honest tongue *Stop Thief* resounds.
So speeds the wily fox, alarmed by fear,
Who lately filched the turkey's callow care;
Hounds following hounds, grow louder as he flies,
And injured tenants join the hunter's cries.
Breathless he stumbling falls: ill-fated boy!
Why did not honest work thy youth employ?

Seized by rough hands, he's dragged amid the rout,
And stretched beneath the pump's incessant spout:
Or plunged in miry ponds, he gasping lies,
Mud chokes his mouth, and plasters o'er his eyes.

OF BALLAD-SINGERS

Let not the ballad-singer's shrilling strain
Amid the swarm thy listening ear detain:
Guard well thy pocket; for these sirens stand,
To aid the labours of the diving hand;
Confederate in the cheat, they draw the throng,
And cambric handkerchiefs reward, the song.
But soon as coach or cart drives rattling on,
The rabble part, in shoals they backward run.
So Jove's loud bolts the mingled war divide,
And Greece and Troy retreats on either side.
. . .

THE DANGER OF CROSSING A SQUARE BY NIGHT

Where Lincoln's Inn, wide space, is railed around,
Cross not with venturous step; there oft is found
The lurking thief, who while the day-light shone,
Made the walls echo with his begging tone:
That crutch which late compassion moved, shall wound
Thy bleeding head, and fell thee to the ground.
Though thou art tempted by the link-man's call,
Yet trust him not along the lonely wall;
In the mid-way he'll quench the flaming brand,
And share the booty with the pilfering band.
Still keep the public streets, where oily rays
Shot from the crystal lamp, o'erspread the ways.
. . .

OF VARIOUS CHEATS FORMERLY IN PRACTICE

Who can the various city frauds recite,
With all the petty rapines of the night?
Who now the guinea-dropper's bait regards,
Tricked by the sharper's dice, or juggler's cards?
Why should I warn thee ne'er to join the fray,
Where the sham-quarrel interrupts the way?
Lives there in these our days so soft a clown,
Braved by the bully's oaths, or threatening frown?
I need not strict enjoin the pocket's care,
When from the crowded play thou lead'st the fair;
Who has not here, or watch, or snuff-box lost,
Or handkerchiefs that India's shuttle boast?

AN ADMONITION TO VIRTUE

O! may thy virtue guard thee through the roads
Of Drury's mazy courts, and dark abodes,
The harlots' guileful paths, who nightly stand,
Where Katherine Street descends into the Strand.
Say, vagrant muse, their wiles and subtle arts,
To lure the stranger's unsuspecting hearts;
So shall our youth on healthful sinews tread,
And city cheeks grow warm with rural red.

HOW TO KNOW A WHORE

'Tis she who nightly strolls with sauntering pace,
No stubborn stays her yielding shape embrace;
Beneath the lamp her tawdry ribbons glare,
The new-scoured manteau, and the slattern air;
High-draggled petticoats her travels show,

And hollow cheeks with artful blushes glow;
With flattering sounds she soothes the credulous ear,
My noble Captain! Charmer! Love! my Dear!
In riding-hood, near tavern doors she plies,
Or muffled pinners hide her livid eyes.
With empty bandbox she delights to range,
And feigns a distant errand from the change;
Nay, she will oft the Quaker's hood prophane,
And trudge demure the rounds of Drury Lane.
She darts from sarcenet ambush wily leers,
Twitches thy sleeve, or with familiar airs,
Her fan will pat thy cheek; these snares disdain,
Nor gaze behind thee, when she turns again.

A DREADFUL EXAMPLE

   I knew a yeoman, who for thirst of gain,
To the great city drove from Devon's plain
His numerous lowing herd; his herds he sold,
And his deep leathern pocket bagged with gold;
Drawn by a fraudful nymph, he gazed, he sighed,
Unmindful of his home, and distant bride;
She leads the willing victim to his doom,
Through winding alleys to her cobweb room.
Thence through the street he reels, from post to post,
Valiant with wine, nor knows his treasure lost.
The vagrant wretch th' assembled watchmen spies,
He waves his hanger, and their poles defies;
Deep in the Round-House pent, all night he snores,
And the next morn in vain his fate deplores.

   Ah hapless swain, unused to pains and ills!
Canst thou forgo roast-beef for nauseous pills?

How wilt thou lift to Heaven thy eyes and hands,
When the long scroll the surgeon's fees demands!
Or else (ye Gods avert that worst disgrace)
Thy ruined nose falls level with thy face;
Then shall thy wife thy loathsome kiss disdain,
And wholesome neighbours from thy mug refrain.

from *The Beggar's Opera*

Since laws were made for every degree,
To curb vice in others as well as me,
I wonder we han't better company
  Upon Tyburn tree.
But gold from law can take out the sting;
And if rich men, like us, were to swing,
'Twould thin the land, such numbers to string
  Upon Tyburn tree.

Anon. (pub. 1719)

The Fair Lass of Islington

There was a lass of Islington,
    As I have heard many tell;
And she would to fair London go
    Fine apples and pears to sell;
And as along the streets she flung
    With her basket on her arm,
Her pears to sell, you may know it right well,
    This fair maid meant no harm.

But as she tripped along the street
    Her pleasant fruit to sell,
A vintner did with her meet
    Who liked this maid full well.
Quoth he, fair maid, what have you there
    In basket deckèd brave?
Fine pears, quoth she, and if it please ye
    A taste, Sir, you shall have.

The vintner he took a taste
    And liked it well, for why;
This maid he thought of all the rest
    Most pleasing to his eye;
Quoth he, fair maid, I have a suit
    That you to me must grant;
Which if I find you be so kind,
    Nothing that you shall want.

Thy beauty doth so please my eye
    And dazzles so my sight,
That now of all my liberty
    I am deprivèd quite;
Then prithee now consent to me,
    And do not put me by;

It is but one small courtesy—
   All night with you to lie.

Sir, if you lie with me one night,
   As you propound to me,
I do expect that you should prove
   Both courteous, kind, and free;
And for to tell you all in short,
   It will cost you five pound.
A match, a match, the vintner said,
   And so let this go round.

When he had lain with her all night
   Her money she did crave;
O stay, quoth he, the other night,
   And thy money thou shalt have.
I cannot stay, nor I will not stay,
   I needs must now be gone.
Why then, thou may'st thy money go look,
   For money I'll pay thee none.

This maid she made no more ado
   But to a justice went,
And unto him she made her moan,
   Who did her case lament;
She said she had a cellar let out
   To a vintner in the town,
And how that he did then agree
   Five pound to pay her down.

But now, quoth she, the case is thus,
   No rent that he will pay;
Therefore, your Worship, I beseech
   To send for him this day;
Then straight the justice for him sent
   And asked the reason why
That he would pay this maid no rent,
   To which he did reply:

Although I hired a cellar of her
    And the possession was mine,
I ne'er put any thing into it
    But one poor pipe of wine;
Therefore my bargain it was hard,
    As you may plainly see;
I from my freedom was debarred—
    Then, good sir, favour me.

This fair maid being ripe of wit,
    She straight replied again:
There were two butts more at the door,
    Why did you not roll them in?
You had your freedom and your will,
    As is to you well known;
Therefore I do desire still
    For to receive my own.

The justice hearing of their case
    Did then give order straight,
That he the money should pay down,
    She should no longer wait.
Withal he told the vintner plain,
    If he a tennant be,
He must expect to pay the same
    For he could not sit rent-free.

But when the money she had got
    She put it in her purse,
And clapped her hand on the cellar door
    And said it was never the worse;
Which caused the people all to laugh,
    To see this vintner fine
Out-witted by a country girl
    About his pipe of wine.

Alexander Pope (1688–1744)

The Alley. An Imitation of Spenser

In every town where Thamis rolls his tide,
A narrow pass there is, with houses low,
Where ever and anon the stream is eyed,
And many a boat soft sliding to and fro.
There oft are heard the notes of infant woe,
The short thick sob, loud scream, and shriller squall:
How can ye, mothers, vex your children so?
Some play, some eat, some cack against the wall,
And as they crouchen low for bread and butter call.

And on the broken pavement, here and there,
Doth many a stinking sprat and herring lie;
A brandy and tobacco shop is near,
And hens, and dogs, and hogs are feeding by,
And here a sailor's jacket hangs to dry.
At every door are sunburnt matrons seen
Mending old nets to catch the scaly fry;
Now singing shrill, and scolding eft between,
Scolds answer foul-mouthed scolds; bad neighbourhood I ween.

The snappish cur (the passenger's annoy)
Close at my heel with yelping treble flies;
The whimpering girl, and hoarser screaming boy,
Join to the yelping treble shrilling cries;
The scolding quean to louder notes doth rise,
And her full pipes those shrilling cries confound:
To her full pipes the grunting hog replies;
The grunting hogs alarm the neighbours round,
And curs, girls, boys and scolds in the deep bass are drowned.

Hard by a sty, beneath a roof of thatch,
Dwelt Obloquy, who in her early days
Baskets of fish at Billingsgate did watch,

Cod, whiting, oyster, mackrel, sprat, or plaice:
There learned she speech from tongues that never cease.
Slander beside her like a magpie chatters,
With Envy (spitting cat), dread foe to peace;
Like a cursed cur, Malice before her clatters,
And, vexing every wight, tears clothes and all to tatters.

Her dugs were marked by every collier's hand,
Her mouth was black as bulldog's at the stall:
She scratchèd, bit, and spared ne lace ne band,
And "bitch" and "rogue" her answer was to all;
Nay, e'en the parts of shame by name would call:
Yea, when she passèd by or lane or nook,
Would greet the man who turned him to the wall,
And by his hand obscene the porter took,
Nor ever did askance like modest virgin look.

Such place hath Deptford, navy-building town,
Woolwich and Wapping, smelling strong of pitch;
Such Lambeth, envy of each band and gown,
And Twickenham such, which fairer scenes enrich,
Grots, statues, urns, and Jo[hnsto]n's dog and bitch:
Ne village is without, on either side,
All up the silver Thames, or all adown;
Ne Richmond's self, from whose tall front are eyed
Vales, spires, meandering streams, and Windsor's towery pride.

A Farewell to London in the Year 1715

Dear, damned, distracting town, farewell!
 Thy fools no more I'll tease:
This year in peace, ye critics, dwell,
 Ye harlots, sleep at ease!

Soft Bethel and rough Craggs, adieu!
 Earl Warwick, make your moan,
The lively Hinchinbrook and you
 May knock up whores alone.

To drink and droll be Rowe allowed
 Till the third watchman's toll;
Let Jervas gratis paint, and Frowde
 Save threepence and his soul.

Farewell Arbuthnot's raillery
 On every learned sot;
And Garth, the best good Christian he,
 Although he knows it not.

Lintot, farewell! thy bard must go;
 Farewell, unhappy Tonson!
Heaven gives thee for thy loss of Rowe,
 Lean Philips, and fat Johnson.

Why should I stay? Both parties rage;
 My vixen mistress squalls;
The wits in envious feuds engage:
 And Homer (damn him) calls.

The love of arts lies cold and dead
 In Halifax's urn;
And not one muse of all he fed,
 Has yet the grace to mourn.

My friends, by turns, my friends confound,
 Betray, and are betrayed:

Poor Younger's sold for fifty pound,
    And Bicknell is a jade.

Why make I friendships with the great,
    When I no favour seek?
Or follow girls seven hours in eight?
    I need but once a week.

Still idle, with a busy air,
    Deep whimsies to contrive;
The gayest valetudinaire,
    Most thinking rake alive.

Solicitous for others' ends,
    Though fond of dear repose;
Careless or drowsy with my friends,
    And frolic with my foes.

Luxurious lobster-nights, farewell,
    For sober, studious days;
And Burlington's delicious meal,
    For salads, tarts, and pease.

Adieu to all but Gay alone,
    Whose soul, sincere and free,
Loves all mankind, but flatters none,
    And so may starve with me.

Epistle to Miss Blount, on her Leaving the Town, after the Coronation

As some fond virgin, whom her mother's care
Drags from the town to wholesome country air,
Just when she learns to roll a melting eye,
And hear a spark, yet think no danger nigh;
From the dear man unwilling she must sever,
Yet takes one kiss before she parts for ever.
Thus from the world fair Zephalinda flew,
Saw others happy, and with sighs withdrew;
Not that their pleasures caused her discontent,
She sighed not that they stayed, but that she went.

    She went to plain-work, and to purling brooks,
Old-fashioned halls, dull aunts, and croaking rooks;
She went from opera, park, assembly, play,
To morning walks, and prayers three hours a day;
To pass her time 'twixt reading and bohea,
To muse, and spill her solitary tea,
Or o'er cold coffee trifle with the spoon,
Count the slow clock, and dine exact at noon;
Divert her eyes with pictures in the fire,
Hum half a tune, tell stories to the squire;
Up to her godly garret after seven,
There starve and pray, for that's the way to heaven.

    Some squire, perhaps, you take delight to rack,
Whose game is whisk, whose treat a toast in sack;
Who visits with a gun, presents you birds,
Then gives a smacking buss and cries,—No words!
Or with his hound comes hollowing from the stable,
Makes love with nods, and knees beneath a table;
Whose laughs are hearty, though his jests are coarse,
And loves you best of all things—but his horse.

    In some fair evening, on your elbow laid,
You dream of triumphs in the rural shade;
In pensive thought recall the fancied scene,

See coronations rise on every green;
Before you pass th' imaginary sights
Of lords, and earls, and dukes, and gartered knights,
While the spread fan o'ershades your closing eyes;
Then give one flirt, and all the vision flies.
Thus vanish sceptres, coronets, and balls,
And leave you in lone woods, or empty walls.
    So when your slave, at some dear, idle time
(Not plagued with head-aches, or the want of rhyme),
Stands in the streets, abstracted from the crew,
And while he seems to study, thinks of you:
Just when his fancy points your sprightly eyes,
Or sees the blush of soft Parthenia rise,
Gay pats my shoulder, and you vanish quite;
Streets, chairs, and coxcombs rush upon my sight;
Vexed to be still in town, I knit my brow,
Look sour, and hum a tune—as you may now.

from *The Dunciad*

BOOK II

High on a gorgeous seat, that far outshone
Henley's gilt tub, or Flecknoe's Irish throne,
Or that where on her Curlls the public pours,
All-bounteous, fragrant grains and golden showers,
Great Cibber sat: the proud Parnassian sneer,
The conscious simper, and the jealous leer,
Mix on his look: all eyes direct their rays
On him, and crowds turn coxcombs as they gaze.
His peers shine round him with reflected grace,
New edge their dulness, and new bronze their face.
So from the sun's broad beam, in shallow urns
Heaven's twinkling sparks draw light, and point their horns.

    Not with more glee, by hands pontific crowned,
With scarlet hats wide-waving circled round,
Rome in her Capitol saw Querno sit,
Throned on seven hills, the Antichrist of wit.

    And now the Queen, to glad her sons, proclaims
By herald hawkers, high heroic games.
They summon all her race: an endless band
Pours forth, and leaves unpeopled half the land.
A motley mixture! in long wigs, in bags,
In silks, in crapes, in garters, and in rags,
From drawing rooms, from colleges, from garrets,
On horse, on foot, in hacks, and gilded chariots:
All who true dunces in her cause appeared,
And all who knew those dunces to reward.

    Amid that area wide they took their stand,
Where the tall maypole once o'erlooked the Strand;
But now (so Anne and piety ordain)
A church collects the saints of Drury Lane.

    With authors, stationers obeyed the call,
(The field of glory is a field for all).
Glory, and gain th'industrious tribe provoke;

And gentle Dulness ever loves a joke.
A poet's form she placed before their eyes,
And bade the nimblest racer seize the prize;
No meagre, muse-rid mope, adust and thin,
In a dun nightgown of his own loose skin;
But such a bulk as no twelve bards could raise,
Twelve starveling bards of these degenerate days.
All as a partridge plump, full-fed, and fair,
She formed this image of well-bodied air,
With pert flat eyes she windowed well its head;
A brain of feathers, and a heart of lead;
And empty words she gave, and sounding strain,
But senseless, lifeless! idol void and vain!
Never was dashed out, at one lucky hit,
A fool, so just a copy of a wit;
So like, that critics said, and courtiers swore,
A wit it was, and called the phantom More.

    All gaze with ardour: some a poet's name,
Others a sword-knot and laced suit inflame.
But lofty Lintot in the circle rose:
"This prize is mine; who tempt it are my foes;
With me began this genius, and shall end."
He spoke: and who with Lintot shall contend?

    Fear held them mute. Alone, untaught to fear,
Stood dauntless Curll; "Behold that rival here!
The race by vigour, not by vaunts is won;
So take the hindmost, Hell."—He said, and run.
Swift as a bard the bailiff leaves behind,
He left huge Lintot, and out-stripped the wind.
As when a dabchick waddles through the copse
On feet and wings, and flies, and wades, and hops;
So labouring on, with shoulders, hands, and head,
Wide as a windmill all his figure spread,
With arms expanded Bernard rows his state,
And left-legged Jacob seems to emulate:
Full in the middle way there stood a lake,

Which Curll's Corinna chanced that morn to make:
(Such was her wont, at early dawn to drop
Her evening cates before his neighbour's shop);
Here fortuned Curll to slide; loud shout the band,
And "Bernard! Bernard!" rings through all the Strand.
Obscene with film the miscreant lies bewrayed,
Fallen in the plash his wickedness had laid:
Then first (if poets aught of truth declare)
The caitiff vaticide conceived a prayer.
      "Hear Jove! whose name my bards and I adore,
As much at least as any god's, or more;
And him and his, if more devotion warms,
Down with the Bible, up with the Pope's Arms."
      A place there is, betwixt earth, air, and seas,
Where, from Ambrosia, Jove retires for ease.
There in his seat two spacious vents appear,
On this he sits, to that he leans his ear.
And hears the various vows of fond mankind;
Some beg an eastern, some a western wind:
All vain petitions, mounting to the sky,
With reams abundant this abode supply;
Amused he reads, and then returns the bills
Signed with that Ichor which from gods distils.
      In office here fair Cloacina stands,
And ministers to Jove with purest hands.
Forth from the heap she picked her votary's prayer,
And placed it next him, a distinction rare!
Oft had the Goddess heard her servant's call,
From her black grottos near the Temple wall,
Listening delighted to the jest unclean
Of link-boys vile, and watermen obscene;
Where as he fished her nether realms for wit,
She oft had favoured him, and favours yet.
Renewed by ordure's sympathetic force,
As oiled with magic juices for the course,
Vigorous he rises; from th' effluvia strong

Imbibes new life, and scours and stinks along;
Repasses Lintot, vindicates the race,
Nor heeds the brown dishonours of his face.

 And now the victor stretched his eager hand
Where the tall nothing stood, or seemed to stand;
A shapeless shade, it melted from his sight,
Like forms in clouds, or visions of the night.
To seize his papers, Curll, was next thy care;
His papers light, fly diverse, tossed in air;
Songs, sonnets, epigrams the winds uplift,
And whisk 'em back to Evans, Young, and Swift.
Th'embroidered suit at least he deemed his prey;
That suit an unpaid tailor snatched away.
No rag, no scrap, of all the beau, or wit,
That once so fluttered, and that once so writ.

 Heaven rings with laughter: of the laughter vain,
Dulness, good Queen, repeats the jest again.
Three wicked imps, of her own Grub Street choir,
She decked like Congreve, Addison, and Prior;
Mears, Warner, Wilkins run: delusive thought!
Breval, Bond, Besaleel, the varlets caught.
Curll stretches after Gay, but Gay is gone,
He grasps an empty Joseph for a John:
So Proteus, hunted in a nobler shape,
Became, when seized, a puppy, or an ape.

 To him the Goddess: "Son! thy grief lay down,
And turn this whole illusion on the town:
As the sage dame, experienced in her trade,
By names of toasts retails each battered jade;
(Whence hapless Monsieur much complains at Paris
Of wrongs from Duchesses and Lady Maries);
Be thine, my stationer! this magic gift,
Cooke shall be Prior, and Concanen, Swift:
So shall each hostile name become our own,
And we too boast our Garth and Addison."

 With that she gave him (piteous of his case,

Yet smiling at his rueful length of face)
A shaggy tapestry, worthy to be spread
On Codrus' old, or Dunton's modern bed;
Instructive work! whose wry-mouthed portraiture
Displayed the fates her confessors endure.
Earless on high, stood unabashed Defoe,
And Tutchin flagrant from the scourge below.
There Ridpath, Roper, cudgelled might ye view,
The very worsted still looked black and blue.
Himself among the storied chiefs he spies,
As from the blanket high in air he flies,
"And oh!" (he cried) "what street, what lane but knows,
Our purgings, pumpings, blankettings, and blows?
In every loom our labours shall be seen,
And the fresh vomit run for ever green!"
    See in the circle next, Eliza placed,
Two babes of love close clinging to her waist;
Fair as before her works she stands confessed,
In flowers and pearls by bounteous Kirkall dressed.
The Goddess then: "Who best can send on high
The salient spout, far-streaming to the sky;
His be yon Juno of majestic size,
With cow-like udders, and with ox-like eyes.
This China jordan let the chief o'ercome
Replenish, not ingloriously, at home."
Osborne and Curll accept the glorious strife,
(Though this his son dissuades, and that his wife.)
One on his manly confidence relies,
One on his vigour and superior size.
First Osborne leaned against his lettered post;
It rose, and laboured to a curve at most.
So Jove's bright bow displays its watery round,
(Sure sign, that no spectator shall be drowned).
A second effort brought but new disgrace,
The wild meander washed the artist's face:
Thus the small jet, which hasty hands unlock,

Spurts in the gardener's eyes who turns the cock.
Not so from shameless Curll; impetuous spread
The stream, and smoking flourished o'er his head.
So (famed like thee for turbulence and horns)
Eridanus his humble fountain scorns;
Through half the heavens he pours th'exalted urn;
His rapid waters in their passage burn.

    Swift as it mounts, all follow with their eyes:
Still happy impudence obtains the prize.
Thou triumph'st, victor of the high-wrought day,
And the pleased dame, soft-smiling, leadst away.
Osborne, through perfect modesty o'ercome,
Crowned with the jordan, walks contented home.

    But now for authors nobler palms remain;
Room for my Lord! three jockeys in his train;
Six huntsmen with a shout precede his chair:
He grins, and looks broad nonsense with a stare.
His honour's meaning Dulness thus expressed,
"He wins this patron, who can tickle best."

    He chinks his purse, and takes his seat of state:
With ready quills the dedicators wait;
Now at his head the dexterous task commence,
And, instant, fancy feels th' imputed sense;
Now gentle touches wanton o'er his face,
He struts Adonis, and affects grimace:
Rolli the feather to his ear conveys,
Then his nice taste directs our operas:
Bentley his mouth with classic flattery opes,
And the puffed orator bursts out in tropes.
But Welsted most the poet's healing balm
Strives to extract from his soft, giving palm;
Unlucky Welsted! thy unfeeling master,
The more thou ticklest, gripes his fist the faster.

    While thus each hand promotes the pleasing pain,
And quick sensations skip from vein to vein;
A youth unknown to Phoebus, in despair,

Puts his last refuge all in heaven and prayer.
What force have pious vows! The Queen of Love
His sister sends, her votress, from above.
As taught by Venus, Paris learnt the art
To touch Achilles' only tender part;
Secure, through her, the noble prize to carry,
He marches off, his Grace's secretary.

    "Now turn to different sports," the Goddess cries,
"And learn, my sons, the wondrous power of noise.
To move, to raise, to ravish every heart,
With Shakespeare's nature, or with Jonson's art,
Let others aim: 'tis yours to shake the soul
With thunder rumbling from the mustard bowl,
With horns and trumpets now to madness swell,
Now sink in sorrows with a tolling bell;
Such happy arts attention can command,
When fancy flags, and sense is at a stand.
Improve we these. Three catcalls be the bribe
Of him, whose chattering shames the monkey tribe:
And his this drum, whose hoarse heroic bass
Drowns the loud clarion of the braying ass."

    Now thousand tongues are heard in one loud din:
The monkey-mimics rush discordant in;
'Twas chattering, grinning, mouthing, jabbering all,
And noise and Norton, brangling and Breval,
Dennis and dissonance, and captious art,
And snipsnap short, and interruption smart,
And demonstration thin, and theses thick,
And major, minor, and conclusion quick.
"Hold," cried the Queen, "a catcall each shall win;
Equal your merits! equal is your din!
But that this well-disputed game may end,
Sound forth my brayers, and the welkin rend."

    As when the long-eared milky mothers wait
At some sick miser's triple-bolted gate,
For their defrauded, absent foals they make

A moan so loud, that all the guild awake;
Sore sighs Sir Gilbert, starting at the bray,
From dreams of millions, and three groats to pay.
So swells each wind-pipe; ass intones to ass,
Harmonic twang! of leather, horn, and brass;
Such as from labouring lungs th' enthusiast blows,
High sound, attempered to the vocal nose;
Or such as bellow from the deep divine:
There Webster! pealed thy voice, and Whitfield! thine.
But far o'er all, sonorous Blackmore's strain;
Walls, steeples, skies, bray back to him again.
In Tottenham fields, the brethren, with amaze,
Prick all their ears up, and forget to graze;
Long Chancery Lane retentive rolls the sound,
And courts to courts return it round and round;
Thames wafts it thence to Rufus' roaring hall,
And Hungerford re-echoes bawl for bawl.
All hail him victor in both gifts of song,
Who sings so loudly, and who sings so long.
    This labour past, by Bridewell all descend,
(As morning prayer, and flagellation end)
To where Fleet Ditch with disemboguing streams
Rolls the large tribute of dead dogs to Thames;
The King of dykes! than whom no sluice of mud
With deeper sable blots the silver flood.
"Here strip, my children! here at once leap in,
Here prove who best can dash through thick and thin,
And who the most in love of dirt excel,
Or dark dexterity of groping well.
Who flings most filth, and wide pollutes around
The stream, be his the *Weekly Journals* bound;
A pig of lead to him who dives the best;
A peck of coals apiece shall glad the rest."
    In naked majesty Oldmixon stands,
And Milo-like surveys his arms and hands;
Then sighing, thus, "And am I now three score?

Ah why, ye gods! should two and two make four?"
He said, and climbed a stranded lighter's height,
Shot to the black abyss, and plunged downright.
The senior's judgment all the crowd admire,
Who but to sink the deeper, rose the higher.

   Next Smedley dived; slow circles dimpled o'er
The quaking mud, that closed, and oped no more.
All look, all sigh, and call on Smedley lost;
"Smedley" in vain resounds through all the coast.

   Then * essayed; scarce vanished out of sight,
He buoys up instant, and returns to light:
He bears no token of the sabler streams,
And mounts far off among the swans of Thames.

   True to the bottom, see Concanen creep,
A cold, long-winded, native of the deep:
If perseverance gain the diver's prize,
Not everlasting Blackmore this denies:
No noise, no stir, no motion canst thou make;
Th' unconscious stream sleeps o'er thee like a lake.

   Next plunged a feeble, but a desperate pack,
With each a sickly brother at his back:
Sons of a day! just buoyant on the flood,
Then numbered with the puppies in the mud.
Ask ye their names? I could as soon disclose
The names of these blind puppies as of those.
Fast by, like Niobe (her children gone)
Sits Mother Osborne, stupefied to stone!
And monumental brass this record bears,
"These are,—ah no! these were, the *Gazetteers!*"

   Not so bold Arnall; with a weight of skull,
Furious he dives, precipitately dull.
Whirlpools and storms his circling arm invest,
With all the might of gravitation blessed:
No crab more active in the dirty dance,
Downward to climb, and backward to advance.
He brings up half the bottom on his head,

And loudly claims the journals and the lead.
    The plunging prelate, and his ponderous Grace,
With holy envy gave one layman place.
When lo! a burst of thunder shook the flood.
Slow rose a form, in majesty of mud;
Shaking the horrors of his sable brows,
And each ferocious feature grim with ooze.
Greater he looks, and more than mortal stares:
Then thus the wonders of the deep declares.
    First he relates, how sinking to the chin,
Smit with his mien, the mud-nymphs sucked him in:
How young Lutetia, softer than the down,
Nigrina black, and Merdamante brown,
Vied for his love in jetty bowers below,
As Hylas fair was ravished long ago.
Then sung, how shown him by the nut-brown maids
A branch of Styx here rises from the shades,
That tinctured as it runs with Lethe's streams,
And wafting vapours from the land of dreams,
(As under seas Alpheus' secret sluice
Bears Pisa's offerings to his Arethuse)
Pours into Thames: and hence the mingled wave
Intoxicates the pert, and lulls the grave:
Here brisker vapours o'er the Temple creep,
There, all from Paul's to Aldgate drink and sleep.
    Thence to the banks where reverend bards repose,
They led him soft; each reverend bard arose;
And Milbourne chief, deputed by the rest,
Gave him the cassock, surcingle, and vest.
"Receive," he said, "these robes which once were mine,
Dulness is sacred in a sound divine."
    He ceased, and spread the robe; the crowd confess,
The reverend flamen in his lengthened dress.
Around him wide a sable army stand,
A low-born, cell-bred, selfish, servile band,
Prompt or to guard or stab, to saint or damn,

Heaven's Swiss, who fight for any god, or man.
   Through Lud's famed gates, along the well-known Fleet
Rolls the black troop, and overshades the street,
Till showers of sermons, characters, essays,
In circling fleeces whiten all the ways:
So clouds replenished from some bog below,
Mount in dark volumes, and descend in snow.
Here stopped the Goddess; and in pomp proclaims
A gentler exercise to close the games.
   "Ye critics! in whose heads, as equal scales,
I weigh what author's heaviness prevails;
Which most conduce to soothe the soul in slumbers,
My Henley's periods, or my Blackmore's numbers;
Attend the trial we propose to make:
If there be man, who o'er such works can wake,
Sleep's all-subduing charms who dares defy,
And boasts Ulysses' ear with Argus' eye;
To him we grant our amplest powers to sit
Judge of all present, past, and future wit;
To cavil, censure, dictate, right or wrong,
Full and eternal privilege of tongue."
   Three college sophs, and three pert templars came,
The same their talents, and their tastes the same;
Each prompt to query, answer, and debate,
And smit with love of poesy and prate.
The ponderous books two gentle readers bring;
The heroes sit, the vulgar form a ring.
The clamorous crowd is hushed with mugs of mum,
Till all tuned equal, send a general hum.
Then mount the clerks, and in one lazy tone
Through the long, heavy, painful page drawl on;
Soft creeping, words on words, the sense compose,
At every line they stretch, they yawn, they doze.
As to soft gales top-heavy pines bow low
Their heads, and lift them as they cease to blow:
Thus oft they rear, and oft the head decline,

As breathe, or pause, by fits, the airs divine.
And now to this side, now to that they nod,
As verse, or prose, infuse the drowsy god.
Thrice Budgell aimed to speak, but thrice suppressed
By potent Arthur, knocked his chin and breast.
Toland and Tindal, prompt at priests to jeer,
Yet silent bowed to Christ's no kingdom here.
Who sat the nearest, by the words o'ercome,
Slept first; the distant nodded to the hum.
Then down are rolled the books; stretched o'er 'em lies
Each gentle clerk, and muttering seals his eyes.
As what a Dutchman plumps into the lakes,
One circle first, and then a second makes;
What Dulness dropped among her sons impressed
Like motion from one circle to the rest;
So from the midmost the nutation spreads
Round and more round, o'er all the sea of heads.
At last Centlivre felt her voice to fail,
Motteux himself unfinished left his tale,
Boyer the state, and Law the stage gave o'er,
Morgan and Mandeville could prate no more;
Norton, from Daniel and Ostroea sprung,
Blessed with his father's front, and mother's tongue,
Hung silent down his never-blushing head;
And all was hushed, as folly's self lay dead.

    Thus the soft gifts of sleep conclude the day,
And stretched on bulks, as usual, poets lay.
Why should I sing what bards the nightly muse
Did slumbering visit, and convey to stews;
Who prouder marched, with magistrates in state,
To some famed round-house, ever open gate!
How Henley lay inspired beside a sink,
And to mere mortals seemed a priest in drink:
While others, timely, to the neighbouring Fleet
(Haunt of the muses) made their safe retreat.

Lady Mary Wortley Montagu (1689–1762)

from *Six Town Eclogues*

SATURDAY

The Small-Pox

FLAVIA

The wretched Flavia, on her couch reclined,
Thus breathed the anguish of a wounded mind.
A glass reversed in her right hand she bore;
For now she shunned the face she sought before.
    "How am I changed! alas! how am I grown
A frightful spectre, to myself unknown!
Where's my complexion? where the radiant bloom,
That promised happiness for years to come?
Then, with what pleasure I this face surveyed!
To look once more, my visits oft delayed!
Charmed with the view, a fresher red would rise,
And a new life shot sparkling from my eyes!
Ah! faithless glass, my wonted bloom restore!
Alas! I rave, that bloom is now no more!
    "The greatest good the gods on men bestow,
Even youth itself, to me is useless now.
There was a time (oh! that I could forget!)
When opera-tickets poured before my feet;
And at the Ring, where brightest beauties shine,
The earliest cherries of the spring were mine.
Witness, O Lillie, and thou, Motteux, tell,
How much japan these eyes have made you sell.
With what contempt ye saw me oft despise
The humble offer of the raffled prize;
For at each raffle still the prize I bore,
With scorn rejected, or with triumph wore.
Now beauty's fled, and presents are no more.

"For me the patriot has the House forsook,
And left debates to catch a passing look;
For me the soldier has soft verses writ;
For me the beau has aimed to be a wit.
For me the wit to nonsense was betrayed;
The gamester has for me his dun delayed,
And overseen the card I would have paid.
The bold and haughty by success made vain,
Awed by my eyes, has trembled to complain:
The bashful squire, touched with a wish unknown,
Has dared to speak with spirit not his own:
Fired by one wish, all did alike adore;
Now beauty's fled, and lovers are no more.

"As round the room I turn my weeping eyes,
New unaffected scenes of sorrow rise.
Far from my sight that killing picture bear,
The face disfigure, or the canvas tear!
That picture, which with pride I used to show,
The lost resemblance but upbraids me now.
And thou, my toilette, where I oft have sat,
While hours unheeded passed in deep debate,
How curls should fall, or where a patch to place;
If blue or scarlet best became my face;
Now on some happier nymph your aid bestow;
On fairer heads, ye useless jewels, glow!
No borrowed lustre can my charms restore,
Beauty is fled, and dress is now no more.

"Ye meaner beauties, I permit you shine;
Go, triumph in the hearts that once were mine;
But, midst your triumphs, with confusion know,
'Tis to my ruin all your charms ye owe.
Would pitying heaven restore my wonted mien,
Ye still might move unthought of and unseen.
But oh, how vain, how wretched is the boast
Of beauty faded, and of empire lost!

What now is left but weeping to deplore
My beauty fled, and empire now no more?
   "Ye cruel chymists, what withheld your aid?
Could no pomatums save a trembling maid?
How false and trifling is that art you boast;
No art can give me back my beauty lost!
In tears, surrounded by my friends I lay,
Masked o'er, and trembling at the light of day;
Mirmillo came my fortune to deplore
(A golden-headed cane well carved he bore):
'Cordials,' he cried, 'my spirits must restore!'
Beauty is fled, and spirit is no more!
Galen the grave, officious Squirt was there,
With fruitless grief and unavailing care:
Machaon too, the great Machaon, known
By his red cloak and his superior frown;
'And why,' he cried, 'this grief and this despair?
You shall again be well, again be fair;
Believe my oath' (with that an oath he swore);
False was his oath! my beauty is no more.
   "Cease, hapless maid, no more thy tale pursue,
Forsake mankind, and bid the world adieu.
Monarchs and beauties rule with equal sway;
All strive to serve, and glory to obey:
Alike unpitied when deposed they grow,
Men mock the idol of their former vow.
   "Adieu, ye parks—in some obscure recess,
Where gentle streams will weep at my distress,
Where no false friend will in my grief take part,
And mourn my ruin with a joyful heart;
There let me live in some deserted place,
There hide in shades this lost inglorious face.
Plays, operas, circles, I no more must view!
My toilette, patches, all the world, adieu!"

Elizabeth Tollet (1694–1754)

On the Prospect from Westminster Bridge, March 1750

Caesar! renowned in silence, as in war,
Look down a while from thy maternal star:
See! to the skies what sacred domes ascend,
What ample arches o'er the river bend;
What vills above in rural prospect lie;
Beneath, a street that intercepts the eye,
Where happy Commerce glads the wealthy streams,
And floating castles ride. Is this the Thames,
The scene where brave Cassibelan of yore
Repulsed thy legions on a savage shore?
Britain, 'tis true, was hard to overcome,
Or by the arms, or by the arts, of Rome;
Yet we allow thee ruler of the Sphere,
And last of all resign thy Julian year.

John Bancks (1709–1751)

A Description of London

Houses, churches, mixed together,
Streets unpleasant in all weather;
Prisons, palaces contiguous,
Gates, a bridge, the Thames irriguous.

Gaudy things enough to tempt ye,
Showy outsides, insides empty;
Bubbles, trades, mechanic arts,
Coaches, wheelbarrows and carts.

Warrants, bailiffs, bills unpaid,
Lords of laundresses afraid;
Rogues that nightly rob and shoot men,
Hangmen, aldermen and footmen.

Lawyers, poets, priests, physicians,
Noble, simple, all conditions:
Worth beneath a threadbare cover,
Villainy bedaubed all over.

Women black, red, fair and grey,
Prudes and such as never pray,
Handsome, ugly, noisy, still,
Some that will not, some that will.

Many a beau without a shilling,
Many a widow not unwilling;
Many a bargain, if you strike it:
This is London! How d'ye like it?

Anon. (1739)

Hail, London!

Hail, London! justly queen of cities crowned,
For freedom, wealth, extent, and arts renowned;
No need of fables to enhance thy praise,
No wandering demi-god thy walls to raise:
Let Rome imperial claim an elder date,
And boast her kindred to the Dardan state;
Thy ancient heroes palms as glorious grace,
Thy British founders, and thy Saxon race.
    Our ancestors, in architecture rude,
Built their first towns of rough unchiselled wood;
No veiny marble yet, no Parian stone,
Nor sculptor's art, nor joiner's skill was known;
These by our Roman visitors were taught,
Which they from Greece, and Greece from Egypt brought.
Soon Thames along her rising shores admires
Her stony battlements, and lofty spires;
Sublime Augusta raised her towery head,
Her Albion's pride, and envying neighbour's dread.
Since founded first, a thousand years twice told,
Two thousand suns have annual circles rolled;
Perpetual growth has stretched her ample bound,
Till scarce seven leagues can mete her circuit round.
A hundred temples for devotion rise,
A hundred steeples glitter in the skies.
Lo! in the midst Wren's wonderous pile appears,
Which, like a mountain, its huge bulk uprears;
Such sure to sailors on a distant stream,
The lofty pike of Tenerife must seem.
Muse, mount with easy flight th' aspiring dome,
And let thy eyes o'er the wide prospect roam.
See how the Thames with dimpling motion smiles,
And from all climes presents Augusta spoils:

Eastward behold! a thousand vessels ride,
Which like a floating city crowd her tide.
See the strong bridge connect the distant shores;
The flood beneath through straitening arches roars:
(Above, amazing sight! two lengthening rows
Of lofty buildings a fair street compose);
Still farther east, large as a town, is seen
The Tower, a strong and copious magazine;
There, in becoming order, ranged remain
Arms oft victorious on the hostile plain;
Drums, cannon, swords and bombs inactive sleep,
And thunders brood which Britain's foes shall weep.
Look all around, and note the bustling throng,
How through each street, like waves, they press along.
There stands Th' Exchange ('tis now the busy time),
Resort of merchants drawn from every clime;
Far west remark our monarch's regal seat,
See there the dome where powerful senates meet:
There, Rufus' ancient hall resounds with law!
And there the Abbey strikes religious awe!
Thus London shines in fame the first and best,
May all who labour for her peace be blest!

Samuel Johnson (1709–1784)

from *London*

A POEM IN IMITATION OF JUVENAL'S THIRD SATIRE

Quis ineptae
Tam patiens urbis, tam ferreus ut teneat se?
    —*Juvenal*

Though grief and fondness in my breast rebel,
When injured Thales bids the town farewell,
Yet still my calmer thoughts his choice commend;
I praise the hermit, but regret the friend,
Resolved at length, from vice and London far,
To breathe in distant fields a purer air,
And, fixed on Cambria's solitary shore,
Give to St. David one true Briton more.

For who would leave, unbribed, Hibernia's land,
Or change the rocks of Scotland for the Strand?
There none are swept by sudden fate away,
But all whom hunger spares, with age decay:
Here malice, rapine, accident, conspire,
And now a rabble rages, now a fire;
Their ambush here relentless ruffians lay,
And here the fell attorney prowls for prey;
Here falling houses thunder on your head,
And here a female atheist talks you dead.

While Thales waits the wherry that contains
Of dissipated wealth the small remains,
On Thames's banks, in silent thought we stood,
Where Greenwich smiles upon the silver flood:
Struck with the seat that gave Eliza birth,
We kneel, and kiss the consecrated earth;
In pleasing dreams the blissful age renew,
And call Britannia's glories back to view;
Behold her cross triumphant on the main,

The guard of commerce, and the dread of Spain,
Ere masquerades debauched, excise oppressed,
Or English honour grew a standing jest.

    A transient calm the happy scenes bestow,
And for a moment lull the sense of woe.
At length awaking, with contemptuous frown,
Indignant Thales eyes the neighbouring town.

    Since worth, he cries, in these degenerate days,
Wants even the cheap reward of empty praise;
In those cursed walls, devote to vice and gain,
Since unrewarded Science toils in vain;
Since hope but soothes to double my distress,
And every moment leaves my little less;
While yet my steady steps no staff sustains,
And life still vigorous revels in my veins;
Grant me, kind heaven, to find some happier place,
Where honesty and sense are no disgrace;
Some pleasing bank where verdant osiers play,
Some peaceful vale with nature's paintings gay;
Where once the harassed Briton found repose,
And safe in poverty defied his foes;
Some secret cell, ye powers, indulgent give.
Let—live here, for—has learned to live.
Here let those reign, whom pensions can incite
To vote a patriot black, a courtier white;
Explain their country's dear-bought rights away,
And plead for pirates in the face of day;
With slavish tenets taint our poisoned youth,
And lend a lie the confidence of truth.

    Let such raise palaces, and manors buy,
Collect a tax, or farm a lottery,
With warbling eunuchs fill a licensed stage,
And lull to servitude a thoughtless age.

    Heroes, proceed! what bounds your pride shall hold?
What check restrain your thirst of power and gold?
Behold rebellious virtue quite o'erthrown,

Behold our fame, our wealth, our lives your own.

   To such, a groaning nation's spoils are given,
When public crimes inflame the wrath of heaven:
But what, my friend, what hope remains for me,
Who start at theft, and blush at perjury?
Who scarce forbear, though Britain's Court he sing,
To pluck a titled poet's borrowed wing;
A statesman's logic unconvinced can hear,
And dare to slumber o'er the *Gazetteer;*
Despise a fool in half his pension dressed,
And strive in vain to laugh at H—y's jest.

   Others with softer smiles, and subtler art,
Can sap the principles, or taint the heart;
With more address a lover's note convey,
Or bribe a virgin's innocence away.
Well may they rise, while I, whose rustic tongue
Ne'er knew to puzzle right, or varnish wrong,
Spurned as a beggar, dreaded as a spy,
Live unregarded, unlamented die.
. . .

   By numbers here from shame or censure free,
All crimes are safe, but hated poverty.
This, only this, the rigid law pursues,
This, only this, provokes the snarling muse.
The sober trader at a tattered cloak,
Wakes from his dream, and labours for a joke;
With brisker air the silken courtiers gaze,
And turn the varied taunt a thousand ways.
Of all the griefs that harass the distressed,
Sure the most bitter is a scornful jest;
Fate never wounds more deep the generous heart
Than when a blockhead's insult points the dart.

   Has heaven reserved, in pity to the poor,
No pathless waste, or undiscovered shore;
No secret island in the boundless main?
No peaceful desert yet unclaimed by Spain?

Quick let us rise, the happy seats explore,
And bear oppression's insolence no more.
This mournful truth is everywhere confessed,
Slow rises worth, by poverty depressed:
But here more slow, where all are slaves to gold,
Where looks are merchandise, and smiles are sold;
Where won by bribes, by flatteries implored,
The groom retails the favours of his lord.

   But hark! th' affrighted crowd's tumultuous cries
Roll through the streets, and thunder to the skies;
Raised from some pleasing dream of wealth and power,
Some pompous palace, or some blissful bower,
Aghast you start, and scarce with aching sight
Sustain th' approaching fire's tremendous light;
Swift from pursuing horrors take your way,
And leave your little all to flames a prey;
Then, through the world a wretched vagrant roam,
For where can starving merit find a home?
In vain your mournful narrative disclose,
While all neglect, and most insult your woes.

   Should heaven's just bolts Orgilio's wealth confound,
And spread his flaming palace on the ground,
Swift o'er the land the dismal rumour flies,
And public mournings pacify the skies;
The laureate tribe in servile verse relate,
How virtue wars with persecuting fate;
With well-feigned gratitude the pensioned band
Refund the plunder of the beggared land.
See! while he builds, the gaudy vassals come,
And crowd with sudden wealth the rising dome;
The price of boroughs and of souls restore,
And raise his treasures higher than before.
Now blessed with all the baubles of the great,
The polished marble, and the shining plate,
Orgilio sees the golden pile aspire,
And hopes from angry heaven another fire.

Couldst thou resign the park and play content,
For the fair banks of Severn or of Trent;
There might'st thou find some elegant retreat,
Some hireling senator's deserted seat;
And stretch thy prospects o'er the smiling land,
For less than rent the dungeons of the Strand;
There prune thy walks, support thy drooping flowers,
Direct thy rivulets, and twine thy bowers;
And, while thy grounds a cheap repast afford,
Despise the dainties of a venal lord:
There every bush with nature's music rings,
There every breeze bears health upon its wings;
On all thy hours security shall smile,
And bless thine evening walk and morning toil.

    Prepare for death, if here at night you roam,
And sign your will before you sup from home.
Some fiery fop, with new commission vain,
Who sleeps on brambles till he kills his man;
Some frolic drunkard, reeling from a feast,
Provokes a broil, and stabs you for a jest.
Yet even these heroes, mischievously gay,
Lords of the street, and terrors of the way,
Flushed as they are with folly, youth, and wine,
Their prudent insults to the poor confine;
Afar they mark the flambeau's bright approach,
And shun the shining train, and golden coach.

    In vain, these dangers past, your doors you close,
And hope the balmy blessings of repose:
Cruel with guilt, and daring with despair,
The midnight murderer bursts the faithless bar;
Invades the sacred hour of silent rest,
And leaves, unseen, a dagger in your breast.

    Scarce can our fields, such crowds at Tyburn die,
With hemp the gallows and the fleet supply.
Propose your schemes, ye Senatorian band,
Whose Ways and Means support the sinking land;

Lest ropes be wanting in the tempting spring,
To rig another convoy for the K—g.
  A single jail, in Alfred's golden reign,
Could half the nation's criminals contain;
Fair justice then, without constraint adored,
Held high the steady scale, but dropped the sword;
No spies were paid, no special juries known,
Blest age! but ah! how different from our own!
  Much could I add,—but see the boat at hand,
The tide retiring, calls me from the land:
Farewell!—When youth, and health, and fortune spent,
Thou fly'st for refuge to the wilds of Kent;
And tired like me with follies and with crimes,
In angry numbers warn'st succeeding times;
Then shall thy friend, nor thou refuse his aid,
Still foe to vice, forsake his Cambrian shade;
In virtue's cause once more exert his rage,
Thy satire point, and animate thy page.

Nursery Rhymes (pub. 18th–19th centuries)

London Bridge

London Bridge is falling down,
Falling down, falling down,
London Bridge is falling down,
My fair lady.

Build it up with wood and clay,
Wood and clay, wood and clay,
Build it up with wood and clay,
My fair lady.

Wood and clay will wash away,
Wash away, wash away,
Wood and clay will wash away,
My fair lady.

Build it up with bricks and mortar,
Bricks and mortar, bricks and mortar,
Build it up with bricks and mortar,
My fair lady.

Bricks and mortar will not stay,
Will not stay, will not stay,
Bricks and mortar will not stay,
My fair lady.

Build it up with iron and steel,
Iron and steel, iron and steel,
Build it up with iron and steel,
My fair lady.

Iron and steel will bend and bow,
Bend and bow, bend and bow,
Iron and steel will bend and bow,
My fair lady.

Build it up with silver and gold,
Silver and gold, silver and gold,
Build it up with silver and gold,
My fair lady.

Silver and gold will be stolen away,
Stolen away, stolen away,
Silver and gold will be stolen away,
My fair lady.

Set a man to watch all night,
Watch all night, watch all night,
Set a man to watch all night,
My fair lady.

Suppose the man should fall asleep,
Fall asleep, fall asleep,
Suppose the man should fall asleep,
My fair lady.

Give him a pipe to smoke all night,
Smoke all night, smoke all night,
Give him a pipe to smoke all night,
My fair lady.

Oranges and Lemons

Gay go up, and gay go down,
To ring the bells of London town.

Bull's eyes and targets,
Say the bells of St. Margaret's.

Brickbats and tiles,
Say the bells of St. Giles'.

Halfpence and farthings,
Say the bells of St. Martin's.

Oranges and lemons,
Say the bells of St. Clement's.

Pancakes and fritters,
Say the bells of St. Peter's.

Two sticks and an apple,
Say the bells at Whitechapel.

Old Father Baldpate,
Say the slow bells at Aldgate.

You owe me ten shillings,
Say the bells at St. Helen's.

Pokers and tongs,
Say the bells at St. John's.

Kettles and pans,
Say the bells at St. Ann's.

When will you pay me?
Say the bells at Old Bailey.

When I grow rich,
Say the bells at Shoreditch.

Pray when will that be?
Say the bells at Stepney.

I am sure I don't know,
Says the great bell at Bow.

Here comes a candle to light you to bed,
And here comes a chopper to chop off your head.

"Pussy cat, pussy cat, where have you been?"

Pussy cat, pussy cat, where have you been?
I've been to London to look at the queen.

Pussy cat, pussy cat, what did you there?
I frightened a little mouse under her chair.

"Poussie, poussie, baudrons"

Poussie, poussie, baudrons,
Where hae ye been?
I've been to London,
Seeing the Queen.
Poussie, poussie, baudrons,
What got ye there?
I got a guid fat mousikie,
Rinning up the stair.
Poussie, poussie, baudrons,
What did ye do wi't?
I put it in my meal-poke,
To eat it to my bread.

"Up at Piccadilly oh!"

Up at Piccadilly oh!
The coachman takes his stand,
And when he meets a pretty girl,
He takes her by the hand;
Whip away for ever oh!
Driver away so clever oh!
All the way to Bristol oh!
He drives her four-in-hand.

"See-saw, sacradown"

See-saw, sacradown,
Which is the way to London town?

One foot up and the other foot down,
That is the way to London town.

"Upon Paul's steeple stands a tree"

Upon Paul's steeple stands a tree
As full of apples as may be;
The little boys of London Town
They run with hooks to pull them down:
And then they run from hedge to hedge
Until they come to London Bridge.

"As I was going o'er London Bridge"

As I was going o'er London Bridge,
I heard something crack;
Not a man in all England
Can mend that.

"As I was going o'er London Bridge"

As I was going o'er London Bridge,
And peeped through a nick,
I saw four and twenty ladies
Riding on a stick.

"I had a little hobby horse, it was well shod"

I had a little hobby horse, it was well shod,
It carried me to London, niddety nod,
And when we got to London, we heard a great shout,
Down fell my hobby horse, and I cried out:
Up again, hobby horse, if thou be a beast,

When we get to our town we will have a feast,
And if there be but little, why thou shalt have some,
And dance to the bagpipes and beating of the drum.

Pop Goes the Weasel

Up and down the City Road,
In and out the Eagle,
That's the way the money goes,
Pop goes the weasel!

Half a pound of tuppenny rice,
Half a pound of treacle,
Mix it up and make it nice,
Pop goes the weasel!

Every night when I go out
The monkey's on the table;
Take a stick and knock it off,
Pop goes the weasel!

William Whitehead (1715–1785)

The Sweepers

I sing of sweepers, frequent in thy streets,
Augusta, as the flowers which grace the spring,
Or branches withering in autumnal shades
To form the brooms they wield. Preserved by them
From dirt, from coach-hire, and th' oppressive rheums
Which clog the springs of life, to them I sing,
And ask no inspiration but their smiles.

   Hail, unowned youths, and virgins unendowed!
Whether on bulk begot, while rattled loud
The passing coaches, or th' officious hand
Of sportive link-boy wide around him dashed
The pitchy flame, obstructive of the joy.
Or, more propitious, to the dark retreat
Of round-house owe your birth, where Nature's reign
Revives, and prompted by untaught desire
The mingling sexes share promiscuous love;
And scarce the pregnant female knows to whom
She owes the precious burden, scarce the sire
Can claim, confused, the many-featured child.

   Nor blush that hence your origin we trace:
'Twas thus immortal heroes sprung of old
Strong from the stolen embrace; by such as you,
Unhoused, unclothed, unlettered and unfed,
Were kingdoms modelled, cities taught to rise,
Firm laws enacted, Freedom's rights maintained,
The gods and patriots of an infant world!

   Let others meanly chant in tuneful song
The blackshoe race, whose mercenary tribes,
Allured by halfpence, take their morning stand
Where streets divide, and to their proffered stools
Solicit wandering feet; vain pensioners,
And placemen of the crowd! Not so you pour

Your blessings on mankind; nor traffic vile
Be your employment deemed, ye last remains
Of public spirit, whose laborious hands,
Uncertain of reward, bid kennels know
Their wonted bounds, remove the bordering filth,
And give th' obstructed ordure where to glide.
   What though the pitying passenger bestows
His unextorted boon, must they refuse
The well-earned bounty, scorn th' obtruded ore?
Proud were the thought and vain. And shall not we
Repay their kindly labours, men like them,
With gratitude unsought? I too have oft
Seen in our streets the withered hands of age
Toil in th' industrious task; and can we there
Be thrifty niggards? Haply they have known
Far better days, and scattered liberal round
The scanty pittance we afford them now.
Soon from this office grant them their discharge,
Ye kind church-wardens! take their meagre limbs
Shivering with cold and age, and wrap them warm
In those blest mansions Charity has raised.
   But you of younger years, while vigour knits
Your labouring sinews, urge the generous task.
Nor lose in fruitless brawls the precious hours
Assigned to toil. Be your contentions who
First in the darkening streets, when Autumn sheds
Her earliest showers, shall clear th' obstructed pass;
Or last shall quit the field when Spring distils
Her moistening dews, prolific there in vain.
So may each lusty scavenger, ye fair,
Fly ardent to your arms; and every maid,
Ye gentle youths, be to your wishes kind.
Whether Ostrea's fishy fumes allure
As Venus' tresses fragrant, or the sweets
More mild and rural from her stall who toils
To feast the sages of the Samian school.

Nor ever may your hearts, elate with pride,
Desert this sphere of love; for should ye, youths,
When blood boils high, and some more lucky chance
Has swelled your stores, pursue the tawdry band
That romp from lamp to lamp, for health expect
Disease, for fleeting pleasure foul remorse,
And daily, nightly, agonising pains.
In vain you call for Aesculapius' aid
From White-cross alley, or the azure posts
Which beam through Haydon-yard; the god demands
More ample offerings, and rejects your prayer.
   And you, ye fair, O let me warn your breasts
To shun deluding men: for some there are,
Great lords of countries, mighty men of war,
And well-dressed courtiers, who with leering eye
Can in the face begrimed with dirt discern
Strange charms, and pant for Cynthia in a cloud.
   But let Lardella's fate avert your own.
Lardella once was fair, the early boast
Of proud St. Giles's, from its ample pound
To where the column points the seven-fold day.
Happy, thrice happy, had she never known
A street more spacious! but ambition led
Her youthful footsteps, artless, unassured,
To Whitehall's fatal pavement. There she plied
Like you the active broom. At sight of her
The coachman dropped his lash, the porter oft
Forgot his burden, and with wild amaze
The tall well-booted sentry, armed in vain,
Leaned from his horse to gaze upon her charms.
   But Fate reserved her for more dreadful ills:
A lord beheld her, and with powerful gold
Seduced her to his arms. What can not gold
Effect, when aided by the matron's tongue
Long tried and practised in the trade of vice,
Against th' unwary innocent! A while

Dazzled with splendour, giddy with the height
Of unexperienced greatness, she looks down
With thoughtless pride, nor sees the gulf beneath.
But soon, too soon, the high-wrought transport sinks
In cold indifference, and a newer face
Alarms her restless lover's fickle heart.
Distressed, abandoned, whither shall she fly?
How urge her former task, and brave the winds
And piercing rains with limbs whose daintier sense
Shrinks from the evening breeze? nor has she now,
Sweet Innocence, thy calmer heart-felt aid
To solace or support the pangs she feels.
    Why should the weeping Muse pursue her steps
Through the dull round of infamy, through haunts
Of public lust, and every painful stage
Of ill-feigned transport, and uneasy joy?
Too sure she tried them all, till her sunk eye
Lost its last languish, and the bloom of health,
Which revelled once on beauty's virgin cheek,
Was pale disease, and meagre penury.
Then loathed, deserted, to her life's last pang
In bitterness of soul she cursed in vain
Her proud betrayer, cursed her fatal charms,
And perished in the streets from whence she sprung.

Oliver Goldsmith (1729–1774)

Description of an Author's Bedchamber

Where the Red Lion, flaring o'er the way,
Invites each passing stranger that can pay;
Where Calvert's butt, and Parson's black champagne,
Regale the drabs and bloods of Drury Lane;
There in a lonely room, from bailiffs snug,
The Muse found Scroggen stretched beneath a rug.
A window, patched with paper, lent a ray
That dimly showed the state in which he lay;
The sanded floor that grits beneath the tread,
The humid wall with paltry pictures spread;
The royal game of goose was there in view,
And the twelve rules the royal martyr drew;
The Seasons framed with listing found a place,
And brave Prince William showed his lamp-black face.
The morn was cold; he views with keen desire
The rusty grate unconscious of a fire;
With beer and milk arrears the frieze was scored,
And five cracked tea-cups dressed the chimney board;
A nightcap decked his brows instead of bay,
A cap by night—a stocking all the day!

William Cowper (1731–1800)

from *The Task*

from BOOK I: THE SOFA

But though true worth and virtue, in the mild
And genial soil of cultivated life
Thrive most, and may perhaps thrive only there,
Yet not in cities oft. In proud and gay
And gain-devoted cities; thither flow,
As to a common and most noisome sewer,
The dregs and feculence of every land.
In cities foul example on most minds
Begets its likeness. Rank abundance breeds
In gross and pampered cities sloth and lust,
And wantonness and gluttonous excess.
In cities, vice is hidden with most ease,
Or seen with least reproach; and virtue, taught
By frequent lapse, can hope no triumph there
Beyond th' achievement of successful flight.
I do confess them nurseries of the arts,
In which they flourish most. Where in the beams
Of warm encouragement, and in the eye
Of public note they reach their perfect size.
Such London is, by taste and wealth proclaimed
The fairest capital of all the world,
By riot and incontinence the worst.
There, touched by Reynolds, a dull blank becomes
A lucid mirror, in which nature sees
All her reflected features. Bacon there
Gives more than female beauty to a stone,
And Chatham's eloquence to marble lips.
Nor does the chisel occupy alone
The powers of sculpture, but the style as much;
Each province of her art her equal care.

With nice incision of her guided steel
She ploughs a brazen field, and clothes a soil
So sterile with what charms soe'er she will,
The richest scenery and the loveliest forms.
Where finds philosophy her eagle eye
With which she gazes at yon burning disk
Undazzled, and detects and counts his spots?
In London; where her implements exact
With which she calculates, computes and scans
All distance, motion, magnitude, and now
Measures an atom, and now girds a world?
In London; where has commerce such a mart,
So rich, so thronged, so drained, and so supplied
As London, opulent, enlarged, and still
Increasing London? Babylon of old
Not more the glory of the earth, than she
A more accomplished world's chief glory now.
    She has her praise. Now mark a spot or two
That so much beauty would do well to purge;
And show this queen of cities, that so fair
May yet be foul, so witty, yet not wise.
It is not seemly, nor of good report
That she is slack in discipline: more prompt
T' avenge than to prevent the breach of law;
That she is rigid in denouncing death
On petty robbers, and indulges life
And liberty, and oft-times honour too,
To peculators of the public gold;
That thieves at home must hang, but he that puts
Into his overgorged and bloated purse
The wealth of Indian provinces, escapes.
Nor is it well, nor can it come to good,
That through profane and infidel contempt
Of holy writ, she has presumed t' annul
And abrogate, as roundly as she may,
The total ordonnance and will of God;

Advancing fashion to the post of truth,
And centering all authority in modes
And customs of her own, till sabbath rites
Have dwindled into unrespected forms,
And knees and hassocks are well-nigh divorced.
   God made the country, and man made the town.
What wonder then, that health and virtue, gifts
That can alone make sweet the bitter draught
That life holds out to all, should most abound
And least be threatened in the fields and groves?
Possess ye therefore, ye who, borne about
In chariots and sedans, know no fatigue
But that of idleness, and taste no scenes
But such as art contrives, possess ye still
Your element; there only ye can shine,
There only minds like yours can do no harm.
Our groves were planted to console at noon
The pensive wanderer in their shades. At eve
The moon-beam gliding softly in between
The sleeping leaves, is all the light they wish,
Birds warbling, all the music. We can spare
The splendour of your lamps; they but eclipse
Our softer satellite. Your songs confound
Our more harmonious notes. The thrush departs
Scared, and th' offended nightingale is mute.
There is a public mischief in your mirth,
It plagues your country. Folly such as your's
Graced with a sword, and worthier of a fan,
Has made, which enemies could ne'er have done,
Our arch of empire, steadfast but for you,
A mutilated structure, soon to fall.

Charles Jenner (1736–1774)

from *Town Eclogues*

from TIME WAS

The spring had now enlivened every scene,
And clad the dusky park in partial green;
Gay opening buds peeped through the winter rust,
And kindly showers half washed off their dust.

On a dull day which, every week, affords
A glut of 'prentices, in bags and swords;
When sober families resort to prayer,
And cits take in their weekly meal of air;
Whilst, eastward of St. Paul's, the well-dressed spark
Runs two long miles, to saunter in the Park:
Prudentio strolling down the mall was seen,
To loll upon a bench, and vent his spleen:
He meets Avaro on the accustomed seat,
And thus, in grumbling strains, the veterans greet.

AVARO
Well met, Prudentio—Come man, sit you down;
How fare you?

PRUDENTIO
Sick, of this confounded town.
. . .
Time was, when tradesmen laid up what they gained,
And frugally a family maintained;
When they took stirring house-wives for their spouses,
To keep up prudent order in their houses;
Who thought no scorn, at night to sit them down,
And make their children's clothes, or mend their own;
Would Polly's coat to younger Bess transfer,
And make their caps without a milliner:
But now a-shopping half the day they're gone,

To buy five hundred things, and pay for none;
Whilst Miss despises all domestic rules,
But lisps the French of Hackney boarding schools;
And every lane around Whitechapel bars
Resounds with screaming notes, and harsh guitars.

PRUDENTIO
Time was too, when the prudent dames would stay
Till Christmas holidays to see a play,
And met at cards, at that glad time alone,
In friendly setts of loo or cheap pope-joan;
Now, every lady writes her invitations
For weekly routs, to all her wise relations,
And every morning teems with fresh delights;
They run the city over, seeing sights;
Then hurry to the play as night approaches,
And spend their precious time in hackney-coaches.

AVARO
Hence spring assemblies with such uncouth names,
At Deptford, Wapping, Rotherhithe, and Shad-Thames,
Where every month the powdered white-gloved sparks,
Spruce haberdashers, pert attornies' clerks,
With deep-enamoured 'prentices, prefer
Their suit to many a sighing millener:
In scrape of plays their passions they impart,
With all the awkward bows they learn from Hart.
'Tis here they learn their genius to improve,
And throw by Wingate for the *Art of Love;*
They frame the acrostic deep, and rebus terse,
And fill the day-book with enamoured verse;
Even learned Fenning on his vacant leaves,
The ill-according epigram receives,
And Cocker's margin hobbling sonnets grace
To Delia, measuring out a yard of lace.

PRUDENTIO

'Tis true, my friend; and thus throughout the nation
Prevails this general love of dissipation:
It matters little where their sports begin,
Whether at Arthur's, or the Bowl and Pin;
Whether they tread the gay Pantheon's round,
Or play at skittles at St. Giles's pound;
The self-same idle spirit drags them on,
And peer and porter are alike undone:
Whilst thoughtless imitation leads the way,
And laughs at all the grave or wise can say.

from THE POET

In vain, alas, shall city bards resort,
For pastoral images, to Tottenham Court;
Fat droves of sheep, consigned from Lincoln fens,
That swearing drovers beat to Smithfield pens,
Give faint ideas of Arcadian plains,
With bleating lambkins and with piping swains.
I've heard of Pope, of Philips and of Gay;
They wrote not pastorals in the king's highway:
On Thames' smooth banks, they framed the rural song,
And wandered free, the tufted groves among;
Culled every flower the fragrant mead affords,
And wrote in solitude, and dined with lords.
Alas for me! what prospects can I find
To raise poetic ardour in my mind?
Where'er around I cast my wandering eyes,
Long burning rows of fetid bricks arise,
And nauseous dunghills swell in mouldering heaps,
Whilst the fat sow beneath their covert sleeps.
I spy no verdant glade, no gushing rill,
No fountain bubbling from the rocky hill;

But stagnant pools adorn our dusty plains,
Where half-starved cows wash down their meal of grains.
No traces here of sweet simplicity,
No lowing herd winds gently o'er the lea,
No tuneful nymph, with cheerful roundelay,
Attends to milk her kine, at close of day;
But droves of oxen through yon clouds appear,
With noisy dogs and butchers in their rear,
To give poetic fancy small relief,
And tempt the hungry bard with thoughts of beef.
From helps like these, how very small my hopes!
My pastorals, sure, will never equal Pope's.
Since, then, no images adorn the plain,
But what are found as well in Gray's Inn Lane,
Since dust and noise inspire no thought serene,
And three-horse stages little mend the scene,
I'll stray no more to seek the vagrant muse,
But even go write at home, and save my shoes.

Anna Letitia Barbauld (1743–1825)

Song for the London Volunteers

Midst golden streets of commerce
Why shines the blaze of arms?
The human hive is stirring;
What cause its peace alarms?

From desk and counter thronging,
From civic feasts and halls,
The Londoners come pouring,
For hark! their country calls.

The thunder of the battle
To them is new and strange;
They're used to the hurry of traffic
And buzz of the crowded 'Change.

They seek not pay or plunder,
They pray that wars may cease;
Their joy is not in slaughter,
For they are sons of peace.

Yet, Frenchmen, dread the onset
When men like these unite;
For they have sworn to perish
Or vanquish you in fight.

Of this land so fair and goodly
Which your ambition craves,
No foot they mean to yield you
But what will find you graves.

Than all your boasted tactics
More strength the thought will lend
That brother stands by brother,
And friend supports his friend.

With tears and blessing covered
Of mothers and of wives,
They go to sell full dearly
Such dearly valued lives.

Their infants smile to see them
In such uncouth attire;
No tongue can tell the fury
Those artless smiles inspire.

Round many an altar kneeling
With fervent lip and eye,
Lo! sires and virgins pleading;
Such prayers ascend on high.

Now sound the trumpets cheerly,
Let all your banners wave;
The Londoners are marching
To glory or a grave.

West End Fair

Dame Charity one day was tired
With nursing of her children three,—
    So might you be
If you had nursed and nursed so long
    A little squalling throng;—
So she, like any earthly lady,
Resolved for once she'd have a play-day.

"I cannot always go about
To hospitals and prisons trudging,
    Or fag from morn to night
    Teaching to spell and write
    A barefoot rout,
Swept from the streets by poor Lancaster,
    My sub-master.

"That Howard ran me out of breath,
And Thornton and a hundred more
    Will be my death:
The air is sweet, the month is gay,
And I," said she, "must have a holiday."

So said, she doffed her robes of brown
In which she commonly is seen,—
    Like French Beguine,—
And sent for ornaments to town:
And Taste in Flavia's form stood by,
Penciled her eyebrows, curled her hair,
Disposed each ornament with care,
And hung her round with trinkets rare,—
She scarcely, looking in the glass,
    Knew her own face.

So forth she sallied, blithe and gay,
And met dame Fashion by the way;
And many a kind and friendly greeting

Passed on their meeting:
Nor let the fact your wonder move,
Abroad, and on a gala-day,
Fashion and she are hand and glove.

So on they walked together;
    Bright was the weather;
Dame Charity was frank and warm;
But being rather apt to tire,
    She leant on Fashion's arm.

And now away for West End fair,
Where whiskey, chariot, coach, and chair,
    Are all in requisition.
    In neat attire the Graces
Behind the counters take their places,
    And humbly do petition
To dress the booths with flowers and sweets,
    As fine as any May-day,
Where Charity with Fashion meets,
    And keeps her play-day.

Charles Dibdin (1745?–1814)

The Jolly Young Waterman

And did you not hear of a jolly young waterman,
    Who at Blackfriars Bridge used to ply?
He feathered his oars with such skill and dexterity,
    Winning each heart and delighting each eye.
He looked so neat and rowed so steadily,
The maidens all flocked to his boat so readily,
And he eyed the young rogues with so charming an air,
That this waterman ne'er was in want of a fare.

What sights of fine folks he rowed in his wherry,
    'Twas cleaned out so nice and so painted withal;
He was always first oars when the fine city ladies
    In a party to Ranelagh went, or Vauxhall.
And oftentimes would they be giggling and leering,
But 'twas all one to Tom, their jibing and jeering;
For loving or liking he little did care,
For this waterman ne'er was in want of a fare.

And yet but to see how strangely things happen,
    As he rowed along thinking of nothing at all,
He was plied by a damsel so lovely and charming,
    That she smiled and so straightway in love did he fall.
And would this young damsel but banish his sorrow,
He'd wed her tonight, before tomorrow;
And how should this waterman ever know care,
When he's married and never in want of a fare?

Poll of Wapping

Your London girls, with all their airs,
Must strike to Poll of Wapping Stairs,
   No tighter lass is going,
From Iron Gate to Limehouse Hole
You'll never meet a kinder soul:
   Not while the Thames is flowing.

And sing Pull away, pull away, Pull! I say,
   Not while the Thames is flowing!

Her father, he's a hearty dog,
Poll makes his flip and serves his grog,
   And never stints his measure;
She minds full well the house affairs,
She seldom drinks, and never swears;
   And isn't that a pleasure?

And sing Pull away, pull away, Pull! I say,
   Not while the Thames is flowing!

And when we wed, the happy time,
The bells of Wapping all shall chime;
   And, ere we go to Davy,
The girls like her shall work and sing,
The boys like me shall serve the King,
   On board Old England's Navy!

And sing Pull away, pull away, Pull! I say,
   Not while the Thames is flowing!

Hannah More (1745–1833)

from *The Gin-Shop; or, A Peep into Prison*

Come, neighbour, take a walk with me
    Through many a London street,
And see the cause of penury
    In hundreds we shall meet.

We shall not need to travel far—
    Behold that great man's door;
He well discerns that idle crew
    From the deserving poor.

He will relieve with liberal hand
    The child of honest thrift;
But where long scores at gin shops stand
    He will withhold his gift.

Behold that shivering female there,
    Who plies her woeful trade!
'Tis ten to one you'll find that gin
    That hopeless wretch has made.

Look down these steps, and view below
    Yon cellar under ground;
There every want and every woe,
    And every sin is found.

Those little wretches, trembling there
    With hunger and with cold,
Were by their parents' love of gin
    To sin and misery sold . . .

To prison dire misfortune oft
    The guiltless debtor brings;
Yet oftener far it will be found
    From gin the misery springs.

See the pale manufacturer there,
   How lank and lean he lies!
How haggard is his sickly cheek,
   How dim his hollow eyes!

He plied the loom with good success,
   His wages still were high;
Twice what the village-labourer gains
   His master did supply.

No book-debts kept him from his cash,
   All paid as soon as due;
His wages on the Saturday
   To fail he never knew.

How amply had his gains sufficed,
   On wife and children spent!
But all must for his pleasures go;
   All to the gin shop went.

See that apprentice, young in years,
   But hackneyed long in sin;
What made him rob his master's till?
   Alas! 'twas love of gin.

That serving-man—I knew him once,
   So jaunty, spruce and smart!
Why did he steal, then pawn the plate?
   'Twas gin ensnared his heart.

But hark! what dismal sound is that?
   'Tis Saint Sepulchre's bell!
It tolls, alas! for human guilt,
   Some malefactor's knell.

O! woeful sound, O! what could cause
   Such punishment and sin?
Hark! hear his words, he owns the cause—
   Bad company and gin.

And when the future lot is fixed
   Of darkness, fire and chains,
How can the drunkard hope to 'scape
   Those everlasting pains?

For, if the murderer's doomed to woe
   As holy writ declares,
The drunkard with self-murderers
   That dreadful portion shares.

Mary Robinson (1757–1800)

London's Summer Morning

  Who has not waked to list the busy sounds
Of summer's morning, in the sultry smoke
Of noisy London? On the pavement hot
The sooty chimney-boy, with dingy face
And tattered covering, shrilly bawls his trade,
Rousing the sleepy housemaid. At the door
The milk-pail rattles, and the tinkling bell
Proclaims the dustman's office; while the street
Is lost in clouds impervious. Now begins
The din of hackney-coaches, waggons, carts;
While tinmen's shops, and noisy trunk-makers,
Knife-grinders, coopers, squeaking cork-cutters,
Fruit-barrows, and the hunger-giving cries
Of vegetable-vendors, fill the air.
Now every shop displays its varied trade,
And the fresh-sprinkled pavement cools the feet
Of early walkers. At the private door
The ruddy housemaid twirls the busy mop,
Annoying the smart 'prentice, or neat girl
Tripping with band-box lightly. Now the sun
Darts burning splendour on the glittering pane,
Save where the canvas awning throws a shade
On the gay merchandise. Now, spruce and trim,
In shops (where beauty smiles with industry)
Sits the smart damsel; while the passenger
Peeps through the window, watching every charm.
Now pastry dainties catch the eye minute
Of humming insects, while the limy snare
Waits to enthral them. Now the lamp-lighter
Mounts the tall ladder, nimbly venturous,
To trim the half-filled lamps, while at his feet
The pot-boy yells discordant! All along

The sultry pavement, the old-clothes-man cries
In tone monotonous, and sidelong views
The area for his traffic: now the bag
Is slyly opened, and the half-worn suit
(Sometimes the pilfered treasure of the base
Domestic spoiler), for one half its worth,
Sinks in the green abyss. The porter now
Bears his huge load along the burning way;
And the poor poet wakes from busy dreams,
To paint the summer morning.

William Blake (1757–1827)

Holy Thursday

'Twas on a Holy Thursday, their innocent faces clean,
The children walking two and two in red and blue and green;
Grey-headed beadles walked before, with wands as white as snow,
Till into the high dome of Paul's they like Thames waters flow.

Oh what a multitude they seemed, these flowers of London town!
Seated in companies they sit, with radiance all their own.
The hum of multitudes was there, but multitudes of lambs,
Thousands of little boys and girls raising their innocent hands.

Now like a mighty wind they raise to heaven the voice of song,
Or like harmonious thunderings the seats of Heaven among.
Beneath them sit the aged men, wise guardians of the poor:
Then cherish pity, lest you drive an angel from your door.

The Chimney Sweeper

When my mother died I was very young,
And my father sold me while yet my tongue
Could scarcely cry *'weep 'weep, 'weep 'weep!*
So your chimneys I sweep, and in soot I sleep.

There's little Tom Dacre, who cried when his head,
That curled like a lamb's back, was shaved; so I said,
"Hush Tom, never mind it, for when your head's bare,
You know that the soot cannot spoil your white hair."

And so he was quiet, and that very night,
As Tom was asleeping he had such a sight—
That thousands of sweepers, Dick, Joe, Ned, and Jack,
Were all of them locked up in coffins of black;

And by came an angel, who had a bright key,
And he opened the coffins and set them all free;
Then down a green plain leaping, laughing, they run,
And wash in a river and shine in the sun.

Then naked and white, all their bags left behind,
They rise upon clouds and sport in the wind.
And the angel told Tom, if he'd be a good boy,
He'd have God for his father and never want joy.

And so Tom awoke, and we rose in the dark,
And got with our bags and our brushes to work.
Though the morning was cold, Tom was happy and warm;
So if all do their duty, they need not fear harm.

London

I wander through each chartered street,
Near where the chartered Thames does flow,
And mark in every face I meet
Marks of weakness, marks of woe.

In every cry of every man,
In every infant's cry of fear,
In every voice, in every ban,
The mind-forged manacles I hear.

How the chimney-sweeper's cry
Every blackening church appalls,
And the hapless soldier's sigh
Runs in blood down palace walls;

But most through midnight streets I hear
How the youthful harlot's curse
Blasts the new-born infant's tear,
And blights with plagues the marriage hearse.

from *Jerusalem*

from PLATE 12

What are those golden builders doing? Where was the burying-place
Of soft Ethinthus? Near Tyburn's fatal tree? Is that
Mild Zion's Hill's most ancient promontory, near mournful
Ever-weeping Paddington? Is that Calvary & Golgotha
Becoming a building of pity & compassion? Lo!
The stones are pity and the bricks well-wrought affections,
Enamelled with love & kindness, & the tiles engraven gold,
Labour of merciful hands. The beams & rafters are forgiveness;
The mortar & cement of the work, tears of honesty; the nails
And the screws & iron braces are well-wrought blandishments,
And well-contrived words, firm fixing, never forgotten,
Always comforting the remembrance; the floors, humility,
The ceilings, devotion; the hearths, thanksgiving.
Prepare the furniture, O Lambeth, in thy pitying looms!
The curtains, woven tears & sighs, wrought into lovely forms
For comfort. There the secret furniture of Jerusalem's chamber
Is wrought; Lambeth! the Bride, the Lamb's wife loveth thee:
Thou art one with her & knowest not of self in thy supreme joy.
Go on, builders in hope, though Jerusalem wanders far away
Without the gate of Los, among the dark Satanic wheels.
. . .

from PLATE 27

The fields from Islington to Marybone,
To Primrose Hill and Saint John's Wood,
    Were builded over with pillars of gold,
And there Jerusalem's pillars stood.

    Her little ones ran on the fields,
The Lamb of God among them seen,
    And fair Jerusalem his bride,
Among the little meadows green.

Pancras & Kentish Town repose
Among her golden pillars high,
   Among her golden arches which
Shine upon the starry sky.

   The Jews-Harp House & the Green Man,
The ponds where boys to bathe delight,
   The fields of cows by Willan's farm,
Shine in Jerusalem's pleasant sight.

   She walks upon our meadows green,
The Lamb of God walks by her side,
   And every English child is seen
Children of Jesus & his Bride,

   Forgiving trespasses and sins,
Lest Babylon with cruel Og,
   With Moral & Self-righteous Law
Should crucify in Satan's Synagogue!

   What are those golden builders doing
Near mournful ever-weeping Paddington,
   Standing above that mighty ruin
Where Satan the first victory won,

   Where Albion slept beneath the fatal tree
And the Druid's golden knife
   Rioted in human gore,
In offerings of human life?

   They groaned aloud on London Stone,
They groaned aloud on Tyburn's brook;
   Albion gave his deadly groan,
And all the Atlantic mountains shook.

   Albion's Spectre from his loins
Tore forth in all the pomp of war,
   Satan his name; in flames of fire
He stretched his Druid pillars far.

Jerusalem fell from Lambeth's Vale,
Down through Poplar & Old Bow,
    Through Maldon & across the sea,
In war & howling, death & woe.
    . . .

from PLATE 34

I behold London, a human awful wonder of God.
He says, "Return, Albion, return, I give myself for thee.
My streets are my Ideas of Imagination.
Awake, Albion, awake, and let us awake up together.
My houses are thoughts; my Inhabitants, Affections,
The children of my thoughts walking within my blood-vessels,
Shut from my nervous form which sleeps, upon the verge of Beulah,
In dreams of darkness, while my vegetating blood, in veiny pipes
Rolls dreadful through the furnaces of Los, and the mills of Satan.
For Albion's sake, and for Jerusalem thy Emanation
I give myself, and these my brethren give themselves for Albion."
So spoke London, immortal Guardian. I heard in Lambeth's shades:
In Felpham I heard and saw the visions of Albion;
I write in South Molton Street, what I both see and hear
In regions of Humanity, in London's opening streets.
    . . .

from PLATE 83

"Our father Albion's land! Oh it was a lovely land! & the Daughters of Beulah
Walked up and down in its green mountains. But Hand is fled
Away, & mighty Hyle, & after them Jerusalem is gone. Awake,
Highgate's heights & Hampstead's, to Poplar, Hackney & Bow,
To Islington & Paddington & the brook of Albion's river.
We builded Jerusalem as a City & a Temple; from Lambeth
We began our foundations, lovely Lambeth! O lovely hills
Of Camberwell, we shall behold you no more in glory & pride,

For Jerusalem lies in ruins & the Furnaces of Los are builded there.
You are now shrunk up to a narrow rock in the midst of the sea;
But here we build Babylon on Euphrates, compelled to build
And to inhabit, our little ones to clothe in armour of the gold
Of Jerusalem's cherubims, & to forge them swords of her altars.
I see London blind & age-bent begging through the streets
Of Babylon, led by a child: his tears run down his beard.
The voice of wandering Reuben echoes from street to street
In all the cities of the nations; Paris, Madrid, Amsterdam.
The corner of Broad Street weeps, Poland Street languishes;
To Great Queen Street & Lincoln's Inn, all is distress & woe . . ."

Joanna Baillie (1762–1851)

London

It is a goodly sight through the clear air,
From Hampstead's heathy height to see at once
England's vast capital in fair expanse,–
Towers, belfries, lengthened streets, and structures fair.
St. Paul's high dome amidst the vassal bands
Of neighbouring spires, a regal chieftain stands;
And over fields of ridgy roofs appear,
With distance softly tinted, side by side
In kindred grace, like twain of sisters dear,
The towers of Westminster, her Abbey's pride:
While far beyond the hills of Surrey shine
Through thin soft haze, and show their wavy line.
Viewed thus, a goodly sight! but when surveyed
Through denser air when moistened winds prevail,
In her grand panoply of smoke arrayed,
While clouds aloft in heavy volumes sail,
She is sublime. She seems a curtained gloom
Connecting heaven and earth,–a threatening sign of doom.
With more than natural height, reared in the sky,
'Tis then St. Paul's arrests the wondering eye;
The lower parts in swathing mist concealed,
The higher through some half-spent shower revealed,
So far from earth removed, that well, I trow,
Did not its form man's artful structure show,
It might some lofty alpine peak be deemed,–
The eagle's haunt, with cave and crevice seamed.
Stretched wide on either hand, a rugged screen
In lurid dimness, nearer streets are seen
Like shoreward billows of a troubled main
Arrested in their rage. Through drizzly rain
Cataracts of tawny sheen pour from the skies,
Of furnace smoke black curling columns rise,

And many-tinted vapours slowly pass
O'er the wide draping of that pictured mass.
So shows by day this grand imperial town,
And, when o'er all the night's black stole is thrown,
The distant traveller doth with wonder mark
Her luminous canopy athwart the dark,
Cast up, from myriads of lamps that shine
Along her streets in many a starry line,
He wondering looks from his yet distant road
And thinks the northern streamers are abroad.
"What hollow sound is that?" Approaching near,
The roar of many wheels breaks on his ear.
It is the flood of human life in motion!
It is the voice of a tempestuous ocean!
With sad but pleasing awe his soul is filled;
Scarce heaves his breast, and all within is stilled,
As many thoughts and feelings cross his mind,—
Thoughts, mingled, melancholy, undefined,
Of restless, reckless man, and years gone by,
And time fast wending to eternity.

William Wordsworth (1770–1850)

The Farmer of Tilsbury Vale

'Tis not for the unfeeling, the falsely refined,
The squeamish in taste, and the narrow of mind,
And the small critic wielding his delicate pen,
That I sing of old Adam, the pride of old men.

He dwells in the centre of London's wide Town;
His staff is a sceptre—his grey hairs a crown;
And his bright eyes look brighter, set off by the streak
Of the unfaded rose that still blooms on his cheek.

'Mid the dews, in the sunshine of morn,—'mid the joy
Of the fields, he collected that bloom, when a boy;
That countenance there fashioned, which, spite of a stain
That his life hath received, to the last will remain.

A Farmer he was; and his house far and near
Was the boast of the country for excellent cheer:
How oft have I heard in sweet Tilsbury Vale
Of the silver-rimmed horn whence he dealt his mild ale!

Yet Adam was far as the farthest from ruin,
His fields seemed to know what their Master was doing;
And turnips, and corn-land, and meadow, and lea,
All caught the infection—as generous as he.

Yet Adam prized little the feast and the bowl,—
The fields better suited the ease of his soul:
He strayed through the fields like an indolent wight,
The quiet of nature was Adam's delight.

For Adam was simple in thought; and the poor,
Familiar with him, made an inn of his door:
He gave them the best that he had,—or, to say
What less may mislead you, they took it away.

Thus thirty smooth years did he thrive on his farm:
The Genius of plenty preserved him from harm:
At length, what to most is a season of sorrow,
His means are run out,—he must beg, or must borrow.

To the neighbours he went,—all were free with their money;
For his hive had so long been replenished with honey,
That they dreamt not of dearth;—He continued his rounds,
Knocked here—and knocked there, pounds still adding to pounds.

He paid what he could with his ill-gotten pelf,
And something, it might be, reserved for himself:
Then (what is too true) without hinting a word,
Turned his back on the country—and off like a bird.

You lift up your eyes!—but I guess that you frame
A judgement too harsh of the sin and the shame;
In him it was scarcely a business of art,
For this he did all in the *ease* of his heart.

To London—a sad emigration I ween—
With his grey hairs he went from the brook and the green;
And there with small wealth but his legs and his hands,
As lonely he stood as a crow on the sands.

All trades, as need was, did old Adam assume,—
Served as stable-boy, errand-boy, porter, and groom.
But nature is gracious, necessity kind,
And, in spite of the shame that may lurk in his mind,

He seems ten birthdays younger, is green and is stout;
Twice as fast as before does his blood run about;
You would say that each hair of his beard was alive,
And his fingers are busy as bees in a hive.

For he's not like an Old Man that leisurely goes
About work that he knows, in a track that he knows;
But often his mind is compelled to demur,
And you guess that the more then his body must stir.

In the throng of the town like a stranger is he,
Like one whose own country's far over the sea;
And Nature, while through the great city he hies,
Full ten times a day takes his heart by surprise.

This gives him the fancy of one that is young,
More of soul in his face than of words on his tongue;
Like a maiden of twenty he trembles and sighs,
And tears of fifteen will come into his eyes.

What's a tempest to him, or the dry parching heats?
Yet he watches the clouds that pass over the streets;
With a look of such earnestness often will stand,
You might think he'd twelve reapers at work in the Strand.

Where proud Covent Garden, in desolate hours
Of snow and hoar-frost, spreads her fruits and her flowers,
Old Adam will smile at the pains that have made
Poor winter look fine in such strange masquerade.

'Mid coaches and chariots, a waggon of straw,
Like a magnet, the heart of old Adam can draw;
With a thousand soft pictures his memory will teem,
And his hearing is touched with the sounds of a dream.

Up the Haymarket hill he oft whistles his way,
Thrusts his hands in a waggon, and smells at the hay;
He thinks of the fields he so often hath mown,
And is happy as if the rich freight were his own.

But chiefly to Smithfield he loves to repair,—
If you pass by at morning, you'll meet with him there.
The breath of the cows you may see him inhale,
And his heart all the while is in Tilsbury Vale.

Now farewell, old Adam! when low thou art laid,
May one blade of grass spring up over thy head;
And I hope that thy grave, wheresoever it be,
Will hear the wind sigh through the leaves of a tree.

The Reverie of Poor Susan

At the corner of Wood Street, when daylight appears,
Hangs a thrush that sings loud, it has sung for three years:
Poor Susan has passed by the spot, and has heard
In the silence of morning the song of the bird.

'Tis a note of enchantment; what ails her? She sees
A mountain ascending, a vision of trees;
Bright volumes of vapour through Lothbury glide,
And a river flows on through the vale of Cheapside.

Green pastures she views in the midst of the dale,
Down which she so often has tripped with her pail;
And a single small cottage, a nest like a dove's,
The one only dwelling on earth that she loves.

She looks, and her heart is in heaven: but they fade,
The mist and the river, the hill and the shade:
The stream will not flow, and the hill will not rise,
And the colours have all passed away from her eyes!

Composed Upon Westminster Bridge, September 3, 1802

Earth has not anything to show more fair:
Dull would he be of soul who could pass by
A sight so touching in its majesty;
This City now doth, like a garment, wear
The beauty of the morning: silent, bare,
Ships, towers, domes, theatres, and temples lie
Open unto the fields, and to the sky;
All bright and glittering in the smokeless air.
Never did sun more beautifully steep
In his first splendour, valley, rock, or hill;
Ne'er saw I, never felt, a calm so deep!
The river glideth at his own sweet will:
Dear God! the very houses seem asleep;
And all that mighty heart is lying still!

from *The Prelude*

There was a time when whatsoe'er is feigned
Of airy palaces and gardens built
By genii of romance, or has in grave
Authentic history been set forth of Rome,
Alcairo, Babylon or Persepolis,
Or given upon report by pilgrim friars
Of golden cities ten months' journey deep
Among Tartarian wilds, fell short, far short,
Of that which I in simpleness believed
And thought of London—held me by a chain
Less strong of wonder and obscure delight.
I know not that herein I shot beyond
The common mark of childhood, but I well
Remember that among our flock of boys
Was one, a cripple from the birth, whom chance
Summoned from school to London—fortunate
And envied traveller! And when he returned,
After short absence, and I first set eyes
Upon his person, verily (though strange
The thing may seem) I was not wholly free
From disappointment to behold the same
Appearance, the same body, not to find
Some change, some beams of glory brought away
From that new region. Much I questioned him,
And every word he uttered on my ears
Fell flatter than a cagèd parrot's note
That answers unexpectedly awry
And mocks the prompter's listening. Marvellous things
My fancy had shaped forth, of sights and shows,
Processions, equipages, lords and dukes,
The King, and the King's palace, and not last
Or least (Heaven bless him!) the renowned Lord Mayor—
Dreams hardly less intense than those which wrought

A change of purpose in young Whittington
When he in friendlessness, a drooping boy,
Sat on a stone, and heard the bells speak out
Articulate music. Above all, one thought
Baffled my understanding: how men lived
Even next-door neighbours (as we say) yet still
Strangers, and knowing not each other's names.

   Oh, wondrous power of words! How sweet they are
According to the meaning which they bring!
Vauxhall and Ranelagh—I then had heard
Of your green groves and wilderness of lamps,
Your gorgeous ladies, fairy cataracts
And pageant fireworks! Nor must we forget
Those other wonders, different in kind
Though scarcely less illustrious in degree:
The river proudly bridged, the giddy top
And Whispering Gallery of St. Paul's, the tombs
Of Westminster, the Giants of Guildhall,
Bedlam and the two figures at its gates,
Streets without end and churches numberless,
Statues with flowery gardens in vast squares,
The Monument and armoury of the Tower.
These fond imaginations of themselves
Had long before given way in season due,
Leaving a throng of others in their stead;
And now I looked upon the real scene,
Familiarly perused it day by day,
With keen and lively pleasure even there
Where disappointment was the strongest, pleased
Through courteous self-submission, as a tax
Paid to the object by prescriptive right—
A thing that ought to be.

           Shall I give way,
Copying the impression of the memory,
(Though things remembered idly do half seem

The work of fancy) shall I, as the mood
Inclines me, here describe for pastime's sake
Some portion of that motley imagery,
A vivid pleasure of my youth, and now,
Among the lonely places that I love,
A frequent daydream for my riper mind?
And first the look and aspect of the place,
The broad highway appearance as it strikes
On strangers of all ages; the quick dance
Of colours, lights, and forms; the Babel din;
The endless stream of men, and moving things;
From hour to hour the illimitable walk
Still among streets, with clouds and sky above;
The wealth, the bustle and the eagerness,
The glittering chariots with their pampered steeds,
Stalls, barrows, porters; midway in the street
The scavenger, who begs with hat in hand;
The labouring hackney-coaches, the rash speed
Of coaches travelling far whirled on with horn
Loud blowing, and the sturdy drayman's team
Ascending from some alley of the Thames
And striking right across the crowded Strand
Till the fore-horse veer round with punctual skill;
Here, there and everywhere a weary throng,
The comers and the goers face to face,
Face after face; the string of dazzling wares,
Shop after shop, with symbols, blazoned names,
And all the tradesman's honours overhead—
Here, fronts of houses, like a title-page,
With letters huge inscribed from top to toe;
Stationed above the door, like guardian saints,
There, allegoric shapes, female or male,
Or physiognomies of real men,
Land-warriors, kings, or admirals of the sea,
Boyle, Shakespeare, Newton, or the attractive head
Of some Scotch doctor, famous in his day.

Meanwhile, the roar continues, till at length,
Escaped as from an enemy, we turn
Abruptly into some sequestered nook
Still as a sheltered place when winds blow loud.
At leisure, thence, through tracts of thin resort
And sights and sounds that come at intervals,
We take our way. A raree-show is here,
With children gathered round; another street
Presents a company of dancing dogs,
Or dromedary with an antic pair
Of monkeys on his back, a minstrel band
Of Savoyards, or, single and alone,
An English ballad-singer. Private courts
Gloomy as coffins, and unsightly lanes
Thrilled by some female vendor's scream (belike
The very shrillest of all London cries),
May then entangle us awhile,
Conducted through those labyrinths unawares
To privileged regions and inviolate
Where from their airy lodges studious lawyers
Look out on waters, walks, and gardens green.

Thence back into the throng, until we reach,
Following the tide that slackens by degrees,
Some half-frequented scene where wider streets
Bring straggling breezes of suburban air.
Here files of ballads dangle from dead walls,
Advertisements of giant-size from high
Press forward in all colours on the sight:
These, bold in conscious merit, lower down,
That—fronted with a most imposing word—
Is peradventure one in masquerade.
As on the broadening causeway we advance,
Behold a face turned up towards us, strong
In lineaments, and red with over-toil.
'Tis one perhaps already met elsewhere,

A travelling cripple, by the trunk cut short
And stumping with his arms. In sailor's garb
Another lies at length beside a range
Of written characters with chalk inscribed
Upon the smooth flat stones. The nurse is here,
The bachelor that loves to sun himself,
The military idler, and the dame
That field-ward takes her walk in decency.

   Now homeward through the thickening hubbub, where
See—among less distinguishable shapes—
The Italian, with his frame of images
Upon his head, with basket at his waist
The Jew, the stately and slow-moving Turk
With freight of slippers piled beneath his arm.
Briefly, we find (if tired of random sights,
And haply to that search our thoughts should turn)
Among the crowd, conspicuous less or more
As we proceed, all specimens of man
Through all the colours which the sun bestows,
And every character of form and face:
The Swede, the Russian; from the genial south
The Frenchman and the Spaniard; from remote
America, the hunter Indian; Moors,
Malays, Lascars, the Tartar and Chinese,
And negro ladies in white muslin gowns.

   At leisure let us view from day to day,
As they present themselves, the spectacles
Within doors: troops of wild beasts, birds and beasts
Of every nature, from all climes convened,
And, next to these, those mimic sights that ape
The absolute presence of reality,
Expressing, as in mirror, sea and land
And what earth is, and what she has to show.
I do not here allude to subtlest craft
By means refined attaining purest ends,

But imitations fondly made in plain
Confession of man's weakness and his loves.
Whether the painter—fashioning a work
To nature's circumambient scenery,
And with his greedy pencil taking in
A whole horizon on all sides—with power
Like that of angels or commissioned spirits
Plant us upon some lofty pinnacle,
Or in a ship on waters (with a world
Of life, and life-like mockery, to east,
To west, beneath, behind us, and before),
Or more mechanic artist represent
By scale exact, in model, wood or clay,
From shading colours also borrowing help,
Some miniature of famous spots and things,
Domestic or the boast of foreign realms:
The Firth of Forth, and Edinborough throned
On crags, fit empress of that mountain land;
St. Peter's Church, or (more aspiring aim)
In microscopic vision, Rome itself;
Or else perhaps some rural haunt, the Falls
Of Tivoli; and high upon that steep
The Temple of the Sibyl—every tree
Through all the landscape, tuft, stone, scratch minute,
And every cottage lurking in the rocks—
All that the traveller sees when he is there.

    Add to these exhibitions, mute and still,
Others of wider scope, where living men,
Music, and shifting pantomimic scenes,
Together joined their multifarious aid
To heighten the allurement. Need I fear
To mention by its name (as in degree
Lowest of these and humblest in attempt,
Though richly graced with honours of its own)
Half-rural Sadler's Wells? Though at that time

Intolerant, as is the way of youth
Unless itself be pleased, I more than once
Here took my seat, and mauger frequent fits
Of irksomeness, with ample recompense
Saw singers, rope-dancers, giants and dwarfs,
Clowns, conjurors, posture-masters, harlequins,
Amid the uproar of the rabblement
Perform their feats. Nor was it mean delight
To watch crude nature work in untaught minds,
To note the laws and progress of belief–
Though obstinate on this way, yet on that
How willingly we travel, and how far!–
To have, for instance, brought upon the scene
The champion, Jack the Giant-killer: lo!
He dons his coat of darkness, on the stage
Walks, and achieves his wonders, from the eye
Of living mortal safe as is the moon
"Hid in her vacant interlunar cave."
Delusion bold!–and faith must needs be coy–
How is it wrought? His garb is black, the word
"Invisible" flames forth upon his chest.
. . .

    I glance but at a few conspicuous marks,
Leaving ten thousand others that do each–
In hall or court, conventicle or shop,
In public room or private, park or street–
With fondness reared on his own pedestal,
Look out for admiration. Folly, vice,
Extravagance in gesture, mien, and dress,
And all the strife of singularity
(Lies to the ear, and lies to every sense),
Of these, and of the living shapes they wear,
There is no end. Such candidates for regard,
Although well pleased to be where they were found,
I did not hunt after or greatly prize,
Nor made unto myself a secret boast

Of reading them with quick and curious eye,
But as a common produce—things that are
Today, tomorrow will be—took of them
Such willing note as, on some errand bound
Of pleasure or of love, some traveller might
(Among a thousand other images)
Of sea-shells that bestud the sandy beach,
Or daisies swarming through the fields in June.

    But foolishness and madness in parade,
Though most at home in this their dear domain,
Are scattered everywhere, no rarities
Even to the rudest novice of the schools.
O friend, one feeling was there which belonged
To this great city by exclusive right—
How often in the overflowing streets
Have I gone forwards with the crowd, and said
Unto myself "The face of everyone
That passes by me is a mystery!"
Thus have I looked, nor ceased to look, oppressed
By thoughts of what and whither, when and how,
Until the shapes before my eyes became
A second-sight procession such as glides
Over still mountains, or appears in dreams,
And all the ballast of familiar life—
The present and the past, hope, fear, all stays,
All laws, of acting, thinking, speaking man—
Went from me, neither knowing me, nor known.
And once, far travelled in such mood, beyond
The reach of common indications, lost
Amid the moving pageant, 'twas my chance
Abruptly to be smitten with the view
Of a blind beggar, who, with upright face,
Stood propped against a wall, upon his chest
Wearing a written paper to explain
The story of the man and who he was.

My mind did at this spectacle turn round
As with the might of waters, and it seemed
To me that in this label was a type
Or emblem of the utmost that we know
Both of ourselves and of the universe;
And, on the shape of this unmoving man,
His fixèd face and sightless eyes, I looked
As if admonished from another world.

    Though reared upon the base of outward things,
These chiefly are such structures as the mind
Builds for itself. Scenes different there are,
Full-formed, which take, with small internal help,
Possession of the faculties: the peace
Of night, for instance, the solemnity
Of nature's intermediate hours of rest
When the great tide of human life stands still,
The business of the day to come unborn,
Of that gone by locked up as in the grave;
The calmness, beauty, of the spectacle,
Sky, stillness, moonshine, empty streets, and sounds
Unfrequent as in deserts; at late hours
Of winter evenings, when unwholesome rains
Are falling hard, with people yet astir,
The feeble salutation from the voice
Of some unhappy woman now and then
Heard as we pass, when no one looks about,
Nothing is listened to. But these I fear
Are falsely catalogued—things that are, are not,
Even as we give them welcome, or assist,
Are prompt or are remiss. What say you then
To times when half the city shall break out
Full of one passion (vengeance, rage, or fear)
To executions, to a street on fire,
Mobs, riots, or rejoicings? From those sights
Take one, an annual festival, the fair

Holden where martyrs suffered in past time,
And named of St. Bartholomew. There see
A work that's finished to our hands, that lays—
If any spectacle on earth can do—
The whole creative powers of man asleep!
For once the muse's help will we implore
And she shall lodge us, wafted on her wings,
Above the press and danger of the crowd,
Upon some showman's platform.

                              What a hell
For eyes and ears, what anarchy and din
Barbarian and infernal—'tis a dream
Monstrous in colour, motion, shape, sight, sound!
Below, the open space, through every nook
Of the wide area, twinkles, is alive
With heads; the midway region and above
Is thronged with staring pictures and huge scrolls,
Dumb proclamations of the prodigies,
And chattering monkeys dangling from their poles,
And children whirling in their roundabouts;
With those that stretch the neck and strain the eyes,
And crack the voice in rivalship (the crowd
Inviting), with buffoons against buffoons
Grimacing, writhing, screaming—him who grinds
The hurdy-gurdy, at the fiddle weaves,
Rattles the salt-box, thumps the kettle-drum,
And him who at the trumpet puffs his cheeks,
The silver-collared negro with his timbrel,
Equestrians, tumblers, women, girls, and boys,
Blue-breeched, pink-vested, and with towering plumes.
All moveables of wonder, from all parts,
Are here: albinos, painted Indians, dwarfs,
The horse of knowledge and the learned pig,
The stone-eater, the man that swallows fire,
Giants, ventriloquists, the invisible girl,

The bust that speaks and moves its goggling eyes,
The wax-work, clock-work, all the marvellous craft
Of modern Merlins, wild beasts, puppet-shows,
All out-o'-the-way, far-fetched, perverted things,
All freaks of nature, all Promethean thoughts
Of man—his dulness, madness, and their feats—
All jumbled up together to make up
This parliament of monsters. Tents and booths
Meanwhile, as if the whole were one vast mill,
Are vomiting, receiving, on all sides,
Men, women, three-years' children, babes in arms.

   Oh, blank confusion, and a type not false
Of what the mighty city is itself
To all except a straggler here and there—
To the whole swarm of its inhabitants—
An undistinguishable world to men,
The slaves unrespited of low pursuits
Living amid the same perpetual flow
Of trivial objects, melted and reduced
To one identity by differences
That have no law, no meaning, and no end—
Oppression under which even highest minds
Must labour, whence the strongest are not free.
But though the picture weary out the eye,
By nature an unmanageable sight,
It is not wholly so to him who looks
In steadiness, who hath among least things
An under-sense of greatest—sees the parts
As parts, but with a feeling of the whole.

James Smith (1775–1839) and Horace Smith (1779–1849)

from *Horace in London*

ODE V: THE JILT

Say, Lucy, what enamoured spark
Now sports thee through the gazing Park
  In new barouche or tandem;
And, as infatuation leads,
Permits his reason and his steeds
  To run their course at random?

Fond youth, those braids of ebon hair,
Which to a face already fair
  Impart a lustre fairer;
Those locks which now invite to love,
Soon unconfined and false shall prove,
  And changeful as the wearer.

Unpractised in a woman's guile,
Thou think'st, perchance, her halcyon smile
  Portends unruffled quiet:
That, ever charming, fond and mild,
No wanton thoughts, or passions wild,
  Within her soul can riot.

Alas! how often shalt thou mourn,
(If nymphs like her, so soon forsworn,
  Be worth a moment's trouble,)
How quickly own, with sad surprise,
The paradise that blessed thine eyes
  Was painted on a bubble.

In her accommodating creed
A lord will always supersede
  A commoner's embraces:
His lordship's love contents the fair,

Until enabled to ensnare
   A nobler prize—his Grace's!

Unhappy are the youths who gaze,
Who feel her beauty's maddening blaze,
   And trust to what she utters!
For me, by sad experience wise,
At rosy cheeks or sparkling eyes,
   My heart no longer flutters.

Chambered in Albany, I view
On every side a jovial crew
   Of Benedictine neighbours.
I sip my coffee, read the news,
I own no mistress but the muse,
   And she repays my labours.

ODE XV: NEW BUILDINGS

Saint George's Fields are fields no more
   The trowel supersedes the plough;
Huge inundated swamps of yore
   Are changed to civic villas now.

The builder's plank, the mason's hod,
   Wide, and more wide extending still,
Usurp the violated sod,
   From Lambeth Marsh to Balaam Hill.

Pert poplars, yew trees, water tubs,
   No more at Clapham meet the eye,
But velvet lawns, acacian shrubs,
   With perfume greet the passer-by.

Thy carpets, Persia, deck our floors,
   Chintz curtains shade the polished pane,
Verandas guard the darkened doors,
   Where dunning Phoebus knocks in vain.

Not thus acquired was Gresham's hoard,
  Who founded London's mart of trade;
Not such thy life, Grimalkin's lord,
  Who Bow's recalling peal obeyed.

In Mark or Mincing Lane confined,
  In cheerful toil they passed the hours;
'Twas theirs to leave their wealth behind,
  To lavish, while we live, is ours.

They gave no treats to thankless kings,
  Many their gains, their wants were few;
They built no house with spacious wings,
  To give their riches pinions too.

Yet sometimes leaving in the lurch
  Sons, to luxurious folly prone,
Their funds rebuilt the parish church—
  Oh! pious waste, to us unknown.

We from our circle never roam,
  Nor ape our sires' eccentric sins;
Our charity begins at home,
  And mostly ends where it begins.

Leigh Hunt (1784–1859)

To Hampstead

Sweet upland, to whose walks, with fond repair,
    Out of thy western slope I took my rise
    Day after day, and on these feverish eyes
Met the moist fingers of the bathing air,—
If health, unearned of thee, I may not share,
    Keep it, I pray thee, where my memory lies,
    In thy green lanes, brown dells, and breezy skies,
Till I return, and find thee doubly fair.

Wait then my coming, on that lightsome land,
    Health, and the Joy that out of nature springs,
        And Freedom's air-blown locks;—but stay with me,
Friendship, frank entering with the cordial hand,
    And Honour, and the Muse with growing wings,
        And Love Domestic, smiling equably.
                 Surrey Jail, August 27, 1813.

Description of Hampstead

A steeple issuing from a leafy rise,
    With farmy fields in front, and sloping green,
    Dear Hampstead, is thy southern face serene,
Silently smiling on approaching eyes.
Within, thine ever-shifting looks surprise,–
    Streets, hills, and dells, trees overhead now seen,
    Now down below, with smoking roofs between,–

A village, revelling in varieties.
Then northward what a range,–with heath and pond,
    Nature's own ground; woods that let mansions through,
And cottaged vales with pillowy fields beyond,
    And clump of darkening pines and prospects blue,
And that clear path through all, where daily meet
Cool cheeks, and brilliant eyes, and morn-elastic feet.

Lord Byron (1788–1824)

from *Childe Harold's Pilgrimage*

from CANTO I

69

    The seventh day this; the jubilee of man.
    London! right well thou know'st the day of prayer:
    Then thy spruce citizen, washed artisan,
    And smug apprentice gulp their weekly air:
    Thy coach of Hackney, whiskey, one-horse chair,
    And humblest gig through sundry suburbs whirl,
    To Hampstead, Brentford, Harrow make repair;
    Till the tired jade the wheel forgets to hurl,
Provoking envious gibe from each pedestrian churl.

70

    Some o'er thy Thamis row the ribboned fair,
    Others along the safer turnpike fly;
    Some Richmond-hill ascend, some scud to Ware,
    And many to the steep of Highgate hie.
    Ask ye, Boeotian shades! the reason why?
    'Tis to the worship of the solemn Horn,
    Grasped in the holy hand of Mystery,
    In whose dread name both men and maids are sworn,
And consecrate the oath with draught, and dance till morn.

from *Don Juan*

from CANTO X

80

. . .

       Juan now was borne,
Just as the day began to wane and darken,
    O'er the high hill which looks with pride or scorn
Towards the great city. Ye who have a spark in
    Your veins of Cockney spirit, smile or mourn
According as you take things well or ill.
Bold Britons, we are now on Shooter's Hill.

81

The sun went down, the smoke rose up, as from
    A half-unquenched volcano, o'er a space
Which well beseemed the "devil's drawing room,"
    As some have qualified that wondrous place.
But Juan felt, though not approaching home,
    As one who, though he were not of the race,
Revered the soil, of those true sons the mother,
Who butchered half the earth and bullied t'other.

82

A mighty mass of brick and smoke and shipping,
    Dirty and dusky, but as wide as eye
Could reach, with here and there a sail just skipping
    In sight, then lost amidst the forestry
Of masts, a wilderness of steeples peeping
    On tiptoe through their sea coal canopy,
A huge, dun cupola, like a foolscap crown
On a fool's head—and there is London town!

from CANTO XI

7

     ... The man who has stood on the Acropolis
       And looked down over Attica, or he
Who has sailed where picturesque Constantinople is,
       Or seen Timbuctoo, or hath taken tea
In small-eyed China's crockery-ware metropolis,
       Or sat amidst the bricks of Nineveh
May not think much of London's first appearance—
But ask him what he thinks of it a year hence?

8

Don Juan had got out on Shooter's Hill,
       Sunset the time, the place the same declivity
Which looks along that vale of good and ill,
       Where London streets ferment in full activity,
While everything around was calm and still,
       Except the creak of wheels, which on their pivot he
Heard, and that bee-like, bubbling, busy hum
Of cities, that boils over with their scum.

9

I say, Don Juan, wrapped in contemplation,
       Walked on behind his carriage o'er the summit,
And lost in wonder of so great a nation,
       Gave way to't, since he could not overcome it.
"And here," he cried, "is Freedom's chosen station.
       Here peals the people's voice, nor can entomb it
Racks, prisons, inquisitions. Resurrection
Awaits it, each new meeting or election.

10

"Here are chaste wives, pure lives. Here people pay
       But what they please, and if that things be dear,
'Tis only that they love to throw away
       Their cash, to show how much they have a year.
Here laws are all inviolate; none lay

Traps for the traveller; every highway's clear,
Here"—he was interrupted by a knife,
With "Damn your eyes! your money or your life!"

11

These freeborn sounds proceeded from four pads
   In ambush laid, who had perceived him loiter
Behind his carriage and like handy lads
   Had seized the lucky hour to reconnoitre,
In which the heedless gentleman who gads
   Upon the road, unless he prove a fighter,
May find himself within that isle of riches
Exposed to lose his life as well as breeches.

12

Juan, who did not understand a word
   Of English, save their shibboleth "God damn!"
And even that he had so rarely heard,
   He sometimes thought 'twas only their "salaam"
Or "God be with you!"—and 'tis not absurd
   To think so, for half English as I am
(To my misfortune), never can I say
I heard them wish "God with you," save that way—

13

Juan yet quickly understood their gesture
   And being somewhat choleric and sudden,
Drew forth a pocket pistol from his vesture
   And fired it into one assailant's pudding,
Who fell, as rolls an ox o'er in his pasture,
   And roared out, as he writhed his native mud in,
Unto his nearest follower or henchman,
"Oh Jack! I'm floored by that 'ere bloody Frenchman!"

14

On which Jack and his train set off at speed,
   And Juan's suite, late scattered at a distance,
Came up, all marvelling at such a deed

And offering as usual late assistance.
Juan, who saw the moon's late minion bleed
    As if his veins would pour out his existence,
Stood calling out for bandages and lint
And wished he had been less hasty with his flint.

15

"Perhaps," thought he, "it is the country's wont
    To welcome foreigners in this way. Now
I recollect some innkeepers who don't
    Differ, except in robbing with a bow,
In lieu of a bare blade and brazen front.
    But what is to be done? I can't allow
The fellow to lie groaning on the road.
So take him up; I'll help you with the load."

16

But ere they could perform this pious duty,
    The dying man cried, "Hold! I've got my gruel!
Oh for a glass of max! We've missed our booty.
    Let me die where I am!" And as the fuel
Of life shrunk in his heart, and thick and sooty
    The drops fell from his death-wound, and he drew ill
His breath, he from his swelling throat untied
A kerchief, crying "Give Sal that!" and died.

17

The cravat stained with bloody drops fell down
    Before Don Juan's feet. He could not tell
Exactly why it was before him thrown,
    Nor what the meaning of the man's farewell.
Poor Tom was once a kiddy upon town,
    A thorough varmint and a real swell,
Full flash, all fancy, until fairly diddled,
His pockets first and then his body riddled.

18

    Don Juan, having done the best he could
      In all the circumstances of the case,
    As soon as "crowner's 'quest" allowed, pursued
      His travels to the capital apace,
    Esteeming it a little hard he should
      In twelve hours' time and very little space
    Have been obliged to slay a freeborn native
    In self-defence. This made him meditative.

19

    He from the world had cut off a great man,
      Who in his time had made heroic bustle.
    Who in a row like Tom could lead the van,
      Booze in the ken, or at the spellken hustle?
    Who queer a flat? Who (spite of Bow Street's ban)
      On the high toby spice so flash the muzzle?
    Who on a lark with black-eyed Sal (his blowing)
    So prime, so swell, so nutty, and so knowing?

20

    But Tom's no more, and so no more of Tom.
      Heroes must die; and by God's blessing 'tis
    Not long before the most of them go home.
      Hail, Thamis, hail! Upon thy verge it is
    That Juan's chariot, rolling like a drum
      In thunder, holds the way it can't well miss,
    Through Kennington and all the other "tons,"
    Which make us wish ourselves in town at once;

21

    Through groves, so called as being void of trees
      (Like *lucus* from no light); through prospects named
    Mount Pleasant, as containing nought to please
      Nor much to climb; through little boxes framed
    Of bricks, to let the dust in at your ease,

With "To be let" upon their doors proclaimed;
Through "Rows" most modestly called "Paradise,"
Which Eve might quit without much sacrifice;

22

Through coaches, drays, choked turnpikes, and a whirl
   Of wheels, and roar of voices and confusion.
Here taverns wooing to a pint of "purl";
   There mails fast flying off like a delusion;
There barber's blocks with periwigs in curl
   In windows; here the lamplighter's infusion
Slowly distilled into the glimmering glass
(For in those days we had not got to gas).

23

Through this and much and more is the approach
   Of travellers to mighty Babylon.
Whether they come by horse or chaise or coach,
   With slight exceptions, all the ways seem one.
I could say more, but do not choose to encroach
   Upon the guidebook's privilege. The sun
Had set some time, and night was on the ridge
Of twilight as the party crossed the bridge.

24

That's rather fine, the gentle sound of Thamis,
   Who vindicates a moment too his stream,
Though hardly heard through multifarious "damme's."
   The lamps of Westminster's more regular gleam,
The breadth of pavement, and yon shrine where Fame is
   A spectral resident, whose pallid beam
In shape of moonshine hovers o'er the pile,
Make this a sacred part of Albion's isle.

25

The Druid's groves are gone—so much the better.
   Stonehenge is not, but what the devil is it?

But Bedlam still exists with its sage fetter,
    That madmen may not bite you on a visit.
The Bench too seats or suits full many a debtor.
    The Mansion House too (though some people quiz it)
To me appears a stiff yet grand erection,
But then the Abbey's worth the whole collection.

26

The line of lights too up to Charing Cross,
    Pall Mall, and so forth, have a coruscation
Like gold as in comparison to dross,
    Matched with the Continent's illumination,
Whose cities night by no means deigns to gloss.
    The French were not yet a lamplighting nation,
And when they grew so, on their new-found lantern,
Instead of wicks, they made a wicked man turn.

27

A row of gentlemen along the streets
    Suspended may illuminate mankind,
As also bonfires made of country seats.
    But the old way is best for the purblind;
The other looks like phosphorus on sheets,
    A sort of *ignis fatuus* to the mind,
Which, though 'tis certain to perplex and frighten,
Must burn more mildly ere it can enlighten.

28

But London's so well lit that if Diogenes
    Could recommence to hunt his honest man,
And found him not amidst the various progenies
    Of this enormous city's spreading spawn,
'Twere not for want of lamps to aid in dodging his
    Yet undiscovered treasure. What I can,
I've done to find the same throughout life's journey,
But see the world is only one attorney.

29

Over the stones still rattling up Pall Mall
    Through crowds and carriages, but waxing thinner
As thundered knockers broke the long-sealed spell
    Of doors 'gainst duns, and to an early dinner
Admitted a small party as night fell,
    Don Juan, our young diplomatic sinner,
Pursued his path and drove past some hotels,
St. James's Palace and St. James's hells.

30

They reached the hotel. Forth streamed from the front door
    A tide of well-clad waiters, and around
The mob stood, and as usual several score
    Of those pedestrian Paphians, who abound
In decent London when the daylight's o'er.
    Commodious but immoral, they are found
Useful, like Malthus, in promoting marriage.
But Juan now is stepping from his carriage

31

Into one of the sweetest of hotels,
    Especially for foreigners and mostly
For those whom favour or whom fortune swells,
    And cannot find a bill's small items costly.
There many an envoy either dwelt or dwells
    (The den of many a diplomatic lost lie),
Until to some conspicuous square they pass
And blazon o'er the door their names in brass.

Percy Bysshe Shelley (1792–1822)

from *Letter to Maria Gisborne*

You are now

In London, that great sea whose ebb and flow
At once is deaf and loud, and on the shore
Vomits its wrecks, and still howls on for more.
Yet in its depth what treasures! You will see
That which was Godwin,—greater none than he
Though fallen—and fallen on evil times—to stand
Among the spirits of our age and land
Before the dread Tribunal of *to come*
The foremost . . . while Rebuke cowers pale and dumb.
You will see Coleridge—he who sits obscure
In the exceeding lustre and the pure
Intense irradiation of a mind
Which, with its own internal lightning blind,
Flags wearily through darkness and despair—
A cloud-encircled meteor of the air,
A hooded eagle among blinking owls.—
You will see Hunt—one of those happy souls
Who are the salt of the Earth, and without whom
This world would smell like what it is, a tomb—
Who is, what others seem—his room no doubt
Is still adorned with many a cast from Shout,
With graceful flowers tastefully placed about,
And coronals of bay from ribbons hung,
And brighter wreaths in neat disorder flung,
The gifts of the most learned among some dozens
Of female friends, sisters-in-law and cousins.
And there is he with his eternal puns,
Which beat the dullest brain for smiles, like duns
Thundering for money at a poet's door.
Alas, it is no use to say "I'm poor!"

Or oft in graver mood, when he will look
Things wiser than were ever read in book,
Except in Shakespeare's wisest tenderness.—
You will see Hogg—and I cannot express
His virtues, though I know that they are great,
Because he locks, then barricades the gate
Within which they inhabit—of his wit
And wisdom, you'll cry out when you are bit.
He is a pearl within an oyster shell,
One of the richest of the deep. And there
Is English Peacock, with his mountain fair,
Turned into a Flamingo, that shy bird
That gleams i' the Indian air—have you not heard
When a man marries, dies, or turns Hindoo,
His best friends hear no more of him?—but you
Will see him, and will like him too, I hope,
With the milk-white Snowdonian antelope
Matched with this cameleopard—his fine wit
Makes such a wound, the knife is lost in it;
A strain too learned for a shallow age,
Too wise for selfish bigots—let his page,
Which charms the chosen spirits of the time,
Fold itself up for the serener clime
Of years to come, and find its recompense
In that just expectation.—Wit and sense,
Virtue and human knowledge, all that might
Make this dull world a business of delight,
Are all combined in Horace Smith.—And these,
With some exceptions, which I need not tease
Your patience by descanting on,—are all
You and I know in London.

from *Peter Bell the Third*

PART III

Hell

Hell is a city much like London—
   A populous and a smoky city;
There are all sorts of people undone,
And there is little or no fun done;
   Small justice shown, and still less pity.

There is a Castles, and a Canning,
   A Cobbett, and a Castlereagh;
All sorts of caitiff corpses planning
All sorts of cozening for trepanning
   Corpses less corrupt than they.

There is a ——, who has lost
   His wits, or sold them, none knows which;
He walks about a double ghost,
And though as thin as Fraud almost—
   Ever grows more grim and rich.

There is a Chancery Court, a King,
   A manufacturing mob; a set
Of thieves who by themselves are sent
Similar thieves to represent;
   An Army;—and a public debt.

Which last is a scheme of Paper money,
   And means—being interpreted—
"Bees, keep your wax—give us the honey
And we will plant while skies are sunny
   Flowers, which in winter serve instead."

There is a great talk of Revolution—
   And a great chance of despotism—
German soldiers—camps—confusion—

Tumults—lotteries—rage—delusion—
    Gin—suicide and methodism;

Taxes too, on wine and bread,
    And meat, and beer, and tea, and cheese,
From which those patriots pure are fed
Who gorge before they reel to bed
    The tenfold essence of all these.

There are mincing women, mewing
    (Like cats, who *amant misere*)
Of their own virtue, and pursuing
Their gentler sisters to that ruin,
    Without which—what were chastity?

Lawyers—judges—old hobnobbers
    Are there—Bailiffs—Chancellors—
Bishops—great and little robbers—
Rhymesters—pamphleteers—stock-jobbers—
    Men of glory in the wars,—

Things whose trade is—over ladies
    To lean, and flirt, and stare, and simper,
Till all that is divine in woman
Grows cruel, courteous, smooth, inhuman,
    Crucified 'twixt a smile and whimper.

Thrusting, toiling, wailing, moiling,
    Frowning, preaching—such a riot!
Each with never ceasing labour
Whilst he thinks he cheats his neighbour
    Cheating his own heart of quiet.

And all these meet at levees;—
    Dinners convivial and political;—
Suppers of epic poets;—teas,
Where small talk dies in agonies;—
    Breakfasts professional and critical;

Lunches and snacks so aldermanic
 That one would furnish forth ten dinners,
Where reigns a Cretan-tongued panic
Lest news Russ, Dutch, or Alemannic
 Should make some losers, and some winners;

At conversazioni—balls—
 Conventicles and drawing-rooms;
Courts of law—committees—calls
Of a morning—clubs—book stalls—
 Churches—masquerades and tombs.

And this is Hell—and in this smother
 All are damnable and damned;
Each one damning, damns the other;
They are damned by one another,
 By none other are they damned.

John Hamilton Reynolds (1794–1852)

Sonnet

On Hearing St. Martin's Bells on My Way Home
from a Sparring Match at the Fives-Court

Beautiful bells! that on this airy eve
    Swoon with such deep and mellow cadences,–
    Filling,–then leaving empty the rapt breeze;–
    Pealing full voiced,–and seeming now to grieve
In distant dreaming sweetness!–ye bereave
    My mind of worldly care by dim degrees;–
    Dropping the balm of falling melodies
    Over a heart that yearneth to receive.
Oh, doubly soft ye seem!–since even but now
    I've left the Fives-Court rush,–the flash,–the rally,–
    The noise of "Go it Jack,"–the stop–the blow,–
The shout–the chattering hit–the check–the sally;–
    Oh, doubly sweet ye seem to come and go;–
    Like peasants' pipes, at peace time, in a valley!

John Keats (1795–1821)

"To one who has been long in city pent"

To one who has been long in city pent
   'Tis very sweet to look into the fair
   And open face of heaven, to breathe a prayer
Full in the smile of the blue firmament.
Who is more happy, when, with heart's content,
   Fatigued he sinks into some pleasant lair
   Of wavy grass and reads a debonair
And gentle tale of love and languishment?
Returning home at evening, with an ear
   Catching the notes of Philomel, an eye
Watching the sailing cloudlet's bright career,
   He mourns that day so soon has glided by,
E'en like the passage of an angel's tear
   That falls through the clear ether silently.

On Seeing the Elgin Marbles

My spirit is too weak—mortality
   Weighs heavily on me like unwilling sleep;
   And each imagined pinnacle and steep
Of godlike hardship tells me I must die
Like a sick eagle looking at the sky.
   Yet 'tis a gentle luxury to weep
   That I have not the cloudy winds to keep
Fresh for the opening of the morning's eye.
Such dim-conceivèd glories of the brain
   Bring round the heart an undescribable feud:
So do these wonders a most dizzy pain,
   That mingles Grecian grandeur with the rude
Wasting of old Time, with a billowy main,
   A sun, a shadow of a magnitude.

Lines on the Mermaid Tavern

Souls of Poets dead and gone,
What Elysium have ye known,
Happy field or mossy cavern,
Choicer than the Mermaid Tavern?
Have ye tippled drink more fine
Than mine host's Canary wine?
Or are fruits of Paradise
Sweeter than those dainty pies
Of venison? Oh, generous food,
Dressed as though bold Robin Hood
Would, with his Maid Marian,
Sup and bowse from horn and can.

I have heard that on a day
Mine host's sign-board flew away,
Nobody knew whither, till
An astrologer's old quill
To a sheepskin gave the story;
Said he saw you in your glory,
Underneath a new old sign
Sipping beverage divine,
And pledging with contented smack
The Mermaid in the Zodiac.

Souls of Poets dead and gone,
What Elysium have ye known,
Happy field or mossy cavern,
Choicer than the Mermaid Tavern?

Thomas Hood (1799–1845)

Moral Reflections on the Cross of St. Paul's

The man that pays his pence, and goes
    Up to thy lofty cross, St. Paul,
Looks over London's naked nose,
      Women and men:
      The world is all beneath his ken,
    He sits above the *Ball.*
He seems on Mount Olympus' top,
Among the Gods, by Jupiter! and lets drop
    His eyes from the empyreal clouds
      On mortal crowds.

Seen from these skies,
How small those emmets in our eyes!
    Some carry little sticks—and one
His eggs—to warm them in the sun:
      Dear! what a hustle,
        And bustle!
And there's my aunt. I know her by her waist,
      So long and thin
      And so pinched in
    Just in the pismire taste.

Oh! what are men?—beings so small,
      That, should I fall
Upon their little heads, I must
Crush them by hundreds into dust!
And what is life? and all its ages—
      There's seven stages!
Turnham Green! Chelsea! Putney! Fulham!
      Brentford! and Kew!
      And Tooting, too!
And oh! what very little nags to pull 'em.
    Yet each would seem a horse indeed,

If here at Paul's tip-top we'd got 'em;
    Although, like Cinderella's breed,
They're mice at bottom.
    Then let me not despise a horse
    Though he looks small from Paul's high cross!
Since he would be,—as near the sky,
    —Fourteen hands high.

What is the world with London in its lap?
    Mogg's Map.
The Thames, that ebbs, and flows in its broad channel?
    A *tidy* kennel.
The bridges stretching from its banks?
    Stone planks.

Oh me! hence could I read an admonition
    To mad Ambition!
But that he would not listen to my call,
Though I should stand upon the cross and *ball!*

The Lord Mayor's Show

How well I remember the ninth of November,
The sky very foggy, the sun looking groggy,
In fact, altogether pea-soup colour's weather.
Shop-windows all shuttered, the pavement all buttered,
Policemen paraded, the street barricaded,
    And a peal from the steeple of Bow!
Low women in pattens, high ladies in satins,
And Cousin Suburbans, in flame-coloured turbans,
Quite up to the attics, inviting rheumatics,
A great mob collecting, without much selecting,
And some, it's a pity, are free of the city,
    As your pockets may happen to know! . . .

Such hustle and bustle, and mobbing and robbing,
All, all to see the Lord Mayor's Show!

How well I remember the ninth of November,
Six trumpets on duty, as shrill as Veluti,
A great City Marshal, to riding not partial,
The footmen, the state ones, with calves very great ones,
The Cook and the Scullion, well basted with bullion,
    And the squad of each Corporate Co.
Four draymen from Perkins, in steel and brass jerkins,
A Coach like lantern, I wonder it *can* turn,
All carved like old buildings, and drawn by six *gildings*,
With two chubby faces, where sword and where mace is,
The late Mayor, the Ex one, a thought that must vex one,
    And the new Mayor just come into blow!

Such hustle and bustle, and mobbing and robbing,
All, all to see the Lord Mayor's Show.

How well I remember the ninth of November,
The fine Lady Mayoress, an Ostrich's heiress,
In best bib and tucker, and dignified pucker,
The learned Recorder, in Old Bailey order,

The Sheriffs together,—with their hanging weather,
    And their heads like John Anderson's pow!
Their Aldermen courtly, and looking "red port"ly,
And buckler and bargemen, with other great large men,
With streamers and banners, held up in odd manners,
A mob running "arter," to see it by "vater,"
    And the Wharfs popping off as they go! ...

Such hustle and bustle, such mobbing and robbing,
All, all to see the Lord Mayor's Show!

Sonnet to Vauxhall

The cold transparent ham is on my fork—
  It hardly rains—and hark the bell!—ding-dingle—
Away. Three thousand feet at gravel work,
  Mocking a Vauxhall shower!—Married and Single
Crush—rush!—Soaked silks with wet white satin mingle.
  Hengler! Madame! round whom all bright sparks lurk,
Calls audibly on Mr. and Mrs. Pringle
  To study the Sublime, &c.—(vide Burke)
All noses are upturned! Whish—ish!—On high
  The rocket rushes—trails—just steals in sight—
Then droops and melts in bubbles of blue light—
  And Darkness reigns—Then balls flare up and die—
Wheels whiz—smack crackers—serpents twist—and then
  Back to the cold transparent ham again.

The Workhouse Clock: An Allegory

There's a murmur in the air,
And noise in every street—
The murmur of many tongues,
The noise of numerous feet—
While round the Workhouse door
The Labouring Classes flock,
For why? the Overseer of the Poor
Is setting the Workhouse Clock.

Who does not hear the tramp
Of thousands speeding along
Of either sex and various stamp,
Sickly, crippled, or strong,
Walking, limping, creeping
From court, and alley, and lane,
But all in one direction sweeping
Like rivers that seek the main?

Who does not see them sally
From mill, and garret, and room,
In lane, and court and alley,
From homes in poverty's lowest valley,
Furnished with shuttle and loom—
Poor slaves of Civilization's galley—
And in the road and footways rally,
As if for the Day of Doom?
Some, of hardly human form,
Stunted, crooked, and crippled by toil;
Dingy with smoke and dust and oil,
And smirched besides with vicious soil,
Clustering, mustering, all in a swarm.
Father, mother, and careful child,
Looking as if it had never smiled—
The Sempstress, lean, and weary, and wan,
With only the ghosts of garments on—

The Weaver, her sallow neighbour,
The grim and sooty Artisan;
Every soul—child, woman, or man,
Who lives—or dies—by labour.

Stirred by an overwhelming zeal,
And social impulse, a terrible throng!
Leaving shuttle, and needle, and wheel,
Furnace, and grindstone, spindle, and reel,
Thread, and yarn, and iron, and steel—
Yea, rest and the yet untasted meal—
Gushing, rushing, crushing along,
A very torrent of Man!
Urged by the sighs of sorrow and wrong,
Grown at last to a hurricane strong,
Stop its course who can!
Stop who can its onward course
And irresistible moral force;
O! vain and idle dream!
For surely as men are all akin,
Whether of fair or sable skin,
According to Nature's scheme,
That Human Movement contains within
A Blood-Power stronger than Steam.

Onward, onward, with hasty feet,
They swarm—and westward still—
Masses born to drink and eat,
But starving amidst Whitechapel's meat,
And famishing down Cornhill!
Through the Poultry—but still unfed—
Christian Charity, hang your head!
Hungry—passing the Street of Bread;
Thirsty—the Street of Milk;
Ragged—beside the Ludgate Mart,
So gorgeous, through Mechanic-Art,
With cotton, and wool, and silk!

At last, before that door
That bears so many a knock
Ere ever it opens to Sick or Poor,
Like sheep they huddle and flock—
And would that all the Good and Wise
Could see the Million of hollow eyes,
With a gleam derived from Hope and the skies,
Upturned to the Workhouse Clock!

Oh! that the Parish Powers,
Who regulate Labour's hours,
The daily amount of human trial,
Weariness, pain, and self-denial
Would turn from the artificial dial
That striketh ten or eleven,
And go, for once, by that older one
That stands in the light of Nature's sun,
And takes its time from Heaven!

Letitia Elizabeth Landon (1802–1838)

Scenes in London: Piccadilly

The sun is on the crowded street,
    It kindles those old towers
Where England's noblest memories meet
    Of old historic hours:

Vast, shadowy, dark and indistinct,
    Tradition's giant fane
Whereto a thousand years are linked
    In one electric chain.

So stands it when the morning light
    First steals upon the skies,
And shadowed by the fallen night
    The sleeping city lies.

It stands with darkness round it cast,
    Touched by the first cold shine;
Vast, vague, and mighty as the past
    Of which it is the shrine.

'Tis lovely when the moonlight falls
    Around the sculptured stone,
Giving a softness to the walls
    Like love that mourns the gone.

Then comes the gentlest influence
    The human heart can know:
The mourning over those gone hence
    To the still dust below.

The smoke, the noise, the dust of day
    Have vanished from the scene;
The pale lamps gleam with spirit ray
    O'er the park's sweeping green.

Sad shining on her lonely path,
   The moon's calm smile above
Seems as it lulled life's toil and wrath
   With universal love.

Past that still hour, and its pale moon,
   The city is alive;
It is the busy hour of noon
   When man must seek and strive.

The pressure of our actual life
   Is on the waking brow;
Labour and care, endurance, strife,
   These are around him now.

How wonderful the common street,
   Its tumult and its throng,
The hurrying of the thousand feet
   That bear life's cares along.

How strongly is the present felt
   With such a scene beside;
All sounds in one vast murmur melt
   The thunder of the tide.

All hurry on—none pause to look
   Upon another's face;
The present is an open book
   None read, yet all must trace.

The poor man hurries on his race,
   His daily bread to find;
The rich man has yet wearier chase,
   For pleasure's hard to bind.

All hurry, though it is to pass
   For which they live so fast—
What doth the present but amass
   The wealth that makes the past?

The past is round us, those old spires
    That glimmer o'er our head;
Not from the present are their fires,
    Their light is from the dead.

But for the past, the present's powers
    Were waste of toil and mind,
But for those long and glorious hours
    Which leave themselves behind.

Winthrop Mackworth Praed (1802–1839)

Goodnight to the Season

Thus runs the world away
      —Hamlet

> Goodnight to the Season! 'tis over!
>   Gay dwellings no longer are gay;
> The courtier, the gambler, the lover,
>   Are scattered like swallows away:
> There's nobody left to invite one,
> Except my good uncle and spouse;
> My mistress is bathing at Brighton,
> My patron is sailing at Cowes:
> For want of a better employment,
> Till Ponto and Don can get out,
> I'll cultivate rural enjoyment,
> And angle immensely for trout.
>
> Goodnight to the Season!—the lobbies,
>   Their changes, and rumours of change,
> Which startled the rustic Sir Bobbies,
>   And made all the Bishops look strange:
> The breaches, and battles, and blunders,
>   Performed by the Commons and Peers;
> The Marquis's eloquent thunders,
>   The Baronet's eloquent ears:
> Denouncings of Papists and treasons
>   Of foreign dominion and oats;
> Misrepresentations of reasons,
>   And misunderstandings of notes.
>
> Goodnight to the Season!—the buildings
>   Enough to make Inigo sick;
> The paintings, and plasterings, and gildings,
>   Of stucco, and marble, and brick;

The orders deliciously blended,
    From love of effect, into one;
The club-houses only intended,
    The palaces only begun;
The hell where the fiend, in his glory,
    Sits staring at putty and stones,
And scrambles from story to story,
    To rattle at midnight his bones.

Goodnight to the Season!—the dances,
    The fillings of hot little rooms,
The glancings of rapturous glances,
    The fancyings of fancy costumes;
The pleasures which Fashion makes duties,
    The praisings of fiddles and flutes,
The luxury of looking at beauties,
    The tedium of talking to mutes;
The female diplomatists, planners
    Of matches for Laura and Jane,
The ice of her Ladyship's manners,
    The ice of his Lordship's champagne.

Goodnight to the Season!—the rages
    Led off by the chiefs of the throng,
The Lady Matilda's new pages,
    The Lady Eliza's new song;
Miss Fennel's Macaw, which at Boodle's
    Was held to have something to say;
Mrs. Splenetic's musical Poodles,
    Which bark "Batti, Batti!" all day;
The pony Sir Araby sported,
    As hot and as black as a coal,
And the Lion his mother imported,
    In bearskins and grease, from the Pole.

Goodnight to the Season!—the Toso,
    So very majestic and tall;

Miss Ayton, whose singing was so so,
  And Pasta, divinest of all;
The labour in vain of the Ballet,
  So sadly deficient in stars;
The foreigners thronging the Alley,
  Exhaling the breath of cigars;
The "loge" where some heiress, how killing
  Environed with Exquisites sits,
The lovely one out of her drilling,
  The silly ones out of their wits.

Goodnight to the Season!—the splendour
  That beamed in the Spanish Bazaar;
Where I purchased—my heart was so tender—
  A card-case,—a pasteboard guitar,—
A bottle of perfume,—a girdle,—
  A lithographed Riego full-grown,
Whom Bigotry drew on a hurdle,
  That artists might draw him on stone,—
A small panorama of Seville,—
  A trap for demolishing flies,—
A caricature of the Devil,—
  And a look from Miss Sheridan's eyes.

Goodnight to the Season!—the flowers
  Of the grand horticultural fête,
When boudoirs were quitted for bowers,
  And the fashion was not to be late;
When all who had money and leisure
  Grew rural o'er ices and wines,
All pleasantly toiling for pleasure,
  All hungrily pining for pines,
And making of beautiful speeches,
  And marring of beautiful shows,
And feeding on delicate peaches,
  And treading on delicate toes.

Goodnight to the Season!—another
   Will come with its trifles and toys,
And hurry away, like its brother,
   In sunshine, and odour, and noise.
Will it come with a rose or a briar?
   Will it come with a blessing or curse?
Will its bonnets be lower or higher?
   Will its morals be better or worse?
Will it find me grown thinner or fatter,
   Or fonder of wrong or of right,
Or married, or buried?—no matter,
   Goodnight to the Season, Goodnight!

Elizabeth Barrett Browning (1806–1861)

from *Aurora Leigh*

Serene and unafraid of solitude,
I worked the short days out,—and watched the sun
On lurid morns or monstrous afternoons
(Like some Druidic idol's fiery brass
With fixed unflickering outline of dead heat,
From which the blood of wretches pent inside
Seems oozing forth to incarnadine the air)
Push out through fog with his dilated disk,
And startle the slant roofs and chimney-pots
With splashes of fierce colour. Or I saw
Fog only, the great tawny weltering fog,
Involve the passive city, strangle it
Alive, and draw it off into the void,
Spires, bridges, streets, and squares, as if a sponge
Had wiped out London,—or as noon and night
Had clapped together, and utterly struck out
The intermediate time, undoing themselves
In the act. Your city poets see such things
Not despicable. Mountains of the south,
When drunk and mad with elemental wines
They rend the seamless mist and stand up bare,
Make fewer singers, haply. No one sings,
Descending Sinai: on Parnassus mount
You take a mule to climb and not a muse
Except in fable and figure: forests chant
Their anthems to themselves, and leave you dumb.
But sit in London at the day's decline,
And view the city perish in the mist
Like Pharaoh's armaments in the deep Red Sea,

The chariots, horsemen, footmen, all the host,
Sucked down and choked to silence—then, surprised
By a sudden sense of vision and of tune,
You feel as conquerors though you did not fight,
And you and Israel's other singing girls,
Ay, Miriam with them, sing the song you choose. . . .

Alfred, Lord Tennyson (1809–1892)

from *In Memoriam*

VII

Dark house, by which once more I stand
   Here in the long unlovely street,
   Doors, where my heart was used to beat
So quickly, waiting for a hand,

A hand that can be clasped no more—
   Behold me, for I cannot sleep,
   And like a guilty thing I creep
At earliest morning to the door.

He is not here; but far away
   The noise of life begins again,
   And ghastly through the drizzling rain
On the bald street breaks the blank day.

from *Ode on the Death of the Duke of Wellington*

I

    Bury the Great Duke
      With an empire's lamentation,
    Let us bury the Great Duke
      To the noise of the mourning of a mighty nation,
    Mourning when their leaders fall,
    Warriors carry the warrior's pall,
    And sorrow darkens hamlet and hall.

II

    Where shall we lay the man whom we deplore?
    Here, in streaming London's central roar.
    Let the sound of those he wrought for,
    And the feet of those he fought for,
    Echo round his bones for evermore.

III

    Lead out the pageant: sad and slow,
    As fits an universal woe,
    Let the long long procession go,
    And let the sorrowing crowd about it grow,
    And let the mournful martial music blow;
    The last great Englishman is low.

IV

    Mourn, for to us he seems the last,
    Remembering all his greatness in the Past.
    No more in soldier fashion will he greet
    With lifted hand the gazer in the street.
    O friends, our chief state-oracle is mute:
    Mourn for the man of long-enduring blood,
    The statesman-warrior, moderate, resolute,
    Whole in himself, a common good.
    Mourn for the man of amplest influence,
    Yet clearest of ambitious crime,
    Our greatest yet with least pretence,

Great in council and great in war,
Foremost captain of his time,
Rich in saving common-sense,
And, as the greatest only are,
In his simplicity sublime.
O good gray head which all men knew,
O voice from which their omens all men drew,
O iron nerve to true occasion true,
O fallen at length that tower of strength
Which stood four-square to all the winds that blew!
Such was he whom we deplore.
The long self-sacrifice of life is o'er.
The great World-victor's victor will be seen no more.

V

All is over and done:
Render thanks to the Giver,
England, for thy son.
Let the bell be tolled.
Render thanks to the Giver,
And render him to the mould.
Under the cross of gold
That shines over city and river,
There he shall rest for ever
Among the wise and the bold.
Let the bell be tolled:
And a reverent people behold
The towering car, the sable steeds:
Bright let it be with its blazoned deeds,
Dark in its funeral fold.
Let the bell be tolled:
And a deeper knell in the heart be knolled;
And the sound of the sorrowing anthem rolled
Through the dome of the golden cross;
And the volleying cannon thunder his loss;
He knew their voices of old.

For many a time in many a clime
His captain's-ear has heard them boom
Bellowing victory, bellowing doom:
When he with those deep voices wrought,
Guarding realms and kings from shame;
With those deep voices our dead captain taught
The tyrant, and asserts his claim
In that dread sound to the great name,
Which he has worn so pure of blame,
In praise and in dispraise the same,
A man of well-attempered frame.
O civic muse, to such a name,
To such a name for ages long,
To such a name,
Preserve a broad approach of fame,
And ever-echoing avenues of song.

Cleopatra's Needle

Here, I that stood in On beside the flow
Of sacred Nile, three thousand years ago!—
A Pharaoh, kingliest of his kingly race,
First shaped, and carved, and set me in my place.
A Caesar of a punier dynasty
Thence haled me toward the Mediterranean sea,
Whence your own citizens, for their own renown,
Through strange seas drew me to your monster town.
I have seen the four great empires disappear.
I was when London was not. I am here.

Anon. (1851)

Have You Been to the Crystal Palace?

In great Hyde Park, like lots of larks,
They work with expedition,
Like swarms of bees, among the trees,
At the great Exhibition;
Talk of Mount Vesuvivus,
Or the Tower of Babylonia,
It is nothing to it, or Noah's Ark,
Or the whale that swallowed Jonah.

I went to see on Sunday last
With every rank and station,
The Palace where is to be the
Exhibition of all Nations.

There I beheld some panes of glass,
So beautifully stained, sirs,
As thick as Nelson's Monument,
And as long as Salisbury Plain, sirs;
I saw a man with seven heads,
With a face as black as tinder,
And five and twenty wooden legs
A peeping through the window.

I saw the tail of a woman's smock,
Which made folks pull wry faces,
Would cover the West India Docks,
And reach to Epsom Races.
I saw a lady's bustle too,
The females to adorn there,
Nine times as thick as Old St. Paul's,
And as wide as Hyde Park Corner.

I saw a prize from Germany,
A sausage made of strength, sirs,

Three hundred and twenty inches thick,
And fifteen miles in length, sirs.
I saw a handsome silver watch,
Made by a man called Jenkin,
Nearly twenty times as big
As the great Tom of Lincoln.

I saw a rat, and two tom cats,
Among the people mingling,
Bigger, my friends, than any bulls
You ever saw in England.
I saw ten thousand men at work,
And numbers more were flocking,
They were so far apart they couldn't
Hear each other knocking.

The prettiest thing I did behold,
My friends depend upon it,
Was a little woman without a head,
Who did not wear a bonnet.
Her husband led a quiet life,
Happy was his position,
He thinks to surely gain a prize
At the National Exhibition.

I saw a pig on thirteen legs
Around the Palace did run,
I saw a teapot seven times
As big as the Tower of London.
I saw a mouse brought from Canton,
As big as a Russian monkey;
And I saw a mite in a Glo'ster cheese,
Five times as big as a donkey.

The prizes all are coming in,
As plainly may be seen, sirs,
And all the towns of England
Are coming up by steam, sirs.

Some bring their bedding on their backs,
Because they will be right slap;
And all who come to town to stop,
Will have to bring their night caps.

I saw a lass, none can surpass,
They call her Madame Chambert,
She had eleven kids in seven months,
As big as old Daniel Lambert.
I saw a pie, it is no lie,
With the crust together knocked hard,
Made of shrimps and sloes, and pigeon's toes,
As big as Woolwich Dock Yard.

I saw a pair of babies shoes,
Believe me what I say now,
I'll take an oath they were as big
As any brewer's dray now.
I saw a handsome frying pan,
The size of half a farden;
And I saw a stunning halfpenny roll,
As big as Covent Garden.

I saw a jew's harp made of gold,
And a silver copper fiddle;
I saw a lady's thing em bob,
All hairy down the middle.
I saw a dandy victorine,
With a yellow, blue, and green coat;
And a pair of lady's ear-rings
Seven times as big as a steam boat.

I have not told you half I saw
The Palace going over,
It would take a sheet of paper that
Would reach from here to Dover.
I saw a man who had twenty wives,

And fed them all on Mondays,
He had one for every day in the week,
And fourteen left for Sundays.

Have you been to see, as well as me,
The wonders in each station,
In great Hyde Park among the trees,
The Exhibition of all Nations.

Robert Browning (1812–1889)

from *Waring*

I

i.

What's become of Waring
Since he gave us all the slip,
Chose land-travel or seafaring,
Boots and chest, or staff and scrip,
Rather than pace up and down
Any longer London-town?

ii.

Who'd have guessed it from his lip,
Or his brow's accustomed bearing,
On the night he thus took ship,
Or started landward, little caring
For us, it seems, who supped together,
(Friends of his too, I remember)
And walked home through the merry weather,
Snowiest in all December;
I left his arm that night myself
For what's-his-name's, the new prose-poet,
That wrote the book there, on the shelf–
How, forsooth, was I to know it
If Waring meant to glide away
Like a ghost at break of day!
Never looked he half so gay!

iii.

He was prouder than the Devil:
How he must have cursed our revel!
Ay, and many other meetings,
Indoor visits, outdoor greetings,
As up and down he paced this London,

With no work done, but great works undone,
Where scarce twenty knew his name.
Why not, then, have earlier spoken,
Written, bustled? Who's to blame
If your silence kept unbroken?
True, but there were sundry jottings,
Stray-leaves, fragments, blurrs and blottings,
Certain first steps were achieved
Already which—(is that your meaning?)
Had well borne out whoe'er believed
In more to come, but who goes gleaning
Hedge-side chance-blades, while full-sheaved
Stand cornfields by him? Pride, o'erweening
Pride alone, puts forth such claims
O'er the day's distinguished names.

iv.

Meantime, how much I loved him,
I find out now I've lost him:
I, who cared not if I moved him,
—Could so carelessly accost him,
Never shall get free
Of his ghostly company,
And eyes that just a little wink
As deep I go into the merit
Of this and that distinguished spirit—
His cheeks' raised colour, soon to sink,
As long I dwell on some stupendous
And tremendous (God defend us!)
Monstr'-inform'-ingens-horrend-ous
Demoniaco-seraphic
Penman's latest piece of graphic.
Nay, my very wrist grows warm
With his dragging weight of arm!
E'en so, swimmingly appears,
Through one's after-supper musings,

Some lost lady of old years,
With her beauteous vain endeavour,
And goodness unrepaid as ever;
The face, accustomed to refusings,
We, puppies that we were. . . . Oh never
Surely, nice of conscience, scrupled
Being aught like false, forsooth, to?
Telling aught but honest truth to?
What a sin had we centupled
Its possessor's grace and sweetness!
No! she heard in its completeness
Truth, for truth's a weighty matter,
And, truth at issue, we can't flatter!
Well, 'tis done with: she's exempt
From damning us through such a sally;
And so she glides, as down a valley,
Taking up with her contempt,
Past our reach; and in, the flowers
Shut her unregarded hours.

Edward Lear (1812–1888)

There Was an Old Person of Putney

There was an old person of Putney,
Whose food was roast spiders and chutney,
Which he took with his tea, within sight of the sea,
That romantic old person of Putney.

There Was an Old Man of Blackheath

There was an old man of Blackheath,
Whose head was adorned with a wreath,
Of lobsters and spice, pickled onions and mice,
That uncommon old man of Blackheath.

There Was a Young Person of Kew

There was a young person of Kew,
Whose virtues and vices were few;
But with blameable haste, she devoured some hot paste,
Which destroyed that young person of Kew.

There Was an Old Person of Bow

There was an old person of Bow,
Whom nobody happened to know;
So they gave him some soap, and said coldly, "We hope
You will go back directly to Bow!"

There Was a Young Lady of Greenwich

There was a young lady of Greenwich,
Whose garments were bordered with Spinach;

But a large spotty Calf, bit her shawl quite in half,
Which alarmed that young lady of Greenwich.

There Was an Old Person of Ealing

There was an old person of Ealing,
Who was wholly devoid of good feeling;
He drove a small gig, with three Owls and a Pig,
Which distressed all the people of Ealing.

There Was an Old Person of Bromley

There was an old person of Bromley,
Whose ways were not cheerful or comely;
He sat in the dust, eating spiders and crust,
That unpleasing old person of Bromley.

There Was an Old Person of Sheen

There was an old person of Sheen,
Whose expression was calm and serene;
He sat in the water, and drank bottled porter,
That placid old person of Sheen.

There Was an Old Man of Thames Ditton

There was an old man of Thames Ditton,
Who called for something to sit on;
But they brought him a hat, and said—"Sit upon that,
You abruptious old man of Thames Ditton!"

Arthur Hugh Clough (1819–1861)

To the Great Metropolis

Traffic, to speak from knowledge but begun,
I saw, and travelling much, and fashion—Yea,
And if that Competition and Display
Make a great Capital, then thou art one,
One, it may be, unrivalled 'neath the sun.
But sovereign symbol of the Great and Good,
True Royalty, and genuine Statesmanhood,
Nobleness, Learning, Piety was none.
If such realities indeed there are
Working within unsignified, 'tis well;
The stranger's fancy of the thing thou art
Is rather truly of a huge Bazaar,
A railway terminus, a gay Hotel,
Anything but a mighty Nation's heart.

In the Great Metropolis

Each for himself is still the rule,
We learn it when we go to school—
    The devil take the hindmost, o!

And when the schoolboys grow to men,
In life they learn it o'er again—
    The devil take the hindmost, o!

For in the church and at the bar,
On 'Change, at court, where'er they are,
    The devil takes the hindmost, o!

Husband for husband, wife for wife,
Are careful that in married life
    The devil take the hindmost, o!

From youth to age, whate'er the game,
The unvarying practice is the same—
    The devil take the hindmost, o!

And after death, we do not know,
But scarce can doubt, where'er we go,
    The devil takes the hindmost, o!

Tol rol de rol, tol rol de ro,
The devil take the hindmost, o!

"Blessed are those who have not seen"

Blessed are those who have not seen,
   And who have yet believed
The witness, here that has not been,
   From heaven they have received.

Blessed are those who have not known
   The things that stand before them,
And for a vision of their own
   Can piously ignore them.

So let me think, whate'er befall,
   That in the city duly
Some men there are who love at all,
   Some women who love truly;

And that upon two million odd
   Transgressors in sad plenty,
Mercy will of a gracious God
   Be shown—because of twenty.

"Ye flags of Piccadilly"

Ye flags of Piccadilly,
  Where I posted up and down,
And wished myself so often
  Well away from you and Town,—

Are the people walking quietly,
  And steady on their feet,
Cabs and omnibuses plying
  Just as usual in the street?

Do the houses look as upright
  As of old they used to be,
And does nothing seem affected
  By the pitching of the sea?

Through the Green Park iron railings
  Do the quick pedestrians pass?
Are the little children playing
  Round the plane-tree in the grass?

This squally wild north-wester
  With which our vessel fights,
Does it merely serve with you to
  Carry up some paper kites?

Ye flags of Piccadilly
  Which I hated so, I vow
I could wish with all my heart
  You were underneath me now!

Anon. (19th century)

from *The Cries of London*

Here's cherries, oh! my pretty maids,
My cherries round and sound;
Whitehearts, Kentish, or Blackhearts
And only two-pence a pound.

Strawberries gathered on a fine morning,
Dear ladies only see,
And only sixpence for a pottle,
Come buy, come buy of me.

Dust or ash this chap calls out,
With all his might and main,
He's got a mighty cinder heap
Somewhere near Gray's Inn Lane.

Here's taters hot, my little chaps,
Now just lay out a copper,
I'm known up and down the Strand,
You'll not find any hotter.

Any old pots or kettles,
Or any old brass to mend?
Come my pretty maids all,
To me your aid must lend.

This man, from Covent Garden comes,
With his green wares early,
Singing out carrots and turnips, oh,
Making a hurly-burly.

Sprats alive, oh! sprats alive,
Just up from Billingsgate;
Come buy some sprats of me, my deary,
For yourself or for your mate.

George Eliot (1819–1880)

In a London Drawingroom

The sky is cloudy, yellowed by the smoke.
For view there are the houses opposite
Cutting the sky with one long line of wall
Like solid fog: far as the eye can stretch
Monotony of surface & of form
Without a break to hang a guess upon.
No bird can make a shadow as it flies,
For all its shadow, as in ways o'erhung
By thickest canvas, where the golden rays
Are clothed in hemp. No figure lingering
Pauses to feed the hunger of the eye
Or rest a little on the lap of life.
All hurry on & look upon the ground,
Or glance unmarking at the passers by.
The wheels are hurrying too, cabs, carriages
All closed, in multiplied identity.
The world seems one huge prison-house & court
Where men are punished at the slightest cost,
With lowest rate of colour, warmth & joy.

Anon. (1869)

Strike of the London Cabmen

Oh! here's a great and glorious row,
All over London, sirs, I vow,
A few words of which I'll tell you now,
    The strike of the London cabmen.
Some days ago they passed an Act,
About the cabs—it is a fact,
Which made old swells and codgers smile,
    That they should ride a tanner a mile;
And if not pleased, then all around
The cabmen had to measure the ground,
And that's the reason, I'll be bound,
    Has caused the strike of the cabmen.

Chorus

    Cut him, slash him, here's a go,
    All over town, come up, gee wo,
    The law was hard you well do know,
        So strike did the London cabmen.

On Tuesday last, oh! what a sight,
The thing was done and all was right,
Just at the hour of twelve at night,
    All strike did the London cabmen.
There was not a cab upon the ground,
And never a cabman to be found,
Swells and cripples on did steer,
    A singing out oh! dear, oh! dear,
They did not know there was a strike,
They bawled and squalled with all their might,
They hunted up and down all night,
    And could not find a cabman.

While coming home from Drury Lane,
I tumbled over Bet and Jane,
Who said the Act was much to blame,
   To cause the strike of the cabmen.
Indeed! indeed! said lovely Kate,
I know they all gave in their plates
And told their masters they would go
   To dwell in South Australia, O.
Behold how dismal is the street,
No cab or carriage can we meet
And we must travel on our feet
   All through the strike of the cabmen.

Now if it comes a thunder shower,
If it rains or if it pours,
You may be about the street for hours
   And never find a cabman,
And won't it too make many fret,
To see the ladies' muslin wet,
And see them through the streets to scud
   With their back behinds all covered with mud,
And won't it cause them to bewail,
To wash their dirty petticoat tails,
'Cause through the dirt they have to trail,
   All through the strike of the cabmen.

Frederick Locker-Lampson (1821–1895)

St. James's Street

St. James's Street, of classic fame,
　For Fashion still is seen there:
St. James's Street? I know the name,
　I almost think I've been there!
Why, that's where Sacharissa sighed
　When Waller read his ditty;
Where Byron lived, and Gibbon died,
　And Alvanley was witty.

A famous Street! To yonder Park
　Young Churchill stole in class-time;
Come, gaze on fifty men of mark,
　And then recall the past time.
The *plats* at White's, the play at *Crock's,*
　The bumpers to Miss Gunning;
The *bonhomie* of Charley Fox,
　And Selwyn's ghastly funning.

The dear old Street of clubs and *cribs,*
　As north and south it stretches,
Still seems to smack of Rolliad squibs,
　And Gillray's fiercer sketches;
The quaint old dress, the grand old style,
　The *mots,* the racy stories;
The wine, the dice, the wit, the bile—
　The hate of Whigs and Tories.

At dusk, when I am strolling there,
　Dim forms will rise around me;
Lepel flits past me in her chair,—
　And Congreve's airs astound me!
And once Nell Gwynne, a frail young Sprite,
　Looked kindly when I met her;

I shook my head, perhaps,—but quite
    Forgot to quite forget her.

The Street is still a lively tomb
    For rich, and gay, and clever;
The crops of dandies bud and bloom,
    And die as fast as ever.
Now gilded youth loves cutty pipes,
    And slang that's rather *scaring;*
It can't approach its prototypes
    In taste, or tone, or bearing.

In Brummell's day of buckle shoes,
    Lawn cravats and roll collars,
They'd fight, and woo, and bet—and lose
    Like gentlemen and scholars:
I'm glad young men should go the pace,
    I half forgive *Old Rapid;*
These louts disgrace their name and race—
    So vicious and so vapid!

Worse times may come. *Bon ton,* indeed,
    Will then be quite forgotten,
And all we much revere will speed
    From ripe to worse than rotten:
Let grass then sprout between yon stones,
    And owls then roost at Boodle's,
For Echo will hurl back the tones
    Of screaming *Yankee Doodles.*

I love the haunts of old Cockaigne,
    Where wit and wealth were squandered;
The halls that tell of hoop and train,
    Where grace and rank have wandered;
Those halls where ladies fair and leal
    First ventured to adore me!
Something of that old love I feel
    For this old Street before me.

Matthew Arnold (1822–1888)

Lines Written in Kensington Gardens

In this lone, open glade I lie,
Screened by deep boughs on either hand;
And at its end, to stay the eye,
Those black-crowned, red-boled pine-trees stand!

Birds here make song, each bird has his,
Across the girdling city's hum.
How green under the boughs it is!
How thick the tremulous sheep-cries come!

Sometimes a child will cross the glade
To take his nurse his broken toy;
Sometimes a thrush flit overhead
Deep in her unknown day's employ.

Here at my feet what wonders pass,
What endless, active life is here!
What blowing daisies, fragrant grass!
An air-stirred forest, fresh and clear.

Scarce fresher is the mountain-sod
Where the tired angler lies, stretched out,
And, eased of basket and of rod,
Counts his day's spoil, the spotted trout.

In the huge world, which roars hard by,
Be others happy if they can!
But in my helpless cradle I
Was breathed on by the rural Pan.

I, on men's impious uproar hurled,
Think often, as I hear them rave,
That peace has left the upper world
And now keeps only in the grave.

Yet here is peace for ever new!
When I who watch them am away,
Still all things in this glade go through
The changes of their quiet day.

Then to their happy rest they pass!
The flowers upclose, the birds are fed,
The night comes down upon the grass,
The child sleeps warmly in his bed.

Calm soul of all things! make it mine
To feel, amid the city's jar,
That there abides a peace of thine,
Man did not make, and cannot mar.

West London

Crouched on the pavement, close by Belgrave Square,
A tramp I saw, ill, moody, and tongue-tied.
A babe was in her arms, and at her side
A girl; their clothes were rags, their feet were bare.

Some labouring men, whose work lay somewhere there,
Passed opposite; she touched her girl, who hied
Across, and begged, and came back satisfied.
The rich she had let pass with frozen stare.

Thought I: "Above her state this spirit towers;
She will not ask of aliens, but of friends,
Of sharers in a common human fate.

She turns from that cold succour, which attends
The unknown little from the unknowing great,
And points us to a better time than ours."

East London

'Twas August, and the fierce sun overhead
    Smote on the squalid streets of Bethnal Green,
    And the pale weaver, through his windows seen
In Spitalfields, looked thrice dispirited;

I met a preacher there I knew, and said:
    "Ill and o'erworked, how fare you in this scene?"
    "Bravely!" said he; "for I of late have been
Much cheered with thoughts of Christ, *the living bread.*"

O human soul! as long as thou canst so
Set up a mark of everlasting light,
Above the howling senses' ebb and flow,

To cheer thee, and to right thee if thou roam,
Not with lost toil thou labourest through the night!
Thou mak'st the heaven thou hop'st indeed thy home.

Dante Gabriel Rossetti (1828–1882)

Tiber, Nile, and Thames

The head and hands of murdered Cicero,
Above his seat high in the Forum hung,
Drew jeers and burning tears. When on the rung
Of a swift-mounted ladder, all aglow,
Fulvia, Mark Antony's shameless wife, with show
Of foot firm-poised and gleaming arm upflung,
Bade her sharp needle pierce that god-like tongue
Whose speech fed Rome even as the Tiber's flow.
And thou, Cleopatra's Needle, that hadst thrid
Great skirts of Time ere she and Antony hid
Dead hope!—hast thou too reached, surviving death,
A city of sweet speech scorned,—on whose chill stone
Keats withered, Coleridge pined, and Chatterton,
Breadless, with poison froze the God-fired breath?

Coventry Patmore (1823–1896)

A London Fête

All night fell hammers, shock on shock;
With echoes Newgate's granite clanged:
The scaffold built, at eight o'clock
They brought the man out to be hanged.
Then came from all the people there
A single cry, that shook the air;
Mothers held up their babes to see,
Who spread their hands, and crowed for glee;
Here a girl from her vesture tore
A rag to wave with, and joined the roar;
There a man, with yelling tired,
Stopped, and the culprit's crime inquired;
A sot, below the doomed man dumb,
Bawled his health in the world to come;
These blasphemed and fought for places;
Those, half-crushed, cast frantic faces,
To windows, where, in freedom sweet,
Others enjoyed the wicked treat.
At last, the show's black crisis pended;
Struggles for better standings ended;
The rabble's lips no longer cursed,
But stood agape with horrid thirst;
Thousands of breasts beat horrid hope;
Thousands of eyeballs, lit with hell,
Burnt one way all, to see the rope
Unslacken as the platform fell.
The rope flew tight; and then the roar
Burst forth afresh; less loud, but more
Confused and affrighting than before.
A few harsh tongues for ever led
The common din, the chaos of noises,
But ear could not catch what they said.

As when the realm of the damned rejoices
At winning a soul to its will,
That clatter and clangour of hateful voices
Sickened and stunned the air, until
The dangling corpse hung straight and still.
The show complete, the pleasure past,
The solid masses loosened fast:
A thief slunk off, with ample spoil,
To ply elsewhere his daily toil;
A baby strung its doll to a stick;
A mother praised the pretty trick;
Two children caught and hanged a cat;
Two friends walked on, in lively chat;
And two, who had disputed places,
Went forth to fight, with murderous faces.

James Thomson (1834–1882)

from *Sunday at Hampstead*

An Idle Idyll by a Very Humble Member of the Great and Noble London Mob

I

This is the Heath of Hampstead,
There is the dome of Saint Paul's;
Beneath, on the serried house-tops,
A chequered lustre falls:

And the mighty city of London,
Under the clouds and the light,
Seems a low wet beach, half shingle,
With a few sharp rocks upright.

Here will we sit, my darling,
And dream an hour away:
The donkeys are hurried and worried,
But we are not donkeys today:

Though all the weary week, dear,
We toil in the murk down there,
Tied to a desk and a counter,
A patient stupid pair!

But on Sunday we slip our tether,
And away from the smoke and the smirch;
Too grateful to God for His Sabbath
To shut its hours in a church.

Away to the green, green country,
Under the open sky;
Where the earth's sweet breath is incense
And the lark sings psalms on high.

On Sunday we're Lord and Lady,
With ten times the love and glee

Of those pale and languid rich ones
Who are always and never free.

They drawl and stare and simper,
So fine and cold and staid,
Like exquisite waxwork figures
That must be kept in the shade:

We can laugh out loud when merry,
We can romp at kiss-in-the-ring,
We can take our beer at a public,
We can loll on the grass and sing. . . .

Would you grieve very much, my darling,
If all yon low wet shore
Were drowned by a mighty flood-tide,
And we never toiled there more?

Wicked?—there is no sin, dear,
In an idle dreamer's head;
He turns the world topsy-turvy
To prove that his soul's not dead.

I am sinking, sinking, sinking;
It is hard to sit upright!
Your lap is the softest pillow!
Good night, my Love, good night!
  . . .

IV

Eight of us promised to meet here
And tea together at five:
And—who would ever believe it?—
We are the first to arrive!

Oh, shame on us, my darling;
It is a monstrous crime
To make a tryst with *others*
And be before our time!

Lizzie is off with William,
Quite happy for her part;
Our sugar in her pocket,
And the sweet love in her heart.

Mary and Dick so grandly
Parade suburban streets;
His waistcoat and her bonnet
Proving the best of treats.

And Fanny plagues big Robert
With tricks of the wildest glee:
O Fanny, *you'll* get in hot water
If you do not bring us our tea!

Why, bless me, look at that table,
Every one of them there!—
"Ha, here at last we have them,
The always behindhand pair!

"When the last trumpet-solo
Strikes up instead of the lark,
They'll turn in their sleep just grunting
Who's up so soon in the dark?"

Babble and gabble, you rabble,
A thousand in full yell!
And this is your Tower of Babel,
This not-to-be-finished Hotel.

"You should see it in the drawing,
You'd think a Palace they make,
Like the one in the *Lady of Lyons*,
With this pond for the lovely lake!"

"I wish it wasn't Sunday,
There's no amusement at all:
Who was here Hot-cross-bun-day?
We had such an open-air ball!

"The bands played polkas, waltzes,
Quadrilles; it was glorious fun!
And each gentleman gave them a penny
After each dance was done."

"Mary is going to chapel,
And what takes her there, do you guess?
Her sweet little duck of a bonnet,
And her new second-hand silk dress."

"*We* went to Church one Sunday,
But felt we had no right there;
For it's only a place for the grand folk
Who come in a carriage and pair.

"And I laughed out loud,—it was shameful!
But Fanny said, *Oh, what lives!*
He must have been clever, the rascal,
To manage seven hundred wives!"

"Suppose we play Hunt-the-Slipper?"
"We can't, there's the crinoline!"–"Phew!
Bother it, always a nuisance!"
"Hoop-de-dooden-do!"

"I think I've seen all the girls here,
About a thousand, or more;
But none of them half so pretty
As our own loving four."

"*Thank* you! and I've been listening
To lots of the men, the knaves;
But none of them half such humbugs
As our devoted slaves."

"Do you see those purple flushes?
The sun will set in state:
Up all! we must cross to the heath, friends,
Before it gets too late.

"We will couch in the fern together,
And watch for the moon and the stars;
And the slim tree-tops will be lighted,
So the boys may light their cigars.

"And while the sunset glory
Burns down in crimson and gold,
Lazy shall tell us a story
Of his wonderful times of old."

V

Ten thousand years ago, *("No more than that?")*
Ten thousand years, *("The age of Robert's hat!"–*
"Silence you gods!"–"Pinch Fanny!"–"Now we're good")
This place where we are sitting was a wood,
Savage and desert save for one rude home
Of wattles plastered with stiff clay and loam;
And here, in front, upon the grassy mire
Four naked squaws were squatted round a fire:
Then four tall naked wild men crushing through
The tangled underwood came into view;
Two of them bent beneath a mighty boar,
The third was gashed and bleeding, number four
Strutted full-dressed in war-paint, *("That was Dick!")*
Blue of a devilish pattern laid on thick.
The squaws jumped up to roast the carcass whole;
The braves sank silent, stark 'gainst root and bole.
The meat half-done, they tore it and devoured,
Sullenly ravenous; the women cowered
Until their lords had finished, then partook.
Mist rose; all crept into their cabin-nook,
And staked the mouth; the floor was one broad bed
Of rushes dried with fox and bearskins spread.
Wolves howled and wild cats wailed; they snored; and so
The long night passed, shedding a storm of snow;
This very night ten thousand years ago.

VI

Ten thousand years before, *("Come, draw it mild!*
Don't waste Conk-ology like that, my child!")
From where we sit to the horizon's bound
A level brilliant plain was spread all round,
As level and as brilliant as a sea
Under the burning sun; high as your knee
Aflame with flowers, yellow and blue and red:
Long lines of palm-trees marked out there the bed
Of a great river, and among them gleamed
A few grey tents. Then four swift horsemen streamed
Out of the West, magnificent in ire,
Churning the meadow into flakes of fire,
Brandishing monstrous spears as if in fight,
They wheeled, ducked, charged, and shouted fierce delight:
So till they reach the camp: the women there
Awaiting them the evening meal prepare;
Milk from the goats and camels, dates plucked fresh,
Cool curds and cheese, millet, sweet broiled kid's flesh.
The spear struck deep hath picketed each barb;
A grave proud turbaned man in flowing garb
Sups with a grave meek woman, humbly proud,
Whose eyes flash empire. Then the solemn crowd
Of stars above, the silent plain below,
Until the East resumes its furnace-glow;
This same night twenty thousand years ago.

VII

Ten thousand years before, *("But if you take*
Such mouthfuls, you will soon eat up Time's cake!")
Where we are sitting rose in splendid light
A broad cool marble palace; from the height
Broad terrace-gardens stairlike sank away
Down to the floor of a deep sapphire bay.
Where the last slope slid greenly to the wave,
And dark rich glossy foliage shadow gave,

Four women—or four goddesses—leaned calm,
Of mighty stature, graceful as the palm:
One stroked with careless hand a lion's mane,
One fed an eagle; while a measured strain
Was poured forth by the others, harp and voice,
Music to make the universe rejoice.
An isle was in the offing seen afar,
Deep-purple based, its peak a glittering star;
Whence rowed a galley (drooped the silken sails),
A dragon-barque with golden burning scales.
Then four bronzed giants leapt to land, embraced
The glorious women, chanting: "Did we haste?
The Cavern-Voice hath silenced all your fears;
Peace on our earth another thousand years!"
On fruits and noble wine, with song's rich flow,
They feasted in the sunset's golden glow;
This same night thirty thousand years ago.

VIII

Ten thousand years before, *("Another ten!*
Good Lord, how greedy are these little men!")
This place where we are sitting *("Half asleep.")*
Was in the sea a hundred fathoms deep:
A floor of silver sand so fine and soft,
A coral forest branching far aloft;
Above, the great dusk emerald golden-green;
Silence profound and solitude serene.
Four mermaids sit beneath the coral rocks,
Combing with golden combs their long green locks,
And wreathing them with little pearly shells;
Four mermen came from out the deep-sea dells,
And whisper to them, and they all turn pale:
Then through the hyaline a voice of wail,
With passionate gestures, "Ever alas for woe!
A rumour cometh down the Ocean-flow,
A word calamitous! that we shall be

All disinherited from the great sea:
Our tail with which like fishes we can swim
Shall split into an awkward double-limb,
And we must waddle on the arid soil,
And build dirt-huts, and get our food with toil,
And lose our happy, happy lives!" And so
These gentle creatures wept "Alas for woe!"
This same night forty thousand years ago.

IX

"Are you not going back a little more?
What was the case ten thousand years before?"
Ten thousand years before 'twas Sunday night;
Four lovely girls were listening with delight,
Three noble youths admired another youth
Discoursing History crammed full of truth:
They all were sitting upon Hampstead Heath,
And monstrous grimy London lay beneath.
"The stupidest story Lazy ever told;
I've no more faith in his fine times of old."
"How do you like our prospects now, my dears?
We'll all be mermaids in ten thousand years."
"Mermaids are beautiful enough, but law!
Think of becoming a poor naked squaw!"
"But in these changes, sex will change no doubt;
We'll all be men and women turn about."
"Then these four chaps will be the squaws?—that's just;
With lots of picaninnies, I *do* trust!"
"If changes go by fifty thousand, yes;
But if by ten, they last were squaws, I guess!"
"Come on; we'll go and do the very beers
We did this night was fifty thousand years."
Thou prophet, thou deep sage! we'll go, we'll go:
The ring is round, Life naught, the World an O;
This night is fifty thousand years ago!

X

As we rush, as we rush in the train,
    The trees and the houses go wheeling back,
But the starry heavens above the plain
    Come flying on our track.

All the beautiful stars of the sky,
    The silver doves of the forest of night,
Over the dull earth swarm and fly,
    Companions of our flight.

We will rush ever on without fear;
    Let the goal be far, the flight be fleet!
For we carry the Heavens with us, Dear,
    While the Earth slips from our feet!

Henry S. Leigh (1837–1883)

A Cockney's Evening Song

Fades into twilight the last golden gleam
Thrown by the sunset on upland and stream;
Glints o'er the Serpentine—tips Notting Hill—
Dies on the summit of proud Pentonville.

Day brought us trouble, but Night brings us peace;
Morning brought sorrow, but Eve bids it cease.
Gaslight and Gaiety, beam for a while;
Pleasure and Paraffin, lend us a smile.

Temples of Mammon are voiceless again—
Lonely policemen inherit Mark Lane
Silent is Lothbury—quiet Cornhill—
Babel of Commerce, thine echoes are still.

Far to the South—where the wanderer strays
Lost among graveyards and riverward ways,
Hardly a footfall and hardly a breath
Comes to dispute Laurence Pountney with Death.

Westward the stream of Humanity glides;—
Buses are proud of their dozen insides.
Put up thy shutters, grim Care, for to-day—
Mirth and the lamplighter hurry this way.

Out on the glimmer weak Hesperus yields!
Gas for the cities and stars for the fields.
Daisies and buttercups, do as ye list;
I and my friends are for music or whist.

Anon. (1893)

Bloomsbury

For me, for me, these old retreats
Amid the world of London streets!
My eye is pleased with all it meets
    In Bloomsbury.

I know how prim is Bedford Park,
At Highgate oft I've heard the lark,
Not these can lure me from my ark
    In Bloomsbury.

I know how green is Peckham Rye,
And Sydenham, flashing in the sky,
But did I dwell there I should sigh
    For Bloomsbury.

I know where Maida Vale receives
The night dews on her summer leaves,
Not less my settled spirit cleaves
    To Bloomsbury.

Some love the Chelsea river gales,
And the slow barges' ruddy sails,
And these I'll woo when glamour fails
    In Bloomsbury.

Enough for me in yonder square
To see the perky sparrows pair,
Or long laburnum gild the air
    In Bloomsbury.

Enough for me in midnight skies
To see the moons of London rise,
And weave their silver fantasies
    In Bloomsbury.

Oh, mine in snows and summer heats,
These good old Tory brick-built streets!
My eye is pleased with all it meets
    In Bloomsbury.

Austin Dobson (1840–1921)

A New Song of the Spring Garden

Come hither ye gallants, come hither ye maids,
To the trim gravelled walks, to shady arcades.
Come hither, come hither, the nightingales call;—
Sing *Tantarara,*—Vauxhall! Vauxhall!

Come hither, ye cits, from your Lothbury hives!
Come hither, ye husbands, and look to your wives!
For the sparks are as thick as the leaves in the Mall;—
Sing *Tantarara,*—Vauxhall! Vauxhall!

Here the 'prentice from Aldgate may ogle a Toast!
Here his Worship must elbow the knight of the post!
For the wicket is free to the great and the small;—
Sing *Tantarara,*—Vauxhall! Vauxhall!

Here Betty may flaunt in her mistress's sack!
Here Trip wear his master's brocade on his back!
Here a hussy may ride, and a rogue take the wall;—
Sing *Tantarara,*—Vauxhall! Vauxhall!

Here Beauty may grant, here Valour may ask!
Here the plainest may pass for a Belle (in a mask)!
Here a domino covers the short and the tall;—
Sing *Tantarara,*—Vauxhall! Vauxhall!

'Tis a type of the world, with its drums and its din;
'Tis a type of the world, for when you come in
You are loth to go out; like the world 'tis a ball;—
Sing *Tantarara,*—Vauxhall, Vauxhall!

Thomas Hardy (1840–1928)

Beyond the Last Lamp

(Near Tooting Common)

I

>   While rain, with eve in partnership,
>   Descended darkly, drip, drip, drip,
>   Beyond the last lone lamp I passed
>   Walking slowly, whispering sadly,
>   Two linked loiterers, wan, downcast:
>   Some heavy thought constrained each face,
>   And blinded them to time and place.

II

>   The pair seemed lovers, yet absorbed
>   In mental scenes no longer orbed
>   By love's young rays. Each countenance
>   As it slowly, as it sadly
>   Caught the lamplight's yellow glance,
>   Held in suspense a misery
>   At things which had been or might be.

III

>   When I retrod that watery way
>   Some hours beyond the droop of day,
>   Still I found pacing there the twain
>   Just as slowly, just as sadly,
>   Heedless of the night and rain.
>   One could but wonder who they were
>   And what wild woe detained them there.

IV

>   Though thirty years of blur and blot
>   Have slid since I beheld that spot,
>   And saw in curious converse there

Moving slowly, moving sadly
 That mysterious tragic pair,
Its olden look may linger on—
All but the couple; they have gone.

V

Whither? Who knows, indeed.... And yet
To me, when nights are weird and wet,
Without those comrades there at tryst
 Creeping slowly, creeping sadly,
 That lone lane does not exist.
There they seem brooding on their pain,
And will, while such a lane remain.

The Coronation

At Westminster, hid from the light of day,
Many who once had shone as monarchs lay.

Edward the Pious, and two Edwards more,
The second Richard, Henrys three or four;

That is to say, those who were called the Third,
Fifth, Seventh, and Eighth (the much self-widowered);

And James the Scot, and near him Charles the Second,
And, too, the second George could there be reckoned.

Of women, Mary and Queen Elizabeth,
And Anne, all silent in a musing death;

And William's Mary, and Mary, Queen of Scots,
And consort-queens whose names oblivion blots;

And several more whose chronicle one sees
Adorning ancient royal pedigrees.

—Now, as they drowsed on, freed from Life's old thrall,
And heedless, save of things exceptional,

Said one: "What means this throbbing thudding sound
That reaches to us here from overground;

"A sound of chisels, augers, planes, and saws,
Infringing all ecclesiastic laws?

"And these tons-weight of timber on us pressed,
Unfelt here since we entered into rest?

"Surely, at least to us, being corpses royal,
A meet repose is owing by the loyal?"

"—Perhaps a scaffold!" Mary Stuart sighed,
"If such still be. It was that way I died."

"—Ods! Far more like," said he the many-wived,
"That for a wedding 'tis this work's contrived.

"Ha-ha! I never would bow down to Rimmon,
But I had a rare time with those six women!"

"Not all at once?" gasped he who loved confession.
"Nay, nay!" said Hal. "That would have been transgression."

"—They build a catafalque here, black and tall,
Perhaps," mused Richard, "for some funeral?"

And Anne chimed in: "Ah, yes: it may be so!"
"Nay!" squeaked Eliza. "Little you seem to know—

"Clearly 'tis for some crowning here in state,
As they crowned us at our long bygone date;

"Though we'd no such a power of carpentry,
But let the ancient architecture be;

"If I were up there where the parsons sit,
In one of my gold robes, I'd see to it!"

"But you are not," Charles chuckled. "You are here,
And never will know the sun again, my dear!"

"Yea," whispered those whom no one had addressed;
"With slow, sad march, amid a folk distressed,
We were brought here, to take our dusty rest.

"And here, alas, in darkness laid below,
We'll wait and listen, and endure the show. . . .
Clamour dogs kingship; afterwards not so!"

1911

In the British Museum

"What do you see in that time-touched stone,
    When nothing is there
But ashen blankness, although you give it
    A rigid stare?

"You look not quite as if you saw,
    But as if you heard,
Parting your lips, and treading softly
    As mouse or bird.

"It is only the base of a pillar, they'll tell you,
    That came to us
From a far old hill men used to name
    Areopagus."

—"I know no art, and I only view
    A stone from a wall,
But I am thinking that stone has echoed
    The voice of Paul;

"Paul as he stood and preached beside it
    Facing the crowd,
A small gaunt figure with wasted features,
    Calling out loud

"Words that in all their intimate accents
    Pattered upon
That marble front, and were wide reflected,
    And then were gone.

"I'm a labouring man, and know but little,
    Or nothing at all;
But I can't help thinking that stone once echoed
    The voice of Paul."

In St. Paul's a While Ago

    Summer and winter close commune
    On this July afternoon
    As I enter chilly Paul's,
    With its chasmal classic walls.
    —Drifts of gray illumination
    From the lofty fenestration
Slant them down in bristling spines that spread
Fan-like upon the vast dust-moted shade.

    Moveless here, no whit allied
    To the daemonian din outside,
    Statues stand, cadaverous, wan,
    Round the loiterers looking on
    Under the yawning dome and nave,
    Pondering whatnot, giddy or grave.
    Here a verger moves a chair,
    Or a red rope fixes there:—
A brimming Hebe, rapt in her adorning,
Brushes an Artemisia craped in mourning;
    Beatrice Benedick piques, coquetting;
    All unknowing or forgetting
    That strange Jew, Damascus-bound,
Whose name, thereafter travelling round
    To this precinct of the world,
    Spread here like a flag unfurled:
Anon inspiring architectural sages
To frame this pile, writ his throughout the ages:
    Whence also the encircling mart
    Assumed his name, of him no part,
    And to his vision-seeing mind
    Charmless, blank in every kind;
And whose displays, even had they called his eye,
No gold or silver had been his to buy;

Whose haunters, had they seen him stand
On his own steps here, lift his hand
In stress of eager, stammering speech,
And his meaning chanced to reach,
Would have proclaimed him as they passed
An epilept enthusiast.

Coming Up Oxford Street: Evening

The sun from the west glares back,
And the sun from the watered track,
And the sun from the sheets of glass,
And the sun from each window-brass;
Sun-mirrorings, too, brighten
From show-cases beneath
The laughing eyes and teeth
Of ladies who rouge and whiten.
And the same warm god explores
Panels and chinks of doors;
Problems with chemists' bottles
Profound as Aristotle's
He solves, and with good cause,
Having been ere man was.

Also he dazzles the pupils of one who walks west,
A city-clerk, with eyesight not of the best,
Who sees no escape to the very verge of his days
From the rut of Oxford Street into open ways;
And he goes along with head and eyes flagging forlorn,
Empty of interest in things, and wondering why he was born.

As seen 4 July 1872

A Refusal

Said the grave Dean of Westminster:
Mine is the best minster
Seen in Great Britain,
As many have written:
So therefore I cannot
Rule here if I ban not
Such liberty-taking
As movements for making
Its grayness environ
The memory of Byron,
Which some are demanding
Who think them of standing,
But in my own viewing
Require some subduing
For tendering suggestions
On Abbey-wall questions
That must interfere here
With my proper sphere here,
And bring to disaster
This fane and its master,
Whose dict is but Christian
Though nicknamed Philistian.

A lax Christian charity—
No mental clarity
Ruling its movements
For fabric improvements—
Demands admonition
And strict supervision
When bent on enshrining
Rapscallions, and signing
Their names on God's stonework,
As if like His own work
Were their lucubrations:
And passed is my patience

That such a creed-scorner
(Not mentioning horner)
Should claim Poets' Corner.

'Tis urged that some sinners
Are here for worms' dinners
Already in person;
That he could not worsen
The walls by a name mere
With men of such fame here.
Yet nay; they but leaven
The others in heaven
In just true proportion,
While more mean distortion.

'Twill next be expected
That I get erected
To Shelley a tablet
In some niche or gablet.
Then—what makes my skin burn,
Yea, forehead to chin burn—
That I ensconce Swinburne!

August 1924

To a Tree in London

(Clement's Inn)

Here you stay
Night and day,
Never, never going away!

Do you ache
When we take
Holiday for our health's sake?

Wish for feet
When the heat
Scalds you in the brick-built street,

That you might
Climb the height
Where your ancestry saw light,

Find a brook
In some nook
There to purge your swarthy look?

No. You read
Trees to need
Smoke like earth whereon to feed. . . .

Have no sense
That far hence
Air is sweet in a blue immense,

Thus, black, blind,
You have opined
Nothing of your brightest kind;

Never seen
Miles of green,
Smelt the landscape's sweet serene.

192–

Christmas in the Elgin Room

British Museum: Early Last Century

"What is the noise that shakes the night,
And seems to soar to the Pole-star height?"
—"Christmas bells,
The watchman tells
Who walks this hall that blears us captives with its blight."

"And what, then, mean such clangs, so clear?"
"—'Tis said to have been a day of cheer,
And source of grace
To the human race
Long ere their woven sails winged us to exile here.

"We are those whom Christmas overthrew
Some centuries after Pheidias knew
How to shape us
And bedrape us
And to set us in Athena's temple for men's view.

"O it is sad now we are sold—
We gods! for Borean people's gold,
And brought to the gloom
Of this gaunt room
Which sunlight shuns, and sweet Aurore but enters cold.

"For all these bells, would I were still
Radiant as on Athenai's Hill."
—"And I, and I!"
The others sigh,
"Before this Christ was known, and we had men's good will."

Thereat old Helios could but nod,
Throbbed, too, the Ilissus River-god,
And the torsos there
Of deities fair,
Whose limbs were shards beneath some Acropolitan clod:

Demeter too, Poseidon hoar,
Persephone, and many more
   Of Zeus' high breed,—
   All loth to heed
What the bells sang that night which shook them to the core.

1905 and 1926

W. H. Hudson (1841–1922)

To a London Sparrow

At dawn thy voice is loud—a merry voice
When other sounds are few and faint. Before
The muffled thunders of the Underground
Begin to shake the houses, and the noise
Of eastward traffic fills the thoroughfares,
Thy voice then welcomes day. Oh, what a day!—
How foul and haggard-faced! See, where she comes
In garments of the chill discoloured mists
Stealing unto the west with noiseless foot
Through dim forsaken streets. Is she not like,
As sister is to sister, unto her
Whose stained cheeks the nightly rains have wet
And made them grey and seamed and desolate,
Beneath the arches of the bitter bridge?
And thou, O Sparrow, from the windy ledge
Where thou dost nestle—creaking chimney-pots
For softly-sighing branches; sooty slates
For leafy canopy; rank steam of slums
For flowery fragrance; and for star-lit woods
This waste that frights, a desert desolate
Of fabrics gaunt and grim and smoke-begrimed,
By goblin misery haunted; scowling towers
Of cloud and stone, gigantic tenements
And castles of despair, by spectral gleams
Of fitful lamps illumined;—from such place
Canst thou, O Sparrow, welcome day so foul?
Ay, not more blithe of heart in forests dim
The golden-throated thrush awakes what time
The leaves atremble whisper to the breath,
The flowery breath, of morning azure-eyed!

Never a morning comes but I do bless thee,
Thou brave and faithful Sparrow, living link
That binds us to the immemorial past;
O blithe heart in a house so melancholy,
And keeper for a thousand gloomy years
Of many a gay tradition; heritor
Of Nature's ancient cheerfulness, for thee
'Tis ever Merry England! Never yet
In thy companionship of centuries
With man in lurid London didst regret
Thy valiant choice;—yea, even from the time
When all its low-roofed rooms were sweet with scents
From summer fields, where shouting children plucked
The floating lily from the reedy Fleet,
Scaring away the timid water-hen.

Robert Bridges (1844–1930)

London Snow

When men were all asleep the snow came flying,
In large white flakes falling on the city brown,
Stealthily and perpetually settling and loosely lying,
    Hushing the latest traffic of the drowsy town;
Deadening, muffling, stifling its murmurs failing;
Lazily and incessantly floating down and down:
    Silently sifting and veiling road, roof and railing;
Hiding difference, making unevenness even,
Into angles and crevices softly drifting and sailing.
    All night it fell, and when full inches seven
It lay in the depth of its uncompacted lightness,
The clouds blew off from a high and frosty heaven;
    And all woke earlier for the unaccustomed brightness
Of the winter dawning, the strange unheavenly glare:
The eye marvelled—marvelled at the dazzling whiteness;
    The ear hearkened to the stillness of the solemn air;
No sound of wheel rumbling nor of foot falling,
And the busy morning cries came thin and spare.
    Then boys I heard, as they went to school, calling,
They gathered up the crystal manna to freeze
Their tongues with tasting, their hands with snowballing;
    Or rioted in a drift, plunging up to the knees;
Or peering up from under the white-mossed wonder,
"O look at the trees!" they cried, "O look at the trees!"
    With lessened load a few carts creak and blunder,
Following along the white deserted way,
A country company long dispersed asunder:
    When now already the sun, in pale display
Standing by Paul's high dome, spread forth below
His sparkling beams, and awoke the stir of the day.
    For now doors open, and war is waged with the snow;

And trains of sombre men, past tale of number,
Tread long brown paths, as toward their toil they go:
    But even for them awhile no cares encumber
Their minds diverted; the daily word is unspoken,
The daily thoughts of labour and sorrow slumber
At the sight of the beauty that greets them, for the charm they have broken.

Trafalgar Square

October, 1917

Fool that I was! my heart was sore,
Yea, sick for the myriad wounded men,
The maimed in the war: I had grief for each one:
And I came in the gay September sun
To the open smile of Trafalgar Square,
Where many a lad with a limb foredone
Lolled by the lion-guarded column
That holdeth Nelson statued thereon
Upright in the air.

The Parliament towers, and the Abbey towers,
The white Horseguards and grey Whitehall,
He looketh on all,
Past Somerset House and river's bend
To the pillared dome of St. Paul,
That slumbers, confessing God's solemn blessing
On Britain's glory, to keep it ours—
While children true her prowess renew
And throng from the ends of the earth to defend
Freedom and honour—till Earth shall end.

The gentle unjealous Shakespeare, I trow,
In his country grave of peaceful fame
Must feel exiled from life and glow,
If he thinks of this man with his warrior claim,
Who looketh on London as if 'twere his own,
As he standeth in stone, aloft and alone,
Sailing the sky, with one arm and one eye.

W. E. Henley (1849–1903)

from *London Voluntaries*

I

GRAVE

St. Margaret's bells,
Quiring their innocent, old-world canticles,
Sing in the storied air,
All rosy-and-golden, as with memories
Of woods at evensong, and sands and seas
Disconsolate for that the night is nigh.
O, the low, lingering lights! The large last gleam
(Hark! how those brazen choristers cry and call!)
Touching these solemn ancientries, and there,
The silent river ranging tide-mark high
And the callow, grey-faced hospital,
With the strange glimmer and glamour of a dream!
The Sabbath peace is in the slumbrous trees,
And from the wistful, the fast-widowing sky
(Hark! how those plangent comforters call and cry!)
Falls as in August plots late roseleaves fall.
The sober Sabbath stir—
Leisurely voices, desultory feet!—
Comes from the dry, dust-coloured street,
Where in their summer frocks the girls go by,
And sweethearts lean and loiter and confer,
Just as they did an hundred years ago,
Just as an hundred years to come they will:—
When you and I, dear Love, lie lost and low,
And sweet-throats none our welkin shall fulfil,
Nor any sunset fade serene and slow;
But, being dead, we shall not grieve to die.

from *London Types*

I

'BUS-DRIVER

He's called *The General* from the brazen craft
And dash with which he *sneaks a bit of road*
And all its fares; challenged, or chafed, or chaffed,
Back-answers of the newest he'll explode;
He reins his horses with an air; he treats
With scoffing calm whatever powers there be;
He *gets it straight,* puts *a bit on,* and meets
His losses with both *lip* and £ *s. d.;*
He arrogates a special taste in *short;*
Is loftily grateful for a flagrant *smoke;*
At all the smarter housemaids winks his court,
And taps them for half-crowns; being *stoney-broke,*
    Lives lustily; is ever *on the make;*
    And hath, I fear, none other gods but *Fake.*

II

LIFE-GUARDSMAN

Joy of the milliner, envy of the Line,
Star of the parks, jack-booted, sworded, helmed,
He sits between his holsters, solid of spine;
Nor, as it seems, though Westminster were whelmed,
With the great globe, in earthquake and eclipse,
Would he and his charger cease from mounting guard,
This Private in the Blues, nor would his lips
Move, though his gorge with throttled oaths were charred!
He wears his inches weightily, as he wears
His old-world armours; and with his port and pride,
His sturdy graces and enormous airs,
He towers, in speech his Colonel countrified,
    A triumph, waxing statelier year by year,
    Of British blood, and bone, and beef, and beer.

III

HAWKER

Far out of bounds he's figured—in a race
Of West End traffic pitching to his loss.
But if you'd see him in his proper place,
Making the *browns* for *bub* and *grub* and *doss,*
Go east among the merchants and their men,
And where the press is noisiest, and the tides
Of trade run highest and widest, there and then
You shall behold him, edging with equal strides
Along the kerb; hawking in either hand
Some artful nothing made of twine and tin,
Cardboard and foil and bits of rubber band:
Some penn'orth of wit-in-fact that, with a grin,
    The careful city marvels at, and buys
    For nurselings in the suburbs to despise!

IV

BEEF-EATER

His beat lies knee-high through a dust of story—
A dust of terror and torture, grief and crime;
Ghosts that are England's wonder, and shame, and glory
Throng where he walks, an antic of old time;
A sense of long immedicable tears
Were ever with him, could his ears but heed;
The stern *Hic Jacets* of our bloodiest years
Are for his reading, had he eyes to read;
But here, where Crookback raged, and Cranmer trimmed,
And More and Strafford faced the axe's proving,
He shows that Crown the desperate Colonel nimmed,
Or simply keeps the Country Cousin moving,
    Or stays such Cockney pencillers as would shame
    The wall where some dead Queen hath traced her name.

V

SANDWICH-MAN

An ill March noon; the flagstones gray with dust;
An all-round east wind volleying straws and grit;
St. Martin's Steps, where every venomous gust
Lingers to buffet, or sneap, the passing cit;
And in the gutter, squelching a rotten boot,
Draped in a wrap that, modish ten-year syne,
Partners, obscene with sweat and grease and soot,
A horrible hat, that once was just as fine;
The drunkard's mouth a-wash for something drinkable,
The drunkard's eye alert for casual *toppers,*
The drunkard's neck stooped to a lot scarce thinkable,
A living, crawling blazoning of Hot-Coppers,
    He trails his mildews towards a Kingdom-Come
    Compact of *sausage-and-mash* and *two-o'-rum!*

VI

'LIZA

'Liza's *old man's* perhaps a little *shady,*
'Liza's *old-woman's* prone to *booze* and cringe;
But 'Liza deems herself *a perfect lady,*
And proves it in her feathers and her fringe.
For 'Liza has a *bloke* her heart to cheer,
With *pearlies* and a *barrer* and a *jack,*
So all the vegetables of the year
Are duly represented on her back.
Her boots are sacrifices to her hats,
Which knock you speechless—*like a load of bricks!*
Her summer velvets dazzle Wanstead Flats,
And cost, at times, a good eighteen-and-six.
    Withal, outside the gay and giddy whirl,
    'Liza's a stupid, straight, hard-working girl.

VII

"LADY"

Time, the old humourist, has a trick today
Of moving landmarks and of levelling down,
Till into Town the Suburbs edge their way,
And in the Suburbs you may scent the Town.
With Mount St. thus approaching Muswell Hill,
And Clapham Common marching with the Mile,
You get a Hammersmith that *fills the bill*,
A Hampstead with a serious sense of style.
So this fair creature, pictured in The Row,
As one of that "gay adulterous world," whose round
Is by the Serpentine, as well would show,
And might, I deem, as readily be found
    On Streatham's Hill, or Wimbledon's, or where
    Brixtonian kitchens lard the late-dining air.

IX

MOUNTED POLICE

Army Reserve; a worshipper of Bobs,
With whom he stripped the smock from Candahar;
Neat as his mount, that neatest among cobs;
Whenever pageants pass, or meetings are,
He moves conspicuous, vigilant, severe,
With his Light Cavalry hand and seat and look,
A living type of Order, in whose sphere
Is room for neither *Hooligan* nor *Hook*.
For in his shadow, wheresoe'er he ride,
Paces, all eye and hardihood and grip,
The dreaded *Crusher*, might in his every stride
And right materialized girt at his hip;
    And they, that shake to see these twain go by,
    Feel that the *Tec*, that plain-clothes Terror, is nigh.

X

NEWS-BOY

Take any station, pavement, circus, corner,
Where men their styles of print may call or choose,
And there—ten times more *on it* than Jack Horner—
There shall you find him swathed in sheets of news.
Nothing can stay the placing of his wares—
Not 'bus, nor cab, nor dray! The very *Slop*,
That imp of power, is powerless! Ever he dares,
And, daring, lands his public neck and crop.
Even the many-tortured London ear,
The much-enduring, loathes his *Speeshul* yell,
His shriek of *Winnur!* But his dart and leer
And poise are irresistible. Pall Mall
   Joys in him, and Mile End; for his vocation
   Is to purvey the stuff of conversation.

XII

FLOWER-GIRL

There's never a delicate nurseling of the year
But our huge London hails it, and delights
To wear it on her breast or at her ear,
Her days to colour and make sweet her nights.
Crocus and daffodil and violet,
Pink, primrose, valley-lily, clove-carnation,
Red rose and white rose, wall-flower, mignonette,
The daisies all—these be her recreation,
Her gaudies these! And forth from Drury Lane,
Traipsing in any of her whirl of weathers,
Her flower-girls foot it, honest and hoarse and vain,
All boot and little shawl and wilted feathers:
   Of populous corners right advantage taking,
   And, where they squat, endlessly posy-making.

XIII

BARMAID

Though, if you ask her name, she says Elise,
Being plain Elizabeth, e'en let it pass,
And own that, if her aspirates take their ease,
She ever makes a point, in washing glass,
Handling the engine, turning taps for *tots,*
And countering change, and scorning what men say,
Of posing as a dove among the pots,
Nor often gives her dignity away.
Her head's a work of art, and, if her eyes
Be tired and ignorant, she has a waist;
Cheaply the Mode she shadows; and she tries
From penny novels to amend her taste;
    And, having mopped the zinc for certain years,
    And faced the gas, she fades and disappears.

Oscar Wilde (1854–1900)

Impression du Matin

The Thames nocturne of blue and gold
  Changed to a Harmony in grey:
  A barge with ochre-coloured hay
Dropped from the wharf: and chill and cold

The yellow fog came creeping down
  The bridges, till the houses' walls
  Seemed changed to shadows, and St. Paul's
Loomed like a bubble o'er the town.

Then suddenly arose the clang
  Of waking life; the streets were stirred
  With country waggons: and a bird
Flew to the glistening roofs and sang.

But one pale woman all alone,
  The daylight kissing her wan hair,
  Loitered beneath the gas lamps' flare,
With lips of flame and heart of stone.

John Davidson (1857–1909)

London

Athwart the sky a lowly sigh
    From west to east the sweet wind carried;
The sun stood still on Primrose Hill;
    His light in all the city tarried:
The clouds on viewless columns bloomed
Like smouldering lilies unconsumed.

Oh sweetheart, see! how shadowy,
    Of some occult magician's rearing,
Or swung in space of heaven's grace
    Dissolving, dimly reappearing,
Afloat upon ethereal tides
St. Paul's above the city rides!

A rumour broke through the thin smoke
    Enwreathing abbey, tower, and palace,
The parks, the squares, the thoroughfares,
    The millon-peopled lanes and alleys,
An ever-muttering prisoned storm,
The heart of London beating warm.

Thirty Bob a Week

I couldn't touch a stop and turn a screw,
    And set the blooming world a-work for me,
Like such as cut their teeth—I hope, like you—
    On the handle of a skeleton gold key;
I cut mine on a leek, which I eat it every week:
    I'm a clerk at thirty bob as you can see.

But I don't allow it's luck and all a toss;
    There's no such thing as being starred and crossed;
It's just the power of some to be a boss,
    And the bally power of others to be bossed:
I face the music, sir; you bet I ain't a cur;
    Strike me lucky if I don't believe I'm lost!

For like a mole I journey in the dark,
    A-travelling along the underground
From my Pillar'd Halls and broad Suburbean Park,
    To come the daily dull official round;
And home again at night with my pipe all alight,
    A-scheming how to count ten bob a pound.

And it's often very cold and very wet,
    And my missis stitches towels for a hunks;
And the Pillar'd Halls is half of it to let—
    Three rooms about the size of travelling trunks.
And we cough, my wife and I, to dislocate a sigh,
    When the noisy little kids are in their bunks.

But you never hear her do a growl or whine,
    For she's made of flint and roses, very odd;
And I've got to cut my meaning rather fine,
    Or I'd blubber, for I'm made of greens and sod:
So p'r'aps we are in Hell for all that I can tell,
    And lost and damned and served up hot to God.

I ain't blaspheming, Mr. Silver-tongue;
    I'm saying things a bit beyond your art:

Of all the rummy starts you ever sprung,
    Thirty bob a week's the rummiest start!
With your science and your books and your theories about spooks,
    Did you ever hear of looking in your heart?

I didn't mean your pocket, Mr., no:
    I mean that having children and a wife,
With thirty bob on which to come and go,
    Isn't dancing to the tabor and the fife:
When it doesn't make you drink, by Heaven! it makes you think,
    And notice curious items about life.

I step into my heart and there I meet
    A god-almighty devil singing small,
Who would like to shout and whistle in the street,
    And squelch the passers flat against the wall;
If the whole world was a cake he had the power to take,
    He would take it, ask for more, and eat it all.

And I meet a sort of simpleton beside,
    The kind that life is always giving beans;
With thirty bob a week to keep a bride
    He fell in love and married in his teens:
At thirty bob he stuck; but he knows it isn't luck:
    He knows the seas are deeper than tureens.

And the god-almighty devil and the fool
    That meet me in the High Street on the strike,
When I walk about my heart a-gathering wool,
    Are my good and evil angels if you like.
And both of them together in every kind of weather
    Ride me like a double-seated bike.

That's rough a bit and needs its meaning curled.
    But I have a high old hot un in my mind—
A most engrugious notion of the world,
    That leaves your lightning 'rithmetic behind:

I give it at a glance when I say "There ain't no chance,
     Nor nothing of the lucky-lottery kind."

And it's this way that I make it out to be:
     No fathers, mothers, countries, climates—none;
Not Adam was responsible for me,
     Nor society, nor systems, nary one:
A little sleeping seed, I woke—I did, indeed—
     A million years before the blooming sun.

I woke because I thought the time had come;
     Beyond my will there was no other cause;
And everywhere I found myself at home,
     Because I chose to be the thing I was;
And in whatever shape of mollusc or of ape
     I always went according to the laws.

I was the love that chose my mother out;
     I joined two lives and from the union burst;
My weakness and my strength without a doubt
     Are mine alone for ever from the first:
It's just the very same with a difference in the name
     As "Thy will be done." You say it if you durst!

They say it daily up and down the land
     As easy as you take a drink, it's true;
But the difficultest go to understand,
     And the difficultest job a man can do,
Is to come it brave and meek with thirty bob a week,
     And feel that that's the proper thing for you.

It's a naked child against a hungry wolf;
     It's playing bowls upon a splitting wreck;
It's walking on a string across a gulf
     With millstones fore-and-aft about your neck;
But the thing is daily done by many and many a one;
     And we fall, face forward, fighting, on the deck.

In the Isle of Dogs

While the water-wagon's ringing showers
Sweetened the dust with a woodland smell,
"Past noon, past noon, two sultry hours,"
Drowsily fell
From the schoolhouse clock
In the Isle of Dogs by Millwall Dock.

Mirrored in shadowy windows draped
With ragged net or half-drawn blind
Bowsprits, masts, exactly shaped
To woo or fight the wind,
Like monitors of guilt
By strength and beauty sent,
Disgraced the shameful houses built
To furnish rent.

From the pavements and the roofs
In shimmering volumes wound
The wrinkled heat;
Distant hammers, wheels and hoofs,
A turbulent pulse of sound,
Southward obscurely beat,
The only utterance of the afternoon,
Till on a sudden in the silent street
An organ-man drew up and ground
The Old Hundredth tune.

Forthwith the pillar of cloud that hides the past
Burst into flame,
Whose alchemy transmuted house and mast,
Street, dockyard, pier and pile:
By magic sound the Isle of Dogs became
A northern isle—
A green isle like a beryl set
In a wine-coloured sea,

Shadowed by mountains where a river met
The ocean's arm extended royally.

There also in the evening on the shore
An old man ground the Old Hundredth tune,
An old enchanter steeped in human lore,
Sad-eyed, with whitening beard, and visage lank:
Not since and not before,
Under the sunset or the mellowing moon,
Has any hand of man's conveyed
Such meaning in the turning of a crank.

Sometimes he played
As if his box had been
An organ in an abbey richly lit;
For when the dark invaded day's demesne,
And the sun set in crimson and in gold;
When idlers swarmed upon the esplanade,
And a late steamer wheeling towards the quay
Struck founts of silver from the darkling sea,
The solemn tune arose and shook and rolled
Above the throng,
Above the hum and tramp and bravely knit
All hearts in common memories of song.

Sometimes he played at speed;
Then the Old Hundredth like a devil's mass
Instinct with evil thought and evil deed,
Rang out in anguish and remorse. Alas!
That men must know both Heaven and Hell!
Sometimes the melody
Sang with the murmuring surge;
And with the winds would tell
Of peaceful graves and of the passing bell.
Sometimes it pealed across the bay

A high triumphal dirge,
A dirge
For the departing undefeated day.

A noble tune, a high becoming mate
Of the capped mountains and the deep broad firth;
A simple tune and great,
The fittest utterance of the voice of earth.

Fog

I love the fog: in every street
    Shrill muffled cries and shapes forlorn,
The frosted hoof with stealthy beat,
    The hollow-sounding motor-horn:

A fog that lasts till, gently wrung
    By Pythian pangs, we realize
That Doomsday somewhere dawns among
    The systems and the galaxies,

And ruin at the swiftest rate
    The chartered destinies pursue;
While as for us, our final fate
    Already fixed with small ado,

Spills on our heads no wrathful cup,
    Nor wrecks us on a fiery shore,
But leaves us simply swallowed up
    In London fog for evermore.

from *The Thames Embankment*

As gray and dank as dust and ashes slaked
With wash of urban tides the morning lowered;
But over Chelsea Bridge the sagging sky
Had colour in it—blots of faintest bronze,
The stains of daybreak. Westward slabs of light
From vapour disentangled, sparsely glazed
The panelled firmament; but vapour held
The morning captive in the smoky east.
At lowest ebb the tide on either bank
Laid bare the fat mud of the Thames, all pinched
And scalloped thick with dwarfish surges. Cranes,
Derricks and chimney-stalks of the Surrey-side,
Inverted shadows, in the motionless,
Dull, leaden mirror of the channel hung:
Black flags of smoke broke out, and in the dead
Sheen of the water hovered underneath,
As in the upper region, listlessly,
Across the viaduct trailing plumes of steam,
The trains clanked in and out.

                                    Slowly the sun
Undid the homespun swathing of the clouds,
And splashed his image on the northern shore—
A thing extravagantly beautiful:
The glistening, close-grained canvas of the mud
Like hammered copper shone, and all about
The burning centre of the mirrored orbs
Illimitable depth of silver fire
Harmonious beams the overtones of light,
Suffused the embossed, metallic river bank.
Woven of rainbows a dewdrop can dissolve
And packed with power a simple lens can wield,
The perfect, only source of beauty, light
Reforms uncouthest shapelessness and turns
Decoloured refuse into ornament;

The leafless trees that lined the vacant street
Had all their stems picked out in golden scales,
Their branches carved in ebony; and shed
Around them by the sanction of the morn
In lieu of leaves each wore an aureole.

Barges at anchor, barges stranded, hulks
Ungainly, in the unshorn beams and rich
Replenished planet of a winter sun,
Appeared ethereal, and about to glide
On high adventure chartered, swift away
For regions undiscovered.

               Huddled wharfs
A while, and then once more a reach of Thames
Visibly flowing where the sun and wind
Together caught the current. Quays and piers
To Vauxhall Bridge, and there the Baltic Wharf
Exhibited its wonders: figureheads
Of the old wooden walls on gate and post—
Colossal torsos, bulky bosoms thrown
Against the storm, sublime uplifted eyes
Telling the stars. As white as ghosts
They overhung the way, usurping time
With carved memorials of the past. Forlorn
Elysium of the might of England! . . .

A. E. Housman (1859–1936)

"From the wash the laundress sends"

From the wash the laundress sends
My collars home with ravelled ends:
I must fit, now these are frayed,
My neck with new ones London-made.

Homespun collars, homespun hearts,
Wear to rags in foreign parts.
Mine at least's as good as done,
And I must get a London one.

Mary E. Coleridge (1861–1907)

In London Town

It was a bird of Paradise,
   Over the roofs he flew.
All the children, in a trice,
Clapped their hands and cried, "How nice!"
   "Look—his wings are blue!"

His body was of ruby red,
   His eyes were burning gold.
All the grown-up people said,
"What a pity the creature is not dead,
   For then it could be sold!"

One was braver than the rest.
   He took a loaded gun;
Aiming at the emerald crest,
He shot the creature through the breast.
   Down it fell in the sun.

It was not heavy, it was not fat,
   And folk began to stare.
"We cannot eat it, that is flat!
And such outlandish feathers as that
   Why, who could ever wear?"

They flung it into the river brown.
   "A pity the creature died!"
With a smile and with a frown,
Thus they did in London town;
   But all the children cried.

Amy Levy (1861–1889)

A March Day in London

The east wind blows in the street today;
The sky is blue, yet the town looks grey.
'Tis the wind of ice, the wind of fire,
Of cold despair and of hot desire,
Which chills the flesh to aches and pains,
And sends a fever through all the veins.

From end to end, with aimless feet,
All day long have I paced the street.
My limbs are weary, but in my breast
Stirs the goad of a mad unrest.
I would give anything to stay
The little wheel that turns in my brain;
The little wheel that turns all day,
That turns all night with might and main.

What is the thing I fear, and why?
Nay, but the world is all awry—
The wind's in the east, the sun's in the sky.
The gas-lamps gleam in a golden line;
The ruby lights of the hansoms shine,
Glance, and flicker like fire-flies bright;
The wind has fallen with the night,
And once again the town seems fair
Thwart the mist that hangs i' the air.

And o'er, at last, my spirit steals
A weary peace; peace that conceals
Within its inner depths the grain
Of hopes that yet shall flower again.

Straw in the Street

Straw in the street where I pass today
Dulls the sound of the wheels and feet.
'Tis for a failing life they lay
　　Straw in the street.

Here, where the pulses of London beat,
Someone strives with the Presence grey;
Ah, is it victory or defeat?

The hurrying people go their way,
Pause and jostle and pass and greet;
For life, for death, are they treading, say,
　　Straw in the street?

London Poets

They trod the streets and squares where now I tread,
With weary hearts, a little while ago;
When, thin and grey, the melancholy snow
Clung to the leafless branches overhead;
Or when the smoke-veiled sky grew stormy-red
In autumn; with a re-arisen woe
Wrestled, what time the passionate spring winds blow;
And paced scorched stones in summer:—they are dead.

The sorrow of their souls to them did seem
As real as mine to me, as permanent.
Today, it is the shadow of a dream,
The half-forgotten breath of breezes spent.
So shall another soothe his woe supreme—
"No more he comes, who this way came and went."

Rudyard Kipling (1865–1936)

In Partibus

> The 'buses run to Battersea,
>   The 'buses run to Bow,
> The 'buses run to Westbourne Grove,
>   And Notting Hill also;
> But I am sick of London Town,
>   From Shepherd's Bush to Bow.

I see the smut upon my cuff,
    And feel him on my nose;
I cannot leave my window wide
    When gentle Zephyr blows,
Because he brings disgusting things,
    And drops 'em on my clo'es.

The sky, a greasy soup-tureen,
    Shuts down atop my brow.
Yes, I have sighed for London Town
    And I have got it now:
And half of it is fog and filth,
    And half is fog and row.

And when I take my nightly prowl,
    'Tis passing good to meet
The pious Briton lugging home
    His wife and daughter sweet,
Through four packed miles of seething vice,
    Thrust out upon the street.

Earth holds no horror like to this
    In any land displayed,
From Suez unto Sandy Hook,
    From Calais to Port Said;
And 'twas to hide their heathendom
    The beastly fog was made.

I cannot tell when dawn is near,
   Or when the day is done,
Because I always see the gas
   And never see the sun,
And now, methinks, I do not care
   A cuss for either one.

But stay, there was an orange, or
   An aged egg its yolk;
It might have been a Pears' balloon
   Or Barnum's latest joke:
I took it for the sun and wept
   To watch it through the smoke.

It's Oh to see the morn ablaze
   Above the mango-tope,
When homeward through the dewy cane
   The little jackals lope,
And half Bengal heaves into view,
   New-washed—with sunlight soap.

It's Oh for one deep whisky-peg
   When Christmas winds are blowing,
When all the men you ever knew,
   And all you've ceased from knowing,
Are "entered for the Tournament,
   And everything that's going."

But I consort with long-haired things
   In velvet collar-rolls,
Who talk about the Aims of Art,
   And "theories" and "goals,"
And moo and coo with womenfolk
   About their blessed souls.

But that they call "psychology"
   Is lack of liver-pill,
And all that blights their tender souls
   Is eating till they're ill,

And their chief way of winning goals
    Consists of sitting still.

Its Oh to meet an Army man,
    Set up, and trimmed and taut,
Who does not spout hashed libraries
    Or think the next man's thought,
And walks as though he owned himself,
    And hogs his bristles short.

Hear now a voice across the seas
    To kin beyond my ken,
If ye have ever filled an hour
    With stories from my pen,
For pity's sake send some one here
    To bring me news of men!

The 'buses run to Islington,
    To Highgate and Soho,
To Hammersmith and Kew therewith,
    And Camberwell also,
But I can only murmur "Bus!"
    From Shepherd's Bush to Bow.

The River's Tale

(PREHISTORIC)

Twenty bridges from Tower to Kew—
(Twenty bridges or twenty-two)—
Wanted to know what the River knew,
For they were young and the Thames was old,
And this is the tale that the River told:

"I walk my beat before London Town,
Five hours up and seven down.
Up I go till I end my run
At Tide-end-town, which is Teddington.
Down I come with the mud in my hands
And plaster it over the Maplin Sands.
But I'd have you know that these waters of mine
Were once a branch of the River Rhine,
When hundreds of miles to the East I went
And England was joined to the Continent.
I remember the bat-winged lizard-birds,
The Age of Ice and the mammoth herds,
And the giant tigers that stalked them down
Through Regent's Park into Camden Town.
And I remember like yesterday
The earliest Cockney who came my way,
When he pushed through the forest that lined the Strand,
With paint on his face and a club in his hand.
He was death to feather and fin and fur.
He trapped my beavers at Westminster.
He netted my salmon, he hunted my deer,
He killed my heron off Lambeth Pier.
He fought his neighbour with axes and swords,
Flint or bronze, at my upper fords,
While down at Greenwich, for slaves and tin,
The tall Phoenician ships stole in,

And North Sea war-boats, painted and gay,
Flashed like dragon-flies, Erith way;
And Norseman and Negro and Gaul and Greek
Drank with the Britons in Barking Creek,
And life was gay, and the world was new,
And I was a mile across at Kew!
But the Roman came with a heavy hand,
And bridged and roaded and ruled the land,
And the Roman left and the Danes blew in—
And that's where your history-books begin!"

London Stone

When you come to London Town,
   (Grieving–grieving!)
Bring your flowers and lay them down
   At the place of grieving.

When you come to London Town,
   (Grieving–grieving!)
Bow your head and mourn your own,
   With the others grieving.

For those minutes, let it wake
   (Grieving–grieving!)
All the empty-heart and ache
   That is not cured by grieving.

For those minutes, tell no lie:
   (Grieving–grieving!)
"Grave, this is thy victory;
   And the sting of death is grieving."

Where's our help, from Earth or Heaven,
   (Grieving–grieving!)
To comfort us for what we've given,
   And only gained the grieving?

Heaven's too far and Earth too near,
   (Grieving–grieving!)
But our neighbour's standing here,
   Grieving as we're grieving.

What's his burden, every day?
   (Grieving–grieving!)
Nothing man can count or weigh,
   But loss and love's own grieving.

What is the tie betwixt us two
    (Grieving–grieving!)
That must last our whole lives through?
"As I suffer, so do you."
    That may ease the grieving.

The Craftsman

Once, after long-drawn revel at The Mermaid,
He to the overbearing Boanerges
Jonson, uttered (if half of it were liquor,
                    Blessed be the vintage!)

Saying how, at an alehouse under Cotswold,
He had made sure of his very Cleopatra
Drunk with enormous, salvation-contemning
                    Love for a tinker.

How, while he hid from Sir Thomas's keepers,
Crouched in a ditch and drenched by the midnight
Dews, he had listened to gipsy Juliet
                    Rail at the dawning.

How at Bankside, a boy drowning kittens
Winced at the business; whereupon his sister—
Lady Macbeth aged seven—thrust 'em under,
                    Sombrely scornful.

How on a Sabbath, hushed and compassionate—
She being known since her birth to the townsfolk—
Stratford dredged and delivered from Avon
                    Dripping Ophelia.

So, with a thin third finger marrying
Drop to wine-drop domed on the table,
Shakespeare opened his heart till the sunrise
                    Entered to hear him.

London waked and he, imperturbable,
Passed from waking to hurry after shadows . . .
Busied upon shows of no earthly importance?
                    Yes, but he knew it!

from *Epitaphs of the War*

BOMBED IN LONDON

On land and sea I strove with anxious care
To escape conscription. It was in the air!

Arthur Symons (1865–1945)

from *London Nights*

PROLOGUE: IN THE STALLS

My life is like a music-hall,
Where, in the impotence of rage,
Chained by enchantment to my stall,
I see myself upon the stage
Dance to amuse a music-hall.

'Tis I that smoke this cigarette,
Lounge here, and laugh for vacancy,
And watch the dancers turn; and yet
It is my very self I see
Across the cloudy cigarette.

My very self that turns and trips,
Painted, pathetically gay,
An empty song upon the lips
In make-believe of holiday:
I, I, this thing that turns and trips!

The light flares in the music-hall,
The light, the sound, that weary us;
Hour follows hour, I count them all,
Lagging, and loud, and riotous:
My life is like a music-hall.

AT THE STAGE-DOOR

Kicking my heels in the street,
Here at the edge of the pavement I wait, and my feet
Paw at the ground like the horses' hoofs in the street.

Under the archway sheer,
Sudden and black as a hole in the placarded wall,

Faces flicker and veer,
Wavering out of the darkness into the light,
Wavering back into night;
Under the archway, suddenly seen, the curls
And thin, bright faces of girls,
Roving eyes, and smiling lips, and the glance
Seeking, finding perchance,
Here at the edge of the pavement, there by the wall,
One face, out of them all.

Steadily, face after face,
Cheeks with the blush of the paint yet lingering, eyes
Still with their circle of black . . .
But hers, but hers?
Rose-leaf cheeks, and flower-soft lips, and the grace
Of the vanishing Spring come back,
And a child's heart blithe in the sudden and sweet surprise,
Subtly expectant, that stirs
In the smile of her heart to my heart, of her eyes to my eyes.

from *Décor de Théâtre*

BEHIND THE SCENES: EMPIRE

To Peppina

> The little painted angels flit,
> See, down the narrow staircase, where
> The pink legs flicker over it!
>
> Blonde, and bewigged, and winged with gold,
> The shining creatures of the air
> Troop sadly, shivering with cold.
>
> The gusty gaslight shoots a thin
> Sharp finger over cheeks and nose
> Rouged to the colour of the rose.
>
> All wigs and paint, they hurry in:
> Then, let their radiant moment be
> The footlights' immortality!

THE PRIMROSE DANCE: TIVOLI

To Minnie Cunningham

> Skirts like the amber petals of a flower,
> A primrose dancing for delight
> In some enchantment of a bower
> That rose to wizard music in the night;
>
> A rhythmic flower whose petals pirouette
> In delicate circles, fain to follow
> The vague aerial minuet,
> The mazy dancing of the swallow;
>
> A flower's caprice, a bird's command
> Of all the airy ways that lie
> In light along the wonder-land,
> The wonder-haunted loneliness of sky:

So, in the smoke-polluted place,
Where bird or flower might never be,
With glimmering feet, with flower-like face,
She dances at the Tivoli.

AT THE FORESTERS

The shadows of the gaslit wings
Come softly crawling down our way;
Before the curtain some one sings,
The music sounds from far away;
I stand beside you in the wings.

Prying and indiscreet, the lights
Illumine, if you chance to move,
The prince's dress, the yellow tights,
That fit your figure like a glove:
You shrink a little from the lights.

Divinely rosy rouged, your face
Smiles, with its painted little mouth,
Half tearfully, a quaint grimace;
The charm and pathos of your youth
Mock the mock roses of your face.

And there is something in your look
(Ambiguous, independent Flo!)
As teasing as a half-shut book;
It lures me till I long to know
The many meanings of your look:

The tired defiance of the eyes,
Pathetically whimsical,
Childish and whimsical and wise;
And now, relenting after all,
The softer welcome of your eyes.

London

The sun, a fiery orange in the air,
Thins and discolours to a disc of tin,
Until the breathing mist's mouth sucks it in;
And now there is no colour anywhere,
Only the ghost of greyness; vapour fills
The hollows of the streets, and seems to shroud
Gulfs where a noise of multitude is loud
As unseen water falling among hills.
Now the light withers, stricken at the root,
And in the evil glimpses of the light
Men as trees walking loom through lanes of night
Hung from the globes of some unnatural fruit.
To live, and to die daily, deaths like these,
Is it to live, while there are winds and seas?

W. B. Yeats (1865–1939)

from *Vacillation*

IV

> My fiftieth year had come and gone,
> I sat, a solitary man,
> In a crowded London shop,
> An open book and empty cup
> On the marble table-top.
> While on the shop and street I gazed
> My body of a sudden blazed;
> And twenty minutes more or less
> It seemed, so great my happiness,
> That I was blessèd and could bless.

Lionel Johnson (1867–1902)

London Town

Let others chant a country praise,
Fair river walks and meadow ways;
Dearer to me my sounding days
    In *London Town:*
To me the tumult of the street
Is no less music, than the sweet
Surge of the wind among the wheat,
    By dale or down.

Three names mine heart with rapture hails,
With homage: *Ireland, Cornwall, Wales:*
Lands of lone moor, and mountain gales,
    And stormy coast:
Yet *London's* voice upon the air
Pleads at mine heart, and enters there;
Sometimes I wellnigh love and care
    For *London* most.

Listen upon the ancient hills:
All silence! save the lark, who trills
Through sunlight, save the rippling rills:
    There peace may be.
But listen to great *London!* loud,
As thunder from the purple cloud,
Comes the deep thunder of the crowd,
    And heartens me.

O gray, O gloomy skies! What then?
Here is a marvellous world of men;
More wonderful than *Rome* was, when
    The world was *Rome!*
See the great stream of life flow by!
Here thronging myriads laugh and sigh,

Here rise and fall, here live and die:
    In this vast home.

In long array they march toward death,
Armies, with proud or piteous breath:
Forward! the spirit in them saith,
    Spirit of life:
Here the triumphant trumpets blow;
Here mourning music sorrows low;
Victors and vanquished, still they go
    Forward in strife.

Who will not heed so great a sight?
Greater than marshalled stars of night,
That move to music and with light:
    For these are men!
These move to music of the soul;
Passions, that madden or control:
These hunger for a distant goal,
    Seen now and then.

Is mine too tragical a strain,
Chanting a burden full of pain,
And labour, that seems all in vain?
    I sing but truth.
Still, many a merry pleasure yet,
To many a merry measure set,
Is ours, who need not to forget
    Summer and youth.

Do *London* birds forget to sing?
Do *London* trees refuse the spring?
Is *London* May no pleasant thing?
    Let country fields,
To milking maid and shepherd boy,
Give flowers, and song, and bright employ:
Her children also can enjoy,
    What *London* yields.

Gleaming with sunlight, each soft lawn
Lies fragrant beneath dew of dawn;
The spires and towers rise, far withdrawn,
      Through golden mist:
At sunset, linger beside *Thames:*
See now, what radiant lights and flames!
That ruby burns: that purple shames
      The amethyst.

Winter was long, and dark, and cold:
Chill rains! grim fogs, black fold on fold,
Round street, and square, and river rolled!
      Ah, let it be:
Winter is gone! Soon comes July,
With wafts from hayfields by-and-by:
While in the dingiest courts you spy
      Flowers fair to see.

Take heart of grace: and let each hour
Break gently into bloom and flower:
Winter and sorrow have no power
      To blight all bloom.
One day, perchance, the sun will see
London's entire felicity:
And all her loyal children be
      Clear of all gloom.

A dream? Dreams often dreamed come true:
Our world would seem a world made new
To those, beneath the churchyard yew
      Laid long ago!
When we beneath like shadows bide,
Fair *London,* throned upon *Thames'* side,
May be our children's children's pride:
      And we shall know.

By the Statue of King Charles at Charing Cross

To William Watson

Sombre and rich, the skies;
Great glooms, and starry plains.
Gently the night wind sighs;
Else a vast silence reigns.

The splendid silence clings
Around me: and around
The saddest of all kings
Crowned, and again discrowned.

Comely and calm, he rides
Hard by his own Whitehall:
Only the night wind glides:
No crowds, nor rebels, brawl.

Gone, too, his Court: and yet,
The stars his courtiers are:
Stars in their stations set;
And every wandering star.

Alone he rides, alone,
The fair and fatal king:
Dark night is all his own,
That strange and solemn thing.

Which are more full of fate:
The stars; or those sad eyes?
Which are more still and great:
Those brows; or the dark skies?

Although his whole heart yearn
In passionate tragedy:
Never was face so stern
With sweet austerity.

Vanquished in life, his death
By beauty made amends:
The passing of his breath
Won his defeated ends.

Brief life, and hapless? Nay:
Through death, life grew sublime.
Speak after sentence? Yea:
And to the end of time.

Armoured he rides, his head
Bare to the stars of doom:
He triumphs now, the dead,
Beholding London's gloom.

Our wearier spirit faints,
Vexed in the world's employ:
His soul was of the saints;
And art to him was joy.

King, tried in fires of woe!
Men hunger for thy grace:
And through the night I go,
Loving thy mournful face.

Yet, when the city sleeps;
When all the cries are still:
The stars and heavenly deeps
Work out a perfect will.

Charlotte Mew (1869–1928)

In Nunhead Cemetery

It is the clay that makes the earth stick to his spade;
    He fills in holes like this year after year;
The others have gone; they were tired, and half afraid
    But I would rather be standing here;

There is nowhere else to go. I have seen this place
    From the windows of the train that's going past
Against the sky. This is rain on my face—
    It was raining here when I saw it last.

There is something horrible about a flower;
    This, broken in my hand, is one of those
He threw in just now; it will not live another hour;
    There are thousands more: you do not miss a rose.

One of the children hanging about
    Pointed at the whole dreadful heap and smiled
This morning, after *that* was carried out;
    There is something terrible about a child.

We were like children, last week, in the Strand;
    That was the day you laughed at me
Because I tried to make you understand
    The cheap, stale chap I used to be
    Before I saw the things you made me see.

This is not a real place; perhaps by-and-by
    I shall wake—I am getting drenched with all this rain:
Tomorrow I will tell you about the eyes of the Crystal Palace train
    Looking down on us, and you will laugh and I shall see what you see again.

    Not here, not now. We said "Not yet
    Across our low stone parapet
Will the quick shadows of the sparrows fall."

But still it was a lovely thing
  Through the grey months to wait for Spring
  With the birds that go a-gypsying
In the parks till the blue seas call.
  And next to these, you used to care
  For the lions in Trafalgar Square,
Who'll stand and speak for London when her bell of Judgement tolls—
  And the gulls at Westminster that were
  The old sea-captains' souls.
Today again the brown tide splashes, step by step, the river stair,
  And the gulls are there!

By a month we have missed our Day:
  The children would have hung about
Round the carriage and over the way
  As you and I came out.

We should have stood on the gulls' black cliffs and heard the sea
  And seen the moon's white track,
I would have called, you would have come to me
  And kissed me back.

You have never done that: I do not know
  Why I stood staring at your bed
And heard you, though you spoke so low,
  But could not reach your hands, your little head.
There was nothing we could not do, you said,
  And you went, and I let you go!

Now I will burn you back, I will burn you through,
  Though I am damned for it we two will lie
  And burn, here where the starlings fly
  To these white stones from the wet sky—;
  Dear, you will say this is not I—
It would not be you, it would not be you!

If for only a little while
  You will think of it you will understand,

If you will touch my sleeve and smile
As you did that morning in the Strand
   I can wait quietly with you
   Or go away if you want me to—
God! What is God? but your face has gone and your hand!
   Let me stay here too.

   When I was quite a little lad
  At Christmas time we went half mad
   For joy of all the toys we had,
And then we used to sing about the sheep
   The shepherds watched by night;
We used to pray to Christ to keep
   Our small souls safe till morning light—;
I am scared, I am staying with you tonight—
    Put me to sleep.

I shall stay here: here you can see the sky;
The houses in the streets are much too high;
  There is no one left to speak to there;
  Here they are everywhere,
And just above them fields and fields of roses lie—
If he would dig it all up again they would not die.

Laurence Binyon (1869–1943)

As I Walked Through London

As I walked through London,
The fresh wound burning in my breast,
As I walked through London,
Longing to have forgotten, to harden my heart, and to rest,
A sudden consolation, a softening light
Touched me: the streets alive and bright,
With hundreds each way thronging, on their tide
Received me, a drop in the stream, unmarked, unknown.
And to my heart I cried:
Here can thy trouble find shelter, thy wound be eased!
For see, not thou alone,
But thousands, each with his smart,
Deep–hidden, perchance, but felt in the core of the heart!
And as to a sick man's feverish veins
The full sponge warmly pressed,
Relieves with its burning the burning of forehead and hands,
So, I, to my aching breast,
Gathered the griefs of those thousands, and made them my own;
My bitterest pains
Merged in a tenderer sorrow, assuaged and appeased.

T. E. Hulme (1883–1917)

The Embankment

(The fantasia of a fallen gentleman on a cold, bitter night)

Once, in finesse of fiddles found I ecstasy,
In a flash of gold heels on the hard pavement.
Now see I
That warmth's the very stuff of poesy.
Oh, God, make small
The old star-eaten blanket of the sky,
That I may fold it round me and in comfort lie.

Ezra Pound (1885–1972)

Portrait d'une Femme

Your mind and you are our Sargasso Sea,
London has swept about you this score years
And bright ships left you this or that in fee:
Ideas, old gossip, oddments of all things,
Strange spars of knowledge and dimmed wares of price.
Great minds have sought you—lacking someone else.
You have been second always. Tragical?
No. You preferred it to the usual thing:
One dull man, dulling and uxorious,
One average mind—with one thought less, each year.
Oh, you are patient, I have seen you sit
Hours, where something might have floated up.
And now you pay one. Yes, you richly pay.
You are a person of some interest, one comes to you
And takes strange gain away:
Trophies fished up; some curious suggestion;
Fact that leads nowhere; and a tale or two,
Pregnant with mandrakes, or with something else
That might prove useful and yet never proves,
That never fits a corner or shows use,
Or finds its hour upon the loom of days:
The tarnished, gaudy, wonderful old work;
Idols and ambergris and rare inlays,
These are your riches, your great store; and yet
For all this sea-hoard of deciduous things,
Strange woods half sodden, and new brighter stuff:
In the slow float of differing light and deep,
No! there is nothing! In the whole and all,
Nothing that's quite your own.
    Yet this is you.

The Garden

En robe de parade.
> —*Samain*

     Like a skein of loose silk blown against a wall
     She walks by the railing of a path in Kensington Gardens,
     And she is dying piece-meal
        of a sort of emotional anaemia.

     And round about there is a rabble
     Of the filthy, sturdy, unkillable infants of the very poor.
     They shall inherit the earth.

     In her is the end of breeding.
     Her boredom is exquisite and excessive.
     She would like some one to speak to her,
     And is almost afraid that I
        will commit that indiscretion.

Simulacra

Why does the horse-faced lady of just the unmentionable age
Walk down Longacre reciting Swinburne to herself, inaudibly?
Why does the small child in the soiled-white imitation fur coat
Crawl in the very black gutter beneath the grape stand?
Why does the really handsome young woman approach me in Sackville Street
Undeterred by the manifest age of my trappings?

from *Hugh Selwyn Mauberley*

YEUX GLAUQUES

Gladstone was still respected,
When John Ruskin produced
"Kings Treasuries"; Swinburne
And Rossetti still abused.

Foetid Buchanan lifted up his voice
When that faun's head of hers
Became a pastime for
Painters and adulterers.

The Burne-Jones cartons
Have preserved her eyes;
Still, at the Tate, they teach
Cophetua to rhapsodize;

Thin like brook-water,
With a vacant gaze.
The English Rubaiyat was still-born
In those days.

The thin, clear gaze, the same
Still darts out faun-like from the half-ruined face
Questing and passive. . . .
"Ah, poor Jenny's case" . . .

Bewildered that a world
Shows no surprise
At her last maquero's
Adulteries.

SIENA MI FE', DISFECEMI MAREMMA

Among the pickled foetuses and bottled bones,
Engaged in perfecting the catalogue,

I found the last scion of the
Senatorial families of Strasbourg, Monsieur Verog.

For two hours he talked of Gallifet;
Of Dowson; of the Rhymers' Club;
Told me how Johnson (Lionel) died
By falling from a high stool in a pub . . .

But showed no trace of alcohol
At the autopsy, privately performed—
Tissue preserved—the pure mind
Arose toward Newman as the whiskey warmed.

Dowson found harlots cheaper than hotels;
Headlam for uplift; Image impartially imbued
With raptures for Bacchus, Terpsichore and the Church.
So spoke the author of "The Dorian Mood,"

M. Verog, out of step with the decade,
Detached from his contemporaries,
Neglected by the young,
Because of these reveries.

XII

"Daphne with her thighs in bark
Stretches toward me her leafy hands,"—
Subjectively. In the stuffed-satin drawing-room
I await The Lady Valentine's commands,

Knowing my coat has never been
Of precisely the fashion
To stimulate, in her,
A durable passion;

Doubtful, somewhat, of the value
Of well-gowned approbation
Of literary effort,
But never of The Lady Valentine's vocation:

Poetry, her border of ideas,
The edge, uncertain, but a means of blending
With other strata
Where the lower and higher have ending;

A hook to catch the Lady Jane's attention,
A modulation toward the theatre,
Also, in the case of revolution,
A possible friend and comforter.
. . .

Conduct, on the other hand, the soul
"Which the highest cultures have nourished"
To Fleet St. where
Dr. Johnson flourished;

Beside this thoroughfare
The sale of half-hose has
Long since superseded the cultivation
Of Pierian roses.

D. H. Lawrence (1885–1930)

Flat Suburbs, S.W., in the Morning

The new red houses spring like plants
    In level rows
Of reddish herbage that bristles and slants
    Its square shadows.

The pink young houses show one side bright
    Flatly assuming the sun,
And one side shadow, half in sight,
    Half-hiding the pavement-run;

Where hastening creatures pass intent
    On their level way,
Threading like ants that can never relent
    And have nothing to say.

Bare stems of street lamps stiffly stand
    At random, desolate twigs,
To testify to a blight on the land
    That has stripped their sprigs.

from *Guards*

A REVIEW IN HYDE PARK, 1910: THE CROWD WATCHES

Where the trees rise like cliffs, proud and blue-tinted in the distance,
Between the cliffs of the trees, on the grey-green park
Rests a still line of soldiers, red, motionless range of guards
Smouldering with darkened busbies beneath the bayonets' slant rain.

Colossal in nearness a blue police sits still on his horse
Guarding the path; his hand relaxed at his thigh,
And skywards his face is immobile, eyelids aslant
In tedium, and mouth relaxed as if smiling—ineffable tedium!

So! So! Gaily a general canters across the space,
With white plumes blinking under the evening grey sky.
And suddenly, as if the ground moved,
The red range heaves in slow, magnetic reply.

Bombardment

The Town has opened to the sun.
Like a flat red lily with a million petals
She unfolds, she comes undone.

A sharp sky brushes upon
The myriad glittering chimney-tips
As she gently exhales to the sun.

Hurrying creatures run
Down the labyrinth of the sinister flower.
What is it they shun?

A dark bird falls from the sun.
It curves in a rush to the heart of the vast
Flower: the day has begun.

Hyde Park at Night, Before the War

CLERKS

We have shut the doors behind us, and the velvet flowers of night
Lean about us scattering their pollen grains of golden light.

Now at last we lift our faces, and our faces come aflower
To the night that takes us willing, liberates us to the hour.

Now at last the ink and dudgeon passes from our fervent eyes
And out of the chambered wilderness wanders a spirit abroad on its
    enterprise.

    Not too near and not too far
    Out of the stress of the crowd
    Music screams as elephants scream
    When they lift their trunks and scream aloud
    For joy of the night when masters are
        Asleep and adream.

    So here I hide in the Shalimar
    With a wanton princess slender and proud,
    And we swoon with kisses, swoon till we seem
    Two streaming peacocks gone in a cloud
    Of golden dust, with star after star
        On our stream.

Embankment at Night, Before the War

CHARITY

By the river
In the black wet night as the furtive rain slinks down,
Dropping and starting from sleep
Alone on a seat
A woman crouches.

I must go back to her.

I want to give her
Some money. Her hand slips out of the breast of her gown
Asleep. My fingers creep
Carefully over the sweet
Thumb-mound, into the palm's deep pouches.

So the gift!

God, how she starts!
And looks at me, and looks in the palm of her hand
And again at me!–
I turn and run
Down the Embankment, run for my life.

But why?–why?

Because of my heart's
Beating like sobs, I come to myself, and stand
In the street spilled over splendidly
With wet, flat lights. What I've done
I know not, my soul is in strife.

The touch was on the quick. I want to forget.

OUTCASTS

The night rain, dripping unseen,
Comes endlessly kissing my face and my hands.

The river slipping between
Lamps, is rayed with golden bands
Half way down its heaving sides;
Revealed where it hides.

Under the bridge
Great electric cars
Sing through, and each with a floor-light racing along at its side.
Far off, oh, midge after midge
Drifts over the gulf that bars
The night with silence, crossing the lamp-touched tide.

At Charing Cross, here, beneath the bridge
Sleep in a row the outcasts,
Packed in a line with their heads against the wall.
Their feet in a broken ridge
Stretched out on the way, and a lout casts
A look as he stands on the edge of this naked stall.

Beasts that sleep will cover
Their face in their flank; so these
Have huddled rags or limbs on the naked sleep.
Save, as the tram-cars hover
Past with the noise of a breeze
And gleam as of sunshine crossing the low black heap,

Two naked faces are seen
Bare and asleep,
Two pale clots swept by the light of the cars.
Foam-clots showing between
The long, low tidal-heap,
The mud-weed opening two pale, shadowless stars.

Over the pallor of only two faces
Passes the gallivant beam of the trams;
Shows in only two sad places
The white bare bone of our shams.

A little, bearded man, peaked in sleeping.
With a face like a chickweed flower.
And a heavy woman, sleeping still keeping
Callous and dour.

Over the pallor of only two places
Tossed on the low, black, ruffled heap
Passes the light of the tram as it races
Out of the deep.

Eloquent limbs
In disarray,
Sleep-suave limbs of a youth with long, smooth thighs
Hutched up for warmth; the muddy rims
Of trousers fray
On the thin bare shins of a man who uneasily lies.

The balls of five red toes
As red and dirty, bare
Young birds forsaken and left in a nest of mud—
Newspaper sheets enclose
Some limbs like parcels, and tear
When the sleeper stirs or turns on the ebb of the flood—

One heaped mound
Of a woman's knees
As she thrusts them upward under the ruffled skirt—
And a curious dearth of sound
In the presence of these
Wastrels that sleep on the flagstones without any hurt.

Over two shadowless, shameless faces
Stark on the heap
Travels the light as it tilts in its paces
Gone in one leap.

At the feet of the sleepers, watching,
Stand those that wait

For a place to lie down; and still as they stand, they sleep;
Wearily catching
The flood's slow gait
Like men who are drowned, but float erect in the deep.

Oh, the singing mansions,
Golden-lighted tall
Trams that pass, blown ruddily down the night!
The bridge on its stanchions
Stoops like a pall
To this human blight.

On the outer pavement, slowly,
Theatre people pass,
Holding aloft their umbrellas that flash and are bright
Like flowers of infernal moly
Over nocturnal grass
Wetly bobbing and drifting away on our sight.

And still by the rotten row of shattered feet,
Outcasts keep guard.
Forgotten,
Forgetting, till fate shall delete
One from the ward.

The factories on the Surrey side
Are beautifully laid in black on a gold-grey sky.
The river's invisible tide
Threads and thrills like ore that is wealth to the eye.

And great gold midges
Cross the chasm
At the bridges
Above intertwined plasm.

Town in 1917

London
Used to wear her lights splendidly,
Flinging her shawl-fringe over the River,
Tassels in abandon.

And up in the sky
A two-eyed clock, like an owl
Solemnly used to approve, chime, chiming
Approval, goggle-eyed fowl!

There are no gleams on the River,
No goggling clock;
No sound from St. Stephen's;
No lamp-fringed frock.

Instead
Darkness, and skin-wrapped
Fleet, hurrying limbs,
Soft-footed dead.

London
Original, wolf-wrapped
In pelts of wolves, all her luminous
Garments gone.

London, with hair
Like a forest darkness, like a marsh
Of rushes, ere the Romans
Broke in her lair.

It is well
That London, lair of sudden
Male and female darknesses,
Has broken her spell.

Frances Cornford (1886–1960)

London Streets

VILLANELLE

The blundering and cruel ways of nature
  —*Charles Darwin*

O Providence, I will not praise,
Neither for fear nor joy of gain,
Your blundering and cruel ways.

This city where the dun fog stays,
These tired faces in the rain,
O Providence, I will not praise.

Here in the mud and wind that slays
In the cold streets, I scan again
Your blundering and cruel ways.

And all men's miserable days,
And all their ugliness and pain,
O Providence, I will not praise.

I will not join the hymns men raise
Like slaves who would avert, in vain,
Your blundering and cruel ways.

At least, in this distracted maze,
I love the truth and see it plain;
O Providence, I will not praise
Your blundering and cruel ways.

Parting in Wartime

How long ago Hector took off his plume,
Not wanting that his little son should cry,
Then kissed his sad Andromache goodbye—
And now we three in Euston waiting-room.

Siegfried Sassoon (1886–1967)

Monody on the Demolition of Devonshire House

Strolling one afternoon along a street
Whose valuable vastness can compare
With anything on earth in the complete
Efficiency of its mammoniac air—
Strolling (to put it plainly) through those bits
Of Londonment adjacent to the Ritz,
(While musing on the social gap between
Myself, whose arrogance is mostly brainy,
And those whose pride, on sunlit days and rainy,
Must loll and glide in yacht and limousine),
Something I saw, beyond a boarded barrier,
Which manifested well that Time's no tarrier.

Where stood the low-built mansion, once so great,
Ducal, demure, secure in its estate—
Where Byron rang the bell and limped upstairs,
And Lord knows what political affairs
Got muddled and remodelled while Their Graces
Manned unperturbed Elizabethan faces—
There, blankly overlooked by wintry strange
Frontage of houses rawly-lit by change,
Industrious workmen reconstructed quite
The lumbered, pegged, and excavated site;
And not one nook survived to screen a mouse
In what was Devonshire (God rest it) House.

T. S. Eliot (1888–1965)

from *The Waste Land*

from I. THE BURIAL OF THE DEAD

> Unreal City,
> Under the brown fog of a winter dawn,
> A crowd flowed over London Bridge, so many,
> I had not thought death had undone so many.
> Sighs, short and infrequent, were exhaled,
> And each man fixed his eyes before his feet.
> Flowed up the hill and down King William Street,
> To where Saint Mary Woolnoth kept the hours
> With a dead sound on the final stroke of nine.
> There I saw one I knew, and stopped him, crying: "Stetson!
> "You who were with me in the ships at Mylae!
> "That corpse you planted last year in your garden,
> "Has it begun to sprout? Will it bloom this year?
> "Or has the sudden frost disturbed its bed?
> "O keep the Dog far hence, that's friend to men,
> "Or with his nails he'll dig it up again!
> "You! hypocrite lecteur!–mon semblable,–mon frère!"

III. THE FIRE SERMON

> The river's tent is broken; the last fingers of leaf
> Clutch and sink into the wet bank. The wind
> Crosses the brown land, unheard. The nymphs are departed.
> Sweet Thames, run softly, till I end my song.
> The river bears no empty bottles, sandwich papers,
> Silk handkerchiefs, cardboard boxes, cigarette ends
> Or other testimony of summer nights. The nymphs are departed.
> And their friends, the loitering heirs of City directors;
> Departed, have left no addresses.
> By the waters of Leman I sat down and wept . . .

Sweet Thames, run softly till I end my song,
Sweet Thames, run softly, for I speak not loud or long.
But at my back in a cold blast I hear
The rattle of the bones, and chuckle spread from ear to ear.

A rat crept softly through the vegetation
Dragging its slimy belly on the bank
While I was fishing in the dull canal
On a winter evening round behind the gashouse
Musing upon the king my brother's wreck
And on the king my father's death before him.
White bodies naked on the low damp ground
And bones cast in a little low dry garret,
Rattled by the rat's foot only, year to year.
But at my back from time to time I hear
The sound of horns and motors, which shall bring
Sweeney to Mrs. Porter in the spring.
O the moon shone bright on Mrs. Porter
And on her daughter
They wash their feet in soda water
Et O ces voix d'enfants, chantant dans la coupole!

Twit twit twit
Jug jug jug jug jug jug
So rudely forc'd.
Tereu

    Unreal City
Under the brown fog of a winter noon
Mr. Eugenides, the Smyrna merchant
Unshaven, with a pocket full of currants
C.i.f. London: documents at sight,
Asked me in demotic French
To luncheon at the Cannon Street Hotel
Followed by a weekend at the Metropole.

    At the violet hour, when the eyes and back
Turn upward from the desk, when the human engine waits

Like a taxi throbbing waiting,
I Tiresias, though blind, throbbing between two lives,
Old man with wrinkled female breasts, can see
At the violet hour, the evening hour that strives
Homeward, and brings the sailor home from sea,
The typist home at teatime, clears her breakfast, lights
Her stove, and lays out food in tins.
Out of the window perilously spread
Her drying combinations touched by the sun's last rays,
On the divan are piled (at night her bed)
Stockings, slippers, camisoles, and stays.
I Tiresias, old man with wrinkled dugs
Perceived the scene, and foretold the rest—
I too awaited the expected guest.
He, the young man carbuncular, arrives,
A small house agent's clerk, with one bold stare,
One of the low on whom assurance sits
As a silk hat on a Bradford millionaire.
The time is now propitious, as he guesses.
The meal is ended, she is bored and tired,
Endeavours to engage her in caresses
Which still are unreproved, if undesired.
Flushed and decided, he assaults at once;
Exploring hands encounter no defence;
His vanity requires no response,
And makes a welcome of indifference.
(And I Tiresias have foresuffered all
Enacted on this same divan or bed;
I who have sat by Thebes below the wall
And walked among the lowest of the dead.)
Bestows one final patronising kiss,
And gropes his way, finding the stairs unlit . . .

  She turns and looks a moment in the glass.
Hardly aware of her departed lover;
Her brain allows one half-formed thought to pass:

"Well now that's done: and I'm glad it's over."
When lovely woman stoops to folly and
Paces about her room again, alone,
She smoothes her hair with automatic hand,
And puts a record on the gramophone.

   "This music crept by me upon the waters"
And along the Strand, up Queen Victoria Street.
O City city, I can sometimes hear
Beside a public bar in Lower Thames Street,
The pleasant whining of a mandoline
And a clatter and a chatter from within
Where fishmen lounge at noon: where the walls
Of Magnus Martyr hold
Inexplicable splendour of Ionian white and gold.

   The river sweats
   Oil and tar
   The barges drift
   With the turning tide
   Red sails
   Wide
   To leeward, swing on the heavy spar.
   The barges wash
   Drifting logs
   Down Greenwich reach
   Past the Isle of Dogs.
     Weialala leia
     Wallala leialala

   Elizabeth and Leicester
   Beating oars
   The stern was formed
   A gilded shell
   Red and gold
   The brisk swell
   Rippled both shores

Southwest wind
Carried down stream
The peal of bells
White towers
 Weialala leia
 Wallala leialala

"Trams and dusty trees.
Highbury bore me. Richmond and Kew
Undid me. By Richmond I raised my knees
Supine on the floor of a narrow canoe."

"My feet are at Moorgate, and my heart
Under my feet. After the event
He wept. He promised 'a new start.'
I made no comment. What should I resent?"

"On Margate Sands.
I can connect
Nothing with nothing.
The broken fingernails of dirty hands.
My people humble people who expect
Nothing."
 la la

To Carthage then I came

Burning burning burning burning
O Lord Thou pluckest me out
O Lord Thou pluckest

burning

from *Sweeney Agonistes*

DUSTY: Do you know London well, Mr. Krumpacker?

KLIPSTEIN: No we never been here before.

KRUMPACKER: We hit this town last night for the first time.

KLIPSTEIN: And I certainly hope it won't be the last time.

DORIS: You like London, Mr. Klipstein?

KRUMPACKER: Do we like London? do we like London!
   Do we like London!! Eh what Klip?

KLIPSTEIN: Say, Miss—er—uh—London's swell.
   We like London fine.

KRUMPACKER: Perfectly slick.

DUSTY: Why don't you come and live here then?

KLIPSTEIN: Well, no, Miss—er—you haven't quite got it
   (I'm afraid I didn't quite catch your name—
   But I'm very pleased to meet you all the same)—
   London's a little too gay for us
   Yes I'll say a little too gay.

KRUMPACKER: Yes London's a little too gay for us
   Don't think I mean anything *coarse*—
   But I'm afraid we couldn't stand the pace.
   What about it Klip?

KLIPSTEIN: You said it, Krum.
   London's a slick place, London's a swell place,
   London's a fine place to come on a visit—

KRUMPACKER: Specially when you got a real live Britisher
   A guy like Sam to show you around.
   Sam of course is at *home* in London,
   And he's promised to show us around.

from *Four Quartets*

from BURNT NORTON

III

Here is a place of disaffection
Time before and time after
In a dim light: neither daylight
Investing form with lucid stillness
Turning shadow into transient beauty
With slow rotation suggesting permanence
Nor darkness to purify the soul
Emptying the sensual with deprivation
Cleansing affection from the temporal.
Neither plenitude nor vacancy. Only a flicker
Over the strained time-ridden faces
Distracted from distraction by distraction
Filled with fancies and empty of meaning
Tumid apathy with no concentration
Men and bits of paper, whirled by the cold wind
That blows before and after time,
Wind in and out of unwholesome lungs
Time before and time after.
Eructation of unhealthy souls
Into the faded air, the torpid
Driven on the wind that sweeps the gloomy hills of London.
Hampstead and Clerkenwell, Campden and Putney,
Highgate, Primrose and Ludgate. Not here
Not here the darkness, in this twittering world.

　　Descend lower, descend only
Into the world of perpetual solitude,
World not world, but that which is not world,
Internal darkness, deprivation
And destitution of all property,
Desiccation of the world of sense,
Evacuation of the world of fancy,

Inoperancy of the world of spirit;
This is the one way, and the other
Is the same, not in movement
But abstention from movement; while the world moves
In appetency, on its metalled ways
Of time past and time future.

Isaac Rosenberg (1890–1918)

Fleet Street

From north and south, from east and west,
Here in one shrieking vortex meet
These streams of life, made manifest
Along the shaking quivering street.
Its pulse and heart that throbs and glows
As if strife were its repose.

I shut my ear to such rude sounds
As reach a harsh discordant note,
Till, melting into what surrounds,
My soul doth with the current float;
And from the turmoil and the strife
Wakes all the melody of life.

The stony buildings blindly stare
Unconscious of the crime within,
While man returns his fellow's glare
The secrets of his soul to win.
And each man passes from his place,
None heed. A shadow leaves such trace.

Richard Aldington (1892–1962)

St. Mary's, Kensington

The orange plane-leaves
Rest gently on the cracked grey slabs
In the city churchyard.

O pitiful dead,
There is not one of those who pass by
To remember you.

But the trees do not forget;
Their severed tresses
Are laid sadly above you.

In the Tube

The electric car jerks;
I stumble on the slats of the floor,
Fall into a leather seat
And look up.

A row of advertisements,
A row of windows,
Set in brown woodwork pitted with brass nails,
A row of hard faces,
Immobile,
In the swaying train,
Rush across the flickering background of fluted dingy tunnel;
A row of eyes,
Eyes of greed, of pitiful blankness, of plethoric complacency,
Immobile,
Gaze, stare at one point,
At my eyes.

Antagonism,
Disgust,
Immediate antipathy,
Cut my brain, as a dry sharp reed
Cuts a finger.
I surprise the same thought
In the brasslike eyes:
"What right have you to live?"

Hampstead Heath

(Easter Monday, 1915)

> Dark clouds, torn into gaps of livid sky,
> Pierced through
> By a swift searchlight, a long white dagger.
> The black murmuring crowd
> Flows, eddies, stops, flows on
> Between the lights
> And the banks of noisy booths.

London

(May, 1915)

Glittering leaves
Dance in a squall;
Behind them bleak immoveable clouds.

A church spire
Holds up a little brass cock
To peck at the blue wheat fields.

Roofs, conical spires, tapering chimneys,
Livid with sunlight, lace the horizon.

A pear-tree, a broken white pyramid
In a dingy garden, troubles me
With ecstasy.

At night, the moon, a pregnant woman,
Walks cautiously over the slippery heavens

And I am tormented,
Obsessed,
Among all this beauty,
With a vision of ruins,
Of walls crumbling into clay.

Whitechapel

Noise;
Iron hoofs, iron wheels, iron din
Of drays and trams and feet passing;
Iron
Beaten to a vast mad cacophony.

In vain the shrill far cry
Of swallows sweeping by;
In vain the silence and green
Of meadows Apriline;
In vain the clear white rain—

Soot; mud;
A nation maddened with labour;
Interminable collision of energies—
Iron beating upon iron;
Smoke whirling upwards,
Speechless, impotent.

In vain the shrill far cry
Of kittiwakes that fly
Where the sea waves leap green.
The meadows Apriline—

Noise, iron, smoke;
Iron, iron, iron.

Eros and Psyche

In an old dull yard near Camden Town,
Which echoes with the rattle of cars and 'buses
And freight-trains, puffing steam and smoke and dirt
To the steaming sooty sky—
There stands an old and grimy statue,
A statue of Psyche and her lover, Eros.

A little nearer Camden Town,
In a square of ugly sordid shops,
Is another statue, facing the Tube,
Staring with heavy purposeless glare
At the red and white shining tiles—
A tall stone statue of Cobden.
And though no one ever pauses to see
What hero it is that faces the Tube,
I can understand very well indeed
That England must honour its national heroes,
Must honour the hero of Free Trade—
Or was it the Corn Laws?—
That I can understand.

But what I shall never understand
Is the little group in the dingy yard
Under the dingier sky,
The Eros and Psyche—
Surrounded with pots and terra-cotta busts
And urns and broken pillars—
Eros, naked, with his wings stretched out
Just lighting down to kiss her on the lips.

What are they doing here in Camden Town
In the midst of all this clamour and filth?
They, who should stand in a sun-lit room
Hung with deep purple, painted with gods,
Paved with dark porphyry,
Stand for ever embraced

By the side of a rustling fountain
Over a marble basin
Carved with leopards and grapes and young men dancing;
Or in a garden leaning above Corinth,
Under the ilexes and the cypresses,
Very white against a very blue sky;
Or growing hoary, if they must grow old,
With lichens and softly creeping moss:
What are they doing here in Camden Town?
And who has brought their naked beauty
And their young fresh lust to Camden Town,
Which settled long ago to toil and sweat and filth,
Forgetting—to the greater glory of Free Trade—
Young beauty and young love and youthful flesh?

Slowly the rain settles down on them,
Slowly the soot eats into them,
Slowly the stone grows greyer and dirtier,
Till in spite of his spreading wings
Her eyes have a rim of soot
Half an inch deep,
And his wings, the tall god's wings,
That should be red and silver
Are ocherous brown.

And I peer from a 'bus-top
As we splash through the grease and puddles,
And I glimpse them, huddled against the wall,
Half-hidden under a freight-train's smoke,
And I see the limbs that a Greek slave cut
In some old Italian town,
I see them growing older
And sadder
And greyer.

Wilfred Owen (1893–1918)

"I am the ghost of Shadwell Stair"

I am the ghost of Shadwell Stair.
    Along the wharves by the water-house
    And through the cavernous slaughter-house,
I am the shadow that walks there.

Yet I have flesh both firm and cool,
    And eyes tumultuous as the gems
    Of moons and lamps in the full Thames
When dusk sails wavering down the Pool.

Shuddering, a purple street-arc burns
    Where I watch always. From the banks
    Dolorously the shipping clanks.
And after me a strange tide turns.

I walk till the stars of London wane,
    And dawn creeps up the Shadwell Stair.
    But when the crowing sirens blare,
I with another ghost am lain.

Sylvia Townsend Warner (1893–1978)

Song from the Bride of Smithfield

A thousand guileless sheep have bled,
A thousand bullocks knelt in fear,
To daub my Henry's cheek with red
And round the curl above his ear.

And wounded calves hung up to drip
Have in slow sweats distilled for him
The dew that polishes his lip,
The inward balm that oils each limb.

In vain I spread my maiden arts,
In vain for Henry's love I pine.
He is too skilled in bleeding hearts
To turn this way and pity mine.

East London Cemetery

Death keeps—an indifferent host—
this house of call,
whose sign-board wears no boast
save Beds for All.

Narrow the bed, and bare,
And none too sweet.
No need, says Death, to air
the single sheet.

Comfort, says he, with shrug,
is but degree,
and London clay a rug
like luxury,

to him who wrapped his bones
in the threadbare hood
blood wove from weft of stones
under warp of foot.

John Rodker (1894–1955)

The Shop

In the evening after work
when I go down the little side street in Battersea,
to the tiny shop
with its packets of Lyons' tea with blue labels
in the window—
and with them
a pink tin or two of salmon;
and the black and brown boot laces
hang from the gas bracket
with its two pale globes,
a little bell jangles
and the Japanese wind bells tinkle furiously for a minute
and my feet strike loudly on the boards.

After a while
a little old woman with grey hair
comes out and sells me matches.

On the counter is a glass case
with collar studs and tins of blacking.
Wood bundles are stacked against the counter
and I smell the tarred string binding them.

In the air is paraffin
and the strong acid of pickles.
Pickles! Red, yellow—
onions, walnuts, gherkins!
their acid smell is poignant
vertiginous ...

Yellow or red—
mustard pickles
or the sickening magenta of red cabbage.

I cannot resist them,
they bite into me,
I too, once lost a love—
and so I take the horrible magenta of the red cabbage
in a piece of newspaper—
and the old lady carefully drains off the vitriol.

And the shop grows sombre
and after a while the little old woman
goes out of the shop
to her bright parlour,
where perhaps she has a parrot.

Such a hollow jangling of the bell when I go out
and the wind bells tinkle, tinkle. . . .

The Searchlight

The searchlights over London
are like the fingers of a woman,
wandering over the dead form of a lover.

She had not thought to do that
while he was living,
to better know his loveliness
or if she had—
he'd stopped her with his kisses—
Now in her great grief
her fingers are to her
sight and sound and hearing.

By all the ways of sense
she knows him lost to her,
yet cannot voice her grief.

Only can she raise white hands towards the heavens
and passionate cursings and great grief,
yet no sign comes, no portent:
O if one blistering tear would come from on high
to crumple up and twist the earth
she'd know her nightly passion not so vain
when her first pang
burst the heavens with howling of guns.

Robert Graves (1895–1985)

Armistice Day, 1918

What's all this hubbub and yelling,
  Commotion and scamper of feet,
With ear-splitting clatter of kettles and cans,
  Wild laughter down Mafeking Street?

O, those are the kids whom we fought for
  (You might think they'd been scoffing our rum)
With flags that they waved when we marched off to war
  In the rapture of bugle and drum.

Now they'll hang Kaiser Bill from a lamp-post,
  Von Tirpitz they'll hang from a tree. . . .
We've been promised a "Land Fit for Heroes"—
  What heroes we heroes must be!

And the guns that we took from the Fritzes,
  That we paid for with rivers of blood,
Look, they're hauling them down to Old Battersea Bridge
  Where they'll topple them, souse, in the mud!

But there's old men and women in corners
  With tears falling fast on their cheeks,
There's the armless and legless and sightless—
  It's seldom that one of them speaks.

And there's flappers gone drunk and indecent
  Their skirts kilted up to the thigh,
The constables lifting no hand in reproof
  And the chaplain averting his eye. . . .

When the days of rejoicing are over,
  When the flags are stowed safely away,

They will dream of another wild "War to End Wars"
    And another wild Armistice day.

But the boys who were killed in the trenches,
    Who fought with no rage and no rant,
We left them stretched out on their pallets of mud
    Low down with the worm and the ant.

A. S. J. Tessimond (1902–1962)

Tube Station

The tube lift mounts,
                sap in a stem,
And blossoms its load,
                a black, untidy rose.
The fountain of the escalator
            curls at the crest,
                      breaks and scatters
A winnow of men,
            a sickle of dark spray.

London

I am the city of two divided cities
Where the eyes of rich and poor collide and wonder;
Where the beggar's voice is low and unexpectant,
And in clubs the feet of the servants are soft on the carpet
And the world's wind scarcely stirs the leaves of *The Times*.

I am the reticent, the private city,
The city of lovers hiding wrapped in shadows,
The city of people sitting and talking quietly
Beyond shut doors and walls as thick as a century,
People who laugh too little and too loudly,
Whose tears fall inward, flowing back to the heart.

I am the city whose fog will fall like a finger gently
Erasing the anger of angles, the strident indecorous gesture,
Whose dusk will come like tact, like a change in the conversation,
Violet and indigo, with strings of lemon streetlamps
Casting their pools into the pools of rain
As the notes of the piano are cast from the top-floor window
Into the square that is always Sunday afternoon.

Summer Night at Hyde Park Corner

Great globes of light spill yellow rain:
    Pencils of gold through purple gloom.
The buses swarm like heavy bees
    Trailing fat bodies. Faces loom,
Moonlike, and fade away among the trees
    Which, lit beneath by lamplight, bloom
High in darkness. Distant traffic
    Sounds with dull, enclosing boom . . .

Sleep extends a velvet forepaw.
    Night spreads out a downsoft plume.

Autumn

Already men are brushing up
    Brown leaves around the saddened parks.
At Marble Arch the nights draw in
    Upon expounders of Karl Marx.

By the Round Pond the lovers feel
    Heavier dews, and grow uneasy.
Elderly men don overcoats,
    Catch cold—sniff—become hoarse and wheezy.

Grey clouds streak across chill white skies.
    Refuse and dirty papers blow
About the gutters. Shoppers hurry,
    Oppressed by vague autumnal woe.

The cats that pick amongst the empty
    Gold Flake boxes, sniffing orts
From frowsy fish-shops, seem beruffled,
    Limp of tail and out of sorts.

Policemen are pale and *fin-de-siècle*.
    The navvy's arm wilts and relaxes.
With more than usual bitterness
    Bus-drivers curse impulsive taxis.

A general malaise descends:
    Desire for something none can say.
And autumn brings once more the pangs
    Of this our annual decay!

The City: Midday Nocturne

The yellow sky
hangs low its awning
on the city spires.

Herded buses
edge through the gloom
with blunt noses.

    A policeman's white forearm

      semaphores slowly.

The men in black coats
who advance up Ludgate Hill
bend their faces
and wonder if this
is the end of the world
at last?

Stevie Smith (1902–1971)

Suburb

How nice it is to slink the streets at night
And taste the slight
Flavour of acrity that comes
From pavements throwing off the dross
Of human tread.
Each paving stone sardonic
Grins to its fellow citizen masonic:
"Thank God they're gone," each to the other cries
"Now there is nothing between us and the skies."
Joy at this state transports the hanging heavens
And down to earth they rain celestial dew
The pavement darkly gleams beneath the lamp
Forgetful now of daylight's weary tramp.
Round about the streets I slink
Suburbs are not so bad I think
When their inhabitants can not be seen,
Even Palmers Green.
Nobody loves the hissing rain as I
And round about I slink
And presently
Turn from the sleek wet pavements to the utter slime
Where jerrybuilders building against time
Pursue their storied way,
Foundations and a pram,
Four walls and a pot of jam,
They have their sentries now
Upon a hundred hillocks.
Night watchman bad and old
Take rheumatism in exchange for gold.
Do you see that pub between the trees
Which advertises gin and cyclists' teas?
Down there I know a lane

Under the padding rain
Where leaves are born again
Every night
And reach maturity
In a remote futurity
Before dawn's light.
I have never seen
Anything quite so green
So close so dark so bright
As the green leaves at night.
I will not show you yet
Lest you should forget,
But when the time is come for your dismembering
I'll show you that you may die remembering.

William Empson (1906–1984)

Homage to the British Museum

There is a Supreme God in the ethnological section;
A hollow toad shape, faced with a blank shield.
He needs his belly to include the Pantheon,
Which is inserted through a hole behind.
At the navel, at the points formally stressed, at the organs of sense,
Lice glue themselves, dolls, local deities,
His smooth wood creeps with all the creeds of the world.

Attending there let us absorb the cultures of nations
And dissolve into our judgement all their codes.
Then, being clogged with a natural hesitation
(People are continually asking one the way out),
Let us stand here and admit that we have no road.
Being everything, let us admit that is to be something,
Or give ourselves the benefit of the doubt;
Let us offer our pinch of dust all to this God,
And grant his reign over the entire building.

John Betjeman (1906–1984)

The Arrest of Oscar Wilde at the Cadogan Hotel

He sipped at a weak hock and seltzer
　　As he gazed at the London skies
Through the Nottingham lace of the curtains
　　Or was it his bees-winged eyes?

To the right and before him Pont Street
　　Did tower in her new built red,
As hard as the morning gaslight
　　That shone on his unmade bed,

"I want some more hock in my seltzer,
　　And Robbie, please give me your hand—
Is this the end or beginning?
　　How can I understand?

"So you've brought me the latest *Yellow Book:*
　　And Buchan has got in it now:
Approval of what is approved of
　　Is as false as a well-kept vow.

"More hock, Robbie—where is the seltzer?
　　Dear boy, pull again at the bell!
They are all little better than *cretins,*
　　Though this *is* the Cadogan Hotel.

"One astrakhan coat is at Willis's—
　　Another one's at the Savoy:
Do fetch my morocco portmanteau,
　　And bring them on later, dear boy."

A thump, and a murmur of voices—
　　("Oh why must they make such a din?")
As the door of the bedroom swung open
　　And TWO PLAIN CLOTHES POLICEMEN came in:

"Mr. Woilde, we 'ave come for tew take yew
  Where felons and criminals dwell:
We must ask yew tew leave with us quoietly
  For this *is* the Cadogan Hotel."

He rose, and he put down *The Yellow Book.*
  He staggered—and, terrible-eyed,
He brushed past the palms on the staircase
  And was helped to a hansom outside.

In Westminster Abbey

Let me take this other glove off
   As the *vox humana* swells,
And the beauteous fields of Eden
   Bask beneath the Abbey bells.
Here, where England's statesmen lie,
Listen to a lady's cry.

Gracious Lord, oh bomb the Germans.
   Spare their women for Thy Sake,
And if that is not too easy
   We will pardon Thy Mistake.
But, gracious Lord, whate'er shall be,
Don't let anyone bomb me.

Keep our Empire undismembered
   Guide our Forces by Thy Hand,
Gallant blacks from far Jamaica,
   Honduras and Togoland;
Protect them Lord in all their fights,
And, even more, protect the whites.

Think of what our Nation stands for,
   Books from Boots' and country lanes,
Free speech, free passes, class distinction,
   Democracy and proper drains.
Lord, put beneath Thy special care
One-eighty-nine Cadogan Square.

Although dear Lord I am a sinner,
   I have done no major crime;
Now I'll come to Evening Service
   Whensoever I have the time.
So, Lord, reserve for me a crown,
And do not let my shares go down.

I will labour for Thy Kingdom,
   Help our lads to win the war,

Send white feathers to the cowards
   Join the Women's Army Corps,
Then wash the Steps around Thy Throne
In the Eternal Safety Zone.

Now I feel a little better,
   What a treat to hear Thy Word,
Where the bones of leading statesmen,
   Have so often been interred.
And now, dear Lord, I cannot wait
Because I have a luncheon date.

Parliament Hill Fields

Rumbling under blackened girders, Midland, bound for Cricklewood,
Puffed its sulphur to the sunset where that Land of Laundries stood.
Rumble under, thunder over, train and tram alternate go,
Shake the floor and smudge the ledger, Charrington, Sells, Dale and Co.,
Nuts and nuggets in the window, trucks along the lines below.

When the Bon Marché was shuttered, when the feet were hot and tired,
Outside Charrington's we waited, by the "STOP HERE IF REQUIRED,"
Launched aboard the shopping basket, sat precipitately down,
Rocked past Zwanziger the baker's, and the terrace blackish brown,
And the curious Anglo-Norman parish church of Kentish Town.

Till the tram went over thirty, sighting terminus again,
Past municipal lawn tennis and the bobble-hanging plane;
Soft the light suburban evening caught our ashlar-speckled spire,
Eighteen-sixty Early English, as the mighty elms retire
Either side of Brookfield Mansions flashing fine French-window fire.

Oh the after-tram-ride quiet, when we heard a mile beyond,
Silver music from the bandstand, barking dogs by Highgate Pond;
Up the hill where stucco houses in Virginia creeper drown—
And my childish wave of pity, seeing children carrying down
Sheaves of drooping dandelions to the courts of Kentish Town.

St. Saviour's, Aberdeen Park, Highbury, London, N.

With oh such peculiar branching and over-reaching of wire
    Trolley-bus standards pick their threads from the London sky
Diminishing up the perspective, Highbury-bound retire
    Threads and buses and standards with plane trees volleying by
And, more peculiar still, that ever-increasing spire
    Bulges over the housetops, polychromatic and high.

Stop the trolley-bus, stop! And here, where the roads unite
    Of weariest worn-out London—no cigarettes, no beer,
No repairs undertaken, nothing in stock—alight;
    For over the waste of willow-herb, look at her, sailing clear,
A great Victorian church, tall, unbroken and bright
    In a sun that's setting in Willesden and saturating us here.

These were the streets my parents knew when they loved and won—
    The brougham that crunched the gravel, the laurel-girt paths that wind,
Geranium-beds for the lawn, Venetian blinds for the sun,
    A separate tradesman's entrance, straw in the mews behind,
Just in the four-mile radius where hackney carriages run,
    Solid Italianate houses for the solid commercial mind.

These were the streets they knew; and I, by descent, belong
    To these tall neglected houses divided into flats.
Only the church remains, where carriages used to throng
    And my mother stepped out in flounces and my father stepped out in spats
To shadowy stained-glass matins or gas-lit evensong
    And back in a country quiet with doffing of chimney hats.

Great red church of my parents, cruciform crossing they knew—
    Over these same encaustics they and their parents trod
Bound through a red-brick transept for a once familiar pew
    Where the organ set them singing and the sermon let them nod
And up this coloured brickwork the same long shadows grew
    As these in the stencilled chancel where I kneel in the presence of God.

Wonder beyond Time's wonders, that Bread so white and small
    Veiled in golden curtains, too mighty for men to see,
Is the Power which sends the shadows up this polychrome wall,
    Is God who created the present, the chain-smoking millions and me;
Beyond the throb of the engines is the throbbing heart of all—
    Christ, at this Highbury altar, I offer myself To Thee.

The Metropolitan Railway

BAKER STREET STATION BUFFET

Early Electric! With what radiant hope
   Men formed this many-branched electrolier,
Twisted the flex around the iron rope
   And let the dazzling vacuum globes hang clear,
And then with hearts the rich contrivance filled
Of copper, beaten by the Bromsgrove Guild.

Early Electric! Sit you down and see,
   'Mid this fine woodwork and a smell of dinner,
A stained-glass windmill and a pot of tea,
   And sepia views of leafy lanes in PINNER,—
Then visualize, far down the shining lines,
Your parents' homestead set in murmuring pines.

Smoothly from HARROW, passing PRESTON ROAD,
   They saw the last green fields and misty sky,
At NEASDEN watched a workmen's train unload,
   And, with the morning villas sliding by,
They felt so sure on their electric trip
That Youth and Progress were in partnership.

And all that day in murky London Wall
   The thought of RUISLIP kept him warm inside;
At FARRINGDON that lunch hour at a stall
   He bought a dozen plants of London Pride;
While she, in arc-lit Oxford Street adrift,
Soared through the sales by safe hydraulic lift.

Early Electric! Maybe even here
   They met that evening at six-fifteen
Beneath the hearts of this electrolier
   And caught the first non-stop to WILLESDEN GREEN,
Then out and on, through rural RAYNER'S LANE
To autumn-scented Middlesex again.

Cancer has killed him. Heart is killing her.
    The trees are down. An Odeon flashes fire
Where stood their villa by the murmuring fir
    When "they would for their children's good conspire."
Of their loves and hopes on hurrying feet
Thou art the worn memorial, Baker Street.

Business Girls

From the geyser ventilators
    Autumn winds are blowing down
On a thousand business women
    Having baths in Camden Town.

Waste pipes chuckle into runnels,
    Steam's escaping here and there,
Morning trains through Camden cutting
    Shake the Crescent and the Square.

Early nip of changeful autumn,
    Dahlias glimpsed through garden doors,
At the back precarious bathrooms
    Jutting out from upper floors;

And behind their frail partitions
    Business women lie and soak,
Seeing through the draughty skylight
    Flying clouds and railway smoke.

Rest you there, poor unbeloved ones,
    Lap your loneliness in heat.
All too soon the tiny breakfast,
    Trolley-bus and windy street!

N.W.5 & N.6

Red cliffs arise. And up them service lifts
Soar with the groceries to silver heights.
Lissenden Mansions. And my memory sifts
Lilies from lily-like electric lights
And Irish stew smells from the smell of prams
And roar of seas from roar of London trams.

Out of it all my memory carves the quiet
Of that dark privet hedge where pleasures breed,
There first, intent upon its leafy diet,
I watched the looping caterpillar feed
And saw it hanging in a gummy froth
Till, weeks on, from the chrysalis burst the moth.

I see black oak twigs outlined on the sky,
Red squirrels on the Burdett-Coutts estate.
I ask my nurse the question "Will I die?"
As bells from sad St. Anne's ring out so late,
"And if I do die, will I go to Heaven?"
Highgate at eventide. Nineteen-eleven.

"You will. I won't." From that cheap nursery-maid,
Sadist and puritan as now I see,
I first learned what it was to be afraid,
Forcibly fed when sprawled across her knee
Locked into cupboards, left alone all day,
"World without end." What fearsome words to pray.

"World without end." It was not what she'ld do
That frightened me so much as did her fear
And guilt at endlessness. I caught them too,
Hating to think of sphere succeeding sphere
Into eternity and God's dread will
I caught her terror then. I have it still.

from *Summoned by Bells*

Great was my joy with London at my feet—
All London mine, five shillings in my hand
And not expected back till after tea!
Great was our joy, Ronald Hughes Wright's and mine,
To travel by the Underground all day
Between the rush hours, so that very soon
There was no station, north to Finsbury Park,
To Barking eastwards, Clapham Common south,
No temporary platform in the west
Among the Actons and the Ealings, where
We had not once alighted. Metroland
Beckoned us out to lanes in beechy Bucks—
Goldschmidt and Howland (in a wooden hut
Beside the station): "Most attractive sites
Ripe for development"; Charrington's for coal;
And not far off the neo-Tudor shops.
We knew the different railways by their smells.
The City and South reeked like a changing-room;
Its orange engines and old rolling-stock,
Its narrow platforms, undulating tracks,
Seemed even then historic. Next in age,
The Central London, with its cut-glass shades
On draughty stations, had an ozone smell—
Not seaweed-scented ozone from the sea
But something chemical from Birmingham.
When, in a pause between the stations, quiet
Descended on the carriage we would talk
Loud gibberish in angry argument,
Pretending to be foreign.

. . .

All silvery on frosty Sunday nights
Were City steeples white against the stars.
And narrowly the chasms wound between
Italianate counting-houses, Roman banks,

To this church and to that. Huge office-doors,
Their granite thresholds worn by weekday feet
(Now far away in slippered ease at Penge),
Stood locked. St. Botolph this, St. Mary that
Alone shone out resplendent in the dark.
I used to stand by intersecting lanes
Among the silent offices, and wait,
Choosing which bell to follow: not a peal,
For that meant somewhere active; not St. Paul's,
For that was too well-known. I liked things dim—
Some lazy Rector living in Bexhill
Who most unwillingly on Sunday came
To take the statutory services.
A single bell would tinkle down a lane:
My echoing steps would track the source of sound—
A cassocked verger, bell-rope in his hands,
Called me to high box pews, to cedar wood
(Like incense where no incense ever burned),
To ticking gallery-clock, and charity bench,
And free seats for the poor, and altar-piece—
Gilded Commandment boards—and sword-rests made
For long-discarded aldermanic pomp.
A hidden organist sent reedy notes
To flute around the plasterwork. I stood,
And from the sea of pews a single head
With cherries nodding on a black straw hat
Rose in a neighbouring pew. The caretaker?
Or the sole resident parishioner?
And so once more, as for three hundred years,
This carven wood, these grey memorial'd walls
Heard once again the Book of Common Prayer,
While somewhere at the back the verger, now
Turned Parish Clerk, would rumble out "Amen."
'Twas not, I think, a conscious search for God
That brought me to these dim forgotten fanes.
Largely it was a longing for the past,

With a slight sense of something unfulfilled;
And yet another feeling drew me there,
A sense of guilt increasing with the years—
"When I am dead you will be sorry, John"—
Here I could pray my mother would not die.
Thus were my London Sundays incomplete
If unaccompanied by Evening Prayer.
How trivial used to seem the Underground,
How worldly looked the over-lighted west,
How different and smug and wise I felt
When from the east I made my journey home!

Louis MacNeice (1907–1963)

from *Autumn Journal*

V

    Today was a beautiful day, the sky was a brilliant
        Blue for the first time for weeks and weeks
    But posters flapping on the railings tell the fluttered
        World that Hitler speaks, that Hitler speaks
    And we cannot take it in and we go to our daily
        Jobs to the dull refrain of the caption "War"
    Buzzing around us as from hidden insects
        And we think "This must be wrong, it has happened before,
    Just like this before, we must be dreaming;
        It was long ago these flies
    Buzzed like this, so why are they still bombarding
        The ears if not the eyes?"
    And we laugh it off and go round town in the evening
        And this, we say, is on me;
    Something out of the usual, a Pimm's Number One, a Picon—
        But did you see
    The latest? You mean whether Cobb has bust the record
        Or do you mean the Australians have lost their last by ten
    Wickets or do you mean that the autumn fashions—
        No, we don't mean anything like that again.
    No, what we mean is Hodza, Henlein, Hitler,
        The Maginot Line,
    The heavy panic that cramps the lungs and presses
        The collar down the spine.
    And when we go out into Piccadilly Circus
        They are selling and buying the late
    Special editions snatched and read abruptly
        Beneath the electric signs as crude as Fate.
    And the individual, powerless, has to exert the
        Powers of will and choice
    And choose between enormous evils, either

Of which depends on somebody else's voice.
The cylinders are racing in the presses,
    The mines are laid,
The ribbon plumbs the fallen fathoms of Wall Street,
    And you and I are afraid.
Today they were building in Oxford Street, the mortar
    Pleasant to smell,
But now it seems futility, imbecility,
    To be building shops when nobody can tell
What will happen next. What will happen
    We ask and waste the question on the air;
Nelson is stone and Johnnie Walker moves his
    Legs like a cretin over Trafalgar Square.
And in the Corner House the carpet-sweepers
    Advance between the tables after crumbs
Inexorably, like a tank battalion
    In answer to the drums.
In Tottenham Court Road the tarts and negroes
    Loiter beneath the lights
And the breeze gets colder as on so many other
    September nights.
A smell of French bread in Charlotte Street, a rustle
    Of leaves in Regent's Park
And suddenly from the Zoo I hear a sea-lion
    Confidently bark.
And so to my flat with the trees outside the window
    And the dahlia shapes of the lights on Primrose Hill
Whose summit once was used for a gun emplacement
    And very likely will
Be used that way again. The bloody frontier
    Converges on our beds
Like jungle beaters closing in on their destined
    Trophy of pelts and heads.
And at this hour of the day it is no good saying
    "Take away this cup";
Having helped to fill it ourselves it is only logic

That now we should drink it up.
Nor can we hide our heads in the sands, the sands have
    Filtered away;
Nothing remains but rock at this hour, this zero
    Hour of the day.
Or that is how it seems to me as I listen
    To a hooter call at six
And then a woodpigeon calls and stops but the wind continues
    Playing its dirge in the trees, playing its tricks.
And now the dairy cart comes clopping slowly—
    Milk at the doors—
And factory workers are on their way to factories
    And charwomen to chores.
And I notice feathers sprouting from the rotted
    Silk of my black
Double eiderdown which was a wedding
    Present eight years back.
And the linen which I lie on came from Ireland
    In the easy days
When all I thought of was affection and comfort,
    Petting and praise.
And now the woodpigeon starts again denying
    The values of the town
And a car having crossed the hill accelerates, changes
    Up, having just changed down.
And a train begins to chug and I wonder what the morning
    Paper will say,
And decide to go quickly to sleep for the morning already
    Is with us, the day is today.

The British Museum Reading Room

Under the hive-like dome the stooping haunted readers
Go up and down the alleys, tap the cells of knowledge—
    Honey and wax, the accumulation of years—
Some on commission, some for the love of learning,
Some because they have nothing better to do
Or because they hope these walls of books will deaden
    The drumming of the demon in their ears.

Cranks, hacks, poverty-stricken scholars,
In pince-nez, period hats or romantic beards
    And cherishing their hobby or their doom
Some are too much alive and some are asleep
Hanging like bats in a world of inverted values,
Folded up in themselves in a world which is safe and silent:
    This is the British Museum Reading Room.

Out on the steps in the sun the pigeons are courting,
Puffing their ruffs and sweeping their tails or taking
    A sun-bath at their ease
And under the totem poles—the ancient terror—
Between the enormous fluted Ionic columns
There seeps from heavily jowled or hawk-like foreign faces
    The guttural sorrow of the refugees.

Goodbye to London

Having left the great mean city, I make
Shift to pretend I am finally quit of her
Though that cannot be so long as I work.
   Nevertheless let the petals fall
   Fast from the flower of cities all.

When I first met her to my child's ear
She was an ocean of drums and tumbrils
And in my nostrils horsepiss and petrol.
   Nevertheless let the petals fall
   Fast from the flower of cities all.

Next to my peering teens she was foreign
Names over winking doors, a kaleidoscope
Of wine and ice, of eyes and emeralds.
   Nevertheless let the petals fall
   Fast from the flower of cities all.

Later as a place to live in and love in
I jockeyed her fogs and quoted Johnson:
To be tired of this is to tire of life.
   Nevertheless let the petals fall
   Fast from the flower of cities all.

Then came the headshrinking war, the city
Closed in too, the people were fewer
But closer too, we were back in the womb.
   Nevertheless let the petals fall
   Fast from the flower of cities all.

From which reborn into anticlimax
We endured much litter and apathy hoping
The phoenix would rise, for so they had promised.
   Nevertheless let the petals fall
   Fast from the flower of cities all.

And nobody rose, only some meaningless
Buildings and the people once more were strangers
At home with no one, sibling or friend.
    Which is why now the petals fall
    Fast from the flower of cities all.

Charon

The conductor's hands were black with money:
Hold on to your ticket, he said, the inspector's
Mind is black with suspicion, and hold on to
That dissolving map. We moved through London,
We could see the pigeons through the glass but failed
To hear their rumours of wars, we could see
The lost dog barking but never knew
That his bark was as shrill as a cock crowing,
We just jogged on, at each request
Stop there was a crowd of aggressively vacant
Faces, we just jogged on, eternity
Gave itself airs in revolving lights
And then we came to the Thames and all
The bridges were down, the further shore
Was lost in fog, so we asked the conductor
What we should do. He said: Take the ferry
Faute de mieux. We flicked the flashlight
And there was the ferryman just as Virgil
And Dante had seen him. He looked at us coldly
And his eyes were dead and his hands on the oar
Were black with obols and varicose veins
Marbled his calves and he said to us coldly:
If you want to die you will have to pay for it.

Stephen Spender (1909–1995)

Hampstead Autumn

In the fat autumn evening street
Hands from my childhood stretch out
And ring muffin bells. The Hampstead
Incandescence burns behind windows
With talk and gold warmth.
Those brothers who we were lie wrapped in flannel,
And how like a vase looks my time then
Rounded with meals laid on by servants
With reading alone in a high room and looking down on
The pleasures of the spoiled pets in the garden—
A vase now broken into fragments,
Little walks which quickly reach their ends,
The islands in the traffic. To questions—I know not what—
Answers hurry back from the world,
But now I reject them all.
I assemble an evening with space
Pinned above the four walls of the garden,
A glowing smell of being under canvas,
The sunset tall above the chimneys,
From behind the smoke-screen of poplar leaves
A piano cutting out its images,
Continuous and fragile as china.

Epilogue to a Human Drama

When pavements were blown up, exposing wires,
And the gas mains burned blue and gold,
And brick and stucco were pulverized—a cloud
Pungent with smells of mice, corpses, anxiety.
When the reverberant emptied façades
Of West End theatres, shops and churches,
Isolated in a vacuum of silence, suddenly
Cracked and blazed and fell with the seven-maned
Lions of Wrath, licking the stony fragments—

Then the sole voice heard through deserted streets
Was the Cassandra bell which rang, released
To quench those fires that ran through city walls.
London burned with unsentimental dignity,
Of resigned kingship. Banks and palaces
Stood near the throne of domed St. Pauls
Like courtiers round the royal sainted martyr.
August shadows of night
And flares of concentrated light
Dropped from the sky to paint a final scene
Illuminated agony of bursting stone.

Who can wonder then that every word
In burning London, stepped out of a play?
On the stage there were heroes, maidens, fools,
Victims, a Chorus. The heroes won medals,
The fools spat quips into the skull of death,
The wounded waited with the humble patience
Of animals trapped within a cellar
For the pickaxes to break with light and water.
The Chorus assisted, bringing cups of tea.

Bernard Spencer (1909–1963)

Regent's Park Terrace

The noises round my house. On cobbles bounding
Victorian-fashioned drays laden with railway goods;
their hollow sound like stones in rolling barrels:
the stony hoofing of dray horses.

Further, the trains themselves; among them the violent,
screaming like frightened animals, clashing metal;
different the pompous, the heavy breathers, the aldermen,
or those again which speed with the declining
sadness of crying along the distant routes
knitting together weathers and dialects.

Between these noises the little teeth
of a London silence.

Finally the lions grumbling over the park,
angry in the night hours,
cavernous as though their throats were openings up from the earth:
hooves, luggage, engines, tumbrils, lions,
hollow noises, noises of travel, hourly these unpick
the bricks of a London terrace, make the ear
their road, and have their audience in whatever
hearing the heart or the deep of the belly owns.

Train to Work

9.20; the Underground groans him to his work;
he sits fumbling a letter; is that
a cheque attached? He is puzzled, frowns
sadly, like Rhesus monkeys, like us. Above
the frown fair hair is thinning. Specially
I celebrate his toes turned in, his worn
shoes splashed with mud (but his hands
are clean and fine), the bottoms of his striped trousers
crumpled by rain.
                           In a little while his station
will syphon him out with others, along, round, away
as a drop goes with its Niagara.
                           And because
he bears the cracking brunt of things he has never willed
and has eight mean hours a day
to live at the bidding of the gods, and is gentle and put upon,
this blindfold bull-fight nag, endearing stranger,
and before long, like others who come to mind,
is condemned to sure death, he sits
(with his mackintosh belt twisted),
poetry roaring from him like a furnace.

Mervyn Peake (1911–1968)

London Buses

> Each day their steep, blood-red abundance winding
> Through corridors of broken stone is binding
> The city's body with a living thread
> That like a vessel weaving through grey flesh
> Its crimson mesh
> Of anger, surges onward like a tide
> Among the empty ruins and the dead—
> And those who have not died.

Kenneth Allott (1912–1973)

Memento Mori

Autumn: by Jack Straw's Castle and the pool,
The toy yachts, the cars, the luxury perambulators.
A white flagstaff is let into a sky of cirrus.
This is a tracking-shot past a hundred faces.
Mile after mile from the heavy manufactures
Up and down by the home for nurses
The retired and pensioned exercising their dogs,
The children, like Pawnees, with an ear for good.

The wind blows off the heath, the birds hang in the wind
Or swerve past the War Memorial to the trees,
Sycamore, plane and chestnut which hide the rich houses,
Where live those to whom charitable appeals
Are always directed: the bluff and kindly zeros,
The baffled gentlemen with the exhausting manners,
Who judge a civilisation by being snug and warm
When a huge wind sits in the north and the water freezes.

The leaves heap up on the fanlight, the lights go on
Hours earlier, the prices of foodstuffs soar;
The doughboy is flying his sex like the Stars and Stripes,
The whore in a soiled shift kneels by a small gas-fire;
The kerbs are wearied by the feet of the gospel poor.
The year is past the age of consent, but still
All that is most abject and most pitiable
Must stand up straight while the black evenings roar.

Time trickled sluggishly past the Piltdown man
To offer us only today a meal of doom.
The map of the future is riddled with bullet-holes.
Behind the rain a blind girl is practising scales
Like an unfortunate beauty. It is not beautiful.
At Geneva the lake looks coldly at the people.

Misery is like locusts or a prairie fire
Deaf to admonishment, leaving a country bare.

The wind tonight is a memento mori;
By Jack Straw's Castle the pool is worried like waves,
A dozen lights are on in the hospital,
A kite is hanging in the telegraph wires;
The leaves are falling, the wind is rising, the leaves
Cannot, any more than we can, tell which way they are going—
Along a gutter or into the face of the stars,
Which are not, any more than we are, grieved by massacres.

Roy Fuller (1912–1991)

First Winter of War

There is a hard thin gun on Clapham Common,
Deserted yachts in the mud at Greenwich,
In a hospital at Ealing notices
Which read WOMEN GASSED and WOMEN NOT GASSED.

The last trains go earlier, stations are like aquaria,
The mauve-lit carriages are full of lust.
I see my friends seldom, they move in nearby
Areas where no one speaks the truth.

It is dark at four and on the peopled streets,
The ornamental banks and turreted offices,
The moon pours a deathly and powdered grey:
The city noises come out of a desert.

It is dark at twelve: I walk down the up escalator
And see that hooded figure before me
Ascending motionless upon a certain step.
As I try to pass, it will stab me with a year.

Battersea: After Dunkirk, June 3, 1940

Smoke corrugated on the steel-blue sky
From the red funnels of the power-station
Is blanched as the shocking bandages one sees
On soldiers in the halted train. Patience!
Still there is nothing definite to say—
Or do, except to watch disintegration,
The rightness of the previous diagnosis,
And guard oneself from pity and isolation.

The generator's titanic vessel floats
Beside the Thames; and smoke continues to pour.
Khaki and white move on as though to hide
In summer. What can keep the autumn fates
From breaking the perfect sky and sending power
For slaves to set against the pyramid?

London Air-Raid, 1940

An ambulance bell rings in the dark among
The rasp of guns, and abstract wrong is brought
Straight to my riveted thought.

Tonight humanity is trapped in evil
Pervasive as plague or devil; hopelessly wages
With pain, like the Middle Ages.

My reading and the alimentary city
Freeze: crouching fear and licking pity's all
Of the handed animal.

Anne Ridler (1912–2001)

Wentworth Place: Keats Grove

The setting sun will always set me to rights . . .
    —Keats, to Benjamin Bailey

> Keats fancied that the nightingale was happy
> Because it sang. So beautiful his garden,
> Behind the gate that shuts the present out
> With all its greed and grimy noise,
> I fall into a like mistake, to think—
> Because there are such depths of peace and greenness,
> Greenness and peace, because the mulberry
> Invites with arms supported like the prophet,
> Because the chestnut candles glimmer crimson—
> That heartache could not flourish among these flowers,
> Nor anguish resist the whisper of the leaves.
>
> Angry for him, blessing his gift, I accuse
> The paradise that could not save him,
> Sickness and grief that sunsets could not heal.

George Barker (1913–1991)

Kew Gardens

There these two
young men stood
together under the
hanging man wood
of Europe, speaking
of gods and doves
and around them one
by one the leaves
the paper leaves of
history fell
until the air
filled with a spell-
binding glitter as of
wings. Whose, whose
aniconic wings
David, were those
that divided the
air into sufferings
like enormous triangles
crushing prisms and the
cyclix agonies?
In the Garden
the mauve and drifting
evening gathered
like pigeons the shifting
shadows together
under the trees and
you David and I and
the dying season
stood unblessed and lost
and trembling in
the descending West

from which only
a dishonoured
faith could ever
rise up in the East
upon our days
again. Deeper the dark
element entered
your younger heart
than mine and centred
all sorrow there
like a swallowed
octopus within your
cave of adoration. Shadowed
the river flashed and shone
among Kew glades
and we stood still.
The worm-worn shades
hissed and sighed around
us, and the green park
and the grass on the ground
took fire at our feet,
and from the boughs above
us, unfolding her
coiled and huge wings
the Knowledge of Evil
tore out our heart strings
and dismembered our love.
I saw the forked
tongue flick and strike
into your eyeball and
saw the knowledge of evil
enter you, David, like
snake piss injected into
your starry systems
curdling the Milky
Way. That Pythian

still coils there in
that black tree of
Kew but nowhere in
those gardens, though
I walk behind you
nor, though I bring
these verses to
remind you, David,
shall I ever again
ever again find you.

Alun Lewis (1915–1944)

Westminster Abbey

Discoloured lights slant from the high rose window
Upon the sightseers and the faithful
And those who shelter from the rain this Sunday.
The clergy in their starched white surplices
Send prayers like pigeons circling overhead
Seeking the ghostly hands that give them bread.

The togaed statesmen on their scribbled plinths
Stand in dull poses, dusty as their fame
Crammed in the chapter of a schoolboy's book;
Their eyes have lost their shrewd and fallible look.

Kneeling by Gladstone is a girl who sobs.
Something profounder than the litany
Moves in the dark beneath the restless steps
Of this pale swirl of human flux.
Soft fingers touch the worn marmoreal stone.
The pale girl reaches out for what has gone.

The thin responsions falter in the air.
Only the restless footsteps hurry on,
Escaping that which was in the beginning,
Is now, and ever shall be.

   —See, the girl
Adjusts her fashionable veil.
The vergers clack their keys, the soldiers go,
The white procession shuffles out of sight.
The incubus is shifted to the stars,
The flux is spun and drifted through the night,
And no one stays within that holy shell
To know if that which IS be good or ill.

Robert Lowell (1917–1977)

from *Redcliffe Square*

1.

LIVING IN LONDON

I learn to live without ice and like the Queen;
we didn't like her buildings when they stood,
but soon Victoria's manly oak was quartered,
knickknacks dropped like spiders from the whatnot,
grandparents and their unmarried staffs decamped
for our own bobbed couples of the swimming twenties,
too giddy to destroy the homes they fled.
These houses, no two the same, tremble up six stories
to dissimilar Flemish pie-slice peaks,
shaped by constructor's pipes and scaffolding—
aboriginal like a jungle gym.
Last century's quantity brick has a sour redness
that time, I fear, does nothing to appease,
condemned by age, rebuilt by desolation.

2.

WINDOW

Tops of the midnight trees move helter-skelter
to ruin, if passion can hurt the classical
in the limited window of the easel painter—
love escapes our hands. We open the curtains:
a square of white-faced houses swerving, foaming,
the swagger of the world and chalk of London.
At each turn the houses wall the path of meeting,
and yet we meet, stand taking in the storm.
Even in provincial capitals,

storms will rarely enter a human house,
the crude and homeless wet is windowed out.
We stand and hear the pummeling unpurged,
almost uneducated by the world—
the tops of the moving trees move helter-skelter.

from *Winter and London*

2.

AT *OFFADO'S*

The Latin Quarter abuts on Belgravia,
three floors low as one, blocks built of blocks,
insular eighteenth century laying down
the functional with a razor in its hand,
construction too practical for conservation.
An alien should count his change here, bring a friend.
Usually on weekend nights I eat alone;
you've taken the train for *Milgate* with the children.
At *Offado's,* the staff is half the guests,
the guitar and singers wait on table,
the artist sings things unconsolable:
"Girls of Majorca. Where is my Sombrero?
Leave me alone and let me talk and love me—
a cod in garlic, a carafe of cruel rosé."

Nicholas Moore (1918–1986)

Monmouth Street

Walking in Monmouth Street I seemed to hear
Among fantastic shops and shuttered doors
The elemental panther gliding near,
Sleekly triumphant, on its padded paws.

I was so young and yet so old: I was
The child who lately in the bluebell wood
Gathered my flowers and I was the man
Of forty-five surrounded by despairs.

I dreamt a room, a monument to those
Distracting fancies. On the mantel-piece
The coloured jugs, the efflorescent vases:
And round the walls exotic fantasies,

Carpets and gilded chairs, and curving snakes,
Queer, muffled birds and the rhinoceros-
Tusk carved with ancient figures; the cold decks
Of fortune-tellers' cards, each deadly ace

Spilled in its pattern, and all harmless there.
For such a room I had devised for you.
All its fantastic furniture was right
To suit your fancy. I was in despair,

Walking down Monmouth Street, to hear the whisper
"Love lights no torch. Young fool, you must forget her.
Love is a lie: old man, you must forget her."
I turned to watch the people hurrying there,

Wearing their masks, all happy in the sun.
The dust was dancing, and the voice was still.
I told myself I was the lucky one,
The winner, gay, unhurt by age or evil:

And yet I stood transfixed, and Monmouth Street
Grinned like an ogre, and the ogling eyes
Of monsters watched me, how lasciviously!
They laughed at the dull echo of my feet.

"You will not win. There's nothing you can do.
Construct your room. Fill it with bric-a-brac.
Transport your monsters, your surrealist
Visions. Still it is everything you lack."

I stood in sunlight, and I did not know
What spoke or whether what it said was true.
I only felt the soft wind in my face,
And heard the panther move a stealthy pace

Beside me. "Then, is all I do no use?
Without choice, without comfort?" "It is so.
There is no truth you cannot come to know.
Yet, even knowing it, what can you choose?"

I gazed at the dark shuttered doors and windows,
And the fantastic curios in shops.
I said "I like these queer, fantastic shapes."
But there was none to hear me but myself.

I heard my steps upon the narrow paving;
I saw my shadow hurrying behind:
And Monmouth Street stretched like an avenue
Leading me back from every hope of you.

John Heath-Stubbs (1918–2006)

London Architecture 1960s

Everyone is complaining
About these featureless new office blocks.
And so am I. Each one recalls
A rather larger than usual poem
By . . . let's call him N. O. Packdrill
The currently fashionable bard.
The poems, you would say, reflect the architecture.
Or does he, like a new Amphion,
Evoke this other Thebes?

Lament for the "Old Swan," Notting Hill Gate

The Old Swan has gone. They have widened the road.
A year ago they closed her, and she stood,
The neighbouring houses pulled down, suddenly revealed
In all her touching pretentiousness
Of turret and Gothic pinnacle, like
A stupid and ugly old woman
Unexpectedly struck to dignity by bereavement.

And now she has vanished. The gap elicits
A guarded sentiment. Enough bad poets
Have romanticized beer and pubs,
And those for whom the gimcrack enchantments
Of engraved glass, mahogany, plants in pots,
Were all laid out to please, were fugitives, doubtless,
Nightly self-immersed in a fake splendour.

Yet a Public House perhaps makes manifest also
The hidden City; implies its laws
Of tolerance, hierarchy, exchange.
Friends I remember there, enemies, acquaintances,
Some drabs and drunks, some bores and boors, and many
Indifferent and decent people. They will drink elsewhere.
Anonymous, it harboured
The dreadful, innocent martyrs
Of megalopolis—Christie or Heath.

Now that's finished with. And all the wide
And sober roads of the world walk sensibly onwards
Into the featureless future. But the white swans
That dipped and swam in each great lucid mirror
Remain in the mind only, remain as a lost symbol.

W. S. Graham (1918–1986)

The Night City

Unmet at Euston in a dream
Of London under Turner's steam
Misting the iron gantries, I
Found myself running away
From Scotland into the golden city.

I ran down Gray's Inn Road and ran
Till I was under a black bridge.
This was me at nineteen
Late at night arriving between
The buildings of the City of London.

And then I (O I have fallen down)
Fell in my dream beside the Bank
Of England's wall to bed, me
With my money belt of Northern ice.
I found Eliot and he said yes

And sprang into a Holmes cab.
Boswell passed me in the fog
Going to visit Whistler who
Was with John Donne who had just seen
Paul Potts shouting on Soho Green.

Midnight. I hear the moon
Light chiming on St. Paul's.

The City is empty. Night
Watchmen are drinking their tea.

The Fire had burnt out.
The Plague's pits had closed
And gone into literature.

Between the big buildings
I sat like a flea crouched
In the stopped works of a watch.

Muriel Spark (1918–2006)

from *A Tour of London*

I. DAYBREAK COMPOSITION

Anyone in this top-floor flat
This morning, might look out upon
An oblong canvas of Kensington
Almost ready for looking at.

Houses lean sideways to the light;
At foreground left, a crowd of trees
Is blue, is a footman, his gloves are white.
The sky's a pair of legs, top-right,
The colour of threadbare dungarees.

All the discrepant churches grind
Four, and in the window frame is
Picasso at least, his scene; its name is
Morning; authentic, but never signed.

II. KENSINGTON GARDENS

Old ladies and tulips, model boats,
Compact babies, mobile mothers,
Distant buses like parakeets,
Lonely men with mackintoshes

Over their arms—where do they go?
Where come from? now that summer's
Paraphernalia and splash is
Out, as if planted a year ago.

III. WHAT THE STRANGER WONDERED

Where does she come from
Sipping coffee alone in London?

The shoes, the hair—I do not think
She has anything in the bank.

Has she a man, where is he then,
Why is she sitting at half-past ten

Reading a book alone in London?
Where does the money come from

That lets her be alone and sipping
Not with a man, not in a job, not with a dog to the grocer tripping?

Keith Douglas (1920–1944)

from *The "Bête Noire" Fragments*

The trumpet man to take it away
blows a hot break in a beautiful way
ought to snap my fingers and tap my toes
but I sit at my table and nobody knows
I've got a beast on my back.

A medieval animal with a dog's face
Notre Dame or Chartres is his proper place
but here he is in the Piccadilly
sneering at the hot musicians' skill. He
is the beast on my back.

Suppose we dance, suppose we run away
into the street, or the underground
he'd come with us. It's his day.
Don't kiss me. Don't put your arm round
and touch the beast on my back.

D. J. Enright (1920–2002)

The Stations of King's Cross

He is seized and bound by the turnstile.

The moving stair writes once, and having writ,
Moves on.

At Hammersmith the nails
At Green Park the tree.

A despatch case which is well named
A square basket made of rattan
Which is a scourge.
The heel of the Serpent bruises Man's instep.

At Earl's Court a Chopper
New, flashing, spotless
It carries hooks and claws and edges
Which wound.

It is hot. Vee
Wipes her face. Cheek to jowl
She wipes the man's on either side.

Rather bear those pills I have
Than fly to others that I know not of.

He speaks to the maidenforms of Jerusalem
Blessed are the paps which never gave suck.

The agony in Covent Garden
He finds them sleeping, for their eyes are heavy.

The first fall, the second fall
The third fall.
And more to come.

A sleeve goes, a leg is torn
A hem is ripped.
This is the parting of garments.

They mock him, offering him vodka.
The effect is shattering.

He is taken down from the strap.
And deposited.

Wilt thou leave him in the loathsome grave?

Philip Larkin (1922–1985)

Deceptions

Of course I was drugged, and so heavily I did not regain my consciousness till the
next morning. I was horrified to discover that I had been ruined, and for some days
I was inconsolable, and cried like a child to be killed or sent back to my aunt.
  —Mayhew, *London Labour and the London Poor*

Even so distant, I can taste the grief,
Bitter and sharp with stalks, he made you gulp.
The sun's occasional print, the brisk brief
Worry of wheels along the street outside
Where bridal London bows the other way,
And light, unanswerable and tall and wide,
Forbids the scar to heal, and drives
Shame out of hiding. All the unhurried day
Your mind lay open like a drawer of knives.

Slums, years, have buried you. I would not dare
Console you if I could. What can be said,
Except that suffering is exact, but where
Desire takes charge, readings will grow erratic?
For you would hardly care
That you were less deceived, out on that bed,
Than he was, stumbling up the breathless stair
To burst into fulfilment's desolate attic.

Naturally the Foundation Will Bear Your Expenses

Hurrying to catch my Comet
　　One dark November day,
Which soon would snatch me from it
　　To the sunshine of Bombay,
I pondered pages Berkeley
　　Not three weeks since had heard,
Perceiving Chatto darkly
　　Through the mirror of the Third.

Crowds, colourless and careworn,
　　Had made my taxi late,
Yet not till I was airborne
　　Did I recall the date—
That day when Queen and Minister
　　And Band of Guards and all
Still act their solemn-sinister
　　Wreath-rubbish in Whitehall.

It used to make me throw up,
　　These mawkish nursery games:
O when will England grow up?
　　—But I outsoar the Thames,
And dwindle off down Auster
　　To greet Professor Lal
(He once met Morgan Forster),
　　My contact and my pal.

Donald Davie (1922–1995)

To Londoners

I get, surprisingly, a sense of space:
As on the rush-hour underground, when in fact
Every one touches, still in his own place
Every one rises above the smirch of contact,
Resolute to assert his self-containment;
A charged field cordons every sovereign will.

The City empty on a July evening,
All the jam-packed commuters gone, and all
The Wren and Hawksmoor spires and steeples shining
In a honeyed light . . . But also mental spaces
As I see now, all energies withdrawn
To hold the frontiers each day menaces.

Trying to hold my own place just inside
The emptied space round Hawksmoor's drawing-board,
I shoulder, I am rancorous, I have tried
Too long, with too much vigour and the wrong
Sort of patience. On the District Line
Budge up a little, tell me I belong!

Gallant baritones whom nothing soured
Between the wars, still hooked on Rupert Brooke
Who adumbrated for the earlier war
A wide and windy Iliad in the embowered
Old garden of the Vicarage, Grantchester . . .
Is that the bugle-note you listen for?

Given a voice thus confident, thus confiding,
As intimate as a commuter's week
And yet as sweeping as imperial war
Or global peace, how spaciously I could
Bind in one *sostenuto* Temple Bar
With Turnham Green, St. Paul's with Chorleywood!

But now or later you will have to say
I am one of yours. Do you not hear the cramp
Of overpopulation, of *mêlée*
In this too tamped-down, pounded-together ramp
Of phrases I manhandle towards what yawning
Yard of what temple, what too void arena?

Dannie Abse (1923–)

Street Scene

(Outside the grocer's, Golders Green Road)

They quarrel, this black-bearded man
and his busy, almost flying wife—
she with her hands, he with proverbs.

"He who never rebukes his son,"
says the bearded man too blandly,
"leads him into delinquency."

And she who hasn't studied nicely
such studied wisdom, now replies,
"You're a, you're a, you're a donkey."

Three or four psychiatrists smile
as they pass the greengrocer's shop.
Again, patient, he quotes the Talmud:

"When one suggests you're a donkey
do not fret; only when two speak thus
go buy yourself a saddle."

But she has thrown appropriate
carrots carrots at his sober head
and one sticks brightly in his beard.

Truce! You have been led into fiction.
Listen! Here comes a violin
and tunes to make a donkey dance.

The bearded man has closed his eyes.
Who's this, disguised as a beggar,
playing a violin without strings?

What music's this, its cold measure?
Who are these, dangling from lamp-posts,
kicking as if under water?

Soho: Saturday Night

Always Cain, anonymous amidst the poor,
Abel dead in his eye, and over his damned sore
a khaki muffler, loiters, a fugitive in Soho,
enters The Golden Calf Club and hears Esau,

dishevelled and drunk, cursing kith and kin.
"A mess of pottage!" Esau strokes an unshaven chin
and strikes a marble table-top. Then hairy hands
fidget dolefully, raise up a glass of gin.

Outside, Joseph, dyspnoeic, regards a star
convexing over Dean Street, coughs up a flower
from ruined lungs—rosy petals on his tongue—
recalls the Pit and wounds of many a colour.

Traffic lights change. With tapping white stick
a giant crosses the road between the frantic
taxis. A philistine pimp laughs. Dancing
in The Nude Show Delilah suddenly feels sick.

Ruth, too, the innocent, was gullibly led,
lay down half-clothed on a brassy railing bed
of Mr. Boaz of Bayswater. Now, too late, weeps
antiseptic tears, wishes she were dead.

Who goes home? Nebuchadnezzar to the doss-
house where, all night, he'll turn and toss.
Lunchtime, in Soho Square, he munched the grass
and now he howls at strangers as they pass.

In Café Babylon, Daniel, interpreter of dreams,
listens to Belshazzar, a shy lad in his teens:
"A soiled finger moved across the lavatory wall."
Growing up is not so easy as it seems.

Prophets, like tipsters, awaiting the Advent.
Beggar Job, under the flashing advertisement
for toothpaste, the spirochaete in his brain,
groans. Chalks a lurid picture on the pavement.

The Golden Calf closes. Who goes home? All
tourists to Nod; psalmists from their pub crawl;
they leave unshaved Soho to its dawn furnace
of affliction, its wormwood and its gall.

James Berry (1924–)

Two Black Labourers on a London Building Site

Been a train crash.
   Wha?
Yeh—tube crash.
   Who the driver?
Not a black man.
   Not a black man?
I check that firs.
   Thank Almighty God.
Bout thirty people dead.
   Thirty people dead?
Looks maybe more.
   Maybe more?
Maybe more.
   An black man didn drive?
No. Black man didn drive.

Beginning in a City, 1948

Stirred by restlessness, pushed by history,
I found myself in the centre of Empire.
Those first few hours, with those packed impressions
I never looked at in all these years.

I knew no room. I knew no Londoner.
I searched without knowing.
I dropped off my grip at the "left luggage."
A smart policeman told me a house to try.

In dim-lit streets, war-tired people moved slowly
like dark-coated bears in a snowy region.
I in my Caribbean gear
was a half-finished shack in the cold winds.
In November, the town was a frosty field.
I walked fantastic stone streets in a dream.

A man on duty took my ten-shilling note
for a bed for four nights.
Inflated with happiness I followed him.
I was left in a close-walled room,
left with a dying shadeless bulb,
a pillowless bed and a smelly army blanket—
all the comfort I had paid for.

Curtainless in morning light, I crawled out of bed
onto wooden legs and stiff-armed body,
with a frosty-board face that I patted
with icy water at the lavatory tap.

Then I came to fellow-inmates in a crowded room.
A rage of combined smells attacked me,
clogging my nostrils—
and new charges of other smells merely
increased the stench. I was alone.
I alone was nauseated and choked in deadly air.

One-legged people stood around a wall of hot plates
prodding sizzled bacon and kippers.
Sore-legged and bandaged people poured tea.
Weather-cracked faces, hairy and hairless, were chewing.
No woman smiled. No man chuckled.
Words pressed through gums and gaps of rusty teeth.

Grimy bundles and bags were pets
beside grimy bulges of people, bowed, and in little clusters.
Though ever so gullible I knew—this was a dosshouse.
I collected back seven shillings and sixpence.
I left the place and its smells, their taste still with me
and again instinct directed me.

I walked without map, without knowledge
from Victoria to Brixton. On Coldharbour Lane
I saw a queue of men—some black—
and stopped. I stood by one man in the queue.
"Wha happenin brodda? Wha happenin here?"

Looking at me he said "You mus be a jus-come?
You did hear about Labour Exchange?" "Yes—I hear."
"Well, you at it! But, you need a place whey you live."
He pointed. "Go over dere and get a room."
So, I had begun—begun in London.

John Ashbery (1927–)

The Tower of London

isn't really a tower. It's a square
building with towers at each
of the four corners. In the thirties
they made a movie of it starring Boris Karloff
as Mord the executioner, who dabbled in torture.
A busy man was Mord. His boss, Richard the Third,
was demanding. Richard had no hump
on his back, but Boris had a club foot,
as though to make up for it. Richard drowned
the Duke of Clarence, whose name wasn't Clarence,
in a tub of malmsey, a sweet-tasting wine.
Clarence had stood in his way. Richard
was determined to kill all who stood in his way,
including the princes in the Tower, two
little boys, practically infants, the sons
of old Henry the Sixth, or maybe of
Richard's half brother, Edward,
played by Ian Hunter. Richard was played by
Basil Rathbone, who also played Sherlock Holmes.

The princes, also named Richard
and Edward, I believe, hadn't done anything.
They didn't deserve to be killed.
But then, none of them did, including old Henry
the Sixth, although he was quite dotty at the time.

Richard's bride was unlike the Queen
in the play *Richard III*. She was played by
Barbara O'Neil, who played Scarlett O'Hara's
mother in *Gone with the Wind,* though she wasn't old
enough to be. That's the way I remember it. Wait, she was
actually Edward's wife. Richard took
unto him the Lady Anne, who was

played by Nan Grey, though she actually
married Wyatt (John Sutton) after they escaped from
the Tower, or the Castle. In the end Richard
killed just about everybody, except Mord,
who got thrown off a cliff by somebody,
a fitting end to a miserable career.

Thom Gunn (1929–2004)

Autobiography

The sniff of the real, that's
what I'd want to get
      how it felt
to sit on Parliament
Hill on a May evening
studying for exams   skinny
seventeen   dissatisfied
      yet sniffing such
a potent air, smell of
grass in heat from
the day's sun

I'd been walking through the damp
rich ways by the ponds
and now lay on the upper
grass with Lamartine's poems

life seemed all
loss, and what was more
I'd lost whatever it was
before I'd even had it

a green dry prospect
distant babble of children
and beyond, distinct at
the end of the glow
St. Paul's like a stone thimble

longing so hard to make
inclusions that the longing
has become   in memory
an inclusion

Talbot Road

(where I lived in London 1964–5)

in memory of Tony White

1

Between the pastel boutiques
of Notting Hill and the less defined
windier reaches of the Harrow Road,
all blackened brick, was the street
built for burghers, another Belgravia,
but eventually fallen
to labourers ("No Coloured or Irish
Need Apply") and then like the veins
of the true-born Englishman
filling with a promiscuous mix:
Pole, Italian, Irish, Jamaican,
rich jostling flow. A Yugoslav restaurant
framed photographs of exiled princes,
but the children chattered with a London accent.
I lived on Talbot Road
for a year. The excellent room
where I slept, ate, read, and wrote,
had a high ceiling, on the borders
stucco roses were painted blue.
You could step through the window
to a heavy balcony and even
(unless the drain was blocked)
sup there on hot evenings.
That's what I call complete access—
to air, to street, to friendship:
for, from it, I could see, blocks away,
the window where Tony, my old friend,
toiled at translation. I too tried
to render obscure passages into clear English,
as I try now.

2

Glamorous and difficult friend,
helper and ally. As students
enwrapt by our own romanticism,
innocent poet and actor we had posed
we had played out parts to each other
I have sometimes thought
like studs in a whorehouse.
—But he had to deal
with the best looks of his year.
If "the rich are different from us,"
so are the handsome. What
did he really want? Ah that question . . .

Two romances going on in London,
one in Northampton, one in Ireland,
probably others. Friends and lovers
all had their own versions of him.
Fantastical duke of dark corners,
he never needed to lie:
you had learned not to ask questions.

The fire of his good looks.
But almost concealed by the fringe of fire,
behind the mighty giving of self,
at the centre of the jollity, there was
something withheld, slow, something—
what? what? A damp smoulder of discontent.
He would speculate about "human relations"
which we were supposed to view
—*vide* Forster, *passim,* etc.—
as an end, a good in themselves.
He did not find them so.

Finally it came to this,
the poses had come undone so far:
he loved you more for your faults

than for anything you could give him.
When once in a pub I lost my temper,
I shouldered my way back from the urinal
and snapped, "I was too angry to piss."
The next day he exclaimed with delight,
"Do you know that was the first time
you have ever been angry with me?"
As some people wait for a sign of love,
he had waited how many years
for a sign of anger,
for a sign of other than love.

3

A London returned to after twelve years.
On a long passage between two streets
I met my past self lingering there
or so he seemed
a youth of about nineteen glaring at me
from a turn of desire. He held his look
as if shielding it from wind.
Our eyes parleyed, then we touched
in the conversation of bodies.
Standing together on asphalt openly,
we gradually loosened into a shared laughter.
This was the year, the year of reconciliation
to whatever it was I had come from,
the prickly heat of adolescent emotion,
premature staleness and self-contempt.
In my hilarity, in my luck,
I forgave myself for having had a youth.

I started to heap up pardons
even in anticipation. On Hampstead Heath
I knew every sudden path from childhood,
the crooks of every climbable tree.
And now I engaged these at night,
and where I had played hide and seek

with neighbour children, played as an adult
with troops of men whose rounds intersected
at the Orgy Tree or in the wood
of birch trunks gleaming like mute watchers
or in tents of branch and bush
surrounded by the familiar smell
of young leaf–salty, explosive.
In a Forest of Arden, in a summer night's dream
I forgave everybody his teens.

4

But I came back, after the last bus,
from Hampstead, Wimbledon, the pubs,
the railway arches of the East End,
I came back to Talbot Road,
to the brick, the cement Arthurian faces,
the area railings by coal holes,
the fat pillars of the entrances.
My balcony filled up with wet snow.
When it dried out Tony and I
would lunch there in the sunshine
on veal-and-ham pie, beer, and salad.
I told him about my adventures.
He wondered aloud if he would be happier
if he were queer like me.
How could he want, I wondered,
to be anything but himself?
Then he would have to be off,
off with his jaunty walk,
where, I didn't ask or guess.

At the end of my year, before I left,
he held a great party for me
on a canal boat. The party slipped
through the watery network of London,
grid that had always been glimpsed
out of the corner of the eye

behind fences or from the tops of buses.
Now here we were, buoyant on it,
picnicking, gazing in mid-mouthful
at the backs of buildings, at smoke-black walls
coral in the light of the long evening,
at what we had suspected all along
when we crossed the bridges we now passed under,
gliding through the open secret.

5

That was fifteen years ago.
Tony is dead, the block where I lived
has been torn down. The mind
is an impermanent place, isn't it,
but it looks to permanence.
The street has opened and opened up
into no character at all. Last night
I dreamt of it as it might have been,
the pavement by the church railings
was wet with spring rain,
it was night, the streetlamps' light
rendered it into an exquisite etching.
Sentimental postcard of a dream,
of a moment between race-riots!

But I do clearly remember my last week,
when every detail brightened with meaning.
A boy was staying with (I would think)
his grandmother in the house opposite.
He was in his teens, from the country perhaps.
Every evening of that week
he sat in his white shirt at the window
—a Gothic arch of reduced proportion—
leaning on his arms, gazing down
as if intently making out characters
from a live language he was still learning,
not a smile cracking his pink cheeks.

Gazing down
at the human traffic, of all nations,
the just and the unjust, who
were they, where were they going,
that fine public flow at the edge of which
he waited, poised, detached in wonder
and in no hurry
before he got ready one day
to climb down into its live current.

Connie Bensley (1929–)

Vauxhall

Pulling through cliffs of windows
We stop at the platform:
Murky, misty; damp haloes round the lights—
The graffiti half lost in dust.

The train gives an orgasmic shudder
And falls silent.
The few passengers gaze vacantly about.
One gives a racking sigh.

Vauxhall. The word blooms in my mind,
Opening up green vistas. Down one of them
My mother, playing the piano,
Waiting for her washing to dry, and singing tremulously:
   When Lady Betty passes by
   I strive to catch her bright blue eye
   At Vauxhall in the morning.

Round her elbow I can just make out the words.
Her hands are crinkly from the soapsuds;
Outside, the roses catch at the blown sheets,
And in Vauxhall, it is all blossom and glances.

I smile out at the grimy wall
(Wogs sod off—Arsenal are shit)
And the train throbs back to life,
Sliding us on to some more ordinary place.

Bottleneck

The bottleneck
in her journey home that night
was the down escalator at Knightsbridge.

He chose to wait there,
looking upwards
for her clocked black stockings,
the red flared skirt,
the swinging plait.

When she saw him
she turned back in a flash,
climbing, stumbling,
passing and re-passing
the bra-and-pantie girl
with her languorous glance
and her cleavage
       cleavage
       cleavage

Peter Porter (1929–2010)

Thomas Hardy at Westbourne Park Villas

Not that I know where in this changed district
    He may have walked under unwarming sun
Through a hedged righteousness already bricked
Up to the pale sky and the many chimneys clouding it,
    Nor where black steeple, tar-gate, and gun-
bright anthracite held back the spring and the exact green to bring it.

Though the smoke's gone now, the old frailty shows
    In people coming unexpectedly out of doors
Hardly renumbered since his time: each house knows
As many stories as in the iron sublime we call
    Victorian. Suicide, lost love, despair are laws
of a visiting Nature raging against proof and practice and changing all.

Here, rather than in death-filled Dorset, I see him,
    The watchful conspirator against the gods
Come to the capital of light on his own grim
Journey into darkness; the dazzle would tell
    Him these were the worst of possible odds—
ordinary gestures of time working on faces the watermark of hell.

U. A. Fanthorpe (1929–2009)

Rising Damp

(for C.A.K. and R.K.M.)

A river can sometimes be diverted, but it is a very hard thing to lose it altogether.
    –J. G. Head: *paper read to the Auctioneers' Institute in 1907*

At our feet they lie low,
The little fervent underground
Rivers of London

Effra, Graveney, Falcon, Quaggy,
Wandle, Walbrook, Tyburn, Fleet

Whose names are disfigured,
Frayed, effaced.

These are the Magogs that chewed the clay
To the basin that London nestles in.
These are the currents that chiselled the city,
That washed the clothes and turned the mills,
Where children drank and salmon swam
And wells were holy.

They have gone under.
Boxed, like the magician's assistant.
Buried alive in earth.
Forgotten, like the dead.

They return spectrally after heavy rain,
Confounding suburban gardens. They infiltrate
Chronic bronchitis statistics. A silken
Slur haunts dwellings by shrouded
Watercourses, and is taken
For the footing of the dead.

Being of our world, they will return
(Westbourne, caged at Sloane Square,

Will jack from his box),
Will deluge cellars, detonate manholes,
Plant effluent on our faces,
Sink the city.

Effra, Graveney, Falcon, Quaggy,
Wandle, Walbrook, Tyburn, Fleet

It is the other rivers that lie
Lower, that touch us only in dreams
That never surface. We feel their tug
As a dowser's rod bends to the source below

Phlegethon, Acheron, Lethe, Styx.

Widening the Westway

Torched, they might have been, in another country
Because the wrong people lived in them;
Or, in quieter times, in homelier places,
Left to slither modestly back to earth.

But this is London. There are guide-lines.
Houses are groomed for a protracted ending.

Some house-man has been on his rounds, diagnosing
The slow-motion stages of a terminal event.
Amputate, he prescribed. First went the more portable shrubs,
The carpets, fittings. Lastly, the people.

Then experts came. They blinded each window
With hardboard, extracted knockers and bells like teeth;
As nurses raise screens in wards to island the dying,
They erected eight-foot boards to segregate.

(And someone has aerosoled *Save us* and *Help,*
Help and *Save us,* along the new wood.)

An avenue-full of confident thirties semis,
Twin-gabled, porched, with double mock-Tudor chimneys,
Who shopped at the Army and Navy, golfed in Ealing,
Dentists, dog-walkers, Dry Fly drinkers—that sort of house.

Now they tremble together, W12 Samsons;
Rooftops flayed of tiles are all you can see.
Tomorrow men in heavy duty yellow jackets
With JCBs will rubbish the garlanded plaster.

(And the forsythia gamely still in flower,
And the houses opposite watching speechless
Like aristos brought too soon in their tumbrils,
Watching the load before them.)

This was the way the world marched on.
This may be how it starts. *Atrocity*
Is what we haven't got used to yet.

Ted Hughes (1930–1998)

Fate Playing

Because the message somehow met a goblin,
Because precedents tripped your expectations,
Because your London was still a kaleidoscope
Of names and places any jolt could scramble,
You waited mistaken. The bus from the North
Came in and emptied and I was not on it.
No matter how much you insisted
And begged the driver, probably with tears,
To produce me or to remember seeing me
Just miss getting on. I was not on it.
Eight in the evening and I was lost and at large
Somewhere in England. You restrained
Your confident inspiration
And did not dash out into the traffic
Milling around Victoria, utterly certain
Of bumping into me where I would have to be walking.
I was not walking anywhere. I was sitting
Unperturbed, in my seat on the train
Rocking towards King's Cross. Somebody,
Calmer than you, had a suggestion. So,
When I got off the train, expecting to find you
Somewhere down at the root of the platform,
I saw that surge and agitation, a figure
Breasting the flow of released passengers,
Then your molten face, your molten eyes
And your exclamations, your flinging arms
Your scattering tears
As if I had come back from the dead
Against every possibility, against
Every negative but your own prayer
To your own gods. There I knew what it was
To be a miracle. And behind you

Your jolly taxi-driver, laughing, like a small god,
To see an American girl being so American,
And to see your frenzied chariot-ride—
Sobbing and goading him, and pleading with him
To make happen what you needed to happen—
Succeed so completely, thanks to him.
Well, it was a wonder
That my train was not earlier, even much earlier,
That it pulled in, late, the very moment
You irrupted onto the platform. It was
Natural and miraculous and an omen
Confirming everything
You wanted confirmed. So your huge despair,
Your cross-London panic dash
And now your triumph, splashed over me,
Like love forty-nine times magnified,
Like the first thunder cloudburst engulfing
The drought in August
When the whole cracked earth seems to quake
And every leaf trembles
And everything holds up its arms weeping.

Epiphany

London. The grimy lilac softness
Of an April evening. Me
Walking over Chalk Farm Bridge
On my way to the tube station.
A new father—slightly light-headed
With the lack of sleep and the novelty.
Next, this young fellow coming towards me.

I glanced at him for the first time as I passed him
Because I noticed (I couldn't believe it)
What I'd been ignoring.

Not the bulge of a small animal
Buttoned into the top of his jacket
The way colliers used to wear their whippets—
But its actual face. Eyes reaching out
Trying to catch my eyes—so familiar!
The huge ears, the pinched, urchin expression—
The wild confronting stare, pushed through fear,
Between the jacket lapels.
                    "It's a fox-cub!"
I heard my own surprise as I stopped.
He stopped. "Where did you get it? What
Are you going to do with it?"
                    A fox-cub
On the hump of Chalk Farm Bridge!

"You can have him for a pound." "But
Where did you find it? What will you do with it?"
"Oh, somebody'll buy him. Cheap enough
At a pound." And a grin.
                    What I was thinking
Was—what would you think? How would we fit it
Into our crate of space? With the baby?
What would you make of its old smell
And its mannerless energy?

And as it grew up and began to enjoy itself
What would we do with an unpredictable,
Powerful, bounding fox?
The long-mouthed, flashing temperament?
That necessary nightly twenty miles
And that vast hunger for everything beyond us?
How would we cope with its cosmic derangements
Whenever we moved?

The little fox peered past me at other folks,
At this one and at that one, then at me.
Good luck was all it needed.
Already past the kittenish
But the eyes still small,
Round, orphaned-looking, woebegone
As if with weeping. Bereft
Of the blue milk, the toys of feather and fur,
The den life's happy dark. And the huge whisper
Of the constellations
Out of which Mother had always returned.
My thoughts felt like big, ignorant hounds
Circling and sniffing around him.
                              Then I walked on
As if out of my own life.
I let that fox-cub go. I tossed it back
Into the future
Of a fox-cub in London and I hurried
Straight on and dived as if escaping
Into the Underground. If I had paid,
If I had paid that pound and turned back
To you, with that armful of fox—

If I had grasped that whatever comes with a fox
Is what tests a marriage and proves it a marriage—
I would not have failed the test. Would you have failed it?
But I failed. Our marriage had failed.

Derek Walcott (1930–)

from *Omeros*

II

He curled up on a bench underneath the Embankment wall.
He saw London gliding with the Thames around its neck
like a barge which an old brown horse draws up a canal

if its yoke is Time. From here he could see the dreck
under the scrolled skirts of statues, the grit in the stone lions'
eyes; he saw under everything an underlying grime

that itched in the balls of rearing bronze stallions,
how the stare of somnolent sphinxes closed in time
to the swaying bells of "cities all the floure"

petalling the spear-railed park where a couple suns
near the angled shade of All-Hallows by the Tower,
as the tinkling Thames drags by in its ankle-irons,

while the ginkgo's leaves flexed their fingers overhead.
He mutters its fluent alphabet, the peaked A of a spire,
the half-vowels of bridges, down to the crumpled Z

of his overcoat draping a bench in midsummer's fire.
He read the inverted names of boats in their element,
he saw the tugs chirring up a devalued empire

as the coins of their wake passed the Houses of Parliament.
But the shadows keep multiplying from the Outer
Provinces, their dialects light as the ginkgo's leaf, their

fingers plucking their saris as wind picks at water,
and the statues raising objections; he sees a wide river
with its landing of pier-stakes flooding Westminster's

flagstones, and traces the wake of dugouts in the frieze
of a bank's running cornice, and whenever the ginkgo stirs
the wash of far navies settles in the bargeman's eyes.

A statue swims upside down, one hand up in response
to a question raised in the House, and applause rises
from the clapping Thames, from benches in the leaves.

And the sunflower sets after all, retracting its irises
with the bargeman's own, then buds on black, iron trees
as a gliding fog hides the empires: London, Rome, Greece.

III

Who decrees a great epoch? The meridian of Greenwich.
Who doles out our zeal, and in which way lies our
hope? In the cobbles of sinister Shoreditch,

in the widening rings of Big Ben's iron flower,
in the barges chained like our islands to the Thames.
Where is the alchemical corn and the light it yields?

Where, in which stones of the Abbey, are incised our names?
Who defines our delight? St. Martin-in-the-Fields.
After every Michaelmas, its piercing soprano steeple

defines our delight. Within whose palatable vault
will echo the Saints' litany of our island people?
St. Paul's salt shaker, when we are worth their salt.

Stand by the tilted crosses of well-quiet Glen-da-Lough.
Follow the rook's crook'd finger to the ivied grange.
As black as the rook is, it comes from a higher stock.

Who screams out our price? The crows of the Corn Exchange.
Where are the pleasant pastures? A green baize-table.
Who invests in our happiness? The Chartered Tour.

Who will teach us a history of which we too are capable?
The red double-decker's view of the Bloody Tower.
When are our brood, like the sparrows, a public nuisance?

When they screech at the sinuous swans on the Serpentine.
The swans are royally protected, but in whose hands
are the black crusts of our children? In the pointing sign

under the harps of the willows, to the litter of Margate Sands.
What has all this to do with the price of fish, our salary
tidally scanned with the bank-rate by waxworks tellers?

Where is the light of the world? In the National Gallery.
In Palladian Wren. In the City that can buy and sell us
the packets of tea stirred with our crystals of sweat.

Where is our sublunar peace? In that sickle sovereign
peeling the gilt from St. Paul's onion silhouette.
There is our lunar peace: in the glittering grain

of the coined estuary, our moonlit, immortal wheat,
its white sail cresting the gradual swell of the Downs,
startling the hare from the pillars on Salisbury Plain,

sharpening the grimaces of thin-lipped market towns,
whitewashing the walls of Brixton, darkening the grain
when coal-shadows cross it. Dark future down darker street.

Alan Brownjohn (1931–)

A202

This coarse road, my road, struggles out
South-east across London, an exhausted
Grey zigzag of stubborn, unassimilable
    Macadam, passing hoardings pasted

With blow-ups of cricket journalists, blackened
And not-quite-Georgian terraces,
Shagged-out Greens of geraniums and
    Floral coats-of-arms, lost pieces

Of genteel façade behind and above
Lyons' shopfronts and "Pullum Promotions,"
—Journeying between wired-off bombed lots glossy
    With parked Consuls, making diversions

Round bus depots and draggled estates
In circumlocutory One-Ways,
Netting aquaria in crammed pet store windows,
    Skirting multi-racial bingo queues,

And acquiring, for its self-hating hoard, old black-railed
Underground bogs advising the Seamen's Hospital,
"Do-it-yourself" shops, "Funerals and Monuments," and
    Victorian Charrington pubs. All

Along its length it despoils, in turn, a sequence
Of echoless names: Camberwell, Peckham,
New Cross Gate; places having no recorded past
    Except in histories of the tram.

It takes out, in cars, arterial affluence
At week-ends, returning it as bad blood
To Monday mornings in town. It is altogether
    Like a vein travelled by hardy diseases, an aged

Canal dredgeable for bodies left behind
On its soulless travels: Sixty-Nine,
Thirty-Six, One-Eight-Five. It takes no clear
    Attitude anyone could easily define

So as to resist or admire it. It seems to hate you
Possessively, want to envelop you in nothing
Distinguishable or distinguished, like its own
    Smothered slopes and rotting

Valleys. This road, generally, is one for
The long-defeated; and turns any ironic
Observer's tracer-isotope of ecology,
    Sociology, or hopeful manic

Verse into a kind of mere
Nosing virus itself. It leaves its despondent, foul
And intractable deposit on its own
    Banks all the way like virtually all

Large rivers, particularly the holy ones, which it
Is not. It sees little that deserves to be undespised.
It only means well in the worst of ways.
    How much of love is much less compromised?

Ruth Fainlight (1931–)

The Same Power

Lush chill of spring in Holland Park.
Dark glassy flesh of the bluebells, hoarse
cry of a peacock strutting his courtship cope
against a wind which flattens it out behind
and ripples the quills like waves on a squally sea.
Striped bark of birch trees' pale trunks
as sharp a white as opening hawthorn flowers.
Vivid rainclouds scudding across the sky.

Which all must be attended to now,
not half-ignored, only recalled later (perhaps)—
that common regret for not having been alert
enough to recognise the one moment
when beauty, truth, life and death became
the same Power: evoked not described.

Geoffrey Hill (1932–)

Churchill's Funeral

I

. . . one dark day in the Guildhall: looking at the memorials of the city's great past &
knowing well the history of its unending charity, I seemed to hear far away in the
dim roof a theme, an echo of some noble melody . . .

Endless London
mourns for that knowledge
under the dim roofs
of smoke-stained glass,

the men hefting
their accoutrements
of webbed tin, many
in bandages,

with cigarettes,
with scuffed hands aflare,
as though exhaustion
drew them to life;

as if by some
miraculous draft
of enforced journeys
their peace were made

strange homecoming
into sleep, blighties,
and untouched people
among the maimed:

nobilmente it
rises from silence,
the grand tune, and goes
something like this.

II

Suppose the subject of inquiry, instead of being House-law (Oikonomia), had been star-
law (Astronomia), and that, ignoring distinction between stars fixed and wandering, as
here between wealth radiant and wealth reflective, the writer had begun thus:

Innocent soul
ghosting for its lost
twin, the afflicted one,
born law-giver;

uncanny wraith
kindled afar-off
like the evening star,
res publica

seen by itself
with its whole shining
history discerned
through shining air,

both origin
and consequence, its
hierarchies of sorts,
fierce tea-making

in time of war,
courage and kindness
as the marvel is
the common weal

that will always,
simply as of right,
keep faith, ignorant
of right or fear:

who is to judge
who can judge of this?
Maestros of the world
not you not them.

III

Los listens to the Cry of the Poor Man; his Cloud Over London in volume terrific low bended in anger.

> The copper clouds
> are not of this light;
> Lambeth is no more
> the house of the lamb.
>
> The meek shall die rich
> would you believe:
> with such poverty
> lavished upon them,
>
> with their obsequies
> the Heinkels' lourd drone
> and Fame darkening
> her theatres
>
> to sirens, laughter,
> the frizzed angels
> of visitation
> powdered by the blast,
>
> the catafalques
> like gin-palaces
> where she entertains
> the comedians.

IV

St. Mary Abchurch, St. Mary Aldermanbury, St. Mary-le-Bow . . .

> Stone Pietà
> for which the city
> offers up incense
> and ashes, blitzed
>
> firecrews, martyrs
> crying to the Lord,

their mangled voices
within the flame;

to which we bring
litanies of scant
survival and all
random mercies,

with the ragwort
and the willow-herb
as edifiers
of ruined things.

V

. . . every minute particular, the jewels of Albion, running down / The kennels of the
streets & lanes as if they were abhorr'd.

The brazed city
reorders its own
destruction, admits
the strutting lords

to the temple,
vandals of sprayed blood—
obliterations
to make their mark.

The spouting head
spiked as prophetic
is ancient news.
Once more the keeper

of the dung-gate
tells his own story;
so too the harlot
of many tears.

Speak now regardless
judges of the hour:

what verdict, what people?
Hem of whose garment?

Whose Jerusalem—
at usance for its bones'
redemption and last
salvo of poppies?

To the High Court of Parliament

November 1994

> —who could outbalance poised
> > Marvell; balk the strength
> of Gillray's unrelenting, unreconciling mind;
> grandees risen from scavenge; to whom Milton
> > addressed his ideal censure:
> once more, singular, ill-attended,
> staid and bitter Commedia—as she is called—
> delivers to your mirth her veiled presence.
>
> None the less amazing: Barry's and Pugin's grand
> dark-lantern above the incumbent Thames.
> You: as by custom unillumined
> > masters of servile counsel.
> Who can now speak for despoiled merit,
> > the fouled catchments of Demos,
> as "thy" high lamp presides with sovereign
> equity, over against us, across this
> densely reflective, long-drawn, procession of waters?

Sylvia Plath (1932–1963)

Parliament Hill Fields

On this bald hill the new year hones its edge.
Faceless and pale as china
The round sky goes on minding its business.
Your absence is inconspicuous;
Nobody can tell what I lack.

Gulls have threaded the river's mud bed back
To this crest of grass. Inland, they argue,
Settling and stirring like blown paper
Or the hands of an invalid. The wan
Sun manages to strike such tin glints

From the linked ponds that my eyes wince
And brim; the city melts like sugar.
A crocodile of small girls
Knotting and stopping, ill-assorted, in blue uniforms,
Opens to swallow me. I'm a stone, a stick,

One child drops a barrette of pink plastic;
None of them seem to notice.
Their shrill, gravelly gossip's funneled off.
Now silence after silence offers itself.
The wind stops my breath like a bandage.

Southward, over Kentish Town, an ashen smudge
Swaddles roof and tree.
It could be a snowfield or a cloudbank.
I suppose it's pointless to think of you at all.
Already your doll grip lets go.

The tumulus, even at noon, guards its black shadow.
You know me less constant,
Ghost of a leaf, ghost of a bird.

I circle the writhen trees. I am too happy.
These faithful dark-boughed cypresses

Brood, rooted in their heaped losses.
Your cry fades like the cry of a gnat.
I lose sight of you on your blind journey,
While the heath grass glitters and the spindling rivulets
Unspool and spend themselves. My mind runs with them,

Pooling in heel-prints, fumbling pebble and stem.
The day empties its images
Like a cup or a room. The moon's crook whitens,
Thin as the skin seaming a scar.
Now, on the nursery wall,

The blue night plants, the little pale blue hill
In your sister's birthday picture start to glow.
The orange pompons, the Egyptian papyrus
Light up. Each rabbit-eared
Blue shrub behind the glass

Exhales an indigo nimbus,
A sort of cellophane balloon.
The old dregs, the old difficulties take me to wife.
Gulls stiffen to their chill vigil in the drafty half-light;
I enter the lit house.

Anne Stevenson (1933–)

Cashpoint Charlie

My office, my crouch, is by the Piccadilly cashpoint where
Clients of the Hong Kong and Shanghai Banking Co.
Facilitate my study of legs as they ebb and flow;
Legs, and the influence of sex and wealth on footwear.

The human foot—wedge-shaped, a mini torso—
Used to be, like the monkey's, toed for zipping
Quickly through jungles. Just how prehensile gripping
Got to be a closed shop for hands I'll never know.

Anyhow, feet are in jail now, shoes' prisoners,
Inviting comparison, ladies, with steel-tipped bullets,
And sadly, gentlemen, with coffins. My tiptop favourites
Are Dr. Martin's hammer-like hoofs and laceless trainers.

It's a proved fact that the shabbily shod give more.
Like knee-slashed jeans give more than knife-creased trousers.
And shivering junkies more than antique browsers.
What? Thanks to a glitch in the chem lab (not a war)

I'm legless. Or as good as . . . it all depends
On where you poke and what you count as me.
To "rise" I use a crutch. It helps the money,
And, like my filthy sleeping bag, offends

Your everyday dainty British git just bad enough
To make him pull his Balaclava face
Hard down over his sweet guilt. I make my case:
OK, if you hate me, you have to hate yourself,

And think it steady at him. Nothing's said, of course.
They never meet your eyes, not even the women

Yanking at their big-eyed kids like I was poison,
And then, with a tight look, opening their purse.

It's crazy, but I love them . . . it . . . taking the piss.
If that old guy, that Greek philosopher in his barrel,
Could see me now, in my sleeping bag, beside a hole
In a wall that spits out money, he'd be envious.

Fleur Adcock (1934–)

Miss Hamilton in London

It would not be true to say she was doing nothing:
she visited several bookshops, spent an hour
in the Victoria and Albert Museum (Indian section),
and walked carefully through the streets of Kensington
carrying five mushrooms in a paper bag,
a tin of black pepper, a literary magazine,
and enough money to pay the rent for two weeks.
The sky was cloudy, leaves lay on the pavements.

Nor did she lack human contacts: she spoke
to three shop-assistants and a newsvendor,
and returned the "Goodnight" of a museum attendant.
Arriving home, she wrote a letter to someone
in Canada, as it might be, or in New Zealand,
listened to the news as she cooked her meal,
and conversed for five minutes with the landlady.
The air was damp with the mist of late autumn.

A full day, and not unrewarding.
Night fell at the usual seasonal hour.
She drew the curtains, switched on the electric fire,
washed her hair and read until it was dry,
then went to bed; where, for the hours of darkness,
she lay pierced by thirty black spears
and felt her limbs numb, her eyes burning,
and dark rust carried along her blood.

Londoner

Scarcely two hours back in the country
and I'm shopping in East Finchley High Road
in a cotton skirt, a cardigan, jandals—
or flipflops as people call them here,
where February's winter. Aren't I cold?
The neighbours in their overcoats are smiling
at my smiles and not at my bare toes:
they know me here.

      I hardly know myself,
yet. It takes me until Monday evening,
walking from the office after dark
to Westminster Bridge. It's cold, it's foggy,
the traffic's as abominable as ever,
and there across the Thames is County Hall,
that uninspired stone body, floodlit.
It makes me laugh. In fact, it makes me sing.

To Marilyn from London

You did London early, at nineteen:
the basement room, the geriatric nursing,
cinema queues, modish fall-apart dresses,
and marriage at Stoke Newington Registry Office,
Spring 1955, on the rebound.

Marrying was what we did in those days.
And soon enough you were back in Wellington
with your eye-shadow and your Edith Piaf records
buying kitchen furniture on hire-purchase
and writing novels when the babies were asleep.

Somehow you're still there, I'm here; and now
Sarah arrives: baby-faced like you then,
second of your four blonde Christmas-tree fairies,
nineteen; competent; with her one suitcase
and her two passports. It begins again.

John Fuller (1937–)

from *London Songs*

1 MISSING

Lonely in London is an endless story,
Tired in the sun on the District Line,
With Barons Court baked beans opened in Ealing,
Tossing in bed and staring at the ceiling,
And: "Yes, Mr. Holdsworth, I'll put you through."
A lot of work and not much glory
And a letter to Mum that says you're fine.

You played me songs on your piana.
Its E was missing like a tooth.
It always rained when I came to see you,
Rained like the mint, the window creaked with rain.
You sat in the window and I told you the truth.

Lonely in London is an endless story.
Where did you go to? Who do you see?
I played at being with you, yes I'm sorry.
Now in this dog's soup I'm less than me,
Miss you, your piana, your piana and your cardigan,
Miss you on Friday, miss you on Monday,
Your cardigan, your tears and the baked-bean smells.
You're like a secret that nobody tells,
Lonely in London, somewhere, now.

2 DUSK

Rain on the river, and this hour of dusk
Settling slowly, imposingly, on London
As though its greatest shopwalker has died
Like a pianist about to play Busoni,
Hands resting in waxen contemplation

In white cuffs quietly upon his knees,
And women, weeping pearls, are gathered now
In Bond Street as the black discreet cortège
Rumbles slowly down to Piccadilly.

Rain on the river, and this hour of dusk
Settling on a city inventive of pleasure,
Secure in pleasure, in its terrible pleasure.

from *The Shires*

MIDDLESEX

Middlesex is mostly roundabouts, the bright
Voice of five P.M., insistent infotainment:
Fingers gallop irritably on the steering-wheel;
The nails make little clicks. Down the line
Of fuming stationary Volvos boys bully with headlines
That tell the drivers all about the place they have come from.

Ken Smith (1938–2003)

from *The London Poems*

MOVIES AFTER MIDNIGHT

From Canning Town to Woolwich
the tall cranes rust. The pub's shut
and the lift's out in the towerblock,
everything you see is up for sale.

But there's a night movie: the well fed
soldiery with fancy weapons come
to stutter out the liberators'
brief philosophy: *up yours Commie.*

Even the prime numbers are giving up,
all the best words have moved to Surrey
and we have just a few at discount now
to make farewells that vanish with us.

CLIPPER SERVICE

In black and white the Isle of Dogs,
slow workless docklands going cheap,
the great outworks of power stations.
I'm living on two eggs and no bacon

here beside the river, smokey as ever,
among strangers. Ships there were son,
and lascars, then as now the afternoon
brought sulphur on the wind and no comfort.

Now the natives are proud and scattered
and lonely in the high rises, living
as they always lived: thieving or work
when there's work. There's none now.

MESSAGE ON THE MACHINE

Your protagonist is not at home just now.
He's out, a one-way window in his head
with everything coming in fast across the city
and always an alarm bell ringing in the buildings

a jammed horn streets away, the town winds
lifting documents along the Broadway,
along Commercial Road a signboard
banging in the night reads *Smack*

Disposal Systems, he fears skinheads
in the drains and angels in the elevator
and the number 5 bus will never come now.
After the tone leave a brief message.

Seamus Heaney (1939–)

The Underground

There we were in the vaulted tunnel running,
You in your going-away coat speeding ahead
And me, me then like a fleet god gaining
Upon you before you turned to a reed

Or some new white flower japped with crimson
As the coat flapped wild and button after button
Sprang off and fell in a trail
Between the Underground and the Albert Hall.

Honeymooning, moonlighting, late for the Proms,
Our echoes die in that corridor and now
I come as Hansel came on the moonlit stones
Retracing the path back, lifting the buttons

To end up in a draughty lamplit station
After the trains have gone, the wet track
Bared and tensed as I am, all attention
For your step following and damned if I look back.

District and Circle

Tunes from a tin whistle underground
Curled up a corridor I'd be walking down
To where I knew I was always going to find
My watcher on the tiles, cap by his side,
His fingers perked, his two eyes eyeing me
In an unaccusing look I'd not avoid,
Or not just yet, since both were out to see
For ourselves.
                    As the music larked and capered
I'd trigger and untrigger a hot coin
Held at the ready, but now my gaze was lowered
For was our traffic not in recognition?
Accorded passage, I would re-pocket and nod,
And he, still eyeing me, would also nod.
❧

Posted, eyes front, along the dreamy ramparts
Of escalators ascending and descending
To a monotonous slight rocking in the works,
We were moved along, upstanding.
Elsewhere, underneath, an engine powered,
Rumbled, quickened, evened, quieted.
The white tiles gleamed. In passages that flowed
With draughts from cooler tunnels, I missed the light
Of all-overing, long since mysterious day,
Parks at lunchtime where the sunners lay
On body-heated mown grass regardless,
A resurrection scene minutes before
The resurrection, habitués
Of their garden of delights, of staggered summer.
❧

Another level down, the platform thronged.
I re-entered the safety of numbers,
A crowd half straggle-ravelled and half strung

Like a human chain, the pushy newcomers
Jostling and purling underneath the vault,
On their marks to be first through the doors,
Street-loud, then succumbing to herd-quiet . . .
Had I betrayed or not, myself or him?
Always new to me, always familiar,
This unrepentant, now repentant turn
As I stood waiting, glad of a first tremor,
Then caught up in the now-or-never whelm
Of one and all the full length of the train.

◦§

Stepping on to it across the gap,
On to the carriage metal, I reached to grab
The stubby black roof-wort and take my stand
From planted ball of heel to heel of hand
As sweet traction and heavy down-slump stayed me.
I was on my way, well girded, yet on edge,
Spot-rooted, buoyed, aloof,
Listening to the dwindling noises off,
My back to the unclosed door, the platform empty;
And wished it could have lasted,
That long between-times pause before the budge
And glaze-over, when any forwardness
Was unwelcome and bodies readjusted,
Blindsided to themselves and other bodies.

◦§

So deeper into it, crowd-swept, strap-hanging,
My lofted arm a-swivel like a flail,
My father's glazed face in my own waning
And craning . . .
                    Again the growl
Of shutting doors, the jolt and one-off treble
Of iron on iron, then a long centrifugal
Haulage of speed through every dragging socket.

And so by night and day to be transported
Through galleried earth with them, the only relict
Of all that I belonged to, hurtled forward,
Reflecting in a window mirror-backed
By blasted weeping rock-walls.
                                    Flicker-lit.

Lee Harwood (1939–)

Rain journal: London: June 65

sitting naked together
on the edge of the bed
drinking vodka

this my first real love scene

your body so good
your eyes sad love stars

but John
now when we're miles apart
the come-down from mountain visions
and the streets all raining
and me in the back of a shop
making free phone calls to you

what can we do?

crackling telephone wires shadow me
and this distance haunts me

and yes—I am miserable
and lost without you

whole days spent
remaking your face
the sound of your voice
the feel of your shoulder

Grey Gowrie (1939–)

Outside Biba's

Flowers after rare rain, boutiques
sprout behind glass in our macadam city
and everyone's talking fashion.

A girl goes by
who must be unmarried but looks so marriageable
her dress is a hurricane of confetti
blown to her from someone else's wedding.

Think of the great skirts of childhood's women,
the New Look that swept the war away . . .

No war now, no one poor under thirty,
all the Cold War babies dressed to kill.

Joseph Brodsky (1940–1996)

from *In England*

NORTH KENSINGTON

The rustle of an *Irish Times* harried by the wind along
railway tracks to a depot long abandoned,
the crackle of dead wormwood, heralding autumn,
a gray tongue of water close by gums of brick.
How I love these sounds—the sounds of aimless
but continuing life, which for long enough
have been sufficient, aside from the crunch of
my own weighty tread on the gravel. And I fling a bolt skyward.
Only a mouse comprehends the delights of waste ground—
a rusting rail, discarded metal pins,
slack wire, reduced to a husky C-sharp,
the defeat of time in the face of metal.
All beyond repair, no further use.
You can only asphalt it over or blast
it clean off the face of the earth, used by now
to grimacing concrete stadia and their bawling crowds.
Then the mouse will come. Slowly, no rush,
out into the middle of the field, tiny as the soul
is in relation to the flesh, and, raising its
little snout, aghast, will shriek, "What is this place?"

Derek Mahon (1941–)

Sunday Morning

We wake and watch the sun make bright
The corners of our London flat—
No sound but the sporadic, surly
Snarl of a car making an early
Dash for the country or the coast.
This is the time I like the most
When, for an hour or two, the strife
And strain of the late bourgeois life

Let up, we lie and grin to hear
The children bickering next door—
Hilarious formulations based
On a weird logic we have lost.
Oil crises and vociferous crowds
Seem as far off as tiny clouds;
The long-range forecast prophesies
Mean temperatures and azure skies.

Out in the park where Celia's father
Died, the Sunday people gather—
Residents towed by Afghan hounds,
Rastafarians trailing "sounds,"
Provincial tourists, Japanese
Economists, Saudi families,
Fresh-faced American college kids
Making out in the green shades.

A chiliastic prick, I prowl
Among the dog-lovers and growl,
Among the kite-fliers and fly
The private kite of poetry—
A sort of winged sandwich board
El-Grecoed to receive the word;

An airborne, tremulous brochure
Proclaiming that the end is near.

Black diplomats with gorgeous wives,
Promenading, notice the natives
Dozing beside the palace gates—
Old ladies under wide straw hats
Who can remember *Chu Chin Chow*
And Kitchener. Exhausted now
By decades of retrenchment, they
Wait for the rain at close of play.

Asia now for a thousand years—
A flower that blooms and disappears
In a sandstorm; every artifact
A pure, self-referential act,
That the intolerant soul may be
Retrieved from triviality
And the locked heart, so long in pawn
To steel, redeemed by flesh and bone.

Hugo Williams (1942–)

Tavistock Square

The Hiroshima silver birch 1963
Is not silver in January.

Mahatma Gandhi looks cold
On his stone shell like a loudspeaker.

They sit down facing him in silence
To talk about their life.

Husband and wife,
Why can't they believe in it?

Bar Italia

to L. S.

This is how we met,
Sheltering from work in this crowded coffee bar.
This is where we sit,
Propped at some narrow shelf,
Each day more crowded than the last
With undesirables.

I wish we could meet again
In two years' time,
Somewhere expensive where they remembered us
From the early days, before the crash.
Instead of here, instead of now,
Facing our reflections in the Bar Italia.

You would be frowning of course,
After all this time,
But then you would hold out your hand and say,
"Well, where are your three pages?"

I haven't written them. One day I will.
Anywhere but here it might seem possible.

Bar Italia

How beautiful it would be to wait for you again
in the usual place,
not looking at the door,
keeping a lookout in the long mirror,
knowing that if you are late
it will not be too late,
knowing that all I have to do
is wait a little longer
and you will be pushing through the other customers,
out of breath, apologetic.
Where have you been, for God's sake?
I was starting to worry.

How long did we say we would wait
if one of us was held up?
It's been so long and still no sign of you.
As time goes by, I search other faces in the bar,
rearranging their features
until they are monstrous versions of you,
their heads wobbling from side to side
like heads on sticks.
Your absence inches forward
until it is standing next to me.
Now it has taken the seat I was saving.
Now we are face to face in the long mirror.

Notting Hill

Notting Hill Gate in the dead of winter.
A woman selling plantain bread.
A man who whispered,
"Sense, sense, sensomilia . . .
Don't you know what sensomilia is?"

He took our twenty quid
and disappeared down a side street,
leaving us with Geraldine,
his junkie teenage sidekick,
who said she hardly knew him.

Iain Sinclair (1943–)

bunhill fields

Secretly, he loved poetry.
  —Tim Hilton *(on Clement Greenberg)*

> the proximate fig shades a shale envelope
> writing I have no intention of writing about this
> heavy leaves green fed with grey fed up
> between showers with being noticed shadows
> where William & Catherine lie loose disinterred
> a glazed brown pot in clay dead flowerheads
> flower-smelling water incoherent autumn
> sunlight free-associating through stone flags when
> the blonde child on her precocious red bicycle
> what did you say these were called again what
> did you say *figs* figs figs but do they have seeds
> confirmation speeds her certain way
> balanced five-in-hand that might have ripened
> juice on the vertical slab unsteady from wine lunch
> a mossy cushion obelisks & peeled plaster faces
> scarlet seeds on a thick black tongue

hurricane drummers: self-aid in haggerston

Ronnie Kray is now in Broadmoor and brother Reggie in Parkhurst from where he is
trying . . . to get a security firm called Budrill off the ground.

> there's a mob of rumours from s. of the river
> challenging the teak and shattering glass
> with dropkicks honed on GLC grant aid—Nike soles
> stamp out likely prints of light, moth-shaped entries
>
> another team of semi-skilled dips work
> the precinct, dry cleaning my credits my
> licences and small wad of royal portraits
> allowing them to collect on unconvincing promises
>
> a couple of vehicles are cased
> and a couple elbowed
>
> in reply the locals can offer
> a squadcar of handy lads looking for lefty,
> cruising on new rubbers that
> give the game away, authentic
> as any red light disco chuck-outs
>
> employment prospects are good
> for the wolf importers the cross-
> breeders of beasts with more
> jaw than brain—the bells! the bells!
>
> charm out in celebration,
> aerobic heels flash high torsion
> round the corner of Queensbridge Road
> "hey, what is it about this place?"
> says the reverend suddenly
> looking out of the window at
> a group of black youths as we

approach Dalston.
"they're smoking reefer on the street!"

"music is music," says Cleveland,
returning to the subject.
"it's the words that separates
gospel from the rest. only the words."

Mimi Khalvati (1944–)

Earls Court

I brush my teeth harder when the gum bleeds.
Arrive alone at parties, leaving early.

The tide comes in, dragging my stare
from pastures I could call my own.

Through the scratches on the record—*Ah! Vieni, vieni!*—
I concentrate on loving.

I use my key. No duplicate of this.
Arrive alone at parties, leaving early.

I brush my teeth harder when the gum bleeds.
Sing to the fern in the steam. Not even looking—

commuters buying oranges, Italian vegetables,
bucket flowers from shores I might have danced in, briefly.

I use my key—a lost belonging on the stair.
Sing to the fern in the steam. I wash my hair.

The tide goes out, goes out. The body's wear and tear.
Commuters' faces turn towards me: bucket flowers.

A man sits eyeing destinations on the train.
He wears Islamic stubble, expensive clothes, two rings.

He talks to himself in Farsi, loudly like a drunk.
Laughs aloud to think where life has brought him.

Eyeing destinations on the train—a lost belonging—
talks to himself with a laugh I could call my own.

Like a drunk I want to neighbour him, sit beside
his stubble's scratch, turn his talking into chatting.

I want to tell him I have a ring like his,
only smaller. I want to see him use his key.

I want to hear the child who runs to him call
Baba! I want to hear him answer, turning

from his hanging coat: *Beeya, Babajune, beeya!*
Ah! Vieni, vieni! . . .

Carol Rumens (1944–)

Pleasure Island, Marble Arch

Time and tarmac have ditched the last
Creaking ghost of Tyburn. A car-swathed island,
Wooded and sown with fine turf, is the navel
Of this oil-fed, pleasure-rich half mile,
Its jewel, a square grey lake, restless as silk
Under the wind. Dull, now, with November,
It wears the haunted, half-resentful look
Of an off-season resort, waiting for life
To be cheap and bright again, a gift of strangers.
Then the fountains will leap like marathon dancers
Pushing white-muscled shoulders and sparkling hair-do's
Hour after desperate hour into the blue,
And the grass lie kindled gold under the plashy
Coloratura of many languages.
Wilkommen, bienvenu, the faded placards
Shout to themselves in the subway corridors—
And a girl will move shyly in front of the fountains,
Smooth back her hair and smile into the future,
To be peeled from its eye, a tiny Hockney
Of blue light, spray and the delicate boldness
Of flesh in a mild climate.
Meanwhile, the grass dims, the stone faucets
Eat leaves. A gardener stoops to his heaped barrow.
The island is ours, though we possess it
Only at a distance, from office windows
Or the tops of circling buses. We approve
Its elegiac mood, its little image
Of transience. Whatever storms tug

Bigger seas to madness, we trust this water
To move within imaginable limits.
It is stamped on our days, part of the pattern,
An opaque poetry, revealing less
Our sense of failure than our certainty
Of what's provincial, gardened, small, enduring.

Wendy Cope (1945–)

Lonely Hearts

Can someone make my simple wish come true?
Male biker seeks female for touring fun.
Do you live in North London? Is it you?

Gay vegetarian whose friends are few,
I'm into music, Shakespeare and the sun.
Can someone make my simple wish come true?

Executive in search of something new—
Perhaps bisexual woman, arty, young.
Do you live in North London? Is it you?

Successful, straight and solvent? I am too—
Attractive Jewish lady with a son.
Can someone make my simple wish come true?

I'm Libran, inexperienced and blue—
Need slim non-smoker, under twenty-one.
Do you live in North London? Is it you?

Please write (with photo) to Box 152.
Who knows where it may lead once we've begun?
Can someone make my simple wish come true?
Do you live in North London? Is it you?

After the Lunch

On Waterloo Bridge, where we said our goodbyes,
The weather conditions bring tears to my eyes.
I wipe them away with a black woolly glove
And try not to notice I've fallen in love.

On Waterloo Bridge I am trying to think:
This is nothing. You're high on the charm and the drink.
But the juke-box inside me is playing a song
That says something different. And when was it wrong?

On Waterloo Bridge with the wind in my hair
I am tempted to skip. *You're a fool.* I don't care.
The head does its best but the heart is the boss—
I admit it before I am halfway across.

Peter Reading (1946–)

from *Perduta Gente*

"SOUTH BANK: SIBELIUS 5'S"

South Bank: Sibelius 5's
incontrovertible end—
five exhalations, bray of expiry,
    absolute silence . . .

Under the Festival Hall is a foetid
    tenebrous concert
    strobed by blue ambulance light.
    PVC/newspapers/rags
insulate ranks of expendables, eyesores,
    winos, unworthies,
one of which (stiff in its cardboard Electrolux
    box stencilled FRAGILE,
    STOW THIS WAY UP, USE NO HOOKS)
officers lug to the tumbril,
    exhaling, like ostlers, its scents:

                squit,

                honk,

                piss,

                meths,

                distress.

"MISSIZ AN ME INDA WARM INDA EUSTON"

missiz an me inda warm inda Euston
    unnerground buskin
fugginwell busted armonica playin
    only da one fing
    over an zover again

missiz gone arse-over-ed on da fuggin
    down eshcalator
tryin to swing for some cuntinna bowler
      wot givver two pee
    bazshd up er face an er arm
    cetched up er sleeve in da fing
    where it gozsh clackety-clack
    mergency stop button presh

mashessa blood inna cetchup da coppers
    draggin er screamin
still wiv er good arm out of er pocket
    bockle uv Strongbow

gizzera fifty or twenny fer fuggsay
    mister a tellya
  savvy dis noosepaper see?
  sonly bed we gotter nigh

"OUTSIDE VICTORIA STATION A QUORUM OF"

Outside Victoria Station a quorum of
    no-hoper foetid
impromptu imbibers is causing a shindy:
    one of the number,
clutching a bottle of Thunderbird, half-full,
    rolls amongst litter
(chip-papers, Pepsi cans, Embassy packets—
    Indian take-out
  remnants adhere to her mac);
  under one arm is a crutch
  (the other is lopped at the elbow);
plaster encases her leg, which a colleague
    (sipping a Carlsberg)
kicks periodically, bellowing "fugg-bag,
    fuggbagging fugg-bag."

Christopher Reid (1949–)

North London Sonnet

for Lucinda

A boom-box blats by,
less music than sonic muscle
assaulting the night sky,
a pumped-up hustle-bustle

which manages to disturb
the twirly, needling alarm
of a car tucked into the kerb—
its mantra, or charm—

but that, too, soon quiets
and you sleep on, proof
against the rumpuses and riots
encircling our roof,

till my switching off the light
prompts a muffled *Good night.*

Exasperated Piety

Majestically indignant, Henry James
    in his preface to *The Altar of the Dead*—
paragraphs I have read and re-read—
    cites instances, but forbears to name names,
as he recalls the gross metropolitan snub
    whereby old friends and associates who had died
were not so much forgotten as denied:
    a frosty ostracism from the club
of the left-over living. I paraphrase crudely
    James's pained, feeling and reasoning prose,
but I too have met the tribal will to impose
    taboos and codes, and have behaved rudely,
invoking my dead wife in dinner-table conversation.
    A beat of silence, of shared fear and sick shock, falls,
a symptom of the malaise that James himself calls
    "the awful doom of general dishumanisation."
He blamed London: "a terrible place to die in";
    "the poor dead, all about one, are nowhere so dead as there."
I see an old writer, gagging on the ghost-rich air
    of a fashionable salon, a terrible place to cry in.

Gillian Allnutt (1949–)

Museum, 19 Princelet Street, Spitalfields

old dull shades of silk on wooden reels
plum, olive, sky-
grey sea they, Huguenot, came hurrying over
hidden in wine-barrels

songbirds, windowsills

later, old leather cases, grandparental
treadle-machine
spool, bobbin
reel

old dull shades of glass, stained, skylit
synagogue light of iron
bare, barley sugar pillars, panels
plain

Lewis Brick died 24th October 1944   £6.6.0
In Memory by his wife and children

altar-gates, closed, with sash cord
chandeliers, kitchen candles
eagles, double-headed
chained

John Agard (1949–)

Toussaint L'Ouverture Acknowledges Wordsworth's Sonnet "To Toussaint L'Ouverture"

I have never walked on Westminster Bridge
or had a close-up view of daffodils.
My childhood's roots are the Haitian hills
where runaway slaves made a freedom pledge
and scarlet poincianas flaunt their scent.
I have never walked on Westminster Bridge
or speak, like you, with Cumbrian accent.
My tongue bridges Europe to Dahomey.
Yet how sweet is the smell of liberty
when human beings share a common garment.
So, thanks brother, for your sonnet's tribute.
May it resound when the Thames' text stays mute.
And what better ground than a city's bridge
for my unchained ghost to trumpet love's decree.

Chilling Out Beside the Thames

Summer come, mi chill-out beside the Thames.
Spend a little time with weeping willow.
Check if dem Trafalgar pigeon still salute
old one-eyed one-armed Lord Horatio.

Mi treat mi gaze to Gothic cathedral
Yet mi cyant forget how spider spiral
Is ladder aspiring to eternal truth . . .
Trickster Nansi spinning from Shakespeare sky.

Sudden so, mi decide to play tourist.
Tower of London high-up on mi list.
Who show up but Anne Boleyn with no head on
And headless Ralegh gazing towards Devon.

Jesus lawd, history shadow so bloody.
A-time fo summer break with strawberry.

Grace Nichols (1950–)

Island Man

(for a Caribbean island man in London who still wakes up to the sound of the sea)

Morning
and island man wakes up
to the sound of blue surf
in his head
the steady breaking and wombing

wild seabirds
and fishermen pushing out to sea
the sun surfacing defiantly

from the east
of his small emerald island
he always comes back   groggily groggily

Comes back to sands
of a grey metallic soar
                              to surge of wheels
to dull North Circular roar

muffling muffling
his crumpled pillow waves
island man heaves himself

Another London day

Charles Boyle (1951–)

The Miracle at Shepherd's Bush

By late afternoon you are standing at the barriers
around a patch of scorched grass, a piece of white clothing,
one shoe, a kite in a tree. The women with armbands

are saying nothing, only that no one
has been hurt or arrested. There's a faint smell of burning,
a lingering pink over Acton

that seems reluctant to call it a day. The choir
of the Pentecostal Church sings unaccompanied gospel hymns
and slowly you become aware just how many people

you live among are blind or dumb or are crippled
in so many ways. Some kneel and pray or weep, others light candles
on a trestle table covered with velvet or dig divots

of grass and soil which they carry off in plastic bags.
Most people are simply curious, they would like the police
or an archbishop to say for sure whether it is one thing

or another, it resembles too closely for comfort a car-boot sale
or minor demonstration against the government—except there lacks
any sense of achievement, of having stood up to be counted.

Blessed by some nuns, warned by a man with a thermos
the end of the world is nigh, you walk home past a couple
in a tent making love. Next day it is in the papers

along with a two-years'-old photo of the boy with his mother
in someone's back garden, not smiling. Eye-witnesses
come forward, though you know for a fact at least two of them

were in the Coningham Arms all day. The lucrative role of father
is claimed by three. It rains, the paths worn in the green
are trodden to mud, wheelchairs get stuck, you overhear jokes

about virgin births and burning bushes. For a week,
maybe two, there are reported sightings of the mother and boy
from Stranraer, Teignmouth, Berwick-upon-Tweed,

Oslo. You think of the boy waking
to the sound of water, the morning light, his fingers
touching skin all over that must scarcely feel his own.

Andrew Motion (1952–)

London Plane

They felled the plane that broke the pavement slabs.
My next-door neighbour worried for his house.
He said the roots had cracked his bedroom wall.
The Council sent tree-surgeons and he watched.
A thin man in the heat without a shirt.
They started at the top and then worked down.
It took a day with one hour free for lunch.
The trunk was carted off in useful logs.

The stump remained for two weeks after that.
A wren sat on it once.
Then back the tree-men came with their machine.
They chomped the stump and left a square of mud.
All afternoon the street was strewn with bits.
That night the wind got up and blew it bare.

Linton Kwesi Johnson (1952–)

Sonny's Lettah

(Anti-Sus Poem)

> Brixtan Prison
> Jebb Avenue
> Landan south-west two
> Inglan

Dear Mama,
Good Day.
I hope dat wen
deze few lines reach yu,
they may find yu in di bes af helt.

Mama,
I really dont know how fi tell yu dis,
cause I did mek a salim pramis
fi tek care a likkle Jim
an try mi bes fi look out fi him.

Mama,
I really did try mi bes,
but nondiles
mi sarry fi tell yu seh
poor likkle Jim get arres.

It woz di miggle a di rush howah
wen evrybady jus a hosel an a bosel
fi goh home fi dem evenin showah;
mi an Jim stan-up
waitin pan a bus,
nat cauzin no fus,
wen all af a sudden
a police van pull-up.

Out jump tree policeman,
di hole a dem carryin batan.
Dem waak straight up to mi an Jim.

One a dem hol awn to Jim
seh him tekin him in;
Jim tell him fi let goh a him
far him noh dhu notn
an him naw teef,
nat even a butn.
Jim start to wriggle
Di police start to giggle.

Mama,
mek I tell yu whe dem dhu to Jim
Mama,
mek I tell yu whe dem dhu to him:

dem tump him in him belly
an it turn to jelly
dem lick him pan him back
an him rib get pap
dem lick him pan him hed
but it tuff like led
dem kick him in him seed
an it started to bleed

Mama,
I jus coudn stan-up deh
an noh dhu notn:
soh mi jook one in him eye
an him started to cry
mi tump one in him mout
an him started to shout
mi kick one pan him shin
an him started to spin
mi tump him pan him chin
an him drap pan a bin

an crash
an ded.

Mama,
more policeman come dung
an beat mi to di grung;
dem charge Jim fi sus,
dem charge mi fi murdah.

Mama,
dont fret,
dont get depres
an doun-hearted.
Be af good courage
till I hear fram you.

I remain
your son,
Sonny.

Jo Shapcott (1953–)

St. Bride's

There is a tower of the winds as tall
as this one in another city, a steeple
filled with fire by the incendiary raids
of a coalition of the unwilling. Nocturnal
shocks pound the citizens who survive,
blast them out of their beds into the streets,
children bundled under their arms. The gutters flame.
Dust is alight. I was born in a city

to come and go safely through the boroughs,
carrying inside me every morning's news: pictures
of soldiers in places they didn't want
to understand, made to fight for loose change,
for the hell of it, for a can of oil. I live here,
the smell of print and ashes in my nose.

Michael Donaghy (1954–2004)

The River Glideth of His Own Sweet Will

Who's this buck of eighteen come up the stairs
squinting from his *Rough Guide*
across the Thames into the late June sun
towards Lambeth, the wheel, the aquarium,

and St. Thomas' Hospital where you lie
in the eighth-floor intensive-care unit
wired up to a heart monitor
staring north to Big Ben's crackled face?

But now the nurse pulls shut the blinds—
not that you'd have clocked one another.
What unaided eyes could possibly connect
thirty years across Westminster bridge
through traffic fumes, crowds,
children, career, marriage, mortgage?

Poem on The Underground

Sirs, as ancient maps imagine monsters
so London's first anatomical charts
displayed the innards of a vast loud animal;
writhing discrete circulatory systems
venous, arterial, lymphatic, rendered
into District, Piccadilly, Bakerloo . . .
But Harry Beck's map was a circuit diagram
of coloured wires soldered at the stations.
It showed us all we needed then to know,
and knew already, that the city's
an angular appliance of intentions, not
the blood and guts of everything that happens.
Commuters found it "easier to read."

My new 3D design improves on Beck,
restoring something of the earlier complexity.
See, here I've drawn the ordinary lines
but crossing these, weaving through the tunnels,
coded beyond the visible spectrum, I've graphed
the vector of today's security alert
due to a suspect package at Victoria,
to the person under a train at Mill Hill East,
with all the circumstantial stops between.

Jeremy Reed (1954–)

Quentin Crisp as Prime Minister

Recalled at last for a pink happening,
the sassy Whitehall ceremonials
proclaim his mordant camp sagacity,
his drag investiture, all brimmish hat—
a UFO concept in mauve felt,
his costume jewellery's glitz vocabulary

pronouncing all values are paste,
but better known for the truth in the lie.
He's come by water, for the river speaks
consolably to the outlawed,
and queened above its moody soup
on purple cushions, he's forgiven all
who spat upon him as a travesty
of mismatched sexes, hunted him through streets
and builder's yards down to the river's crawl.

From barge to a pink-frosted limousine,
he's had the car stand under foggy trees
in St. James's Park, and kept it back
until irreverence returned
to his coquettish dignity.
He dispenses red roses to the crowd,
bitches with performing artistes

who mob his progress, and all over town
the streets are scented with Chanel,
the army disbanded and cloned in drag.
They're waiting for his inaugural speech,

an end to biz-speak rhetoric
and ministerial duplicity.

His timing's perfect, and his drawl appropriate
to London's liberation, and he points
to absence of the police, and higher up
to roses trailing smoochily
round Downing Street's redoubtably barred gates.

from *Sainthood: Elegies for Derek Jarman*

LOVE IN DEATH

All day, the traffic's ambient decibels
surf around Phoenix House, its flat facade
presenting on the street. A white-noise shell,

the building's atomized by toxic haze,
its windows click-tracked by the diesel mash
of black cabs streaming up to Centre Point . . .

Somebody's absent from the honeycomb,
and uncontactable. He's gone away,
leaving a trail of sand down Brewer Street,

as though he'd walked in beach-shoes to his death,
thinking the sea was on the other side,
a blue invasion at Piccadilly.

The inspirational genus locus gone
from his packed studio, we have the word
resituate his fireballed energies

in every meeting-place where we collect
to burn a torch beside the river's groove,
or wait for love to hurry through the rain . . .

Say that we recreate the little things
that gave an apple-polish to his life,
a coffee-tang to being just a man

alert and vulnerable to everything,
then he's still here, beating in every heart,
catching the raindrops and making them sing.

SITES

A warehouse burns in solid orange flame,
erupts at Bankside, a black cumulus
of tented smoke pyramiding the Thames.

He sits and contemplates biography,
a Persian carpet rages in the sky,
voluted purples peacocked into green,

a fuming skylight over Canon Street.
A city's dawn is always visionary,
he strokes atomized stardust on his skin,

as though chasing gold embers from his pores.
His studio is torched. The years go by
memoried under bridges, blued with tears,

the same trains hustling into Charing Cross,
the changes registered inside his blood.
A day is like a pick-up which won't stay

faithful to anyone, despite the need
to have it open out into a friend.
Bugloss and borage present to his eyes . . .

He paces memory like it's a room
in which the furniture comes clear at dawn,
a blue vase loaded with redundant dreams,

a red one choked with flowers, he clears the lot
to know the moment, catch his breath again,
and feel the city fit him like a boot.

John Stammers (1954–)

John Keats Walks Home Following a Night Spent Reading Homer with Cowden Clarke

Brother, your comely hypotheses trouble
the quiet waters of dawn streets; as mercury
integrates to a constant self-fascination,
so a puddle's surface would retain the home-bent form:
here passed one whose shape was graven in rainwater.

Your rough coat gripped round you on that solitary march,
your attention is elsewhere to the moment while you travel
not by Cripplegate or Leadenhall but Troy:
the thousand walled narratives of a city slumbering and silent
before day and the dead clap of bronze on bronze,

the flat plain of Finsbury Pavement fell away to sand,
and Patroclus come to a young death on Mars' field. Apothecary,
you let the fevered blood of your imaginings into verse.
These are visions, visions born to survive, as you beetle
beneath the fixed planets across London Bridge.

God blind me, the star-struck heavens you contemplate
contemplate you in their turn, singular beacon
whose unrepeatable illumination inspires
ordinary readers at this particular remove,
so countenance that innocent vanity

which claims an association to a special realm.
Now at your desk, you lift your pen,
mutter something lost and begin to write.
Daylight finds you trophied in ink, clouded in near-sleep.
By first post, you will be a masterpiece.

Carol Ann Duffy (1955–)

Woman Seated in the Underground, 1941

after the drawing by Henry Moore

> I forget. I have looked at the other faces and found
> no memory, no love. *Christ, she's a rum one.*
> Their laughter fills the tunnel, but it does not
> comfort me. There was a bang and then
> I was running with the rest through smoke. Thick, grey
> smoke has covered thirty years at least.
> I know I am pregnant, but I do not know my name.
>
> Now they are singing. *Underneath the lantern*
> *by the barrack gate.* But waiting for whom?
> Did I? I have no wedding ring, no handbag, nothing.
> I want a fag. I have either lost my ring or I am
> a loose woman. No. Someone has loved me. Someone
> is looking for me even now. I live somewhere.
> I sing the word *darling* and it yields nothing.
>
> Nothing. A child is crying. Mine doesn't show yet.
> Baby. My hands mime the memory of knitting.
> Purl. Plain. I know how to do these things, yet my mind
> has unravelled into thin threads that lead nowhere.
> In a moment I shall stand up and scream until
> somebody helps me. The skies were filled with sirens, planes,
> fire, bombs, and I lost myself in the crowd. Dear God.

Alan Jenkins (1955–)

from *The London Dissector*

ART LOVER

She wants to see St. Paul's, Trafalgar Square, the Tower.
Instead, in the Tate you lectured her for an hour
On Bacon's rawness, his grasp of Renaissance Rome,
Of *the things that happen with two people in a room* . . .

Almost all, these days, best forgotten. To forget,
You walk the streets, or drink; but streets bring back
The rooms things happened in, or might have, you forget—
An attic in Holland Park, a basement in Hackney. Back

To square one, the room above a shrub-lined square
In Pimlico, or was it Primrose Hill? She lay in black
Bra and slip, still, not sleeping.—It's quite a scare;
So you try drinking. On the way to the pub, willows

Through sunlit drifts of smoke weep their reflections
Into water. (She buried her face in the pillows.
And important suddenly, her foreign inflections,
Her stillness, her weeping. Do you get the picture yet?)

RHYMER

It's called the Cheshire Cheese but it's a *chop-house,*
You explain between mouthfuls; not a *cheese*-shop.
A chop sits on your plate, and blood, in little eddies, swirls
Towards the middle . . . Your soul, which low culture has nourished,

Feels at home here—though you're one of too many,
Though it's Fleet Street: not *where Dr. Johnson flourished*
But where everything screams *Failure* at you, where
You think you might have shared a mattress with two girls . . .

Her room's across the bridge, one of the murky streets near Guy's.
You have a drink and start on Keats and resurrection-men
And the *London Dissector:* read out the bit where he dies
Coughing bright red, like your dear dead daddy; but when

You try to stagger to your feet you haven't any,
You fall back, blubbing, gaping at her pair of red pants
Draped—a red rag to a bull, or *danger*—on the chair
To dry, and here it is, the drooping soul of romance . . .

EAST ENDER

When she tried on an old dress of her mother's, you wrote
(This was in your *First Love* phase), "It's strange,
The way they dress each other for the sacrifice."
And now you name names, candidates who range

From lunatics to royalty to Gull, your favourite;
You want to trace each doorway, entry and courtyard
Where one of "five unfortunates" was drawn and quartered,
The final, blood-flecked, sweating room, the festoons

He hung around it, made of her intestines,
The banner of meat, bleeding; the ruined face
And always the stark white body spread on grey,
Greasy mattress-ticking, on a narrow bed of stains . . .

She is open, vulnerable; you drag her to the soaked stones
Of Smithfield, *meat-cathedral,* run full-tilt into an aisle
Of grinning sheep's heads—your own sickly smile,
She's scared, she wants—better she went home, you agree.

RHYMER II (NINETIES)

Remember nights you breezed into the Café Royal
For gins and absinthes with the poetry crowd,

Poured wine and *bons mots* down Lydias and Giselles?
Then tottered back, weeks later, to your rooms

Through a Nocturne by Whistler, turned up wicks on lamps
And penned a few impressions in tetrameter, with rhymes?
London was a gaslit jewel, pearl-amber, *whence arose
A palette of perfumes mixed with lilies scented white*

As swansdown skin that in the darkness palely glows—
Good, that. Naturally, the girls were all gazelles.
Morning brought the pile of envelopes and stamps,
A hock-and-seltzer, then: *My dear Symons/Dowson/Gosse* . . .

(They're all dead, stupid; gone where everyone goes,
The scribblers and the muses, to ash or mulch, to shite.
Who writes letters now? Get down the Cow & Crud
With Mick and Simon, for a pint of something *real.*)

Jamie McKendrick (1955–)

Occupations of Bridewell

The loafers, the forgers, the feckless, the fickle,
The vagabond that will abide in no place,
The rioter that consumeth all,
Shall make tennis balls, bonnets, featherbeds and lace.

Ruffians, cutpurses and dissolute women
Shall find there a fresh field of exercise
Spinning wealth from packthread or cotton
So out of crime may come forth merchandise.

Penal Architecture

There are in London . . . notwithstanding we are a nation of liberty, more publick
and private prisons and houses of confinement, than any city in Europe, perhaps as
many as in all the capital cities of Europe put together . . .

—Daniel Defoe, *A Tour through England and Wales*

And of course the exterior was magnificent, even sublime—about that all
contemporary commentators were agreed. After its completion they would also
agree that it was a bad prison from any other point of view. In particular the interior
was close, airless and insalubrious.

—Robin Evans, *The Fabrication of Virtue*

With a touch of excess or overkill,
George Dance the younger
had actual iron chains
pinned to the rusticated stone
on either side of the double door
of Newgate Gaol.

Drawing the pediment
he thought of Dante,
just a consonant away,
and Milton's gates of adamant.
He was after a kind of
sombre, frozen music,
a literal metaphor—
turning the flow of words
back into things.

The mind is its own place
and can stress
the lock not the hinge
in the idea of door.

The Deadhouse

(SOMERSET HOUSE)

Ooliths in a Jurassic bath of micrite:
the palatial, weathered white of Portland stone.
I too would prefer to watch the work of masons

than hear sermons. Watch them mallet down
the granite paving cubes, dress limestone,
engrave the slab of the Queen's Lady-in-Waiting:

CY GIST LE CORPS DE DEFUNCTE CATHERINE
GUILERMET. PRIEZ DIEU POUR SON AME.

Catchpool of sound in the sheer lightwell.
Catchpool of light in the deep soundwell.
A faint swell of water at the palace roots.

Ting-tang, the quarter chimes from the birdcage
cast frame in the West Wing, clock work
by Vulliamy. Its silent fellow in the East.

The rivergate now a sweeping arch left on
the stone manuscript. Bricked in, the river embanked.

Creases of thick water, iron-filed and polished.
Silken rucks as the river eases and edges past
the bridge, glistened, scuffed and scored like a zinc plate

half-cleared of ink. Fiddleheads of swirls,
fishtail eddies. Its own level. Sea level.
Rolled up seacharts like telescopes

in the Navy Board storeroom.
The thrumming engine of empire.

Mind-forged, unreal city. The weight
of stone on each square foot of earth.
At least the river is its own weight, give or take

the passing traffic. Makes a silvery tear
where the light floods in, pools in the soundwell.
Scaresome the outreach of its administrations,

the intent skulking in its bridges' shadows, its
tentacular, inky dusk with fishlamps scowling.
◦§
Loath to be lured to the glove of the falconer
with a strip of bush-meat the Harris hawk,
employed to chase pigeons from the Dead Room,

perches on a lagged pipe, settles its gold tail-feathers
and glares at the tombstone of the king's priest.
Upstairs the taxes rendered unto Caesar

his own minted image or hologram,
while the river, withdrawn to a new margin,
reflects gold glass from the wavering,

hollow towers of commerce where the profiteers
long for their "strong and stable government."
The skaters wait till winter for their rink.

Mick Imlah (1956–2009)

Cockney

How heightened the taste!—of champagne at the piano; of little side-kisses to
    tickle the fancy
At the party to mark our sarcastic account of the overblown *Mass of the
    Masses* by Finzi
(An aristocrat who betrayed what he stood for and set up in Bow with his
    matchgirl fiancée);

Moreover, the skit I had chosen to grace the occasion ("*My Way*—in the Set-
    ting for Tuba by Mahler")
Had even the Previns in generous stitches (it seemed an acceptable social
    milieu
If only because it was something like six million light years away from the
    planet of Millwall)

When the buffet arrived; and as we applauded the *crudités* carved into minia-
    ture flats and sharps
There crept into mind for a desperate moment the ghost of me mum shuffling
    back from the shops
With a Saturday treat—"Look! We got sausages, beans, an' *chips!*"

So I mentally told her to stuff it, and turned, with a shivering reflex of anger
To harangue a superior brace of brunettes for their preference of Verdi to
    Wagner;
But again she appeared at the door, with the salt and the sacred vinegar

And I was reclaimed. "You!" she demanded, "You who last month in the Sey-
    chelles
Took drinks with a Marquess, and studded the spine of Lucinda with sea-
    shells—
You are the same little boy that I sent out in winter with *Cockney* inscribed on
    your satchel!"

And as she dispersed, one or two of my neighbours were squinting at me as
    you do a bad odour,

And even my friendly advances were met by a flurry of coughs and a mutter of
   Oh, dear—
For try as I might I just couldn't assemble the sounds that came out in a deli-
   cate order:

ALL ROYT MOY SAHN! HA'S YOR FARVAH?
LEN YOU TEN NOWTS?–CALL IT A FOIVAH!
TRAVELLED IN TEE-ASCANY?–DO ME A *FIVAH!*

And worse was to follow. For over this bleak ostinato of base-born vowels
I detected the faraway strains of a disco remix of *The Dance of the Seven Veils*
And felt the lads egging me on to enact what a tug at the Seventh reveals—

Yes, down came the pants of old Rotherhithe's rugged Salomé,
And pointing it straight at the toff who was leading the charge to assail me
Out of my shirtfront I prodded two-thirds of a purple salami . . .
❦
Sometimes, there's a song in my head as I sit down at tea, and I know what
   the tune is
But can't catch the words. And when I get tired of the humming, it's off down
   to Terry's, or Tony's,
A couple of pints, then across to the club till it closes, for snooker with Paki-
   stanis.

Sarah Maguire (1957–)

Almost the Equinox

and the Thames so emptied of current
it shows bare flanks of sand. Beige sand. A beach.
The sudden vertigo of hardness when we're cupped
over the walls of the Embankment

examining the strange cream stones below,
driftwood, bottle-tops, crockery, one sodden boot.
And the slow mud opens its mouth.
Jets long departed, their con-trails fire

across the fierce blue skies, unfurling
into breath. The very last weather of a summer
spent impatient for change,
waiting for a sign, an alignment.

Beneath our feet, a hemisphere away,
the full moon tugs fluids into tides, and stops
another night in its tracks,
hours before it climbs over London—

the constant pull of elsewhere
mooring us outside ourselves. The colchicums
come naked into the early autumn air.
Bruised into mauve and purple,

their frail blooms admit the memory of harm
in their risky flight to beauty. Packed bulbs
underground harbour their secrets.
Now that we have witnessed

the flare of that ginkgo spilling up
beside St. Paul's—its roots woven
deep beneath a graveyard of graves,
its slim knotted branches, sleeved

with airy, fantail leaves—
it will return to us, suddenly,
years from now. Anomalous Jurassic relic,
its origins are as ancient as these slabs

of blackening Whin-bed Portland Stone,
set here by Wren to stamp out Fire and Plague.
As a child, I climbed all the stairs
to the Whispering Gallery, laid my cheek

against the painted plaster of the dome,
and let those perfected acoustics bear my changed voice
back to myself. The huge nave
reminds you of the Great Mosque in Kabul—

sunlight falling on pillars of stone, the hushed intentness
of prayer. Shattered, war-torn, it's still standing,
somehow, next to the river by the Bridge of Bricks,
just as Wren's great dome once soared above the Blitz,

intact. Tonight, we will look up to see
Mars, that old harbinger of war, come so close to us
it rivets the southern sky with its furious,
amber flare. Sixty-thousand years ago it lit

these heavens and looked down
on ice. Next convergence, nothing will be left of us
leaning on this bridge of wires and tempered steel,
wondering at the river and the city and the stars,

here, on the last hot night before this planet tilts us
into darkness, our cold season underground.
The tide has turned, the Thames comes inching back,
drowning everything it will reveal again.

for Yama

Michael Hofmann (1957–)

From Kensal Rise to Heaven

Old Labour slogans, *Venceremos,* dates for demonstrations
like passed deadlines—they must be disappointed
to find they still exist. Halfway down the street,
a sign struggles to its feet and says Brent.

The surfaces are friable, broken and dirty, a skin unsuitable
for chemical treatment. Building, repair and demolition
go on simultaneously, indistinguishably. Change and decay.
—When change is arrested, what do you get?

The Sun, our Chinese takeaway, is being repainted.
I see an orange topcoat calls for a pink undercoat.
A Chinese calendar girl, naked, chaste and varnished,
simpers behind potplants like a jungle dawn.

Joy, local, it says in the phone-booth, with a number
next to it. Or *Petra.* Or *Out of Order,* and an arrow.
This last gives you pause, ten minutes, several weeks . . .
Delay deters the opportunist as much as doubt.

In an elementary deception, the name of the street
is taken from a country town, and when I get up
I find my education is back to haunt me: Dickens House,
Blake Court, Austen House, thirteen-storey giants.

Some Sunday mornings, blood trails down the street
from the night before. Stabbing, punch-up or nosebleed,
it's impossible to guess, but the drops fell thickly and easily
on the paving-stones, too many for the rules of hopscotch.

The roadway itself is reddish, the faded spongy brick
of the terrace is overpowered by the paintwork's
sweet dessert colours. They spoil it, but you understand
they are there as the sugar in tomato soup is there.

Clouds come over from the West, as always in England
the feeling that the sea is just beyond the next horizon:
a thick, Byzantine crucifix on a steep schoolhouse roof,
the slippery, ecclesiastical gleam of wet slate.

Dogs vet the garbage before the refuse collectors.
Brazen starlings and pigeons, "flying rats," go over
what is left. Rough-necked, microcephalous, they have
too much white on their bodies, like calcium defectives.

The pigeons mate in full view: some preliminary billing,
then the male flutters his wings as though to break a fall . . .
They inhabit a ruined chiropodist's, coming and going freely
through broken windows into their cosy excremental hollow.

The old man in the vest in the old people's home
would willingly watch us all day. In their windows,
a kind of alcove, they keep wine bottles and candlesticks,
Torvill and Dean, a special occasion on ice.

The motor-mews has flat roofs of sandpaper or tarpaper.
One is terraced, like three descending trays of gravel.
Their skylights are angled towards the red East,
some are truncated pyramids, others whole glazed shacks.

From A to B and Back Again

The Northern Line had come out into the open,
was leaving tracks like a curving cicatrice.
There was Barnet, my glottal stop, trying hard
to live up to its name, colloquial and harmless and trite.

The place was sunny and congested, brick and green trim,
it had the one-of-everything-and-two-butchers
of a provincial town. First, I dropped into
the maternity hospital by accident . . .

The porter was an analphabete, but together
we found your name, down among the Os,
and there you were, my brave love,
in a loose hospital gown that covered nothing;

pale; on an empty drip; and eager to show me
your scars, a couple of tidy crosses
like grappling hooks, one in the metropolis,
the other some distance away, in the unconcerned suburbs.

Malvern Road

It's only a short walk, and we'll never make it,
the street where we first set up house—
set up maisonette—together . . . do you remember
the grim Tuesday *Guardian* Society-section aspect of it,
the crumbly terrace on one side,
then the road, modern and daunting but somehow in truce,

and the high-rises and multi-storey garages opposite
that gave us our view, and in winter,
like a periscope five miles away due south,
the GPO tower obliterated by Paddington Rec the rest of the time,
and that was the only way to go from where we were,
"barely perched on the outer rim of the hub of decency,"

probably we were happy but in any case
we were beyond dreams in the strange actualness of everything,
a tyro salary, a baby mortgage, such heartstopping fun,
the place too intimate and new and connected to us
for us to think of "entertaining"
and we liked the stairs best of everything anyway,

the *ancien* lino kitchen
where I cooked out of *The Pauper's Cookbook*
—"a wealth, or should it be, a poverty of recipes"—
the bedroom barely wide enough to take our bed crosswise,
so we lay next to the window, the window making a third,
the creased cardboard blind bleaching like jeans,

everything cheap and cheerful,
your jaunty primary touches everywhere, fauve and mingled,
my room a grave navy ("Trafalgar") with my vast desk
like an aircraft carrier that I had to saw the legs off
to get upstairs, and then fitted the stumps on casters
so when I wrote it rolled,

the muso downstairs and on the ground floor
the night cook with a farouche squint,

his placid Spanish wife and their little Sahara,
how frightening everything was,
and with how much faith, effort and heart
we went out to meet it anyway,

the corner pub we probably never set foot in,
the health centre padlocked and grilled like an offie,
the prefab post office set down at an odd angle,
the bank that closed down, the undertaker who stayed open,
the idealistic delicatessen before God and Thatcher created the zuppie,
the tremulous restaurant my best friend proposed in,

the sun breeding life from dirt like Camus,
the pepper-fruited scrawny alder with two yellow days of pollen,
the nights of your recurring dream
where you whimpered comfort to your phantom baby boy
you didn't have and said you'd mind him, as now,
to my shame, you have and you do.

Maura Dooley (1957–)

Smash the Windows

OR, TEN SOUTH LONDON FIDDLE TUNES

1. The Misted Pane
2. Egg on a Bap
3. Knock at the Door
4. A Draught of Air
5. Turd on the Step
6. Fox in a Wheelie Bin
7. Toke on the Swings
8. Parakeet in the Oak
9. The Short Way Home
10. Glass on the Pavement

David Kennedy (1959–)

The Bombs, July 2005

Trying to join words
to four bombs,

words that are not,
words that are not,

words that are not,
that are not,

are not
like carnage,

atrocity, screens
around the bombs.

Or trying to join words
to four men,

words that are not,
like jihad, cell,

screens
around the men.

Or trying to start
from the same point:

how much
they hated

us: our fierce,
pointless individualisms.

Trying to join words
to four bombs,

to four men,
words that are not,

trying I stood up
in a room

nine days later,
before a reading,

and said something
about a line

with "harm" at one end
and, at the other,

"care" where
poetry is

showing us care.
I stood up

trying to join words
that would stand.

Standing,
I tried to word joins.

Balanced
on the tip

of trying,
I tried to join words,

words that won't
make the living

or the dead cringe
and crawl away

and turn their faces
to the wall.

Fred d'Aguiar (1960–)

Home

These days whenever I stay away too long,
anything I happen to clap eyes on,
(that red telephone box) somehow makes me
miss here more than anything I can name.

My heart performs a jazzy drum solo
when the crow's feet on the 747
scrape down at Heathrow. H.M. Customs . . .
I resign to the usual inquisition,

telling me with Surrey loam caked
on the tongue, home is always elsewhere.
I take it like an English middleweight
with a questionable chin, knowing

my passport photo's too open-faced,
haircut wrong (an afro) for the decade;
the stamp, British Citizen not bold enough
for my liking and too much for theirs.

The cockney cab driver begins chirpily
but can't or won't steer clear of race,
so rounds on Asians. I lock eyes with him
in the rearview when I say I live with one.

He settles at the wheel grudgingly,
in a huffed silence. Cha! Drive man!
I have legal tender burning in my pocket
to move on, like a cross in Transylvania.

At my front door, why doesn't the lock
recognise me and budge? I give an extra
twist and fall forward over the threshold
piled with the felicitations of junk mail,

into a cool reception in the hall.
Grey light and close skies I love you;
chokey streets, roundabouts and streetlamps
with tyres chucked round them, I love you.

Police officer, your boots need re-heeling.
Robin Redbreast, special request—a burst
of song so the worm can wind to the surface.
We must all sing for our suppers or else.

Lavinia Greenlaw (1962–)

River History

Even then the river carried cargo,
Saxon corn shipped to storehouses on the Rhine.
Taxes were paid in pepper and cloth by the Easterlings,
the German merchants trading from the Steelyard
demolished in the fire of 1666.
Wharves burned like touchpaper, packed
with resin, sulphur, pitch.
The daily catch between London and Deptford
was salmon, eel, smelt and plaice
but the Port Authority preferred to dine
at the Tavern on the best turtle soup in the City
as they argued the height of the wall to be built
against the Mudlarks, Plunderers and Peterboatmen,
intent on their nightly specialized percentage:
cloves from Zanzibar, mother-of-pearl,
tortoiseshell, South American iodine,
West Indian rum, the heavy iron bottles
of Spanish quicksilver, and, from Ivory House,
the occasional mammoth tusk unfrozen in Siberia.
The Empire expanded, cess-pits were banned,
water grew thick with steamships and sewage
and the docks pushed east out into the marshes,
breaking the horizon with a forest of cranes
that unloaded meat, cloth, tobacco and grain
from countries my school atlas still colours pink.
At the Crutched Friars Deposit Office records were kept
of ships in berth, noted daily
by a row of clerks crouched under gaslight
and seven-foot ceilings. Records were kept
of each member of the Union, the fight to be paid

a tanner an hour and not have to climb each day
on another's back and shout to be chosen.
There was always the army.
The Luftwaffe bombed Surrey Commercial Docks
for fifty-seven nights and the timber blazed
for more days than most people kept counting.
Even when every magnetic mine
had been located and cleared, there were dangers.
Centuries of waste had silted the river
till the water ran black over Teddington weir
and a bag of rubbish thrown from London Bridge
took six weeks to ride a dying current
out to the estuary. No swimming, no fish,
and those who fell in had to be sluiced out.
No ships, no work. The industry found itself
caught in the net of passing time,
watching mile after mile of dockland fill
with silence and absence. Land changed hands
in an estate agent's office, short-lease premises
with "Upstream" and "Downstream" carved above the doors.
Now the tidal traffic is a slow weekday flow of cars
channeled into streets built before cars were thought of.
They inch round corners, nudge against kerbs,
then settle tight packed against the pavement.
On Butler's Wharf, the only machinery
now in daily use is the tow-away truck:
cruising yellow lines, it pauses to hoist
the solid engineering of a badly parked BMW
into the air with illogical ease.
In Coriander Building, an agency
maintains the plants, the colour scheme is neutral
but the smell of new paint has yet to sink in,
like the spice that still seasons the air after rain.
A film crew arrives, on a costly location shoot

for *Jack the Ripper*. It's a crowded night.
Intent on atmosphere, they've cluttered the alleys
with urchins, trollops and guttersnipes
who drift to the waterfront when they're not working
and gaze across at the biggest, emptiest office block in Europe
and its undefendable, passing light.

Glyn Maxwell (1962–)

The Fires by the River

Just say you went beside the fires by the river,
in neither night nor day, insofar as
violet and lime were the shades of the air that
    steamed or anchored over
the slurping water, and this was the River Thames
    you somehow knew it.

And people had turned to people of those days,
though moreso, now you walked and heard
the actual cursing, the splattered effluents,
    not far from you in the rose-
grey coloured mud that sloped to the pale Thames
    to be its banks.

Just say the place was a mezzanine or less
up from hell, and who wasn't a thug was a child.
And there was a drug called drug, and a drug that went
    by day in a blue guise;
and there was a boat of cocktailers on the Thames
    staring at this point—

at lolling homes, and clapboard warehouses
shot with mice or riddled with the likes
of Monks and Sikes, who mutter by the wharf—
    skin-crawling passages—
all, just say so, that was real as the Thames
    is, by any life:

what would you do with your clean hands and drowned
feet in the place? Remove them to a room?
Remove them to a room. And sit, forget
    the city-licking sound
of water moving slowly through the Thames
    like years in thought.

Simon Armitage (1963–)

KX

Northerner, this is your stop. This longhouse
of echoing echoes and sooted glass,
this goth pigeon hangar, this diesel roost
is the end of the line. Brace and be brisk,
commoner, carry your heart like an egg
on a spoon, be fleet through the concourse, primed
for that point in time when the world goes bust,
when the unattended holdall or case
unloads its cache of fanaticised heat.

Here's you after the fact, found by torchlight,
being-less, heaped, boned of all thought and sense.
The camera can barely look. Or maybe,
just maybe, you live. Here's you on the News,
shirtless, minus a limb, exiting smoke
to a backdrop of red melt, onto streets
paved with gilt, begging a junkie for help.

Alice Oswald (1966–)

Another Westminster Bridge

go and glimpse the lovely inattentive water
discarding the gaze of many a bored street walker

where the weather trespasses into strip-lit offices
through tiny windows into tiny thoughts and authorities

and the soft beseeching tapping of typewriters

take hold of a breath-width instant, stare
at water which is already elsewhere
in a scrapwork of flashes and glittery flutters
and regular waves of apparently motionless motion

under the teetering structures of administration

where a million shut-away eyes glance once
restlessly at the river's ruts and glints

count five, then wander swiftly
away over the stone wing-bone of the city

Daljit Nagra (1966–)

Yobbos!

The first step towards lightening THE WHITE MAN'S burden is through teaching the virtues of cleanliness.

—Pears Soap advert, 1899

A right savage I was—sozzled
to the nose with sprightly
Muldoon, squeezed into the communal

sweat of a Saturday tube home—
I'm up to p. 388 of his sharp lemon-skinned
Collected Poems

when some scruffy looking git pipes to his crew—
Some Paki shit, like,
eee's loookin into!

My blood rising, especially when my head's
done in with words like
"Badhbh" ... "Cailidin" ... "Salah-eh-din,"

I nearly get blunt, as one of them—
Well mate, this Paki's more British than that inde-
cipherable, impossibly untranslatable

sod of a Paddy—
only I don't 'cos I catch my throat gungeing
on its Cromwellian vile, my tongue foaming for soap . . .

Nick Laird (1975–)

The Tip

You climbed in at Oxford Circus
and out on Willesden Lane.
Even now you get a kick
from doing it, from hailing.

You note how you adopt
the superhero's posture
and slow the vehicle up
as if your hand shot forth

an electro-subatomic ray
and it drew the taxi in,
stopped the nuclear bomb
and saved the heroine,

now her shopping's done.
The cab indicates you've won.
∾ऽ
Also histrionic, this,
and a category of thing your class,
the ones at home in camouflage,
find marginally embarrassing

like any act you've only seen
effected in the movies
and thus feel false attempting
for yourself, as if all you could

repeat for good were the gestures
of your father, and him his,
keeping some path walked,
some tiny circuit lit.

But look: the cab pulls up,
the door swings back.

You met a cabbie once who claimed
to have a perfect memory.
He said that on the morning
you were born, it rained,

then described
the clothes he'd worn,
what he'd eaten, what he'd done.

You were lugging
legal documents in boxes
from his cab onto the kerb.

He said it was a curse,
the sort of thing, honestly,
he wouldn't wish on anyone,
even his enemy.

Inside the cab the driver's back
is far away and higher up,
as if he drove a horse and trap
or you sat behind a magistrate,

to transcribe every argument
and silence of his travels
along the district circuit,
around the same chambers,
the different cases.

The people on the pavement
are all hurry and dissolve.
You draw up to the lights and pause
as the centre slips,
and the sound stops.

Heather Phillipson (1978–)

German Phenomenology Makes Me Want to Strip and Run through North London

Page seven—I've had enough of *Being and Time*
and of clothing. Many streakers seek quieter locations
and Marlborough Road's unreasonably quiet tonight.
If it were winter I'd be intellectual, but it's Tuesday
and I'd rather be outside, naked, than learned—
rather lap the tarmac escarpment of Archway Roundabout
wearing only a rucksack. It might come in useful.
I can't take any more of Heidegger's *Dasein*-diction,
I say as I jettison my slippers.

When I speak of my ambition
it is not to be a Doctor of Letters
or to marry Friedrich Nietzsche, it turns out,
or to think better.
It is to give up this fashion for dressing.
It is to drop my robe on the communal stairs
and open the front door onto the commuter hour,
my neighbour, his Labrador, and say nothing
of what I know or do not know, except what my body announces.

Ben Borek (1980–)

from *Donjong Heights*

South London has its reputation:
No tube, a multitude of guns,
And hence this Johnsonesque quotation:
"When Peckham tires one simply runs
On up to Hoxton and carouses
In trendy noveau-cool warehouses
And listens to Electro Funk
Affecting toned down retro-punk."
Don't get me wrong, it's no Soweto
Down south, it's not all crack and pillage—
Just take a look at Dulwich Village—
But for the common man it's Netto,
Not Conran, tea, not mochaccino,
And Asda jeans, not Valentino.

Now Reader, focus on a room;
Mix cinematic metaphors
With bookish ones, engage your zoom
And speed up pockmarked streets, through doors
That open for the lens politely,
Skim rooftops high above the nightly
Dramatics in the streets below
(The pubs call time, the usual show
Of fights and mawkish "au revoirs!"),
Then hurtle up, the revellers melt
And fade behind, Orion's belt
Is slalomed briskly and the stars
Are left to their portentous glowing
As, Reader, look, the camera's slowing . . .

It crawls towards a grotty dwelling,
An edifice of brick and rot,
Pads through a smashed-in doorway smelling—

Predictably, I know, but not
Untrue—whichever one that you're in,
All council estates reek of . . . urine.
The lift is out of order, so
The camera has to boldly go
Up nine levels and past nine landings
On stairs now lacking banisters,
Now strewn with needles, canisters
That once held paint (now used for brandings
Of off-white walls with "YPB,"
"Regret," "KondemOne RIP"),

And spins round ninety slow degrees,
Meanders on through several halls
Where dust-soaked amber filigrees
From strip-lights bolted to the walls
Provide our scene's dim source of lighting.
One doorway bares a plaque inviting:
Come on Punk, rob me, make my day.
And now the soundtrack starts to play
With added, looming, grave intensity—
As you'll have noted, there's not been
A tune picked for this opening scene . . .
Choose one yourself with the propensity
To build a sense of introspection
And melancholy from your collection . . .

Perhaps a moody saxophone
From John Coltrane, perhaps some strings,
A cello's poignant rising drone,
Some ambient electronic pings,
A Deep House track that hypnotises
Or Radiohead's "No Surprises,"
Or anything by Portishead,
Or Leonard Cohen . . . As I've said,
The choice is yours . . . but just make sure
That now you fade it out quite gently . . .

As here the camera stops intently
Before our goal, a mottled door;
It hovers, ponders what to do . . .
With one last surge it ghosts right through.

Inside, beneath a pale fluorescent
Lamp-glow: our tale's protagonist.
His smoking—furious, incessant—
Has filled the scene with fine-knit mist.
The camera, now with gentle panning,
Investigates the chamber: spanning
One wall, above the fireplace,
A giant print: Schiele's *Embrace;*
Three photographs (a girl with braided
Blond hair, a coastal shot of Nice,
A sunset) share the mantelpiece;
Some books . . . but here the shot grows faded . . .
And after all, it's getting late . . .
Our subject speaks. Let him narrate.

Tom Chivers (1983–)

Big Skies over Docklands

High noon expectancy.

Tower Hill
Limehouse

Toytown Poplar
and the road crumples out of view.

From the train the water is not real,
does not move. The people, real enough.

Mudflats the colour of petrol.
Twenty years of stains on concrete.

The distant shimmer of a broker
as oddly familiar as a white man
in Cherokee territory.

Stilled cranes turned to public art
like the cradling arms of an angel.
◦§
To journey here
is to listen and recant:
Mudchute, Crossharbour.

Herons Quay, reminding me of
home, the hunter,
locked away
in these names we use
to tie us to the land;
to this configuration of land
and water.

Our third city
awakens into steel
and pound.

Ahren Warner (1986–)

Διόνυσος

Girl with ridiculous earrings   why do you bother
to slap the boy   we all assume is your boyfriend
and is lolling over   that bus seat   shouting

it's a London thing.   He is obviously a knob
but a happy one   and that   it seems to me
is the important   though not localisable   thing.

Credits

Laurence Binyon
"As I Walked Through London" used by permission of the Society of Authors as the literary representative of the Estate of Laurence Binyon.   491

Ezra Pound
"Portrait d'une Femme," "The Garden," and "Simulacra" from *Personae*, copyright © 1926 by Ezra Pound. Reprinted by permission of New Directions Publishing Corp. and Faber and Faber, Ltd. "Yeux Glauques," "Siena Mi Fe, Disfecemi Maremma," and "XII" excerpted from *Hugh Selwyn Mauberley*, from *Personae*, copyright © 1926 by Ezra Pound. Reprinted by permission of New Directions Publishing Corp. and Faber and Faber, Ltd.   493

Frances Cornford
"London Streets" from *Poems* and "Parting in Wartime" from *Travelling Home* used by permission of the J. P. Cornford Trust.   508

Siegfried Sassoon
"Monody on the Demolition of Devonshire House" from *Collected Poems of Siegfried Sassoon* by Siegfried Sassoon. Copyright 1918, 1920 by E. P. Dutton. Copyright 1936, 1946, 1947, 1948 by Siegfried Sassoon. Used by permission of Viking Penguin, a division of Penguin Group (USA) Inc. Copyright Siegfried Sassoon used by kind permission of the Estate of George Sassoon.   510

T. S. Eliot
Excerpts from "The Waste Land," "Sweeney Agonistes," and "Burnt Norton" used by permission of Faber and Faber, Ltd.   511

Isaac Rosenberg
"Fleet Street" used by permission of Bernard Warwick and the Isaac Rosenberg Estate.   519

Richard Aldington
"St. Mary's, Kensington," "In the Tube," "Hampstead Heath," "London," "Whitechapel," and "Eros and Psyche" used by permission of Rosica Colin, Ltd.   520

Wilfred Owen
"I am the ghost of Shadwell Stair . . ." from *The Collected Poems of Wilfred Owen.* Copyright © 1963 by Chatto & Windus, Ltd. Reprinted by permission of New Directions Publishing Corp. Used by permission from *Wilfred Owen: The Complete Poems & Fragments,* ed. Jon Stallworthy (London: Chatto & Windus, 1983).   527

Sylvia Townsend Warner
"Song from the Bride of Smithfield" and "East London Cemetery" reprinted with permission from *New Collected Poems* by Sylvia Townsend Warner, ed. Claire Harman (Carcanet Press Limited, 2008).   528

© Roy Fuller, reprinted with permission from *New and Collected Poems 1934 to 1984* (Secker and Warburg, 1985).   571

Anne Ridler
"Wentworth Place: Keats Grove" reprinted with permission from *Collected Poems* by Anne Ridler (Carcanet Press Limited, 1997).   574

George Barker
"Kew Gardens" used by permission of Elspeth Barker.   575

Alun Lewis
"Westminster Abbey" from *Collected Poems* by Alun Lewis, used by permission.   578

Robert Lowell
Excerpts from "Redcliffe Square" and "Winter and London" from *Collected Poems* by Robert Lowell. Copyright © 2003 by Harriet Lowell and Sheridan Lowell. Reprinted by permission of Farrar, Straus and Giroux, LLC.   579

Nicholas Moore
"Monmouth Street" reprinted with permission from *Longings of the Acrobats* by Nicholas Moore (Carcanet Press Limited, 1990).   582

John Heath-Stubbs
"London Architecture 1960s" and "Lament for the 'Old Swan,' Notting Hill Gate" used with permission of David Higham Associates.   584

W. S. Graham
"The Night City" used by kind permission of Michael Snow.   586

Muriel Spark
"A Tour of London (I, II, III)" by Muriel Spark, from *All the Poems of Muriel Spark.* Copyright © 1953, 1957, 1958, 1961, 1964, 1967, 1985, 1987, 1989, 1994, 1995, 1996, 1997 by Muriel Spark. Copyright © 1985 by Copyright Administration Limited. Reprinted by permission of New Directions Publishing Corp.   588

Keith Douglas
"C" from "The 'Bête Noir' Fragments" from *Complete Poems* by Keith Douglas. Copyright © 2000 by Keith Douglas. Reprinted by permission of Faber and Faber, an affiliate of Farrar, Straus and Giroux, LLC, and Faber and Faber Ltd.   590

D. J. Enright
"The Stations of King's Cross" courtesy of Watson, Little Ltd.   591

Philip Larkin
"Deceptions" and "Naturally the Foundation Will Bear Your Expenses" from *Collected Poems* by Philip Larkin. Copyright © 1988, 2003 by the Estate of Philip Larkin. Reprinted by permission of Farrar, Straus and Giroux, LLC, and Faber and Faber, Ltd.   593

Donald Davie
"To Londoners" reprinted with permission from *Collected Poems* by Donald Davie (Carcanet Press Limited, 1990).   595

Dannie Abse

> "Street Scene" and "Soho: Saturday Night" from *New and Collected Poems* (Hutchinson, 2003). Copyright © Dannie Abse 2003. Reproduced by permission of United Agents (www.unitedagents.co.uk) on behalf of Dannie Abse.   597

James Berry

> "Two Black Labourers on a London Building Site" from *Hot Earth Cold Earth* and "Beginning in a City, 1948" from *Windrush Songs* by James Berry. Reprinted by permission of Peters Fraser & Dunlop (www.petersfraserdunlop.com) on behalf of James Berry.   600

John Ashbery

> "The Tower of London" from *Planisphere* by John Ashbery. Copyright © 2009 by John Ashbery. Reprinted by permission of HarperCollins Publishers.   603

Thom Gunn

> "Autobiography" and "Talbot Road" from *Collected Poems* by Thom Gunn. Copyright © 1994 by Thom Gunn. Reprinted by permission of Farrar, Straus and Giroux, LLC, and Faber and Faber Ltd.   605

Connie Bensley

> "Vauxhall" and "Bottleneck" reprinted with permission from *Central Reservations: New & Selected Poems* by Connie Bensley (Bloodaxe Books, 1990).   612

Peter Porter

> "Thomas Hardy at Westbourne Park Villas" copyright © Peter Porter. Reproduced by permission of the author, c/o Rogers, Coleridge & White Ltd., 20 Powis Mews, London W11 1JN.   614

U. A. Fanthorpe

> "Rising Damp" and "Widening the Westway" used by permission.   615

Ted Hughes

> "Fate Playing" and "Epiphany" from *Birthday Letters* by Ted Hughes. Copyright © 1998 by Ted Hughes. Reprinted by permission of Farrar, Straus and Giroux, LLC, and Faber and Faber Ltd.   618

Derek Walcott

> "I" and "II" from *Omeros* by Derek Walcott. Copyright © 1990 by Derek Walcott. Reprinted by permission of Farrar, Straus and Giroux, LLC, and Faber and Faber Ltd.   622

Alan Brownjohn

> "A202" reprinted with permission from *The Saner Places: Selected Poems* (Enitharmon Press, 2011).   625

Ruth Fainlight

> "The Same Power" used by permission of the author.   627

Geoffrey Hill

> "Churchill's Funeral" and "To the High Court of Parliament" from *Canaan* by Geoffrey Hill. Copyright © 1996 by Geoffrey Hill. Used by permission of Houghton Mifflin Harcourt Publishing Company and Penguin Books. All rights reserved.   628

Sylvia Plath

"Parliament Hill Fields" from *Crossing the Water* by Sylvia Plath. Copyright © 1961 by Ted Hughes. Reprinted by permission of HarperCollins Publishers and Faber and Faber Ltd.   634

Anne Stevenson

"Cashpoint Charlie" reprinted with permission from *Poems 1955–2005* by Anne Stevenson (Bloodaxe Books, 2005).   636

Fleur Adcock

"Miss Hamilton in London," "Londoner," and "To Marilyn from London" reprinted with permission from *Poems 1960–2000* by Fleur Adcock (Bloodaxe Books, 2000).   638

John Fuller

"Missing" and "Dusk" excerpted from *London Songs* and "Middlesex" excerpted from *The Shires,* from *Collected Poems* by John Fuller, published by Chatto & Windus. Reprinted by permission of the Random House Group Ltd.   641

Ken Smith

Excerpts from "The London Poems" reprinted with permission from *Shed: Poems 1980–2001* by Ken Smith (Bloodaxe Books, 2002).   644

Seamus Heaney

"The Underground" from *Opened Ground: Selected Poems 1966–1996* by Seamus Heaney. Copyright © 1998 by Seamus Heaney. Reprinted by permission of Farrar, Straus and Giroux, LLC, and Faber and Faber Ltd. "District and Circle" from *District and Circle* by Seamus Heaney. Copyright © 2006 by Seamus Heaney. Reprinted by permission of Farrar, Straus and Giroux, LLC, and Faber and Faber Ltd.   646

Lee Harwood

"Rain journal: London: June 65" from *Collected Poems* (Shearsman Books, 2004). Used by permission of Shearsman Books and the author.   650

Grey Gowrie

"Outside Biba's" reprinted with permission from *Third Day: New and Selected Poems* by Grey Gowrie (Carcanet Press Limited, 2008).   651

Joseph Brodsky

"North Kensington" from *Collected Poems in English* by Joseph Brodsky. Copyright © 2000 by the Estate of Joseph Brodsky. Reprinted by permission of Farrar, Straus and Giroux, LLC.   652

Derek Mahon

"Sunday Morning" from *New Collected Poems* (2011). By kind permission of the author and the Gallery Press, Loughcrew, Oldcastle, County Meath, Ireland.   653

Hugo Williams

"Tavistock Square," "Bar Italia" (to L. S.), "Bar Italia," and "Notting Hill" reprinted with permission of Faber and Faber Ltd.   655

Iain Sinclair

"bunhill fields" from *Penguin Modern Poets 10* (1996); "hurricane drummers: self-aid in haggerston" from *Autistic Poses* (Hoarse Commerce, 1985). Both poems were reprinted in *The Firewall: Selected Poems 1979–2006* (Etruscan Books). Used with permission.   659

Mimi Khalvati

"Earls Court" reprinted with permission from *Selected Poems* by Mimi Khalvati (Carcanet Press Limited, 2000).   662

Carol Rumens

"Pleasure Island, Marble Arch" used by permission of the author.   664

Wendy Cope

"Lonely Hearts" and "After the Lunch" reprinted by permission of United Agents on behalf of Wendy Cope.   666

Peter Reading

Excerpts from "Perduta Gente" reprinted with permission from *Collected Poems Volume 2: 1985–1996* by Peter Reading (Bloodaxe Books, 1996).   668

Christopher Reid

"North London Sonnet" reprinted with permission of Faber and Faber Ltd. "Exasperated Piety" from *A Scattering* (Arete, 2009). Reprinted by permission.

Gillian Allnutt

"Museum, 19 Princelet Street, Spitalfields" reprinted with permission from *How the Bicycle: New & Selected Poems* by Gillian Allnutt (Bloodaxe Books, 2007).   672

John Agard

"Toussaint L'Ouverture Acknowledges Wordsworth's Sonnet 'To Toussaint L'Ouverture'" and "Chilling Out Beside the Thames" reprinted with permission from *Alternative Anthem: Selected Poems with Live DVD* by John Agard (Bloodaxe Books, 2009).   674

Grace Nichols

"Island Man" copyright © Grace Nichols, 1984. Used with permission.   675

Charles Boyle

"The Miracle at Shepherd's Bush" used with permission of Faber and Faber Ltd.   676

Andrew Motion

"London Plane" by Andrew Motion from *The Cinder Path* (Faber & Faber). Copyright © Andrew Motion. Reproduced by permission of United Agents (www.unitedagents.co.uk) on behalf of Andrew Motion.   678

Linton Kwesi Johnson

"Sonny's Lettah" © Linton Kwesi Johnson. Republished by kind permission of LKJ Music Publishers Ltd.   679

Jo Shapcott

"St. Bride's" used by permission of Faber and Faber Ltd.   682

Michael Donaghy
   "The River Glideth of His Own Sweet Will" and "Poem on The Underground" reprinted with permission from *Collected Poems* by Michael Donaghy (Pan Macmillan, 2009).   683

Jeremy Reed
   "Love in Death" and "Sites" (excerpted from *Sainthood: Elegies for Derek Jarman*) and "Quentin Crisp as Prime Minister" first published in *Patron Saint of Eyeliner* (London: Creation Books, 2000). Reproduced with permission.   685

John Stammers
   "John Keats Walks Home Following a Night Spent Reading Homer with Cowden Clarke" from *Stolen Love Behavior* by John Stammers (Pan Macmillan, 2005). Used by permission.   689

Carol Ann Duffy
   "Woman Seated in the Underground, 1941" copyright © Carol Ann Duffy 2004. Reproduced by permission of the author c/o Rogers, Coleridge & White Ltd., 20 Powis Mews, London W11 1JN   690

Alan Jenkins
   Art Lovers, Rhymers, Whitechapel and Nineties from "The London Dissector" in *A Short History of Snakes*. Copyright © 2001 by Alan Jenkins. Used by permission of Grove/Atlantic, Inc. Excerpts from "The London Dissector" from *Greenheart* by Alan Jenkins, published by Chatto & Windus. Reprinted by permission of the Random House Group Ltd.   691

Jamie McKendrick
   "Occupations of Bridewell" and "Penal Architecture" used by permission of Faber and Faber Ltd. "The Deadhouse" reproduced with permission of the author.   694

Mick Imlah
   "Cockney" used by permission of Faber and Faber Ltd.   698

Sarah Maguire
   "Almost the Equinox" from *The Pomegranates of Kandahar* by Sarah Maguire, published by Chatto & Windus. Reprinted by permission of the Random House Group Ltd.   700

Michael Hofmann
   "From Kensal Rise to Heaven," "From A to B and Back Again," and "Malvern Road" from *Selected Poems* by Michael Hofmann. Copyright © 2008 by Michael Hofmann. Reprinted by permission of Farrar, Straus and Giroux, LLC, and Faber and Faber Ltd.   702

Maura Dooley
   "Smash the Windows" reprinted with permission from *Life Under Water* by Maura Dooley (Bloodaxe Books, 2008).   707

David Kennedy
   "The Bombs, July 2005" used by permission of Salt Publishing.   708

Fred d'Aguiar
   "Home" used by permission of the author.   710

Lavinia Greenlaw

"River History" used by permission of Faber and Faber Ltd.   712

Glyn Maxwell

"The Fires by the River" from *The Boys at Twilight: Poems 1990–1995* by Glyn Maxwell. Copyright © 1990, 1992, 1995, 2000 by Glyn Maxwell. Reprinted by permission of Houghton Mifflin Harcourt Publishing Company. All rights reserved. Reprinted by permission from *The Boys at Twilight: Poems 1990–1995* by Glyn Maxwell (Bloodaxe Books, 2000)

Simon Armitage

"KX" by Simon Armitage, copyright © Simon Armitage 2006. Used by permission of Faber and Faber Ltd.   716

Alice Oswald

"Another Westminster Bridge" reprinted by permission of United Agents on behalf of Alice Oswald.   717

Daljit Nagra

"Yobbos!" used by permission of Faber and Faber Ltd.   718

Nick Laird

"The Tip" used by permission of Faber and Faber Ltd.   719

Heather Phillipson

"German Phenomenology Makes Me Want to Strip and Run through North London" used by permission of the author.   721

Ben Borek

"Donjong Heights" used by permission of Egg Box Publishing.   722

Tom Chivers

"Big Skies over Docklands" used by permission of Salt Publishing.   725

Ahren Warner

"Διόνυσος" used by permission of the author.   726

Index of Poets

Index of Titles